SHERWOOD BOYS

Corporal Ronald Somerville, 5th Sherwood Foresters.

SHERWOOD BOYS

Biography of a Battalion
Volume 1
April 1939–August 1943

Michael Somerville

First published in Great Britain in 2025 by
Fonthill
An imprint of
Pen & Sword Books Ltd
Yorkshire – Philadelphia

Copyright © Michael Somerville 2025

ISBN 978-1-78155-964-2

The right of Michael Somerville to be identified as Author of this work has been asserted by him in accordance with the Copyright, Designs and Patents Act 1988.

A CIP catalogue record for this book is available from the British Library.

All rights reserved. No part of this book may be reproduced, transmitted, downloaded, decompiled or reverse engineered in any form or by any means, electronic or mechanical including photocopying, recording or by any information storage and retrieval system, without permission from the Publisher in writing. NO AI TRAINING: Without in any way limiting the Author's and Publisher's exclusive rights under copyright, any use of this publication to "train" generative artificial intelligence (AI) technologies to generate text is expressly prohibited. The Author and Publisher reserve all rights to license uses of this work for generative AI training and development of machine learning language models.

The Publisher's authorised representative in the EU for product safety is Authorised Rep Compliance Ltd., Ground Floor, 71 Lower Baggot Street, Dublin D02 P593, Ireland.
www.arccompliance.com

For a complete list of Pen & Sword titles please contact

PEN & SWORD BOOKS LIMITED
47 Church Street, Barnsley, South Yorkshire, S70 2AS, England
E-mail: enquiries@pen-and-sword.co.uk
Website: www.pen-and-sword.co.uk
or
PEN AND SWORD BOOKS
1950 Lawrence Road, Havertown, PA 19083, USA
E-mail: uspen-and-sword@casematepublishers.com
Website: www.penandswordbooks.com

Preface

Although this book deals with military history, its origins lie in a completely different form of historical research. Back in 2017 I had just completed my doctorate in military history and also retired from my job as an IT consultant. My wife, Gillian, who is an avid family historian, decided that this meant I had some free time to investigate my own family and persuaded me to get my father's military service record. I knew that he had served in Italy with the Sherwood Foresters during the Second World War, but like so many veterans he had never really talked about his experiences. Even though I had developed an interest in military history at a young age, I respected his silence. With the records provided by the MoD, I was now able to determine the specific battalion in which he served and decided to investigate further their part in the war.

Initially this seemed relatively easy, a matter of locating and finding the battalion war diaries in the National Archives and combining the contents with existing campaign narratives. I had a vague idea I might produce a book from this research, but thought that it would not be particularly onerous. But in looking for further information on the battalion, I also wrote to both the regimental and county archives asking them what material they held, and arranged visits to them both.

What I found there completely changed the scope of the project. This is largely down to the extraordinary efforts of one man, Wally Binch. A private in the battalion during the war, he became the secretary of the battalion association, which under his enthusiastic leadership from the 1980s onwards became very active, particularly in the Nottingham and Derby area. As a result of Wally's work, I found in the archives a treasure trove of material, in particular three collections of personal stories covering every period of the battalion's history, from its pre-war formation in Derbyshire to its post-war demobilisation in Austria, and almost every rank and role in the unit. There were also personal diaries, individuals' accounts of their war service and hundreds of photographs putting faces to their names. Through Wally, the members of the association had also made an enormous contribution to the Imperial War Museum's collection of sound archives, resulting in over 150 hours of tape interviews about their time in the battalion. I am most grateful to Wally's son, Edward Binch, for permission to use some of his father's extensive material in this book.

This was no longer just a unit history; it was a detailed personal and local history. The accounts covered many aspects of military life usually omitted from standard accounts. I saw the opportunity to give broader context to these experiences, to give background to readers unfamiliar with the detailed course of the war, but also to show how the unit and its members had trained, fought and changed over the duration of the conflict. I believe the result is the most complete story of a single battalion yet written, which will appeal to specialist and non-specialist readers alike. This first volume covers the battalion's actions in the Dunkirk and Tunisian campaigns, but also examines in detail its formation and training in the UK, and the motivation of the young men who joined up to serve in the unit. The second volume will describe its operations in Italy, where my father joined it, in Greece and Austria, and the post-war experiences of the main characters in the story.

Through Jennifer Brookman, the regimental archivist, and Andrew McDougall of the Mercian Regiment I was also fortunate enough to be put in touch with Major (retd) John Cotterill MBE, who has over the last six years given me an enormous amount of support and encouragement. As well as providing additional unpublished material from his own collection of photos and documents, he has been kind enough to review, correct and comment on every chapter as it has been written. As an experienced battlefield guide and former officer in the regiment, he has been able to provide valuable insights into the battalion's operations and the careers of some of its members. Other former members of the regiment who have contributed through their comments and support are Roger Stockton OBE, John Hughes-Wilson and Edward Wilkinson, and thanks are also due to Peter Lockwood for providing me with these further contacts.

As well as Jennifer's assistance, there are staff at several other archives who have helped. Most important among these is the Nottinghamshire Archives, where thanks are due to Richard Burman, Nick Clark, Luke Danes, Jaime McMurtrie, Alexa Rees and Linda Webster. Elizabeth Smith and her staff in the research rooms at the Imperial War Museum helped with access to the sound archive there, and Andrew Webb with the provision of photographs. Other assistance has come from Angela Tarnowski (9th/12th Royal Lancers Museum, Derby), Emma Nesbitt (BBC People's War website), Charlotte Crooks (Royal College of Defence Studies [RCDS]) and Kirsty McGill (Bedford Archive). I am grateful to Brigadier (Retd) John Drewienkiewicz for granting access to his RCDS thesis on the Territorial Army.

Contemporary maps are from the Perry-Castañeda Library, University of Texas, and are understood to be in the public domain. Use is courtesy of the University of Texas Libraries, The University of Texas at Austin; all edits and annotations are by myself. The GSGS (Geographical Section, General Staff) series of maps in the British Library has been consulted for additional material, with the assistance of Daniel Wilkinson and others. The PoW camp location maps are with permission of the British Red Cross Museum and Archives, with thanks to Mehzebin Adam-Suter.

Historians and battlefield guides who have reviewed and commented on different chapters include James Holland, Tim Lynch, Ian Mitchell, Frank da Palma, Gary Sheffield and Malcolm Tudor. I have also had input from correspondents on the WW2 Talk forum, where there are several threads on the activities of the 2/5th Foresters and other battalions in the regiment; these include Daniel Bamford, Richard John Cox, Chris Harris, Nick Pitman and Gary Tankard. My good friend Richard Butler provided me with accommodation during visits to the Nottinghamshire and Derbyshire area, as well as providing local knowledge when visiting sites in the counties. Through Chris Clegg, Derek Thomas and Andrew Timms at the Friends of Oignies organisation, I met Thierry Lariviere, who guided me around the Oignies battlefield and provided me with material from the local history society, ONYACUM.

Sadly, I began work on the battalion history too late to have the opportunity of speaking to any surviving veterans. But as it evolved from a family history project, through using various genealogy sites and techniques, I have been fortunate enough to make contact with a number of their descendants. Some knew next to nothing of their fathers' and grandfathers' experiences. At the opposite extreme, several had already carried out significant research of their own and were able to provide me with further personal information including photographs, memorabilia, letters, diaries and personal reminiscences. In a few cases, they have even provided short histories of their relative's lives. Whatever their knowledge, the reception that I have received from family members for my project has been overwhelmingly positive. Among those who have assisted are Julie Armstrong (née Seibert), John Blore, Sharon Bridge, Peter William Bryan, Charlotte Burchell, Malcolm Campbell, Niall Campbell, Emma Chapman, Tony and Sharon Clark, Gillian Coope, Leonie and Tim Cousin, Ian Willis Dixon, Catherine Dunn, Richard Everard, Paul Foreman, Diane Holt, Mary Jackson, Susan Mary Lane, John, Mark, and Tanya Mardell, Tony Mellors, William Newton, Martha Serena Page, Fiona Robertson (née Collen), Jon Roth, Pauline Scott Garrett, Connie and Peter Sharpe, Martin Steel, Jeremy Stroud, Ann Suttie, Andy Timms, Richard and Norma Tomlinson (née Barratt), Jayne Waterworth, Dave Watkin, Patricia Willis (née Enser) and Joanne Womack. My apologies to anyone who I have omitted.

My thanks to Jay Slater at Fonthill Media for commissioning the work, and to Jasper Hadman for his guidance throughout the production process.

I will close these acknowledgements where I started, with my wife, Gillian. Not only was she there at the conception of this project, she has persevered with me through its gestation. She has proofread every chapter (often several times) and made suggestions on how to improve them, especially for a non-technical reader. She has tolerated long periods when I have been absent at archives or cloistered away at the computer, and accompanied me on many of the trips to Europe to look at the sites of the battalion's operations. Without her assistance and encouragement, this book would probably not have been completed.

Contents

Preface	5
List of Maps	10
Main Characters	11
1 Heritage: 1741–March 1939	15
2 Birth: Derbyshire, March 1939–March 1940	24
3 First Steps: France, April–May 1940	43
4 Evacuation: Dunkirk, May–June 1940	72
5 Education: Scotland and England, June 1940–September 1942	83
6 Deaths in the Family: Norway, North Africa and the Far East, April 1940–July 1942	107
7 Leaving Home: Tunisia, January–February 1943	115
8 Examinations: Tunisia, March 1943	139
9 Graduation: Tunisia, March–May 1943	160
10 Captives: Germany and Italy, June 1940–August 1943	177
11 Time Out: North Africa, June–August 1943	190
Extract from Volume 2	200
Notes	202
Bibliography	206
Index	211

List of Maps

1	Derbyshire, 1939	34
2	Northern France and Belgium, 1940	56
3	Oignies, 26 May 1940	64
4	The Dunkirk Perimeter, 28 May–2 June 1940	77
5	Scotland, winter 1940	87
6	East Anglia, 1941	95
7	South-east England, 1942	101
8	Northern Tunisa, January 1943	128
9	Sedjenane, 2 March 1943	142
10	Tamera, 17 March 1943	166
11	PoW camps in Italy, 1943	181
12	Exercise 'Conqueror', June 1943	193

 Richard Garrett

 Ernie Gibson

 Willoughby Gilliver

 Eddie Hallett

 Richard Hammond MBE

 George Hampton

 Fred Hirst

 Fred Hutt

 Fred Jeffrey

 Stan Knight

 Frank Lees

 Pat McKay

Frank Mardell

Reg Markham

Harold Mellors

Eric Morral

Dick Newell

Patrick O'Sullivan

Allan Orme

Philip Palmer MC

Bert Pinnock

Phil Plowright

John Watts Potter DSO

George Price

1
Heritage: 1741–March 1939

According to the great American general, William Tecumseh Sherman, every army, as well as every individual, has a soul. For the British army, however, Sherman's observation needs to be modified, for it has not one soul but many, one for each of its constituent regiments. The regimental system is more than just an organisational or administrative structure. It is the basis for the army's traditions, culture and ethos. The regiment becomes a surrogate family for its members, and often many generations of the same family serve within its ranks. Just as when writing a personal biography it is customary to describe a person's family and lineage, when writing the history of a battalion it is necessary to briefly tell the history of its parent regiment.

The story begins, therefore, with Colonel Daniel Houghton, who in 1741 raised a regiment of foot of 1,000 men to serve King George II in the War of the Austrian Succession. It was recruited in the Buckingham and Aylesbury area, only the Lincoln green facings on its scarlet uniform giving any remote prediction of its future regional associations. When the foot regiments were first arranged in order of precedence in 1747, it was ranked the 56th Regiment of Foot, amended to the 45th the following year, and in 1751 this became its formal title. There were about a hundred infantry regiments active in the British army at any one time in this period, and the 45th was the epitome of an average regiment. Its early service was also no more than average. After garrison duty at Gibraltar in 1745, it was posted to Nova Scotia, where it joined in the siege of Louisbourg in 1758 and the taking of Quebec in 1759. It saw further action when the American colonies declared independence in 1776, and by 1778 it was reduced to less than 100 men and returned to England.

At Nottingham, a group of prominent locals had resolved to raise subscriptions to support a regiment. The 45th was sent to the city on the agreement that if 300 men were found to serve 'with the assistance and influence and bounty of the chief residents of the county', it would be given the county name.[1] It thereupon took the title of the 45th (1st Nottinghamshire) Regiment. During the French

Revolutionary Wars, it served in the West Indies, and then in 1807 took part in an attack against Buenos Aires. But it was in the Peninsular War that it first truly gained fame, winning thirteen battle honours. At Talavera (July 1809), it was stationed on outpost duty and seriously delayed the assault of the advancing French columns. 'Upon this occasion the steadiness and discipline of the 45th Regiment were conspicuous', wrote the Duke of Wellington, and the regiment thus earned its first nickname, 'The Old Stubborns'.[2] It was not only in stubborn defence that the regiment won honour. At the siege of Badajoz (1812), one of the fiercest engagements fought by the British army in Spain and Portugal, the 45th were the first to enter the castle, hoisting an officer's red coat to signal its capture. Badajoz Day (6 April) became one of the most significant celebrations in the regiment's calendar.

The first half of the nineteenth century saw the regiment deployed overseas in Burma and South Africa. In 1867, it took part in the Abyssinian Expedition, marching some 300 miles in twenty-four days, including one route march of 70 miles in four days over mountainous terrain to be present at the final battle of the campaign at Magdala. By this time, the regimental association with the Nottingham area had been further strengthened with the addition of the title 'The Sherwood Foresters', which had been in use by the Nottinghamshire Militia since 1813.

The British regimental system in 1867 would still have been familiar to Colonel Houghton, but by the mid-nineteenth century it was no longer fit for purpose. Regiments in European armies usually had three battalions (the tactical unit in battle), which served together in war. Apart from the twenty-five senior regiments of foot, which had two battalions, British regiments had a single battalion, only grouped together into three-battalion brigades when on active service. Although several regiments, like the 45th, had adopted local affiliations, these were still informal. Men joining the army could be drafted into any regiment, a deterrent to recruitment as they preferred to serve in units with a local connection and with others from the same area. This changed in 1871 when the secretary of state for war, Edward Cardwell, initiated reforms which allocated regiments to counties. All regiments were now to have two battalions, the idea being that one would serve overseas and the other stay at home for recruitment and training. This was achieved by the simple expedient of linking single-battalion regiments together. The 45th, serving in India at the time, was exceptional in being linked to the 17th (Leicestershire) Regiment, which already had two battalions. This anomaly was corrected in 1881 under further reforms initiated by the war secretary, Hugh Childers. Under his system, the regiments also lost their numbering (though retaining their order of precedence in the army) and replaced them with a distinctive, usually regional, name. The 45th from Nottinghamshire was now joined with the 95th from neighbouring Derbyshire, forming the 1st Battalion Sherwood Foresters (Derbyshire Regiment).

The regiment now linked to the 45th was technically a much more recent formation. It had only been raised in 1823, initially in Winchester. Like its Nottinghamshire sibling, its earliest years had been spent serving either at home or on overseas garrison duties. In 1825, it was given its territorial designation as the 95th (Derbyshire) Regiment of Foot. Then in 1854 it joined the British force sent to the Crimea, where it was in the forefront of the assault on the Russian lines at the Battle of the Alma and took heavy casualties. The regimental colours ended up being carried by a private soldier rather than a junior officer, as was then the normal practice, and as a result it became a regimental tradition that on Alma Day (20 September) the colours were handed over to a private soldier. Subsequent to this, the army in the Crimea issued instructions not to carry the colours in battle, but the 95th apparently did not receive the order, as the regiment still carried them at Inkerman in November 1854, the last regiment to do so in a major action. By the end of that battle there were less than a hundred men remaining, but the unit continued to serve in the trenches before Sebastopol. 'There may be few of the 95th left but those are as hard as nails', wrote a British officer, and so the regiment acquired its own nickname, 'The Nails'.[3] A few years later, the regiment was on its way to South Africa when the mutiny broke out in India. Re-routed to Bombay, the unit saw action with the Central Indian Field Force in a series of largely forgotten engagements notable for two events: the regiment's first Victoria Cross (VC), won by Private Bernard McQuirt at Rowa, and the acquisition of the regimental mascot. At the siege of Kotah, the 95th adopted a ram, named 'Derby', which was present at six actions and even received the India campaign medal. Under Cardwell's reforms, the unit was redesignated the 2nd Battalion Sherwood Foresters (Derbyshire Regiment) in 1881, with headquarters at Normanton Barracks, Derby

Although the 95th (Derbyshire) Regiment had only a brief history before amalgamation, it was the sixth regiment in the army to hold that number. Most famous of these had been the 95th Rifles, which had served in the Light Brigade under Wellington in the Peninsular War. The new regiment had adopted several traditions from its more illustrious predecessor, notably the Maltese Cross, which forms part of the regimental crest, and the regimental march, the Rifle Quickstep 'I'm Ninety-Five'. The Rifle connotations also led to the regiment acquiring its most famous scion, General Horace Smith-Dorrien, commander of the British II Corps at Le Cateau in 1914 and subsequently the Second Army at Ypres in 1915. Having graduated from the Royal Military Academy, Smith-Dorrien was asked to choose to which regiment he wanted to be posted and wrote down '95th', believing this to be the Rifle Brigade—and ended up in the rather less prestigious Sherwood Foresters. He apparently became reconciled to his choice, as after the First World War he became their Colonel and his three sons also served in the regiment.

*

It was not only the regular battalions of the 45th and 95th Foot that came together to create the Sherwood Foresters. The regular army formed only one component amongst many in the British armed forces. They were at the time the only troops that were available for overseas service, but in the event of an invasion of Britain, other forces, albeit less well armed and trained, were also available. The main component of these were the county militias, originally created back in the seventeenth century and selected by ballot, and which had been the principal home defence force during the Napoleonic Wars. Since these were already established on a local basis, Childers incorporated them into the county regiments. The 2nd Battalion Derbyshire Militia became the 3rd Battalion Sherwood Foresters and the Nottinghamshire Militia the 4th Battalion. The 1st Derbyshire Militia briefly became the first incarnation of the 5th Sherwood Foresters, before being amalgamated into the 3rd Battalion a few years later.

In 1870, Prussia had shocked the European political system order by rapidly defeating France and establishing the German Empire. That empire could put millions of trained troops into the field, compared to mere hundreds of thousands in the British army. The militia, largely drawn from poorly educated agricultural labouring classes and officered by the local gentry, were felt to be a poor match for the new professional continental armies. A French invasion scare in the late 1850s had already seen the creation of many independent and locally raised volunteer units. In comparison to the militia, they were mostly from the urban artisan and professional classes, with a higher standard of living, education, and economic and social status. They provided their own arms and were often innovative in their adoption of both tactics and technology. Derbyshire was prominent in the volunteer movement. In 1859, a request had been made to the great local landowner, the Duke of Devonshire, to form a volunteer company, and as a result it became the sixth county to form such a unit. Eventually, twenty-three companies of the Derbyshire Rifle Volunteer Corps would be formed, each with its own headquarters and drill locations around the county, and each organising its own funds and uniforms. For administrative purposes, they were grouped into three battalions (reduced to two in 1869), which during annual reviews were often brigaded together. Nottinghamshire had a similar setup of two battalions. These units were also incorporated into Childers' scheme of localisation. When in 1888 a mobilisation plan for the volunteer force was formed, it was natural that the four volunteer battalions affiliated to the Sherwood Foresters were grouped together as the North Midlands Brigade, to be assembled at Derby and placed under the Northern Command.

The volunteers' capability as a home defence force, like that of the militia, was never tested. But at the end of the century, when war broke out in South Africa and it was realised that large numbers of men would be needed to defeat the Boers, volunteer units made up those numbers. Neither the militia nor the volunteers were obliged to serve overseas, but contingents from the Volunteer Corps were formed as service companies of up to a hundred men and went to South Africa with the 1st Battalion.

In 1904, fear of the rising military and industrial power of Germany drove together the old rivals, Britain and France, in the Entente Cordiale. For the first time since the Napoleonic era, involvement in a continental war began to be seriously considered in British military planning. The problem of the lack of reserves for the regular army once more loomed large, resulting in 1907 in yet another series of reforms initiated by Richard Burdon Haldane, the war secretary. The old militia was abolished; the 3rd and 4th battalions became reserve battalions, feeding recruits, and in time of war reinforcements, into the regular battalions. The volunteers were replaced by a new organisation, the Territorial Force (TF). On 1 April 1908, the 1st Volunteer Battalion Sherwood Foresters became the 5th (Territorial Force) Battalion, the others the 6th through to 8th battalions.

Regimental histories mostly focus upon the activities of regular battalions, but the importance of the militia and volunteers to the regimental culture should not be overlooked. Volunteer units purposefully mimicked their regular equivalents in their titles and traditions. The 6th Sherwood Foresters had their own ram mascot, and the volunteers sometimes adopted slouch hats as a nod to their involvement in South Africa. Until the conscription system was introduced in 1916 to meet the enormous manpower demands of the Great War, the volunteer principal—whether in the regular army or the 'part time soldiers' of the TF—was fundamental to the British approach to raising troops. Even after conscription was introduced, the attitude of the British soldier still reflected the amateur tradition of the volunteers more than the professional military rigour of the German or French armies. It was largely seen as a means of sharing the burden of national service equally among the population, compared to the forced service of an authoritarian regime.

In 1914, there were about 250,000 men in the TF, giving the army its first extensive trained reserve. It was organised into formal brigades and divisions, providing a more effective mobilisation structure. The TF was a big advance on the archaic systems it replaced, but still had its limitations and critics. Like the old volunteers, enlistment was part-time and voluntary; like the old militia, there was no compulsion on the men in the TF to serve overseas—although when the call to arms came in 1914, the majority elected to do so. Regular officers were inclined to dismiss the training and efficiency of the part-time soldiers and were even more derisive of their officers. These opinions were most clearly demonstrated by Lord Kitchener, who in 1914 chose to create a 'New Army' of service battalions (commonly known as 'Pals' battalions) for overseas service, intending to retain the territorials for home defence. But while the 'Pals' get most of the attention in the popular history of the First World War, territorial battalions fulfilled much of the army's demand for more men in the front line throughout 1915 and early 1916.

*

The First World War saw the largest ever expansion in the British army in order to wage war on a continental scale. It was indicative of how the regimental system was considered essential to maintain *esprit de corps* and recruitment numbers that this was not done by creating new infantry regiments, but by adding new battalions to the existing ones. The territorial component of the regiment did this through the replication of battalions. Thus, for example, the 1/5th Battalion was the first-line battalion sent to France in 1915; the 2/5th was created as a second-line battalion for home service, but due to the shortage of manpower also went to France in 1917; while the 3/5th Battalion stayed in the UK as a training unit for reserves. In addition to the pre-war territorials, Kitchener's mass recruitment generated eleven service battalions numbered from the 9th upwards. These were even more localised; for example, the 16th (Chatsworth Rifles) was raised by the Duke of Devonshire from men on his estate, and the 17th (Welbeck Rangers) was formed by the Lord Mayor of Nottingham. In all, the regiment comprised thirty battalions during the war, twenty of which served overseas. The details of their service are too extensive to go into here, but a few examples are noteworthy for comparison with that of the 5th Foresters from 1939–45.

The unprecedented losses suffered by the regular divisions in 1914 meant that the country could not wait until Kitchener's New Army was ready to reinforce the army in France. Consequently, the four territorial battalions, brigaded together in 139 (Forester) Brigade of the 46th (North Midlands) Division, went to the Western Front in February 1915. For the 1/5th Battalion, their first day in the trenches was 5 March 1915; they suffered their first casualty the very same day. Their first major action was an ill-judged and ill-fated assault on a heavily fortified German position called the Hohenzollern Redoubt during the Battle of Loos on 13 October 1915. Although the brigade played only a supporting role in the attack, it took 430 casualties. The brigade also saw action on the first day of the Battle of the Somme, 1 July 1916; not in the main assault on the German lines, but as part of a diversionary attack on the Gommecourt salient, 5 miles to the north. Of course, the men involved were not informed that they were a diversion. They went into the attack without the seven-day artillery bombardment which was a feature of the main attack, and against largely uncut barbed wire. The 1/5th Foresters were amongst the lead assaulting battalions, and in less than two hours of fighting took 431 casualties in killed, wounded and missing, including the commanding officer and his adjutant—about 80 per cent of the attacking force. Of those who had managed to enter the enemy trenches, only one officer and twenty-four other ranks (ORs) returned. The attack did not even fulfil its objective of diverting the enemy's attention. Being so obviously a feint and so easily held by the German troops immediately available, the local German artillery was able to turn its fire onto the British advance to the south. It would not be the last time in their history that the Foresters lost heavily in a sideshow.

The disaster at Gommecourt, on the back of the failure at the Hohenzollern Redoubt, undeservedly gave the 46th Division a poor reputation. However, on the 1/5th Foresters' front, the German second-line was entered in places and the casualties on both sides indicate that the fighting was fiercer than anywhere else in the sector. Two years later, the division was back on the attack during the Hundred Days Offensive, redeeming itself with one of the most spectacular victories achieved by any British formation in the war, the breaking of the Hindenburg Line at the Battle of the St Quentin Canal on 29 September 1918. It captured over 4,000 prisoners for the loss of 800 men, and more importantly laid the way for the opening of the front and the war of movement that had been the holy grail of the generals since 1914. Lieutenant Colonel Bernard Vann of the 1/6th Battalion won the VC on that day for leading his battalion across the canal in thick fog. Vann lost his life a few days later, on 3 October, in the Forester Brigade's final major operation of the war, the breaking of the Beaurevoir–Fonsomme line, the third and last of the successive Hindenburg Line defences. The battalion advanced some 3,000 yards to the village of Montbrehain, where it was checked by strong resistance. Following heavy street fighting, Lieutenant John Watts Potter led his platoon in a bayonet charge against a German artillery battery. They could not progress any further because of more artillery and machine guns, so they dug in and held on to the village. Potter, just turned twenty-two, was awarded the Distinguished Service Order (DSO) for his leadership and bravery. The Foresters had outrun the units on both their flanks, so the brigadier decided to withdraw his exhausted troops into a more tenable defensive position. Nevertheless, the actions of the Forester Brigade against the Hindenburg Line defences show how effective a fighting force the British infantry had become by 1918.

The second-line territorials started out on home defence duties, which included action in Dublin against the Easter Rising of 1916 by the 2/7th and 2/8th battalions, and then went to France in 1917. The experiences of the service battalions varied, but they were present at most of the major campaigns of the war. The 12th Sherwood Foresters arrived in France in August 1915 as a pioneer battalion attached to the 24th Division and was stationed at Loos. While on occasion they were called upon to fight, the men of the battalion were more famous for producing the satirical front-line newspaper *The Wipers Times*. The story of the 11th Battalion is also worthy of note, given the regiment's service in the Second World War. It served on the Western Front at Loos, the Somme and Passchendaele. Then in November 1917, the Italian army collapsed in the face of a German–Austrian offensive at Caporetto (modern-day Kobarid in

Slovenia). British and French troops, including the 11th Foresters, were rushed to Italy to bolster their ally. Fighting in the southern Alps, the battalion lived up to its regimental traditions by winning renown for a stubborn stand against the Germans on 15 June 1918 on the Piave River. Their 26-year-old commanding officer, Lieutenant Colonel Charles Edward Hudson, was awarded the VC for personally leading a counterattack.

Around 140,000 men, almost all from Nottinghamshire or Derbyshire, served with the regiment in the Great War; 11,409 lost their lives. The casualties from wounds, gas, frostbite and sickness amounted to some three times that number. They earned fifty-seven battle honours and over 2,000 individual gallantry awards, including nine Victoria Crosses. A monument to those who had served was erected on a hill near the village of Crich, chosen because the point was visible from a large area of both Derbyshire and Nottinghamshire. Dedicated on 6 August 1923 by the Bishop of Southwell, it became a site of remembrance to the sacrifice made by the men of the two counties.

*

The huge losses of 1916–18 meant that towards the end of the war, several battalions, particularly the second-line territorial units, had already been reduced to cadre strength, disbanded or merged with other battalions. When peace came, as the vast army that had been created to beat Germany and its allies was no longer needed, the service battalions were also rapidly disbanded. This left the regiment with two regular battalions, two reserve battalions and four territorial battalions, the same structure as in 1914, but with fewer troops. The 2nd Battalion served mostly overseas, while the 1st Battalion stayed at home and after 1919 was rarely above half-strength. It was mainly stationed either in Northern Ireland or south-east England, although Normanton Barracks in Derby was the regiment's depot and training centre. The fact that neither regular battalion was based locally weakened the relationship between them and the Territorial Force, which had begun to reorganise on a peace footing from June 1919. The 5th Battalion had its base in Derby, the 6th and 7th in Nottingham and the 8th in Newark, and they remained grouped in the same brigade.

The Territorial Force (renamed the Territorial Army, or TA, in 1920) suffered from massive funding cuts post-war. With this came a reduction in pay, limitations on equipment and, as a result, a decline in numbers. In August 1920, the 5th Battalion mustered sixteen officers and 380 ORs for its first post-war camp at Scarborough. This included a small cadre of First World War veteran officers, non-commissioned officers (NCOs) and soldiers. Soldiering was now an unpopular occupation and there was a shortage of recruits across the TA overall, although numbers held up reasonably well in the Nottinghamshire and Derbyshire area. Officers joined as much for the social element of the organisation as any interest in the profession, and recruitment in the ranks may have reflected the harsh economic environment rather than any active interest in military life. Nevertheless, in 1933, the 5th and 8th battalions were awarded the *Daily Telegraph* Cup for 100 per cent attendance at camp, which in the words of the regiment's official historian, 'shows clearly the spirit of enthusiasm in the TA battalions of the Foresters at a time when they were given little official encouragement'.[4]

Since 1914–18 had supposedly been the war that would end all wars, the very role of the TA was being questioned in political and military circles. Its primary obligation remained home defence, but it was decided by the War Office that it would be both the army's reserve force and the sole framework for future expansion in time of crisis. A more controversial remit was the support of civil authorities. On 12 April 1920, around 400 reservists had been called up during a coal strike, reinforcing the 1st Battalion in London. In 1926, the army was called upon again to run essential services during the General Strike, but the government decided not to deploy the TA. In Derbyshire and Nottinghamshire, such an action would have been problematic, exposing divided loyalties. Some territorials enrolled as special constables, as much for economic reasons as political, and there were supposedly cases of individuals being a territorial, a special constable and a striker!

Although the regiment saw some organisational change and new equipment in the 1930s, this was slow to arrive, even in the regular battalions, and almost unknown within the TA. One major exception was the selection of the 6th and 7th battalions in December 1936 to convert to searchlight troops, in recognition of the future importance of airpower and the need for specialist air defence units rather than infantry to defend Britain. On 12 December, they transferred to the Royal Engineers. Nevertheless, since this was the British army, they retained that all-important link to their heritage in the unit names, the 40th (Sherwood Foresters) and 42nd (Robin Hood) AA battalions. This reduced the TA component of the regiment to a mere two battalions, the 5th and 8th, which in 1939 were brigaded with the 5th Leicesters in 148 Infantry Brigade, 49th Division, just as the threat of war loomed once again over Europe.

2
Birth: Derbyshire, March 1939–March 1940

The series of international crises that culminated in the outbreak of war in Europe in September 1939 has been discussed in so many books and television documentaries that the story needs little retelling here, other than to give context to the creation in March 1939 of a new battalion of the Sherwood Foresters, the 2/5th. The Treaty of Versailles in June 1919 had left Germany stripped of its overseas colonies and the border provinces of Alsace, Lorraine and parts of Pomerania; its armed forces reduced to insignificance; and its economy hamstrung by the need to pay reparations to the victorious powers. While the victors may have seen 1914–18 as the war to end all wars, many Germans saw the treaty as an insult that must be overturned, by military force if necessary. The situation was compounded by fear of communism and then the economic crisis of the Great Depression after 1929, allowing Hitler and the Nazi party to present their fascist and antisemitic doctrine as patriotic policies for national recovery. Assisted into power by traditional conservative political factions, Hitler almost immediately began to reverse the 1919 treaty by proclaiming a rearmament policy, and in 1936 took the next step by reoccupying the demilitarised Rhineland region with his fledgling new army.

While Nazi Germany embarked on an armaments programme to spend its way out of the Depression, Britain saw military spending as an unaffordable luxury in times of economic deprivation. All the armed forces were starved of funds during the early 1930s. Germany was still relatively weak, and there were those who saw the new regime as a bulwark against communism and sympathised with some of the criticisms of Versailles. From 1936, however, a policy of rearmament was gradually adopted. By 1938, British military spending was four times that of 1934, but the army saw relatively little of this new funding. Priority was given to the Royal Navy and Royal Air Force (RAF). Radar and new fighters for the air defence of Britain, and new battleships and aircraft carriers for the navy, were all capital-intensive programmes with long lead times. Perhaps more importantly, British policy still did not envisage sending the army back into Europe to fight another campaign in France. The blockade and the bomber were the core of British offensive strategy; fear of the enemy's bombers dominated defensive thought, as demonstrated by the conversion of the two Foresters' TA battalions from infantry to air defence. In the short-term, Britain was neither militarily nor emotionally prepared for war by 1938, which led the new prime minister, Neville Chamberlain, to buy time for rearmament with the now discredited policy of appeasement.

In March 1938, Hitler marched his troops into Austria and incorporated that country into his new Reich. Austria, Hitler's birth country but never part of the Kaiser's German Empire, had been even more harshly treated under the 1919 Treaty of Saint-Germain than Germany had been under Versailles, leaving it as the German-speaking rump of the once-powerful Austro-Hungarian Empire. Austria had been similarly demilitarised, lost access to the sea and been shorn of provinces that may not have been ethnically German but which had been part of the Habsburg monarchy for centuries. *Anschluss* (union) with Germany had been forbidden under the peace treaties, but many Austrians saw Nazism as their own route back to prosperity and national respect. Hitler's next target was another former Austrian possession, and another one that was ethnically German. When the new country of Czechoslovakia had been carved out of the Habsburg Empire in 1919, a large German-speaking minority had been created in the Sudeten mountains that formed the borderland with Germany. The Nazi regime portrayed these as a repressed minority of their own and appropriated the principle of self-determination applied in 1919 for its own ends. Still unprepared to go to war for a country which had no strategic interest for Britain, at a four-way meeting of the great European powers (Britain, France, Germany and Italy) in Munich in September 1938, Chamberlain negotiated away the Sudetenland to buy peace. Now almost universally condemned, it was at the time presented as a diplomatic victory and was popular with much of the British public.

In hindsight, it was also Chamberlain's last concession to Hitler. In the following months, British policy turned from one of appeasement and reconciliation to one of containment and preparation for war. Rearmament was stepped up, particularly regarding air raid precautions. Most significantly, on 6 February 1939, Chamberlain announced that Britain would give military support to France in Europe. This signalled a new intent to stand up to German aggression. It also reflected the anti-German sentiment in the country since the agreement signed in Munich the previous year, exacerbated by a growing awareness of the true nature of the Nazi regime following events such as the *Kristallnacht* pogrom against the Jews in November 1938. While not wanting war, the British public was beginning to realise that Hitler's Germany was a threat to peace and might have to be fought. This view was endorsed on 15 March 1939 when Hitler's forces, in breach of the Munich agreement, marched into Prague and occupied the remnant of the Czechoslovak state. On 31 March, Chamberlain gave military guarantees to the anticipated target of Hitler's next aggressive move, Poland.

*

The commitment to France in the aftermath of Munich resulted in changes in British war plans. The most important of these was a political decision to send a new British Expeditionary Force (BEF) to France in the event of war, a commitment that previous governments had tried to avoid. The Committee of Imperial Defence and the Imperial General Staff now persuaded Leslie Hore-Belisha, the Secretary of State for War, that a continental expeditionary force was essential—perhaps mainly to reassure the French of British sincerity as the army was still far too weak to send a substantial number of troops to assist them in the event of war. In February 1939, the cabinet agreed a field force of nine divisions. The following month, however, Hore-Belisha announced in parliament that it would eventually consist of six regular and thirteen territorial divisions, and that the TA divisions would have the same strength and level of equipment as the regulars. This was a huge undertaking, the military authorities estimating that it would take between a year and eighteen months to train and equip such a force to be put into the field. The peace-time establishment of the TA was only 130,000 men, its war establishment 170,000. Thirteen divisions would absorb almost all this manpower into the planned BEF, leaving nothing for home defence. Hore-Belisha therefore proposed the doubling of the TA to 340,000 men, a force of twenty-six divisions, all equipped to regular standards. Although the existing TA system was at the time the favoured means of expansion, because volunteers, rather than conscripts, were considered to make the best material for soldiers, there were still many who doubted the TA's capability. The War Office had been considering alternative plans based upon conscription, and the pledge to the territorials that they would be allowed to serve in their own chosen unit restricted the army's flexibility in manpower planning. The huge expansion had extraordinary implications, as every new territorial battalion would require accommodation, equipment, training and—perhaps most important—officers.

In the case of Derbyshire, new recruits were initially used to bring the existing 5th Battalion of the Sherwood Foresters up to its establishment strength. Recruitment was brisk, and this was achieved by midday on Friday, 28 April 1939. Then the creation of a second-line battalion was begun, meaning a further 500 men. This was similar in some respects to the creation of second- and even third-line territorial battalions in 1914–18, but in Derbyshire the arrangements had a local flavour which also reflected the 'Pals' phenomenon of 1914. Recruitment for the new unit specifically looked to enlist men from areas of the county under-represented in the original battalion. C Company, based in Ripley and Belper, became the HQ Company of the new unit, the 2/5th Sherwood Foresters, and a new rifle company was raised in the Swadlincote area to replace it in the original battalion, now designated the 1/5th. Four more companies were to be recruited to complete the 2/5th Battalion. These were based in Glossop and the Hope Valley (A Company), Buxton (B), Chesterfield (C) and Heanor (D). Chesterfield, a town of 65,000 people, had not had a territorial infantry company since the conversion of the 6th Battalion to AA (anti-aircraft) defence, while in Glossop and the Hope Valley, recruitment took place for the first time since the Great War. Enthusiasm in the different areas was mixed. In Buxton, seventy men had volunteered by 24 July, and that same weekend the Hope Valley contingent paraded fifty-strong. In Chesterfield, however, where the new infantry company had to compete for volunteers with the local signals platoon and the AA battalion, only forty had joined up.

This method of expanding the TA was controversial. Critics denounced it for redistributing the experienced men of the first-line units, thereby creating two poor battalions in place of one good battalion. C Company was widely regarded as the best in the original 5th Battalion, winning most of the prizes in the annual shooting competition at Belper, so its loss was particularly keenly felt. However, a cadre of more experienced officers and men was essential to command and train the new intake, and taking the best of the rifle companies from the original battalion—leaving the rest of it mostly intact—had its merits, and gave officers and men in the new HQ Company the opportunity to learn new skills. There was an alternative view that the process added to the morale of the new battalion by making it seem less 'second-line'. It was even suggested that rather than being named the 2/5th, with its aura of inferiority, it should adopt the traditional designation of the 6th Sherwood Foresters. This was not approved by the War Office, although the 2/8th Battalion, then forming in Nottinghamshire, did become the 9th Battalion. There were also significant advantages from an administrative perspective: the 1/5th was now based in the south of the county, the 2/5th in the north. This meant less time travelling to training for the men, and when war did break out they could initially be billeted at home.

Other evidence supports the view that the process was disruptive and detrimental. Particularly damaging were changes to the summer training camp programme. Originally, the three battalions of 148 Brigade had all been scheduled to train at Holyhead for two weeks at the end of July. After the doubling of battalions, the numbers simply could not be accommodated and the camp was extended to six weeks. The first- and second-line battalions from each unit attended together for two weeks each—from 13–27 August 1939 in the case of the 1/5th and 2/5th Foresters. This perhaps levelled up the training of the two battalions to an extent, but it sacrificed exercises above battalion level, which were always limited in peacetime to begin with. The 1/5th went to camp with twenty-nine officers and 584 other ranks, the 2/5th rather fewer with twenty-two officers and 465 ORs. Apart from the HQ Company, it was reported that all the 2/5th had been recruited within the last few weeks, necessitating a much higher proportion of elementary drill than normal. In particular, new officers and NCOs had to undergo extensive special training, with almost every specialist post in the battalion having to be filled from scratch. One of the youngest recruits was 18-year-old Reg Markham, who had signed up on 15 June 1939 at the Chesterfield drill hall. Although he had left school aged 14, Reg volunteered for the role of company clerk, which earned him the rank of lance corporal—though without the extra pay. At the Holyhead camp, he was appointed acting company quartermaster sergeant (CQMS). This was a substantial position of responsibility for someone so young, placing Markham in charge of all the company pay, rations and stores, including kit issues and inspections, and disciplinary action over damages and loss. As he had no real experience, he was taught the basics at the camp by the company sergeant major (CSM), then had to learn the rest on the job. Fortunately, he had a good head for numbers and was quick at mental arithmetic, despite his lack of formal qualifications. His youth did not endear him to the regimental sergeant major (RSM), the senior NCO in the battalion, a 50-year-old regular who disliked territorials in general. But critically he won the confidence and support of his company commander, Captain Victor Ward, after Reg took the blame for an accounting error made by Ward.

It had quickly become clear that relying on traditional volunteering could not produce the numbers now needed by the army. On 26 April 1939, the government introduced a form of conscription through the Military Training Act. This required all 20-year-old men to undertake six months of military training, followed by three-and-a-half years in the TA. They were to register at their local labour exchange, and to be liable for call up any time within the following twelve months. Service could be postponed or anticipated with good reason, such as completion or expectation of an apprenticeship or academic study. Anyone in the military was exempt, as were those not now serving but who had already completed six months' military service since the age of 17, and any territorials enlisted up to 27 April. For the army, compulsory service had the benefit that the restrictions that applied within the TA, particularly the fact that they were not liable for overseas service unless they volunteered for it, did not apply to those who entered the army under the Military Training Act. Unlike in the First World War, where the regulars, territorials and New Army had acted almost as separate organisations, the army in 1939 was moving towards having a common basis for service throughout.

What motivated the young men of Derbyshire to join up? The sense of national emergency was of course important. Throughout most of the decade, military service had not been popular in the county, but the army shared in the change of national sentiment due to the events of 1938. Recruitment numbers for the regulars in that year were more than double those for 1937. A similar rise was shown in the number of men enrolled in the TA in the county, up from 1,654 (in all units) in 1937 to 3,555 in May 1939. But the initial March recruitment drive for the TA drew in less than half the number of volunteers needed, which, together with Hore-Belisha's expansion plans, led to a further campaign in April with the slogan 'Double up Derbyshire'. Although under the Military Training Act the new 'militiamen', as they were termed (to distinguish them from regular recruits but also perhaps to avoid the term 'conscript'), could not be sent out of the UK, and were guaranteed security in their peacetime employment (employees had to reinstate them at the end of their training), there was a rush in recruitment later that month, which suggests that some joined the TA to avoid compulsory service. On 26 April, there were seventeen men recruited for the Foresters at the Derby Drill Hall, and no fewer than fifty-seven at the HQ of the Derbyshire Yeomanry, an armoured car unit. After that date, recruits could not join the TA at all if aged 20 or 21, and if younger they were still not exempt from compulsory service when they reached 20. Volunteers for the TA could also choose the unit or service they wanted to join. This was particularly important to those choosing to serve in the yeomanry, artillery, signals or engineers. These units had generally reached their war establishment by June 1939, while the infantry units were still understrength. But even in the infantry, there were those wanting to ensure enlistment in their local regiment. The introduction of compulsory service did not stop the territorials' recruitment drive; instead, it was hoped that it would stimulate recruiting of those between the ages of 21 and 25.

There were other factors involved in any individual's decision to join up. Although by definition the territorials were part-time soldiers who had other employment, financial incentives may have played some part. A recruit was required to attend a minimum of forty training drills in his first year and to attend a three-week annual camp. Successful completion of this was rewarded by a bounty of £3. There was no payment for attending the drills themselves, which took place at evenings or weekends. Expenses could be claimed, but only for the first fifteen drills. While at camp, the TA men also received regular rates of pay—which could be up to 8s 3d (42p) per day for a senior sergeant, although it started at only 2s (10p) daily for a private. Married men got an additional 17s (85p) per day allowance for their wife, and additional sums if they had children. Trying to equate these to modern wages and prices is difficult. The nominal Consumer Price Inflation rate valued a 1939 pound at £54.09 in 2023, which would imply that the bounties were relatively small sums. But the average weekly earnings for a man in 1938 were £3.50, compared to about £861 in 2023. Looking at it in these terms, the bounty was worth slightly less than an average week's wages, the equivalent of £738.[1] The attendance payments may therefore have been attractive to younger men with a low-paid job or those in industries still struggling to recover from the Depression of the early 1930s. Reg Markham reckoned that he had never been so well off in his life. Nonetheless, money was unlikely to be the main attraction for service for those in full-time work.

The army used some clever marketing strategies in its recruitment drive, not unlike today's television adverts for the armed forces which promote service careers as both a lifestyle and education opportunity. It was presented as a modern fighting force in which young men could develop their skills and personal potential. In the aftermath of Munich, National Service Weeks were held around the country. The one in Derby was scheduled to take place from 12–18 March 1939, but was extended into the following week—perhaps in response to the occupation of Czechoslovakia. Displays included army vehicles of the 5th Sherwood Foresters and armoured cars of the Derbyshire Yeomanry. There were also searchlights, anti-aircraft guns and barrage balloons from local air defence units, and aircraft from the nearby RAF base at Hucknall. An example more directly related to the raising of men for the 2/5th Battalion took place early in April, when a contingent from Normanton Barracks toured around villages in Derbyshire to demonstrate the army's new equipment and give displays of physical training. According to the local paper, the exhibits included the new Bren light machine gun (although it was incorrectly described as an automatic rifle), 2-inch and 3-inch mortars and anti-tank rifles, but also less warlike items such as Norton motorcycles, petrol cookers and diet sheets indicating the improved quality of army food. The exhibition also included sports equipment and regimental trophies. The Foresters had a strong sporting tradition, particularly in football, but the 5th Battalion also boasted the champion cook in the whole of the TA, Private J. Crooks, prompting the rather unlikely claim in one local newspaper that the army's menus 'would do credit to many an hotel'.[2] Displays such as these sought to entice young men attracted to adventure and sport, and perhaps by a uniform to impress the local girls—that was why 19-year-old Bill Sheppard, a miner's son from Chesterfield, signed up with D Company in June. Recruits were mostly young—the local papers reported 17-year-olds demonstrating machine-gun drills. For those of a more serious disposition, the army offered the opportunity to learn a trade or skill, such as operating a wireless or driving and maintaining motor vehicles, which may seem commonplace now but were not so readily available to young men in rural Derbyshire in the 1930s. With the replacement of horsed transport in the army, many of the men attending the summer camp had to be trained to drive the new trucks, Bren gun carriers and motorcycles. Harry Higton, a 20-year-old iron foundry worker, was an avid reader of Basil Liddell Hart, one of the leading military British theorists on tank and air warfare. Harry attended one of the recruiting shows and was keen to join up, but his mother, Fanny, stopped him. She had lost a husband and seven of her eleven children to the hard times of the 1920s and '30s, and needed her eldest son to help out in the successful fish-and-chip shop she now ran in Ilkeston with Harry's stepfather.

Local pride also had its part to play. In April, there was an appeal for recruits from the Duke of Devonshire, who expressed that he had 'no doubt that Derbyshire will maintain its old tradition of service'.[3] Local businesses also supported recruitment drives: five staff at Bourne and Sons in Ripley (now the Denby Pottery) were enticed by the company's offer of holidays for training and a bonus of £5 for each man who joined up. In Belper, meanwhile, thirty employees of Brettle's hosing and stocking factory had signed up by May. When 18-year-old Chesterfield baker George Hampton joined the TA in June, it was together with a number of cousins, friends and neighbours. The most significant example of local patronage was across the county border in Nottinghamshire, where Captain Claude Granville Lancaster, MP for Fylde—a former officer in the Horse Guards, and chairman and managing director of BA Collieries Ltd—recruited 85 per cent of the new second-line battalion of the 8th Foresters from the men in his firm, and became its lieutenant colonel. This resulted in it rapidly reaching full strength and having a high *esprit de corps* from its inception. For its part, the army played both the territorial card and that of the regiment's heritage. The 5th Battalion's band was a popular attraction at many gatherings, and an appeal was launched to purchase new instruments—not perhaps as useful in war as tanks and machine guns, but bringing in £298 by the middle of August and demonstrating the local support for the battalion.[4] The 2nd Battalion, which had long been absent from the region either overseas or in the south of England, but in which 80 per cent of the men came from Derbyshire and Nottinghamshire, toured the area during the summer, parading with the regimental mascot Derby XVI. On 15 July, when the first 150 militiamen arrived at Normanton Barracks—all of them from North Derbyshire, Nottinghamshire or Burton upon Trent—sixty-eight of them attended a service at the Crich Memorial the next day. A crowd of 2,000 gathered, despite heavy rain, to hear the colonel of the regiment, Sir Frederick Maurice, declare that 'Derbyshire and Nottinghamshire have always set an example to the country of service and duty well performed', and call upon a new generation to emulate the sacrifices of those of 1914–18. They would not have long to wait. On 1 September 1939, Hitler's forces launched their onslaught on Poland.

*

The outbreak of war in the summer of 1939 did not take the British government by surprise, as it had twenty-five years earlier. The army had in fact started mobilising even before Hitler made his move. Territorial AA units, which had already been deployed during the Munich crisis in 1938, were called up in June 1939 because of the fear of a possible surprise air attack, and were fully mobilised on 21 August. The war diary of the Foresters' Infantry Training Centre (ITC) at Derby, which was responsible for organising the call-up and allocation of reservists, dates from 24 August, when Hore-Belisha began a further mobilisation to protect 'vulnerable points' (VPs). On that day, the ITC organised a reconnaissance of VPs in the region, estimated the number of guards required for each and began to call up reservists to the regular battalions. The following day, some key personnel of TA units were called up, including acting CQMS Reg Markham; the 18-year-old's job was so important. Preparations for Passive Air Defence (PAD)—such as the digging of trenches or shelters—started to be put into effect, and on 31 August the Army Reserve and Supplementary Reserve were called out. Then at 2.30pm on 1 September, the HQ of the 2/5th Foresters received the codeword 'Clive', the signal to implement the national Civil Defence Scheme, including mobilisation of the TA. (For some reason, the ITC only recorded receiving the 'Clive' signal at 7.25pm, with the signal for full mobilisation arriving thirty-five minutes later.) Call-up papers were delivered by hand, but since it had only just returned from the summer camp at Holyhead, the 2/5th Battalion was able to react quickly. The nominal strength of the unit was twenty-one officers and 458 other ranks, and by 2 September—*before* war was declared on Germany—all twenty-one officers and 408 ORs had reported for duty.

As well as replicating the individual battalions in the TA, Hore-Belisha's expansion programme had also included the duplication of the higher-level formations. In the case of 49th Division, this meant resurrecting the number of the famous 46th Division from the Great War, which had been converted to an AA formation in 1936. Within the new second-line division, initially commanded by 56-year-old Major General Algernon Lee Ransome, 148 Brigade was duplicated as 139 Brigade, under Brigadier Henry Alastair Fergusson Crewdson. Wounded twice as a lieutenant in the Coldstream Guards in the First World War, Crewdson came from a Nottinghamshire family and had transferred to the 8th Sherwood Foresters in 1917. He commanded the battalion from 1936 before being given 139 Brigade on the outbreak of war. At 41, Crewdson was significantly younger than most senior officers in the TA formations, who on average were Ransome's age. Although these divisional and brigade structures had been provided for prior to the war, they did not have a permanent establishment—even in the original TA divisions, the brigades were run at only 30–40 per cent of their requirements in peacetime. Instead, officers and men were assigned to brigade-level duties from within the constituent units. With little more than a skeleton staff, 139 Brigade HQ opened on 15 September at 6 Clinton Terrace, Nottingham. Among those assigned over the next few weeks was Jack Schofield from Hathersage, serving with A Company of the 2/5th Foresters. Schofield was the second youngest of seven children, and his father Harry had served with the Coldstream Guards on the Somme. He had signed up in May 1939 when the company had been formed, centred upon the Hope Valley, with its HQ in the village of Bamford. Eighteen-year-old Schofield had clearly been singled out as a potential leader by the company commander, Captain Thomas Hardy McCall, another Hathersage man, and by Sergeant Jukes, its regular army instructor; after the August camp, Schofield had been appointed lance corporal and sent on a Physical Training Instructors course. On 22 September, he arrived in Nottingham, along with George Quin of the 2/5th Leicesters and Jim Poyle of the 9th Foresters, to join the brigade HQ. He would be the only one of the three to survive the war. Billeted in an empty house and sleeping on bare boards, they were nevertheless 'light hearted and care free', spending their 2s per day wages in Nottingham's plentiful pubs, in the company of girls from the John Player's cigarette factory.

The TA effectively ceased to exist as of 5 September 1939, and all units and formations became part of a single army. The wearing of the distinctive 'T' badge by TA units was suspended. Though resented by some, there were obvious security reasons for its removal. TA recruiting stopped and conscription became the normal means of bringing more men into the service. Most importantly, all previous arrangements whereby territorials were guaranteed to remain within their units were cancelled under the new Armed Forces (Conditions of Service) Act. The army now reserved the right to move men between units, and even change the role of entire units, according to the necessities of the war.

When it came to the practical deployment of men and units in 1939, regulars and former territorials were treated entirely differently due to their levels of training and experience. The second-line TA units of 139 Brigade were initially assigned to guard VPs across Derbyshire and Nottinghamshire, formally taking over these duties at midnight on 23 September from 148 Brigade. The most important of these, the Rolls Royce factory at Derby which manufactured Merlin engines for Spitfires, was allocated not to the locals of the Sherwood Foresters but to the 2/5th Leicesters, who took up billets in the town. The 9th Foresters were given responsibility for the RAF airfields and fuel dumps in the Nottingham area. This left the 2/5th with rather less glamorous locations to guard throughout Derbyshire. A and D companies were sent to guard internment camps (ICs) at Swanwick and Donnington Hall respectively—though neither camp yet contained any internees! C Company was given the task of guarding the Totley Tunnel in the Hope Valley, a 3½-mile-long feature on the Midland Railway's line between Sheffield and Manchester. B Company received perhaps the most important and certainly the largest task, which was to guard the RAF's new fuel dump at Dove Holes Quarry, between Buxton and Chapel-en-le-Frith, intended to hold 12 million gallons of fuel. An attempted attack on the site had already occurred in June, probably associated with the Irish Republican Army (IRA), which was active in Britain in the late 1930s. The Derbyshire Police also investigated an Irish private soldier (unit unnamed) for possible IRA affiliations, though none were identified and he was allowed to continue with his duties. The first men from B Company arrived at Dove Holes on 18 September.

The allocation of VPs to the different companies roughly matched their recruitment areas, which meant that many of the men could be billeted at home. When on VP guard duty, men were to have three nights per week in bed and one

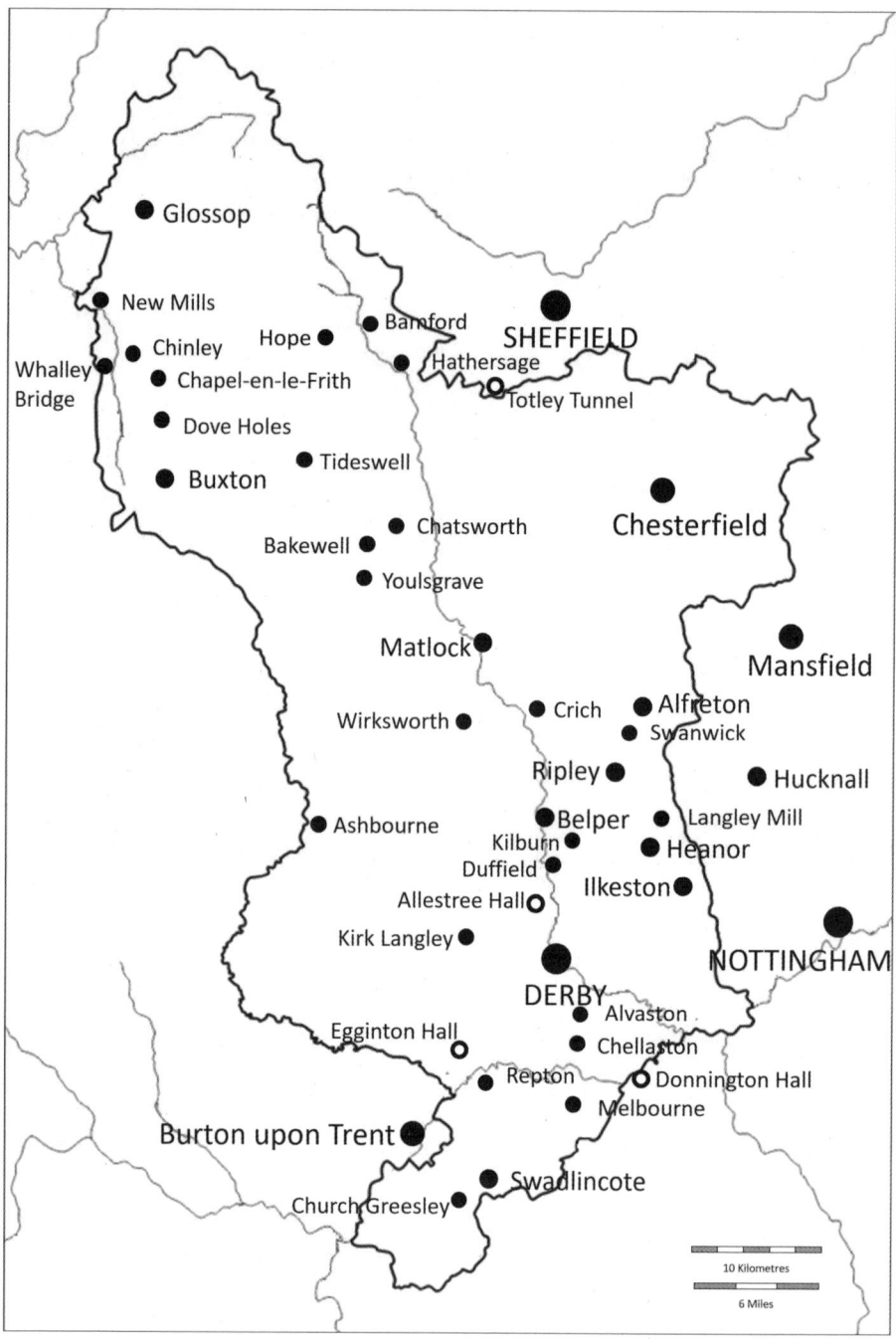

Derbyshire, 1939.

week in four off. The few alarms reported were trivial—a 'suspicious incident' at the Swanwick IC on 1 October; a man seen at Rolls Royce with a 'very large camera' on 6 October, who subsequently proved to be a company employee; and barbed wire being cut along the railway lines near Derby on 12 October. Nevertheless, the duties were acknowledged to be irksome, and as the wet autumn weather in the Peak District set in they also became uncomfortable. The average age of the guards in October was less than 19, and they were considered unsuitable for the work. There were several cases of individuals deserting their posts, and the importance of the activity to the war effort had to be stressed to the men. Claude Lancaster, now acting commander of 139 Brigade, wrote in November that the duties had a 'negative effect on discipline, health and keenness' of the men and stated the 'desirability at the earliest moment of some authoritative statement as to their prospects of being trained and playing their part on active service, for which they are so naturally impatient'. He considered that 'the discipline, enthusiasm and esprit de corps of the B[attalio]ns' formed over the summer had been 'of very high standard', and the officers and men 'of superior quality on physique and intelligence to their counterparts in the first-line Units', though not, he admitted, in their level of training and effectiveness.[5] Requests to use the new conscript classes for guard duty instead of the more highly motivated TA volunteers were rejected, however, as the army was intent upon getting those men trained as soon as possible.

Dove Holes was the least hospitable post of those guarded by the 2/5th Foresters, as well as the most important. Extensive building activity was still taking place, and rain and construction traffic turned the roads and paths in the quarry leading to the sentry posts into quagmires. As winter drew on, the plan was to have reliefs every half-hour. The site was so large that it was impossible to hear the sentries' whistles at the command post, so Very lights had to be requested for signalling. Meanwhile, the RAF was anxious to get the site completed and tried to initiate round-the-clock working with floodlights. The Foresters objected that this would potentially silhouette the guards walking their rounds, so refused to allow it unless the perimeter was surrounded by barbed wire fence. However, such a fence around the railhead at Doves Hole village did little to add to the security of the site, as it was frequently crossed by men taking a shortcut to avoid the mud at the entrance. Three officers and ninety-nine men were assigned to guard the dump, but the officer commanding reckoned that it would require 260 men to mount a proper guard.

The battalion's resources were being stretched thin. C Company had given up its responsibility for the Totley Tunnel but had taken on that of RAF Hucknall, while a further 110 men had to be found for a Balloon Barrage Depot at Alvaston. This would have made it all but impossible to fulfil their other main role under the Civil Defence Scheme, to help defend the country against the air attacks which were thought sure to come soon. The role of the army in the event of heavy aerial attack was to support the civil powers in quelling disturbances, supplement the local authorities in response to air raids and, perhaps most important of all, to steady the morale of the civilian population just through being visible on the streets. Very few troops—and they did not include the 2/5th Foresters—were either trained or equipped for Air Raid Precautions (ARP) work or to clear bomb damage, so they were only expected to perform ancillary duties such as forming cordons, rescuing trapped civilians, traffic control, crowd control and managing refugees. They were instructed to always deploy in formed bodies of at least company strength, from which platoon-sized groups could then be detached. They were to carry live ammunition, but only rifles and side-arms. Automatic weapons were not to be carried, except for use in air defence, and second-line TA units still had very few of these anyway. Importantly, instructions stated that the troops 'will not be used in aid of the civil power to overawe or suppress the civil population'.[6] Although troops were told to report any parachutists to the police—even if in British uniform—there was little expectation of meeting the enemy.

The country was organised into a number of regions, each under a civilian Regional Commissioner, who was supported by a Regional Committee and a military liaison officer. Number 3 North Midland Region covered Northamptonshire, Lincolnshire, Leicestershire, Rutlandshire, Nottinghamshire and most of Derbyshire (excluding Glossop, Buxton, New Mills, Whalley Bridge and Chapel-en-le-Frith). Lord Trent (the head of Boots the Chemists) was the commissioner, with his headquarters in the Nottingham Main Post Office. The region was then divided into sub-areas, which were individually assessed for risk of air attack and graded on a five-point scale. Derby, which contained the important Rolls Royce works, was given the second-highest grading (Grade II), with a risk that it could be the target for up to 25 per cent of the enemy's military effort on any single day. Nottingham was also classed as a Grade II target, Chesterfield ranked as Grade III and Mansfield as Grade IV. Civilian requests for assistance from the army were to come from the Chief Constable of the county; these would then be passed to the Regional HQ, to the military liaison officer, and then to the local sub-area commander, who would allocate military resources. Only if this chain of command broke down were local police officers authorised to call directly upon the local military. Within 139 Brigade, whose area of responsibility covered most of Nottinghamshire and Derbyshire, the 2/5th Leicesters were responsible for the south, the 9th Foresters the north and the 2/5th Foresters the west.

*

On 12 September 1939, Private Stanley Waine Darwent, from the Hope Valley, appeared in court to give evidence at an inquest into the death of a man he had seen killed while on sentry duty the previous weekend. After the hearing, he was given a few hours' leave and went to visit friends in the village of Tideswell with his stepbrother. While returning to barracks, Darwent crashed his motorcycle into a wall near the hamlet of Windmill, north of the village. He suffered a fractured skull and other severe injuries and was unconscious in Sheffield Royal Infirmary for fourteen hours. This was probably the battalion's first casualty of the war. Its first fatality occurred on 17 October 1939 and was equally mundane, not the result of either enemy action or an accident, but of disease. Twenty-year-old Private Ernest Briggs Hill of B Company, from Chinley near Chapel-en-le-Frith, died at Dove Holes of cerebro-spinal fever—now better known as meningitis. This had been almost unknown in the British army prior to the First World War, but had become a serious health threat from 1914–18, with a very high mortality rate because of the lack of experience with the disease within the Royal Army Medical Corps (RAMC) and absence of a testing regime or effective serums. By the Second World War, the RAMC was better prepared to manage the highly contagious disease, but the case must still have caused concern within the battalion in October 1939, not least because it seems not to have had its own medical officer (MO) until the end of the month. There was also a suspected case of diphtheria at Castle Donnington the following week, though this tested negative. These medical issues temporarily prevented the transfer of men between battalions and companies. There was an outbreak of scarlet fever amongst the guard at Hucknall in early December, but other than these incidents the health of the battalion appears to have been remarkably good throughout the harsh winter of 1939–40.

While the battalion may not have suffered many casualties during the early months of the war, there was significant turnover within its ranks. As soon as men had been called up, there began a process of 'combing out' those who were in reserved occupations or were simply unfit to serve, having failed their medical. The latter would have regrettably included some of the longer-serving and more experienced pre-war TA men. The number 'combed out' in the 2/5th is not clear, but since it predominantly contained new recruits, it was probably less affected than the original 1/5th Battalion. A second reason for turnover arose from the army's policy against sending very young troops abroad. Within the ranks of the 1/5th Foresters were several men under the age of 19, and these were not allowed to serve overseas. Towards the end of September, fifty-three of these 'immatures' were transferred to the 2/5th, while the same number of older men were transferred in the other direction to keep the first-line battalion up to strength. A further 133 men went from the 2/5th to the 1/5th in October, but this time only ninety-two were received in return, all of them under 19 on 1 January 1940. The original request had been to transfer even more men to the 1/5th, but they could not be spared from guard duty. By the end of November, it was reported that in the whole of 139 Brigade there were only 200 trained men—the remainder being immatures or new conscripts.

The initial pre-war intake of 'militia' had, after basic training, mostly gone to the regular or at least the first-line territorial battalions. Wartime intakes began to be posted to the second-line battalions in the new year. Amongst the group that had been called up on 16 October, and inspected the following week by Brigadier Crewdson—who was 'favourably impressed by the type and their enthusiasm'—was 20-year-old Alan Orme.[7] Most of the intake was from Nottingham, but Orme was a miner's son from Belper. He had left school at 14 and gone down the pit, but after an accident at the colliery he had left to work at an iron foundry in Derby. Many of his friends had joined the TA, but Orme had a well-paid job, a girlfriend and was studying at night school, so had waited as long as possible after receiving the initial conscription papers in July. After a few weeks of basic training at Normanton Barracks, Orme went to Egginton Hall, a country house in the south of the county near Burton, where the men were taught to shoot using .22 rifles at the local range and generally 'toughened up' by the commanding officer at the Hall, Captain Geoffrey 'Goofy' Gofton-Salmond, a pre-war regular officer. The winter of 1939–40 gave many opportunities for toughening up; it was the most severe since 1895. The temperature dropped below zero on 27 December and stayed there or thereabouts until mid-February, and the north of the country suffered from an exceptionally heavy snowfall on 28 January. The freezing conditions, as well as ammunition and weapon shortages, severely restricted further training. Frank Offiler, called up from his job at Player's Cigarettes in the same month as Orme, never fired a shot while at Egginton, and there were no opportunities for learning field craft or even basic platoon-level exercises. Orme and the others were instead sent down to Birmingham to clear the railway lines of snow, which had brought the network to a standstill. At Allestree Hall north of Derby, another country house requisitioned by the army, conscript and former miner Willis Dixon spent his time shifting snow as well as carrying and chopping wood for the cookhouse. The new wartime intakes were substantially larger than those of the summer. Horace Hansell, who had tried to enlist while underage in 1935, entered the army for a second time in November as part of a group of around 800 at Normanton Barracks, where they were drilled for several weeks before moving on to Egginton Hall.

For the TA men, relief from the tedium of guard duty eventually arrived in the form of men from the National Defence Companies. In June 1939, an appeal had gone out for men to enlist in these formations as part of the TA reserve, with 100 men wanted from the Derby district alone. They were attached to TA units and received the same pay, but because they would receive little training (a mere six drills per year, compared to the forty expected of the bulk of the TA), they were only open to ex-servicemen between the ages of 45 and 55. Recruitment was mostly through the Sherwood Foresters Association and other ex-servicemen's organisations. The expectation had been that these companies would be called up before the TA. However, it was not until late November

1939 that they began to take responsibility for VPs, by which time they had been organised into a separate battalion, the 10th (Home Defence) Battalion Sherwood Foresters.

The need to find guards and to prepare for Home Defence duties had a damaging effect on basic military training. The detachments at each post—usually organised into groups of twelve men, including NCOs—were in theory meant to do one-and-a-half days of training in every four, and after any session of guard duty they were to have received at least a full night's rest. This allowed for substantially less training than that received by the conscripts, which compressed a full year of regular drills and skills training into six months. The pre-war 'militia' intake had been divided into squads of thirty and received daily weapons training and shooting practice in the afternoon and evening. After two months, the first drafts had gone to Bordon for another two months' training with the 2nd Battalion, prior to two months of specialist training. The outbreak of war, plus the severe weather in January and February, curtailed this to some extent, but as already mentioned, the army strongly resisted any requests for the conscripts to take on VP guard duties. In contrast, the expectations for the territorials were much lower, perhaps a misjudgement, given that as volunteers they were probably more motivated. The emphasis was put on acquiring 'basic military qualities'—discipline, *esprit de corps* and alertness. There was little opportunity to teach more specialist skills. In November, the brigade reported a shortage of personnel to form signals platoons, although it was trying to arrange what training it could. More difficult still was developing leadership and military skills among officers and NCOs. The dearth of experience among officers may explain the attachment of Captain J. W. Bee from the University of Reading Officer Training Corps (OTC) to the battalion on 27 November. NCOs had to be trained within their companies because of the demands of other duties. Junior officers, on the other hand, were occasionally sent away on courses held at brigade or division level, which were also sometimes attended by NCOs and ORs from brigade HQ. Second Lieutenant Richard Garrett, who in the winter of 1939–40 had just been posted to the 8th Foresters in Nottingham but would later join the 2/5th, went off to Ripon in Yorkshire for a two-week crash course on being an officer, and his equivalents in the 2/5th did the same or similar. Jack Schofield found himself with some of them in early February 1940 at the Nottingham College of Art, attending a course on map reading, field sketching and camouflage.

*

On 17 February 1940, the Civil Defence Scheme was cancelled and a new Home Defence Scheme issued, but it did not substantially change the battalion's role. The civil structure remained as before, while the military were allocated to three tiers of response: a 'first line', a local reserve and an area reserve. Military operations were expected to be coordinated by battalion COs or above, although lower-ranking officers would be allowed to carry out urgent tasks if reference to higher echelons would delay a response. The scenarios envisaged were those of seaborne attack, airborne attack and sabotage. A seaborne invasion was to be met with an immediate counterattack, but for the men of the 2/5th Foresters, based well inland, their role would have been limited to keeping roads clear of refugees and preventing civilian motor transport entering the invasion area. Anti-saboteur activity was the role of the Home Defence battalions guarding the VPs. This meant that the focus of the battalion was guarding against air attack, either in the form of an extended attritional campaign or a concentrated offensive, both referred to as 'home security' duties.

Aside from the possibility of saboteurs dropped by parachute, three forms of air attack were considered: high-level raids by bombers using high explosive, incendiaries or gas; low-flying attacks with the same munitions; and the dropping of airborne troops with the intent of capturing one or more airfields. Opposing the bombers was down to RAF Fighter Command, supported by the army's AA Command. Specialist parties of Royal Engineers were responsible for bomb disposal, and a proportion of reserves—again mostly Engineers—were earmarked for ARP clearance and rescue duties. The RAF was responsible for crashed aircraft. Troops such as the 2/5th Foresters were merely expected to assist with public morale, maintaining order, preventing sabotage and looting, and maintaining communications and essential services. Low-level aerial attacks would be tackled in a similar fashion, with the difference that the main responsibility for dealing with these rested with the AA troops rather than the RAF.

The risk of enemy action against RAF stations was also assessed in the new scheme. Four levels of attack were considered possible, the last of which involved only sabotage originating from within Britain. The next-lowest category was isolated raids by up to forty airborne troops. Cottesmore, Finningley and Hucknall aerodromes were judged to be possible targets for such an operation. The next level of risk, a raid at battalion level (400 troops) on ten to twelve airfields, was considered negligible in the region. The final possibility, since the Germans were believed to have some 4,000 paratroopers and another 6,000 air-landing troops available, was a full-scale attack against the east-coast aerodromes to destroy fighter bases or seize airfields or landing beaches in advance of a seaborne invasion by up to 20,000 men carried on up to twenty-five ships. The Humber estuary was expected to be the most likely target for such an attempt in Northern Command. Any naval force would require some twelve to fourteen hours to cross the North Sea, and a further seven to disembark. Unsurprisingly, the scheme included the assessment that 'it seems unlikely that the enemy would attempt a large-scale invasion without preliminary action to neutralise our fighters and bombers and to drive our naval forces from the North Sea'.[8]

Unlikely or not, plans were made to defend against such an invasion, and the 2/5th Foresters were part of them. 'Julius' would be the codeword issued giving warning of a possible attack; it would result in the immediate cancellation of all leave and the start of preparations for a response to 'Caesar', the codeword for an imminent attack. Upon receipt of this, all units would go onto standby, issue ammunition and collect their transport. The 46th Division was allocated responsibility for the southern sector of Northern Command, with 23rd Division to its north, a light armoured brigade in Command reserve and 55th Division in general reserve. The ITCs within the region were also allocated to the divisions for local defence. Given its distance from the coast, the division's role was again limited to home security, which meant dispersion of the troops. Two companies (less than 200 men) of the 2/5th Foresters were allocated to be a sub-area reserve, covering the whole of Derbyshire, Nottinghamshire, Leicestershire and Rutlandshire. In addition to this reserve, a mobile detachment of up to 250 was earmarked for the retaking of Hucknall aerodrome, should it be attacked.

The battalion's involvement in this new plan was short lived, however, as Brigadier Crewdson was advised by secret letter from 46th Division on 7 March that his brigade was to be on three weeks' notice to move to France, and that any remaining VP guards were to be transferred to 55th Division. The orders were for a move as a formation, rather than battalions being split up as drafts to existing units, and units were expected to go at war establishment but without any immediate reserve (in army parlance, 'first reinforcements'). No officers were to go on courses that would end after 12 April, and while men were allowed to go on Easter leave at the end of March, it would constitute their entitlement to four days of embarkation leave. Initially, the information was restricted to company commanders and above, who were advised upon matters such as discipline during the move and liaison with the French. The men were only told of the move on 21 March, two weeks before the battalion's home defence responsibilities ended on 5 April.

These orders caused Crewdson great consternation. He pointed out to the division commander that on 29 March, 139 Brigade would be only 1,250 strong—460 in the 2/5th Leicesters, 440 in the 9th Foresters and a mere 350 in the 2/5th. This was less than half the war establishment. With these low levels of manpower, merely organising companies for routine activities would be very difficult. The response was to add men at the last minute from training establishments. Among these new men were Orme, Offiler and Hansell. Stationed in Market Harborough in Leicestershire, they realised something was up when they received tetanus and tuberculosis jabs. After allowing for the loss of 'immatures' not eligible to go overseas, these reinforcements bought the battalion up to something like war strength, but in terms of personnel it was a substantially different battalion to that which had mustered at the start of the war. It was still overwhelmingly comprised of men from Nottinghamshire and Derbyshire, and some of the companies still retained their association with particular towns and villages resulting from the recruitment drives of 1939. B Company, for example, contained a large proportion of men from Buxton. But less than half of the troops had been with the battalion more than six months, and its overall level of training and experience was low. It was also overwhelmingly young, mostly comprised of 20-year-olds in the ranks. Many of its junior officers were as young and inexperienced as the men they were now expected to lead, while its senior officers were Great War veterans from the pre-war TA. Such was the state of the battalion as it prepared to take its first steps to becoming a true fighting unit.

3

First Steps: France, April–May 1940

The British forces in France at the start of April 1940 had grown to a strength of over 280,000 men. However, only about 140,000 of these were front-line troops in the ten infantry divisions, a number scarcely larger than that of the BEF which had fought in autumn 1914 after only a few weeks of war.[1] In large part this was due to the vastly increased complexity of warfare compared to a generation earlier. The BEF of 1940 was not particularly well equipped with tanks, but there were nevertheless several armoured units, along with the necessary maintenance and support depots. The RAF, independent since 1918, was still largely reliant upon the army to construct its airfields in France, and then to provide support and protection for them in the form of AA and searchlight battalions. Then there were the specialist chemical warfare troops, since everyone expected that gas would be used again, as it had been in the last war. Gas masks were issued to both soldiers and civilians in 1939, and soldiers carried further counter-measures; these included an oilskin gas cape, a tin of ointment to use against mustard gas burns and a pack of eyeshields.

Behind the fighting units were a whole range of services needed by a modern army to provide communication, construction and logistics support. There were telegraph and telephony units, and despatch riders (DRs) on motorcycles, from the Royal Signals. To build and run the military railways, there were surveying companies, construction and maintenance companies, and workshops and operation companies, from the Royal Engineers. There were stevedore companies to work in the docks. There were also the field bakeries and butcheries, and a range of motor transport units, of the Royal Army Service Corps (RASC); the hospitals, ambulances, laboratories and field hygiene units of the Royal Army Medical Corps (RAMC); and the stores and ammunition depots manned by the Royal Army Ordnance Corps (RAOC).

In the First World War, the BEF's main lines of communication had passed through the Channel ports, but in 1939 the decision had been made to establish its logistics train in Brittany. The primary reason for this was because of the perceived threat to the Channel route from enemy air action. There was a further benefit that it meant both the French and British supply lines to northern France ran roughly parallel in a north–south direction. The city of Rennes, the largest railway marshalling yard in western France, was the logical choice for the BEF's main depot. From here, the supply line ran to Le Mans, then via Rouen and Amiens to Arras. This was a much longer route than in 1918, requiring many more men to construct and operate it. Among the units so deployed in 1939 was the 1/5th Foresters, based in Nozay near the port of St Nazaire.

The period from September 1939 to April 1940 is popularly known as the 'Phoney War', since little fighting took place between the French and British forces and the Germans. The First World War had instilled a methodical, cautious and mostly defensive approach to modern war in the Allied armies, especially the French, who had constructed the massive and technically sophisticated line of fortifications known as the Maginot Line along the German border. However, this permanent defensive line stopped south of Luxembourg, leaving the French border with Belgium undefended. The expectation was that in the event of war, the Germans would invade Belgium and the Allies would go to its aid. Nevertheless, as Belgium held a strictly neutral diplomatic stance, there was no plan either for cooperation with its army or to occupy its defences. So during this period the French and the British began construction of hundreds of miles of trenches and pillboxes along the Belgian frontier to extend and protect the flank of the Maginot Line. In the British sector, where 40 miles of anti-tank obstacles and around 400 pillboxes were constructed, this became known as the 'Gort Line', after the BEF commander, Lord Gort VC. Creation of the Gort Line required yet more troops to be diverted to construction work rather than combat training.

The Phoney War period ended in April 1940 with the German invasion of Norway. Not only were troops sent to Norway from Britain, including the 8th Foresters, but there were also suggestions that one or more of the divisions already in France might need to be sent to support operations there.

The overall result of this was that with over 280,000 troops in France, none of whom were actually fighting the enemy, the BEF found itself short of men. The answer to this was to be found in the ranks of the second-line territorial units that remained in the UK. Although not yet trained to fight, they could still be used to build roads, railways and airfields; to construct barracks and warehouses; to dig trenches; or simply to direct traffic. The decision was made to send nine of these battalions, organised into three divisions (the 12th, 23rd and 46th), to France: not to fight, but as labour battalions.

*

Before describing the experience of the 2/5th Sherwood Foresters in their first campaign, it is appropriate to explain the organisation and equipment of the British infantry at this stage of the war. Most of the privates in the battalion were in one of its rifle sections. In 1940, each of these contained eight men, considered to be the largest group that could be directly commanded by a single man on the modern battlefield, and it formed the basic component of infantry tactics. It also formed the focus of the soldier's social life. Most men fought not for king and country, not for the honour of their regiment, but so as not to let down their mates in their section. Head of this surrogate family was the corporal. In a 1940 TA unit, these would have consisted of a few regulars backed up by the longer-serving territorials, but in a second-line battalion like the 2/5th, they were unlikely to be significantly older or more experienced than the privates. Bill Sheppard got the rank mostly because his father had been in the old 6th Battalion, so he knew the basics of soldiering before joining up. Second in command was a lance corporal. In the British army at this time, this was an appointment, not an actual rank. Men were appointed lance corporals by their commanding officers if they were thought to be more intelligent than their peers, or to have the leadership qualities that gave them the potential for later promotion. Although Britain had universal and compulsory education, many youngsters still left school at 14, and some recruits lacked the basic numeracy and literacy skills to carry out the functions required of these junior NCOs, such as reporting stores or passing on written orders.

Two of the men in the section at this time were still designated as 'bombers', a legacy of the trench fighting of the First World War, where the hand grenade had been as important as the rifle. The standard weapon with which all the men were armed was the .303 Short Magazine Lee-Enfield (SMLE) rifle. This would also have been familiar to veterans of the last war; in fact, the basic design was some fifty years old. Weighing just under 9lb, with an effective range of 600 yards and a maximum of 2,000, it was still an accurate weapon in trained hands but lacked the rate of fire of more modern semi-automatic rifles. The normal rate of fire was five aimed rounds per minute, while rapid fire was simply as fast as the soldier could fire with accuracy—up to fifteen rounds per minute for well-trained troops. Many of the 2/5th had received little or no instruction with the Lee-Enfield; at best they had shot .22 rifles at Totley or Trent Bridge.

The primary weapon of the section was neither the rifle nor the hand grenade, but the Bren light machine gun. A pre-war Czech design, weighing 26lb, firing up to 450 rifle-calibre bullets per minute and with a range up to 2,000 yards, this was one of the mainstays of the rearmament programme of the late 1930s. Section tactics were built around the Bren gun, with the accompanying rifleman there to give support and covering fire as the two-man Bren team moved from position to position in order to bring its fire down upon the enemy, keeping him suppressed until the riflemen could make a final assault. The Bren was robust and highly accurate, but the latter was not necessarily a good attribute for a machine gun. Its German equivalent, the MG34, fired more rounds per minute and its bullets spread over a wider field of fire. But in 1940, there was a more serious problem. In the rush to rearm, Bren guns were in short supply, and the second-line territorials were last in line to receive the new weapons. The 2/5th had only eighteen Bren guns in total, rather than the fifty they should have had. They were, after all, a labour battalion.

Three rifle sections formed a platoon. In addition to the Lee-Enfields and Bren guns of the rifle sections, the small six-man Platoon HQ was also allocated a Boys anti-tank rifle and a 2-inch mortar. The former was a heavy-calibre (.55), high-velocity bolt action magazine rifle, capable of nine rounds per minute in trained hands, with a maximum range of 500 yards. It was unpopular with troops, partly because of its weight (36lb), but also because it kicked like a mule. Although not intended as a specialist weapon, to hit a moving tank required considerable training, and its penetration capability (24mm at best and around 9–10mm in practice) was poor even in 1940. The 2/5th had ten, slightly less than one per platoon, compared to the twenty-two that it should have had. The 2-inch mortar weighed about 24lb and fired a 2lb shell up to 470 yards. Its chief use was to produce smoke to cover an attack, though it also provided a reserve of high explosive (HE) firepower to take out enemy points of resistance. The labour battalions were told to take any 2-inch mortars which they possessed to France and that, once there, they would have further weapons issued for training. This training never materialised, and it is unlikely the 2/5th had received any 2-inch mortars before leaving the UK.

Each platoon was led by a subaltern—a lieutenant or, more usual in 1940, a 2nd lieutenant. In the 2/5th in April 1940, these fell into two distinct groups. The first were those who had been in the TA prior to the outbreak of war, local men such as Lieutenant Doug Cousin from Basford, Nottingham, and Lieutenant Michael Paling Smith from Little Hallam, Ilkeston. Most platoon commanders seem to have come from the second group, those who had joined the army after September 1939 and had been given Emergency Commissions. Some of these were also local men, such as 2nd Lieutenant David James ('Jim') Quixano Henriques, who despite his Spanish-sounding name was the son of a textile manufacturer from Buxton. Others were from further afield and had been posted to the battalion from other regiments, including Lieutenant John Kerly from Surrey, who had initially signed up with the Inns of Court Regiment in London, part of the Royal Armoured Corps. The territorial officers, who usually had more experience, tended to be allocated to more senior or specialist roles. The platoon commanders were mostly in their early twenties—at 32, Cousin was an exception. They would rely upon the support of their platoon sergeants to help them lead their men. Usually in their early thirties, few if any of the sergeants had experience from the First World War, but some might have been former regulars or have spent significant time in the territorials.

The twelve platoons were numbered consecutively from 7 to 18 (platoons 1 to 6 being specialist units, which will be covered later), and three rifle platoons formed a rifle company, identified by the letters A through to D. Thus, for example, Platoons 10 to 12 made up B Company. Each company was led by a captain. The most experienced of these commanded C Company, 44-year-old Captain John Watts Potter, who had won the DSO at Montbrehain in 1918. But he had only just been recalled to the colours from the regiment's Territorial Reserve; in September 1939, he had been manager of a knitting mill in Matlock. He bought considerable experience to the battalion, but from over twenty years earlier. John Wyndham Hartigan, commanding B Company, was a regular officer from the 2nd Foresters and came from a military family—his father had been a major in the Royal Munster Fusiliers and later commanded a unit of South African light horse in East Africa during the First World War. Only just appointed a lieutenant in August 1939, aged 24, he had immediately been promoted to captain on the outbreak of war and had served in France before transferring battalions. The two other company commanders, Captain Phillip ('Dolly') Armstrong (A Company) and Captain Victor Ward (D Company), were territorials in their early thirties. The captains commanding the rifle companies formed the backbone of the battalion's officers, and a major weakness was that they were all new to the battalion. Hartigan had joined sometime after January and the others on 24 April 1940. They were still in the process of getting to know their officers and men when sent to France. Each company commander was supported by a company sergeant major (CSM) and a company sergeant.

In addition to the four rifle companies, there was HQ Company, comprising platoon numbers 1 to 6. These were a mixture of fighting and administrative units. The most important was the Carrier (number 4) Platoon. In a full-strength battalion, this contained three sections, each of nine men, and three Bren gun carriers, plus a further two officers, twelve men and one carrier as a platoon HQ. The lightly armoured, fully tracked Bren carrier was another major component of the rearmament programme, and their inclusion in the infantry battalions was unique to the British army in 1940. With ten light machine guns, four anti-tank rifles, four 2-inch mortars and fifty-eight rifles, the platoon gave the battalion a substantial amount of mobile firepower, which could be used for reconnaissance, for fire support in an attack, for plugging breaks in the line or for counterattack in defence. One problem was that in the absence of other armoured support, the carriers were sometimes used as a substitute for tanks, a role for which they were neither intended nor suited, being open-topped. This was not, however, an option for the 2/5th in April 1940, for the simple reason that they did not have any. Once again, the second-line battalions were bottom of the list for new equipment; even if they had them, the labour battalions were ordered not to take their carriers to France.

No 3 Platoon should have been armed with two 3-inch mortars. Weighing 125lb and throwing a 10lb HE charge up to 1,600 yards, this provided indirect fire support for the rifle companies, since the battalion had no integrated artillery support. The provision of mortars to the infantry represented another lesson from the First World War, where they had been invaluable in trench warfare. The movement orders sending the battalion to France instructed them to take any mortars which they had, but there is no mention of these weapons in the 2/5th Battalion records in either the UK or France, and it is highly unlikely that they had them at this time. They do, however, seem to have possessed four Bren guns for anti-aircraft use, which was the role of 2 Platoon.

No 1 Platoon was the Signals Platoon, but there was no signalling equipment. The battalion signals officer, 2nd Lieutenant Cecil Wall, another pre-war territorial from Matlock, would have to do his best with a DR on a motorcycle and any bicycles he could scrounge.

In addition to these fighting units, there was the Pioneer Platoon (number 5), which would play an important role in any labour duties allocated to the battalion, as well as undertaking more mundane and less savoury tasks such as laying out camp sites and the digging of latrines. It included several specialists: a blacksmith, a mason, a bricklayer and six carpenters, as well as ten generalist pioneer privates.

Finally, HQ Company had a large administrative platoon (number 6), around ninety men at full strength. This contained the Quartermaster (QM), Captain Richard (Dick) Hammond, and his team of QM sergeants and storemen, the battalion's clerical staff and the ten battalion cooks. There were also smaller teams of cooks within the individual companies, including Private George Hampton, who with his baking experience had been allocated to this role in C Company. Numerically however, the largest component in a full war establishment HQ Platoon was the battalion's drivers, up to fifty-five of them, under motor transport officer (MTO) Joseph Richard (Dick) Newell. The labour battalions only had about a quarter of their establishment transport, so it can be assumed that the number of drivers was also correspondingly less. Many of the men in the HQ Company were more elderly than those in the fighting platoons. Frank Hession was 37, just too young to have served in the First World War, and had been a bus driver in Chesterfield before the war. This was a reserved occupation and he was too old to be conscripted, but he was tired of the work, especially the hours, and joined the army at the outbreak of war, claiming to be an invoice clerk. Frank had learnt both shorthand and typing when young and was assigned to the orderly room on clerical duties. He received no basic military training but was immediately made a lance corporal, probably due to his age and supposed clerical experience. By the time he went to France, he was a sergeant.

The commanding officer of the HQ Company was 44-year-old Major Thomas Hardy McCall from Hathersage in the Peak District, who before the war had been a director of a steel-making company in Sheffield. In the First World War, he had served as a captain in the Leeds Rifles, a battalion of the West Yorkshire

Regiment, and been wounded twice. He was a visual reminder of that conflict, which had left him with one arm 2 inches shorter than the other. Formerly the commander of A Company when the battalion had formed in 1939, he was a popular as well as experienced officer.

The battalion's commanding officer (CO) was Lieutenant Colonel Henry Breedon Everard. A railway engineer in civilian life, Everard was another veteran of the Great War, where he had served as a captain in the Rifle Brigade. In January 1940, Everard was attached for a week to the 2nd Foresters in France, together with Victor Ward of D Company, but this was his only experience of modern military operations. He had taken command of the battalion on 24 August 1939, so had time to get to know his officers and men, when they did not keep changing around him. Hession found him a decisive character who did not stand for any inefficiency.

The second in command (2iC), in contrast, was new to the battalion, having only been appointed on 24 April. Major Eric Noel Deall had an unusual First World War. At the age of only 17, he had enlisted in September 1914 as a private in the Seaforth Highlanders. He went to France but was beset with medical problems, which effectively prevented him from front-line service. Discharged in August 1916 because of chronic bronchitis, young Deall was still determined to serve his country. He therefore obtained a commission as a 2nd lieutenant in the Suffolk Regiment, with which he served in the UK during 1917 and 1918. After the war, he became a territorial officer with the 7th Sherwood Foresters, staying with them when they converted to a searchlight battalion. Thus, Deall had a history in the Foresters and as an infantry officer, although nominally he was a Royal Engineer in 1939.

The battalion adjutant was Major Myles Harry Cooper. This was a critical role, for as well as being responsible for discipline and administration the adjutant of a battalion was the CO's right-hand man and executive officer. Cooper had been made adjutant in July 1939, on the eve of war. His assistant was 2nd Lieutenant William Roger Newton, who had joined the TA immediately prior to the war at the age of 33. Eight years his junior in age but nine days his senior in the army, 2nd Lieutenant John Harvey Walker was the battalion's intelligence officer (IO). The senior leadership of the battalion was completed by Lieutenant Kenneth Ian Bruce of the RAMC and Captain Reverend Harold Norman Barratt of the Royal Army Chaplaincy Department, non-fighting personnel but vital to the physical and moral well-being and efficiency of the unit.

The war establishment of a British infantry battalion in early 1940 was twenty-two officers and 752 men. On 1 April 1940, the 2/5th reported thirty-two officers and 418 other ranks present. Two groups of reinforcements arrived, with 230 men on 18 April and 150 four days later, as well as Deall, Armstrong, and Potter on 24 April. On 1 May, however, in France, the battalion strength was reported as twenty-nine officers and 515 other ranks. This suggests that a large number of men were left behind in Britain, perhaps as a cadre to train further reinforcements, because they were unfit to travel or, most likely in the case of the private soldiers, they were still too young for overseas service. One teenage soldier who did go to France was Derrick Farnell from Buxton, who had only just turned 18, so probably lied about his age. What is certain is that many, probably a majority, of the men in the battalion were very new recruits. According to Private Ernie Gibson, who joined C Company in France, half of them had only three months' training and many had not even fired their rifles. Private Sydney Cooper of A Company admitted that 'we weren't much of a fighting unit at the time, mostly militia men (myself included) all locals and some territorials'.[2]

Three infantry battalions together formed an infantry brigade, which was the smallest formation at the operational level of command. Brigadier Crewdson's 139 Brigade comprised the 2/5th and 9th Foresters and the 2/5th Leicesters, all second-line territorial battalions formed in 1939. The brigade HQ was staffed by officers and men from its three component battalions like Jack Schofield.

Consisting as it did of only infantry battalions, the brigade was still not an all-arms force capable of fully independent action. The lowest-level formation of which this was true was the division; 139 Brigade was grouped with 137 and 138 Brigades into the 46th Division. Although taking the same number as the North Midland Division that had broken the Hindenburg Line in 1918, it did not adopt the regional title, but it did choose as its divisional badge a Sherwood Forest oak tree. Major General Henry Osborne Curtis MC was appointed to command the division in December 1939. He had seen service in France, Salonika and Palestine in 1914–18, and previously commanded a brigade in the BEF in France.

Infantry divisions did not have their own tanks, but they did have a range of other supporting arms. These could include a machine-gun battalion, with roughly the strength of a standard infantry battalion but armed with the Vickers medium machine gun, another weapon from the First World War. They also had an anti-tank regiment of the Royal Artillery, with four batteries of twelve 2-pounder anti-tank guns. Small by later standards, these were quite capable of taking on most if not all German tanks in service in 1940. Most importantly, an infantry division had its own artillery—two or three field regiments of the Royal Artillery, each with two batteries of twelve guns. Ideally, these were the excellent new 25-pounder gun, which was just coming into service, but failing that they were reconditioned 18-pounders of 1918 vintage.

The 46th Division had none of these. The divisional artillery did not accompany it, and its anti-tank regiment was left behind. It did have four companies of the Royal Engineers attached—obviously of value for supervising construction work—and its own field ambulance and field hygiene units. There was a small signals detachment too, but it consisted of DRs rather than radio operators. It had a fraction of the transport normally allocated to a division as it was not expected to fight until it had completed its training. It was merely a labour division.

In fairness, the 2/5th Foresters were probably no worse than some of the second-line German infantry battalions in 1940. These also consisted of recently conscripted, semi-trained young men, as the German army too had expanded rapidly in preparation for war. But the Foresters would not fight second-line German troops. Instead, the under-equipped and under-trained soldiers would find themselves up against some of the elite of the German army, veterans of the Polish campaign or even the Spanish Civil War.

*

The 2/5th Battalion left its barracks at Kedleston Hall at 2am on Friday, 26 April 1940, and marched to Derby station to entrain for London. An advance party of about twenty men under Captain Hartigan had already left for France on 11 April to prepare transportation and accommodation. Arriving at Southampton in the early afternoon, the main body of the battalion embarked, with bands playing, on the 3,104-GRT *Lady of Mann*, a former Isle of Man passenger steamer, which would take them to France. The rest of 139 Brigade would be in the same convoy: Jack Schofield and the brigade HQ, together with the 9th Foresters, on the troopship *Duke of York*, and the 2/5th Leicesters on the *Viking*. The battalions' AA platoons posted their machine guns around the ships for defence. Although the ships sailed that afternoon, forming up inside the anti-submarine boom at Portsmouth, they were delayed leaving the Solent because of thick fog, and it was not until about 9am the next morning that the weather cleared and the small convoy of six ships, escorted by the destroyer HMS *Wivern*, set sail across the Channel. The voyage was uneventful. A solitary French seaplane arrived to guide them into Cherbourg, the main port for landing British personnel, where the 2/5th Foresters disembarked at 4.15pm.

It is often said that the BEF was the only fully mechanised army in 1940. This is true to the extent that, unlike both the French and German armies, it did not use any horse-drawn transport. But it did not mean that every battalion had its own motor transport. In the more fully equipped regular divisions, transport was provided for the infantry's heavy equipment and baggage, but if the men were also to travel by truck, these were usually centrally provided through the RASC. Once again, things were much worse in the three labour divisions. The labour battalions were allocated eight 15cwt trucks, but after allowing for those carrying such things as pioneers' tools, cooking equipment and other stores, it meant that there was only one of these per rifle company, rather than the one per rifle platoon that there should have been. The men of the 2/5th loaded their heavier gear onto these trucks, slung a camouflage net over the top, then travelled the same way as their predecessors had done in the Great War. They were marched to the local station, where they embarked in railway wagons, whose stencilled marking '*40 Hommes 8 Chevaux*' (40 men 8 horses) was indicative both of capacity and the level of comfort that could be expected. More than one passenger was convinced that they must have had square wheels. The trains took them to Rennes, from where they got RASC transport to their accommodation, neat rows of tents in a field outside the village of Bruz that had been established by the advance party. Crewdson, Schofield and the brigade HQ set up residence in the Chateau de la Haie in the nearby village of Merdelle.

Again in imitation of the Great War, the British soldiers mangled the local names into something more familiar. Bruz inevitably became 'Boozer', somewhat inappropriately as the camp itself was dry, while the army rations were mostly bully beef and biscuits. The Foresters managed to find alternative sites to refresh themselves in the local bars and cafes, washing down the local bread and cheese with cider or *bier brun* (brown beer), at 4d per litre, though how men used to the ales produced by the renowned breweries of Burton upon Trent reacted to their French equivalent seems not to have been recorded.

During the first two weeks of May, further reinforcements joined the battalion, bringing it up to a strength of 617 ORs. Some of these new men came from the regiment's training depots in the UK, but others, such as Ernie Gibson, joined from a holding battalion in the south of France. The plan was for a nine-week regime consisting of six weeks of fatigue duties and three weeks of training. The 9th Foresters were scheduled to be the first to receive training, followed by the 2/5th Leicesters. The 2/5th Foresters were last in line, with their training not due to start until Monday, 10 June. Meanwhile, they mostly provided road working parties in the Rennes area, although when not so employed they may have received some basic training—maybe even being taught to fire their rifles. Morale was good nevertheless, with the Royal Engineer officers who were supervising the works commending 'the excellent spirit of the men and the manner in which the task was carried out'.[3] Nearby, however, was one dark portent that this would turn out to be a different war to the last. Next door to 'Boozer' was a Jewish refugee camp, and many of its residents showed their neighbours the tattoos and scars they had received in the concentration camps back in Germany. The refugees had been formed into an 'Alien Pioneer Unit' and worked alongside the British troops.

In the pleasant late spring weather, the men settled down to the routine of construction work. Saturdays were full working days, but the men had Sundays free after church parade and a half-day on Wednesdays. The Foresters had a proud sporting tradition, Schofield playing for an army team in a football match against Rennes FC. There were inspection visits by Brigadier Crewdson, Major General Curtis and the South District Sub-Area Commander, Brigadier G. E. C. Rasch. On 8 May, Major McCall, Captain Armstrong and Lieutenant Cedric Colver presided over the court martial of a sergeant of the 9th Foresters at St Thurial.

And then the war changed.

First Steps: France, April–May 1940

*

On Friday, 10 May 1940, Lieutenant Doug Cousin was in the mess with other officers being entertained by Brigadier Crewdson when the news came through that the Germans had attacked Holland and Belgium. Other ranks learned about the invasion in similar circumstances: Sydney Cooper was drinking cider with a few mates in a local cafe. While both recalled the battalion then being rushed to the front, the initial report of hostilities did not cause too much consternation at Rennes. A German offensive in the Low Countries had long been expected. In November 1939, a German plane had crashed in Belgium, which had fortuitously provided the Allies with detailed plans for such an offensive. Secure in the knowledge that the powerful fortifications of the Maginot Line prevented any direct attack on France, the British and French high command prepared their response, a rapid advance by their best-trained and most mobile troops—including the BEF—to join up with the Belgian army and hold the line of the River Dyle, which would protect Brussels and important Belgian industrial areas. As events unfolded from 10–14 May, this response seemed to be going to plan. True, the Belgian army had not held up the German advance as much as had been hoped, and the Allied air forces had suffered heavy losses trying to disrupt the enemy lines of communication by attacking the bridges over the Albert Canal. Furthermore, Holland surrendered on 15 May, its army hopelessly outclassed by the Germans and its civilian morale broken by the bombing of Rotterdam. But wherever the British and French forces had engaged the enemy on level terms, they had generally proved the equal of the Germans.

In Bruz, therefore, time continued to pass relatively uneventfully. There was an alert issued from brigade HQ on 11 May of parachutists landing in the Rennes area, requiring all battalions to take precautions against attack, but this proved a false alarm. It was followed by a Warning Order the next day that the brigade might be called upon to move, but this was cancelled at a brigade-level conference on 13 May. The brigade continued with its pioneer and training activities; on 14 May, several officers attended a divisional Tactical Exercise Without Troops (TEWT). General Curtis was determined to get into the war, however. According to several accounts, during a telephone call to Lord Gort that same day, he told the field marshal that his division was ready to fight, which if true says more about Curtis' fighting spirit than his military judgement, as the division lacked every requisite for modern warfare.

How much this call may have influenced decisions at HQ is not clear, but at 11pm that night, 46th Division HQ at St Nicholas de Redon received orders from South District command that 139 Brigade was to move north at once. In the small hours of the morning, the orders were relayed down to the battalion adjutants. Advance parties were to set off as soon as possible in all the motor transport available, with the rest of the brigade following by train. As the orders filtered down to the men, Sydney Cooper recalled that they caused panic stations: 'Despatch riders coming in with orders, everyone rushing around, the QM ordering everybody to go to the cobblers to get their boots studded as there was no telling when there would be another chance, as there could be a lot of marching ahead of us.'[4] To make matters worse, the good weather ended; it poured with rain on 15 May, making a misery of the process of packing kit, loading it up onto the few battalion vehicles and marching to the station. Given the short notice, it was creditable that the battalion entrained at Rennes at 6.30pm for its transfer to the forward areas, followed eight hours later by the 9th Foresters.

What had caused this sudden panic? The initial apparent success of the Allied advance into Belgium had been illusory. While the German orders captured in November had been real, their loss had resulted in a complete change in the German plan. A substantial force would still advance through Holland and Belgium, but it would no longer be the main attack. That would come further south, through the Ardennes forest and crossing the Meuse river at Sedan. The French high command had dismissed this sector of the front as being impractical for any major operations. Under their methodical doctrine, learnt in the last war, the heavily wooded terrain and primitive road network would make it impossible for the enemy to bring forward sufficient heavy artillery to break down a resolute defence before it could be reinforced. The border around Sedan was held by second-line French troops, low in morale, for the most part poorly led, and even after eight months of war many of the defences were incomplete.

The German troops that made the attack were not constrained by First World War doctrine. Seven out of their ten armoured panzer divisions, the elite corps of the army, spearheaded the assault. Their commanders, men such as Heinz Guderian and Erwin Rommel, pushed on regardless of traffic jams and used their tanks and massed attacks by the Stuka dive-bombers of the Luftwaffe to overawe and overwhelm the French defenders, rather than wait for their artillery. The first assault on the Meuse began on 13 May. By the following evening, the panzers had broken a hole 10 miles wide in the French lines.

The French and British reaction to this remained set in First World War doctrine. Superficially, the situation was not dissimilar to the one faced in March 1918 when the German Michael offensive had broken through between Cambrai and St Quentin. The Sedan sector now formed a hinge between the static defences of the Maginot Line and the mobile forces holding the Dyle Line in Belgium. With the hinge broken, troops to the south of the breakthrough had to fall back to prevent the Maginot Line being outflanked, just as in 1918 the French had withdrawn south to cover Paris. The forces holding the Dyle north of the breach would also have to fall back westwards to avoid being outflanked, just as in 1918 the British army fell back west to cover the Channel. Meanwhile, any available troops would be fed in to maintain a continuous line between the two. In 1918, due to the heroic defence of the troops directly in the path of the Germans that delayed their advance, and by diverting every available reserve, the line had held. Hence the calling forward of 139 Brigade.

It does not appear that the brigade was intended to fight, but to free up better-trained troops currently doing rear-echelon duties for front-line service. This was shown by its orders, which did not keep the brigade or even the battalions together as a cohesive formation. On the way north, packed into the bone-rattling *40 Hommes 8 Chevaux* railway trucks, the men of the 2/5th Foresters laughed and joked and were in good spirits, glad to be going to do their bit as their predecessors had done in 1914–18. Two days later they arrived at Seclin, an important railhead 5 miles south of Lille in northern France, at 2.30pm on 17 May. The town was being subjected to an air raid by Heinkel and Junkers bombers of the Luftwaffe. The 2/5th was met by Brigadier Crewdson and was split up and sent off by motor transport to four different locations in Belgium. Transport was limited, so the battalions left behind non-essential items such as the band's instruments, as well as some more useful equipment like blankets. A Company was posted at Tournai, while B Company was the most advanced at the town of Ath, some 20 miles east. C Company and the HQ Company were at Leuze, and D Company at the nearby village of Thieulain, both about halfway between Tournai and Ath. Their primary task was to perform traffic control.

This seemingly trivial use of infantry, even partly trained ones, was actually vitally important, because it was quickly becoming clear that the situation was not at all like March 1918. The German breakthrough was much more rapid, and British or French reserves available to form a line to hold it almost non-existent. No plans had been made for refugees, as the Belgian and French authorities thought that their civilians would obey instructions to stay put. Instead, they jammed the roads trying to escape the enemy advance, a situation deliberately encouraged and exacerbated by the Germans with air attacks. Carrying whatever possessions they could on carts, wheelbarrows, prams, donkeys or just by hand, these frightened civilians were a pathetic sight. Posted at key crossroads or strung out along the roadside, with a breakdown lorry and an ambulance if available and keeping in touch with other sections by bicycle, the Foresters tried to keep the civilian traffic off the roads to allow military transport to get through. Much of this was no less a problem than the civilians, as also streaming south and west were disorganised units of the Belgian army; cyclists, machine gunners and horse artillery, all in full retreat. On 18 May, orders were issued that both refugees and the Belgian army were to be turned off the road. An officer in the 9th Foresters, who were carrying out similar duties, wryly observed that 'by then there was little difference between the two'.[5] The BEF was retiring in somewhat better order, but it too was falling back, to take up new positions on the River Escaut.

A Company arrived in the ancient town of Tournai to find it under air attack and in flames. The attitude of the Belgian population to the British troops was mixed; an old couple brought Sydney Cooper and his mates cups of coffee as

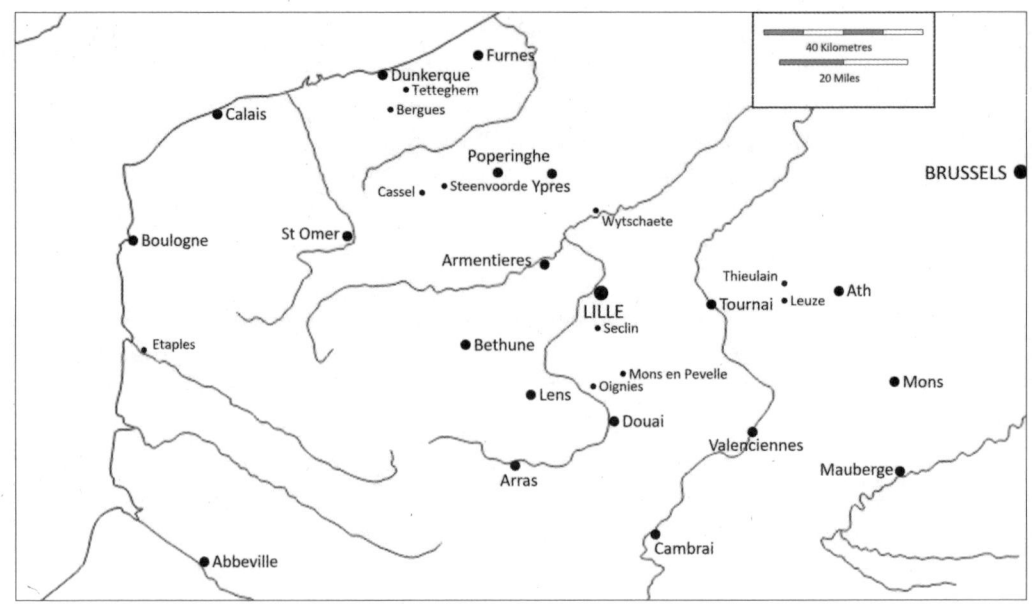

Northern France and Belgium, 1940.

they directed traffic, whereas a bevy of young girls taunted them with the First World War song 'Good Byee'. Several houses had white sheets hanging from their first-floor windows, though whether to signify surrender or just because it was washing day was not clear. As Lance Corporal Fred Jeffery and his section patrolled the town, they were fired upon from an upstairs window. Leaving the rest of the section to cover him from the front, Jeffery crept in through the back of the house and cleared out the snipers with grenade and rifle. According to Jeffery, these were Belgian fifth columnists, although he and his section later encountered regular German troops. At around the same time, the 9th Foresters recorded capturing four enemy parachutists dressed as civilians, who were shot as spies. The men killed by Jeffery may also have been German. However, there is no corroborative evidence of airborne landings this far west, and it is possible some or all of those shot may have simply been Belgian civilians unfortunate to have been in the wrong place at the wrong time; victims of the widespread panic, fear and confusion. Rumours of spies and fifth columnists were rife throughout the campaign, and in this tense situation the soldiers were particularly suspicious of the number of nuns seen amongst the refugees—of course, Belgium and France being Catholic countries, these were naturally more numerous than back in the UK.

At Ath, an old Vauban fortress town once besieged by the Duke of Marlborough, the men of B Company were also being introduced to the Luftwaffe. Private Willis Dixon had the company Bren gun mounted for AA use, but when he fired it the tripod bounced around on the cobblestones. He grabbed some sandbags to hold it firm, to the consternation of some local women who had placed them to protect their cellar. Not long after, orders came to retire; upon leaving the town, Dixon gave the women their sandbags back. When his company marched back through Tournai, they were continually attacked by Stuka dive-bombers and Messerschmitt fighters. The only major building left standing in the city appeared to be the cathedral.

The other forward companies also fell back to Tournai before the German advance. C Company took over a disused building in the town square, and shortly afterwards a convoy arrived with seven days' rations for the battalion. Before any issues could be made, however, there was a report of German tanks entering the town and the rations had to be left behind, except for some tea and sugar which the men were able to salvage. CQMS Reg Markham managed to keep a pack of this tea throughout the whole campaign and evacuation, giving it to his family back in England to supplement their ration. The men of C Company were thankful for Captain Potter's experience and leadership, and his smattering of French, as they tried to find their way back through the maze of blazing buildings and rubble into which the town's medieval streets had been transformed. They only just made it back across the last bridge over the Scheldt river before it was blown by the Royal Engineers.

Further south, meanwhile, there was little to stop the German breakthrough. The motorised panzer divisions were able to exploit the break in the Allied lines far faster than the British and French generals—basing their responses on First World War timeframes—were able to anticipate. By the evening of 16 May, Guderian's leading troops were 55 miles west of Sedan. Rommel's men continued their advance overnight to take Le Cateau the following morning. On the next day, both St Quentin and Cambrai fell and the Germans were now poised to take Amiens, scene of the decisive battles of 1918, but more importantly in 1940 the critical rail centre through which the British supply line ran. The German advance was also putting a strain on the Anglo-French relationship. On 19 May, Gort began to make preparations to withdraw British forces from Belgium, ordering 'useless mouths' to be sent back to the UK. Vice Admiral Sir Bertram Ramsay, Flag Officer commanding Dover, began contingency planning for an evacuation if necessary, codenamed Operation Dynamo. Gort's primary concern now was preserving the BEF.

The threat to the British supply lines meant that every available man needed to be put into combat to try to defend them from the German advance, and this included the labour divisions. So far, 139 Brigade had been lucky, detraining in Seclin before the German advance had got so far west. The troops of the 12th and 23rd Divisions, who had left Brittany later, arrived in the area directly in the Germans' path. Like the 46th, these were divisions in name only, totally unprepared to take on the panzers. On 20 May, 36 Infantry Brigade (12th

Division) was destroyed at Doullens, while a battalion of the Royal Sussex Regiment (23rd Division) was lost as Guderian's men took Amiens. The Germans acknowledged the determined defence put up by the British, but under-equipped and almost untrained, there could be only one result. It was little short of a massacre.

Faced with the threat to their communications and rear, and with the regular divisions of the BEF still under pressure from the German advance in Belgium, the British now improvised a series of formations to attempt to hold a defensive line on their southern flank. The units which made up these forces were drawn from various line-of-communication troops, in which the labour battalions were prominent, stiffened by some fighting units, mostly artillery, drawn from the divisions to the north. 'Petreforce', under Major General P. L. Petre, would hold Arras, another vital communication centre. General Curtis, whose 46th Division was hopelessly split up across north-west France and Belgium, was appointed to command a force to defend St Pol ('Polforce'). The largest of these formations was 'MacForce', under Gort's Director of Military Intelligence, Major General F. N. Mason-MacFarlane, with orders to defend the road north from Cambrai to Marchiennes, the crossings of the River Scarpe from St Amand to Râches, and the town of Orchies. The 2/5th Foresters would join MacForce.

These ad hoc formations were a common feature of British army practice during the first half of the war, and their use is controversial. On the one hand, they demonstrated the flexibility and resourcefulness of British commanders, a legacy of many years of small-scale colonial operations. But their component units were drawn from various higher-level formations, they had no previous experience of working together and they lacked the time to set up effective administration and communication organisations. This obviously reduced their effectiveness in combat. Gort has been criticised for creating these temporary forces, but in the situation that the British found themselves in May 1940, it is difficult to see what other options were available. As soon as possible, some regular formations were extricated from Belgium to bolster the southern front, but in the meantime the breach had to be plugged with anything available.

This included the men of 139 Brigade. Having only just arrived at its destination in Belgium, it received orders on 18 May to move west of the River Escaut and then to the south around Orchies, where it would join Macforce. As part of this move, the 2/5th Foresters began to march. At 7pm on 18 May, they bivouacked for the night in a wood near Baisieux, 7 miles east of Tournai. It is unlikely that B Company made it this far that day; both it and C Company seem to have spent longer in the Tournai area. A further march next day of about 15 miles took the battalion to the villages of Allennes and Chemy, south-west of Seclin. It did not arrive until about 11pm, but at least that night the men got billets in the villages. The following afternoon, 20 May, the battalion moved into the Forêt de Flines, north of the Canal de la Haute (Upper) Deule and the town of Douai, where it set

First Steps: France, April–May 1940

up bivouacs between 3 and 5pm. Just a few hours later, Guderian's tanks reached the coast at Abbeville, near the mouth of the River Somme. The BEF, together with two French armies, was now cut off in a huge pocket some 40 miles wide and 80 miles long. The 2/5th Foresters were in its extreme south-east corner.

During this march, the battalion had its first casualty of the campaign, but once again not due to enemy action. At 34, 2nd Lieutenant George Cripps was considerably older than the average subaltern, and he came not from the East Midlands but from Dunmow in Essex. Both he and his younger brother, Percival, had joined the army as members of the Artists Rifles, a famous London-based territorial unit which had its origins in the nineteenth century, when many painters, writers and sculptors had joined its ranks. With a higher proportion of middle-class recruits, the unit developed a reputation as a training ground for officers, and the Cripps brothers were both given emergency war commissions and posted to the Sherwood Foresters; Percival to the 1/5th Battalion and George to the 2/5th. George was a popular officer with a good sense of humour. At some time during the move south, he was climbing into one of the battalion's trucks when one of the men behind, who had a live round in his rifle and had left the safety off, accidentally shot him. George died of his wounds on 20 May.

On 21 May, the battalion deployed for the first time in a defensive position against the enemy. It had arrived in this location two days ahead of the other units in its brigade, so it was temporarily attached to 138 Brigade. The frontage occupied was along the Canal de la Haute Deule between Oignies and Auby, with the battalion HQ set up in an abandoned brewery in the village of Evin Malmaison. To their left was the 6th Lincolnshire Regiment and to their right the 6th York and Lancaster Regiment. The total length of the brigade front was 14 miles, and it included fourteen bridges. Three of these, all prepared for demolition but not blown, were in the Foresters' sector of 3½ miles, as well as a footbridge that had been blocked but not prepared for demolition. Each was guarded by a platoon of infantry under an officer. Field guns and anti-tank guns were also deployed to cover the bridges at ranges of as little as 50–100 yards. Although the bridges were prepared for destruction, there were still French troops south of the canal, so except in the case of immediate attack, when the officer responsible could use his discretion, they were only to be blown if ordered by Macforce. The canal was also still in use by barges, which in places were so numerous it was possible to walk across on them. Efforts were made to move all these barges to the north bank, but the Germans were still able to use some of them to cross the canal when they later attacked the British positions.

On the same day, at the town of Arras south-west of Oignies, the British were making their only major counterattack of the campaign, by 1 Army Tank Brigade supported by two battalions of the Durham Light Infantry (DLI). The attack briefly discomfited Rommel's 7th Panzer Division, but was far too small to seriously impact the German advance. The British and French headquarters tried to make plans to free up more sizeable forces to counterattack both north and south of the panzer corridor, but with the Germans pressing them on all fronts, limited mobile reserves, a road network jammed with refugees and a command structure incapable of acting quickly enough, these plans came to nothing. The best that the new troops moving south could do was to stiffen the defensive line that was being formed along the rivers and canals along the southern edge of the pocket.

With Arras under imminent threat and the need to move the lines of communication to run through the Channel ports rather than from the south, the transport priority was for supplies of small-arms ammunition, artillery and anti-tank shells and explosives to prepare the bridges over the River Scarpe for demolition. It was decided that it was impossible to get regular rations to the troops in the Oignies area, and on 21 May they were instructed to live off the land. Fortunately, they had no problem in so doing, there being a 'plentiful supply of cattle, pigs and poultry which units slaughtered (generally with a rifle or Bren gun) as they needed. Bread, tea and sugar were the only items over which any anxiety was felt.'[6] The Foresters had a partial solution to the bread problem: George Hampton located a bakery in Evin Malmaison and was able to use his pre-war skills to provide some fresh bread for the battalion. The food situation would not improve much for the rest of the campaign, and on 25 May the whole of the BEF went on to half-rations.

The next two days passed relatively quietly, though not comfortably. There were heavy bombing raids on Douai to the front, held by the French, and on Carvin and Libercourt to the rear. Every now and then, aircraft would machine-gun the bridges, either to draw fire and expose the defenders' positions or to panic the refugees who still crossed them in both directions. Around this time, there were a number of attacks seemingly made by aircraft with British markings; either these were cases of friendly fire or, as the soldiers believed, captured British aircraft being used by the Germans. On 23 May, the Lincolns and the York and Lancs withdrew and the 2/5th Foresters temporarily took over the whole 14-mile line, but later in the day the men were relieved and marched back to the village of Thumeries, while the Battalion HQ remained at Evin Malmaison. The night was cold and wet, so the men were probably glad not to be in the front line.

The rest of 139 Brigade now arrived in the area to hold the line from Râches to Carvin, along the line of the La Bassée Canal and River Scarpe. They were now under the command of Brigadier Raleigh Charles Joseph Chichester-Constable DSO, who had been on General Curtis' staff and had replaced Crewdson on 21 May. It seems probably that like many senior TA officers, Crewdson's skills were considered better suited to peacetime than wartime and Curtis was looking to appoint a fighting soldier. The new commander was described as 'a tower of strength' in subsequent operations—'he appeared to be Brigade Commander, Battalion and Platoon Commander all in one and inspired everyone with confidence'.[7]

On 25 May, the 2/5th Foresters headed back towards the front, digging trenches in a position behind the French. Some of these were on the site of First World War defences, probably German rear positions as the main front line in 1914–18 ran west of Loos and La Bassée (coincidentally, the 46th Division had held the British lines in this area for much of 1917). Lance Corporal George Price of the Signals Platoon remembered coming upon traces of barbed wire while digging, and Schofield, with the brigade HQ in the village of Mons-en-Pévèle, found himself creeping through First World War trenches on a night patrol. Willis Dixon 'found some ready-made trenches, reinforced with sandbags full of concrete. The bags had rotted away, but you could still see the pattern of the weave.'[8] Dixon and his mates did not avoid digging that evening as a result of their find though, as they ended up constructing latrines in a wood behind their position.

Both MacForce and Polforce were now dissolved and 139 Brigade once more came under the command of General Curtis' 46th Division. The division at least now had some artillery, in the form of twenty-four 25-pounders of 16th Field Regiment RA, and a further twelve guns of 225 Field Battery RA. It also had 2 and 8 Anti-Tank Batteries RA, with twenty 2-pounder anti-tank guns between them. But whatever relief Curtis may have had at being in charge of something resembling a proper division was offset by the confused responsibilities for the defence of the area. He had been instructed to hold a 20-mile front from east of La Bassée (held by the British 2nd Division) to the village of Râches. But this area of the front was already occupied by several French units, including two infantry regiments, the 1st Moroccan Division and the French V Corps. Some British units, like the 2/5th Foresters, held supporting positions back from the canal line behind French troops, while in other places the French and British positions were intermixed. There were also French units south of the canal as far as Douai—3 miles in front of the line Curtis was instructed to hold. When Curtis met with General René Altmayer, the V Corps commander, the Frenchman not only expressed surprise that the British were in his defensive area, but also confessed that the two French regiments and the Moroccans did not come under his command. Such a situation was a recipe for disaster, which was not long in coming.

*

The River Deule, behind which the 2/5th Foresters deployed, is canalised for its entire length between Lille and Douai. Running south from Lille, near the town of Beauvin it is joined by the Canal d'Aire, which runs west to La Bassée and beyond. Three miles further south, at the Pont du Vendin, it turns to run almost due east to the Pont de la Batterie (Battery Bridge), which connects the two mining towns of Oignies and Courrières. From here it turns south-east to Douai, where it is linked by canal to the River Scarpe. Also canalised, this runs north to Belgium, where it becomes the Escaut and later the Scheldt. Between 20 and 50 yards wide, the three canals formed a significant obstacle, especially to tanks. The terrain each side of the canals was not so favourable for defence, being for the most part extremely flat—Oignies, 50 miles from Dunkirk on the coast, is a mere 80 feet above sea level. About 2 miles south-west of Courrières, the land rises to a low ridge on which sit the suburbs of the city of Lens, especially the mining town then known as Henin-Liétard (now Henin-Beaumont). On the northern side of the canal, starting some 4 miles north-east of Oignies and running to the north-east parallel with the Scarpe, is the Pévèle ridge. Between this ridge and Oignies there was a semi-circle of woodland, much of which has now been replaced with modern housing and industrial estates. Apart from this, the area had seen enough fighting during the First World War to be largely denuded of trees. There were, however, some small stands of woodland south of the canal, at Pont du Vendin and at Courrières; north of the canal near the Pont de la Batterie; and on both sides of the canal for about 4 miles north-west of Douai. These offered some cover to the attacking German troops. Other than this, the plain is bereft of natural features, but has several prominent spoil heaps from the extensive coal mines in the area. This was the most important mining area in the whole of France, and in 1915 the British territorials had seen their first actions here in the brickworks and pitheads during the battles of Loos and Lens. A quarter of a century later, the next generation would follow in their footsteps.

The positions held that evening by 139 Brigade, as best as can be determined from the various unit diaries, was as follows. On the extreme left, north of Douai, with the dubious distinction of being the British troops furthest from Dunkirk, were the 9th Foresters, with three companies forward between the villages of Râches and Auby, and one in reserve. During the day, additional British troops retreating from Arras arrived in this sector; these were formed into a 'foreign legion' of about 100 men under Captain Chadwick of the 5th Green Howards and added to the reserves. Also in the area were troops of the French 99th Infantry Regiment. This formed a strong defensive position which anchored the left flank of the 2/5th Foresters, who were dug in between the villages of Auby and Estevelles, 2 miles east of the Pont du Vendin, on a front of some 15,000 yards. To put this in perspective, that was roughly the recommended defensive frontage for two whole divisions. On 25 May, it was held by only two infantry battalions, the 2/5th Foresters and the 2nd Battalion of the French 7th Régiment Tirailleurs Marocains (RTM), the latter at least 30 per cent below strength, supported by a squadron of *spahis* (North African horsed cavalry) from the 80th Groupe de Reconnaissance de Division d'Infanterie (GRDI) with two anti-tank guns. The 2/5th Foresters were probably also deployed with three companies forward and one in reserve. The Battalion HQ may still have been at Evin Malmaison, well to the left of the position, although another possibility is that it had moved to the Villa Les Floralies, on the road between Oignies and the important Pont de la Batterie in the centre of the battalion's line. This bridge was also initially covered by five guns from 2 Anti-Tank Battery RA, but these were withdrawn during the night of 25 May, as they had been reallocated to 2nd Division. On the 2/5th Foresters' right, the 2/5th Leicesters completed the brigade dispositions. Their right flank was in the village of Salome, about 2 miles east of La Bassée, and their positions also extended over a 15,000yd front. Their Battalion HQ was at Buqueux, north-east of the town of Carvin and some 4 miles behind the front line, making communication extremely difficult. Intermingled with the Leicesters were two more battalions of the 1st Moroccan Division.

Brigadier Chichester-Constable had set up 139 Brigade HQ in the village of Mons-en-Pévèle, at the southern end of the Pévèle ridge. This was ideally sited to observe the country to the south and south-east, but was 5 to 7 miles from the battalion HQs and no less than 15 miles from the extreme right of the line at Salome. Communication both within the battalions and back to the brigade HQ, it must be remembered, was by runner or DR. Also around Mons-en-Pévèle were the twelve anti-tank guns of 8 Anti-Tank Battery RA. The 16th Field Regiment's HQ was at La Vacquerie, about a mile to the south, with 27/72 Battery at Gorguechon to its left and 34/86 Battery at Le Thelu to its right. These were well placed to support the 2/5th Foresters, being about 5,000 yards back from the battalion HQ. The artillery put liaison officers with the infantry battalions, sent out roving observers with radios and came into action that night. To the rear of the Leicesters was the British 151 Infantry Brigade, comprising three battalions of the Durham Light Infantry (DLI); the 9th at Carvin, the 8th at Provin and the 6th further north at Don. These territorial troops had already proven themselves in combat during the fighting around Arras. But the brigade was in general reserve, not under 46th Division command, and was due to move north the next morning.

French reserves in the area to the north-west of Oignies included the 11th Zouave Regiment and 40th Artillery Regiment, from the 2nd Division Infanterie Nord Africaine. The 106th Motorised Infantry Regiment of the 12th (Motorised) Infantry Division, which was further north around the town of Avelin, was also later sent as a reserve to Oignies. Finally, as a result of enemy activity, tanks and motorised infantry of the 3rd Division Légère Mécanique, from the French Cavalry Corps, were moved overnight on 25 May to support the Moroccans around Carvin. While there were plenty of Allied troops in the area between La Bassée and Douai, they came from many different formations. With neither clear lines of communication nor procedures for cooperation between them, they were severely handicapped in their response to the German attacks.

During 25 May, the Germans made a frontal attack on the canal line around the Pont de la Batterie with tanks and infantry supported by artillery fire from the direction of Henin-Liétard. This was repulsed with heavy losses by the French and English defenders. The French retired from those positions that they still held south of the canal in preparation for pulling back towards Lille, blowing

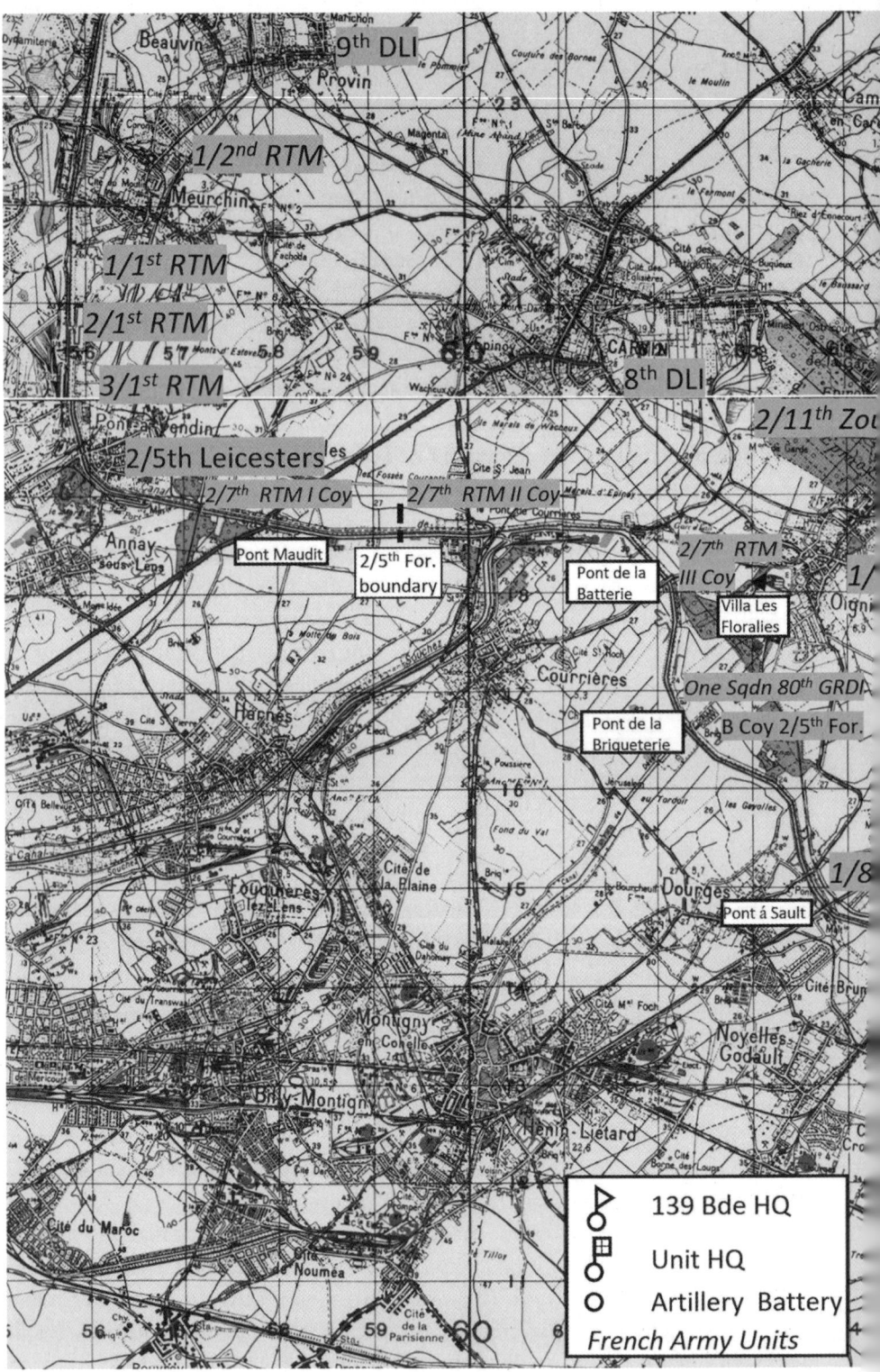

First Steps: France, April–May 1940

Oignies, 26 May 1940.

up several bridges behind them. The Moroccan troops warned the British that a further enemy attack was probable the following day. In the evening, the German artillery was very active, particularly firing into the woods north of Oignies, where the DLI had their transport. According to French accounts, the British infantry was severely tested by this fire as they were not sufficiently well dug in—evidence of their inexperience and lack of training.

White signal lights could be seen going up overnight, and German patrols infiltrated across the canal at the Pont Maudit south of Estevelles, capturing some of the 2/5th Leicesters outposts. This was the prelude to a more substantial attack the following morning between 7 and 8.30am, when German troops attacked in force, supported by a heavy artillery bombardment. According to British accounts, the Moroccan troops had retired from this sector during the night, leaving the Leicesters holding far too large a frontage for a single battalion. Their isolated posts were incapable of mutual support and they took heavy casualties. By 10.30am, the German attack had crossed the canal by two more bridges to the north, the Pont à Sault and Pont de Beauvin, and were pushing east towards Carvin. They had driven in the exposed right flank of the 2/5th Foresters, who responded by altering their front to face west, taking up positions along a railway embankment. This new line was covered on its right by Captain Chadwick and his 'foreign legion', sent by the CO of 9th Foresters, allegedly after stragglers from the 2/5th had arrived at their HQ, although this was a long way from the 2/5th's original positions. Reinforcement from the British left was possible because the weight of the German attack had been directed against the western end of the positions held by 139 Brigade. They had only sent light patrols forward on the 9th Foresters' front, which had been easily driven off by the French forces in that sector. The new line held by the 2/5th was also well supported by the 25-pounders of 16th Field Regiment RA, which together with French artillery batteries were putting a heavy fire down on the town of Courrières and the approaches to the Pont de la Batterie, held by a company of the 7th RTM and some Foresters. This artillery support was essential as the Germans were still making frontal assaults in this sector. A section from B Company of the 2/5th and the squadron of French *spahis* from the 80th GRDI were also holding on to their positions at the next bridge south, the Pont de la Briqueterie, named from its position next to a brickworks.

By late morning, it was clear that the Leicesters had been all but destroyed. Some French Algerian troops were still holding out in Carvin, supported by the carrier platoon of the 8th DLI. This battalion had originally been ordered to pull back north to Armentières, near the Belgian border, that day, but those instructions were now hurriedly overridden at 10.45am. The DLI were placed under 46th Division, with orders to counterattack the German troops on the north bank of the canal, supported by French tanks. By 4.30pm, despite some ongoing indecision at divisional level over whether to hold or retire, the DLI had successfully stabilised the position at the south-west outskirts of Carvin, although the Algerian divisional commander would not advance further without more tank and artillery support. Offsetting this successful counterattack, the position at the Pont de la Briqueterie had been lost around 4pm, with most of the defenders captured.

Thunderstorms now caused a brief lull in the fighting, during which 46th Division HQ planned a further counterattack to fully restore the positions on the canal. The main attack would come once again from 151 Infantry Brigade, with the 8th DLI to continue attacking south, joined by the 9th DLI on their left and supported by French tanks. It would be directed towards Estevelles and Henin-Liétard, the latter objective somewhat optimistic as it was some 2 or 3 miles south of the canal. Once the original defence line had been regained, the 2/5th Foresters were to move north-west along the canal line to reoccupy Estevelles. The attack was fixed for 6pm, but at the last minute it was cancelled—according to the British, because the French were unable to provide the tanks as planned. In the confused command situation, the cancellation orders did not reach the Foresters until 6.30pm. But they had already started their forward movement as planned, expecting support from the DLI and the French.

B Company spearheaded the advance and took the brunt of the enemy fire. As one group led by Lieutenant Jim Henriques neared the edge of a wood, machine-gun fire whipped past them from both sides. Henriques quickly consulted with his sergeant, Fred Kellett, saying 'I think we should attack', not knowing that apart from Stanley Storey and one other private, the men behind him had dived for cover into a ditch. The four men ran along one side of the embankment, hidden from view of the enemy, then Kellett charged over the bank with bayonet fixed, followed by Henriques. The fourth man ran the other way, while Storey cautiously climbed the bank a few yards further on, only to see the lieutenant and the sergeant sprawled dead across the railway line, a German soldier only feet away, gun in hand. Storey decided discretion was the better part of valour and zig-zagged his way back to the rest of the platoon.

The ditch into which the men of B Company had dived to escape the enemy fire turned out to be a sewer. 'Better shit than shot,' quipped Sergeant Harry Brown from Derby as the men with him disturbed its contents. The Foresters had been taken by surprise and split into several small groups, but they were not in a mood to give up or run away. Private Percy Scott shot a German officer calling on them to surrender, while Captain Hartigan twice tried to rally his men for a bayonet charge. Hartigan led his men according to the tradition of the regular army, from the front, and was last seen firing a Bren gun from the hip. He was posthumously mentioned in dispatches for his gallantry. Also killed was Lieutenant Smith, leaving 2nd Lieutenant Charles Arthur Wellesley Williamson as the only surviving officer to lead the withdrawal of B Company. Some of the men ended up in a firefight in a mining pit-yard, but to their dismay the German bullets came straight through the pit props that they were using for cover. Williamson, a schoolmaster at Trent College in Nottingham before the war, regrouped the survivors again in a field 20 yards in front of a battery of French 75mm field guns. Firing over open sights, the artillery broke up any concentrations of German troops, while the Foresters picked off those who tried to infiltrate the position in ones and twos. But when the French had fired off all their ammunition, they attached their guns to their horse-drawn limbers and moved off. B Company withdrew again, to a field where A Company commander Captain Armstrong had organised further defensive positions.

Worse was to come. In an effort to find out the situation, Lieutenant Colonel Everard and the IO (Information Officer), 2nd Lieutenant Walker, went forward in Everard's civilian shooting brake car to carry out a reconnaissance. Passing through Oignies, they came under enemy fire and Everard's driver, young Derek Farnell, was shot dead as they tried to take cover. Everard was taken prisoner and Walker was missing; he was later reported killed in action. The battalion 2iC, Major Deall, was also taken prisoner during the German attack, while Major McCall died the following day as the result of a German mortar barrage. According to the battalion war diary, the total losses in the action around Oignies were seven officers and forty-nine men. Of these, five officers and fourteen men were killed, five of them from Buxton, including 18-year-old Derrick Farnell. Also among the dead were Frederick and Laban Jones, cousins from the mining communities of Belper and Heage, both of whom had just turned 21. Some of the forty-nine were only missing and would eventually rejoin the battalion. The final casualty toll—killed, wounded and captured—was seven officers and forty men. Other battalions fighting in France and Belgium in 1940 suffered much worse losses than this. What was crippling, especially for a partially trained unit like the 2/5th Foresters, was the loss of more than half of its most experienced officers—Everard, Deall, McCall and Hartigan. It had been decapitated.

Although the British blamed their French allies for the cancellation of the counterattack that led to these losses, it is questionable whether they deserve this. The war diary accounts are not consistent. The 46th Division diary blames the unavailability of tanks, that of 139 Brigade simply says it was cancelled by the French, while the 2/5th Foresters' diarist suggests the movement was cancelled because 'the French Commander did not think it was necessary'.[9] But neither of the DLI war diaries mention the planned second attack at all, although that of the 8th DLI does say that the commander of the Algerians would not attack without tanks. The overall confusion of command at all levels and the exposed position of both French and British troops around Oignies and Douai were the underlying reasons for the failure. The very day of the battle, the British War Cabinet back in London had decided that the BEF had to be evacuated. Both the British and French commanders within the northern pocket were already planning to pull back to the line of the River Lys in order to shorten their lines—

the scheduled move of 151 Brigade was part of this. The French also received orders to withdraw from their exposed positions during the day. The 7th RTM was ordered to retire at 4pm, and according to the 8th DLI the French pulled back from Carvin at 7pm. The 46th Division received orders from Lord Gort at BEF HQ to pull out at about 6pm, within minutes of the planned time of the Foresters' advance. Since there was no overall Allied commander in the Oignies sector, and Curtis and the local French commanders did not have direct command even of all their own country's troops in the area, the conflicting objectives of holding the canal line and withdrawing to the Lys could only cause confusion. Furthermore, several French units continued to hold out for up to two more days, even after being ordered to withdraw.

The action at Carvin–Oignies is largely omitted from British histories of the campaign, or at best seen as part of the French action to hold the Lille salient. Actions at Arras, Boulogne, Calais, Ypres and Cassel, amongst others, figure more highly in British accounts, though one historian considers that Oignies was the most dangerous penetration of the Allied lines made on 26 May.[10] The efforts of the 2/5th Foresters and the other British and French units along the Canal de la Haute Deule were, however, an essential part of the many rearguard actions which in combination saved the BEF. A French author said of the resistance on the canal that 'it stemmed the enemy advance for several days, thus affording precious time for our armies falling back on the port of Dunkirk'.[11] Gort himself had been only 5 miles north of the battle during the day, at Attiches, south-west of Seclin, where he was discussing withdrawal arrangements with General Georges Blanchard, commander of the northern group of French armies. A breakthrough could have had catastrophic consequences.

The Germans were certainly frustrated by the stubborn defence, taking it out on the local population with one of those vicious acts of reprisal that had begun to appear even this early in the war. Following the British retirement on 27 May, the French had been reinforced by the 11th Zouave Regiment, which held out at Oignies until nightfall, losing at least thirty-five killed during the battle. The Germans were incensed by the fact that they had been held up by a relatively small number of troops, and local accounts suggest that a machine gun was sited in the tower of the church in Oignies, which may have given rise to suspicion that the civilian population had assisted the French soldiers. Nazi racist ideology also played a part. At Carvin, the captured commander of the 2/7th RTM was criticised for allowing his Moroccan troops to kill white German soldiers. Many of the community in Oignies were of Polish descent, having come there in the early 1920s to work in the mines. They spoke or at least understood German; some may even have fought for the Kaiser in 1914–18; and were therefore regarded as traitors. Some of the German troops at Oignies were from Pomerania, part of which had been given to Poland under the 1919 Versailles Treaty, which may have heightened the animosity felt. Groups of these Polish workers were pressed into service on 27 May to carry ammunition to German troops fighting their way into Oignies, where they came under machine-gun fire and several were killed or wounded.

The following morning, at 6am, troops under 31-year-old Hauptmann (Captain) Horst Kolrep arrived in the town. Although some accounts describe them as belonging to the SS (Kolrep did become an SS officer later in in the war), these belonged to 6th Company, II/497th Infantry Regiment, part of the second-line 267th Infantry Division. Kolrep gave orders for the male population to be killed and the town razed to the ground. Eighty of the townsfolk were shot, ranging in age from 17 to 70, including four women. Some 380 houses were destroyed. Another sixty or more civilians were killed in Courrières and Carvin. As inhabitants of Oignies were led down the road going south to Dourges, they passed a wounded British soldier lying at the roadside, who asked for water. According to eyewitness accounts, the German officer leading the column instead shot him in the head.

There was a second atrocity involving a British soldier. While civilian prisoners were being escorted to Courrières down the road leading to the Pont de la Batterie, as they passed the Villa Les Floralies they heard screaming from inside. Although the Germans had placed armed guards around the villa, some people were able to catch sight of a soldier tied to a chair being tortured. His captors then proceeded to douse him in petrol and set it alight, burning the man alive. Since the floor of the villa was made of reinforced concrete, it survived the flames and some remains of the victim of the atrocity were found. Buttons from his tunic identified him as a British officer, while a watch was found bearing the inscription 'Keith Davenport'. The hands were stopped at 5.15.

There was an officer named Davenport fighting with the 2/5th Foresters at Oignies. Second Lieutenant George Arthur Keith Davenport had joined the battalion from the Artists Rifles in November 1939, the same day as George Cripps, and he was serving in D Company. For some sixty years, the people of Oignies assumed that the officer burnt alive (commemorated on the memorial to the massacre in the town cemetery only as '*officer inconnu*', and presumably also the unknown soldier among the Commonwealth War Graves there) was Lieutenant Davenport. There is one problem with this. Davenport survived not only the battle but also the war, later marrying and settling down in Dorking, Surrey, until his death in 1990. Furthermore, there are no other casualties recorded in the battalion at this time who do not have a known grave. Therefore, the identity of the victim is unknown. He may have been an officer from another unit in the area, or he may have been a private soldier who had put on an officer's uniform in the hope of getting better treatment. There is another theory that he was in fact an enemy spy who was tortured and killed because he had been guilty of treachery. None of these explain Davenport's watch. The mystery is now unlikely ever to be solved.

All of this was unknown to the men of the 2/5th Foresters who had escaped death or capture. Major Cooper had taken over command of the battalion on the evening of 26 May. His immediate task was to extricate them from the new pocket around Lille which the German attack threatened to create. Orders to pull out arrived at 7.30pm, and overnight the battalion marched back some 6 miles to Mons-en-Pévèle. Operation Dynamo had been put into effect, and the Foresters would need to retire to Dunkirk, from where the navy would transport them to England. Provided, of course, that the Germans did not get there first.

4

Evacuation: Dunkirk, May–June 1940

Over 800,000 children were evacuated from British cities in the first few days of the war due to fear of bombing raids. Barely a year old itself, the 2/5th Battalion was now also facing a life-or-death evacuation under the threat of intense air attacks. In the confusion of the retreat north, some of the unit had inevitably become separated. Private George Hampton was with Lance Corporal Fred Tomlinson in one of the battalion's 30cwt lorries, loaded with rations including two full sides of beef and cases of NAAFI whisky, which they dared not touch. Bringing up the rear of the convoy, the truck was separated from the main body and fell into a ditch while trying to make its way past the throng of civilians. It was eventually righted with the help of some refugees, but the rest of the battalion was by then long gone. Without maps, instructions or even any idea of where the battalion was heading, Hampton and Tomlinson now faced a personal odyssey to get to the coast and away. Another man left behind was signaller Steve Loach, who had simply fallen asleep from exhaustion when the column stopped for a break. Lance Corporal George Price and his mates tried to wake him but could not, and they reluctantly had to leave him and catch up with the disappearing column. Loach survived to rejoin the battalion in England, but some wounded men were left behind as transport was not available for them. These included Private Ronald Bradley, who died in August as a prisoner of war (PoW).

The roads were jammed with civilian and army transport, and Private Stanley Storey attempted to take advantage of the slow-moving traffic to take a rest on one of the battalion's few vehicles. Throwing his rifle on board before jumping on, he was horrified to see the truck speed up, leaving him without his weapon. His reward for the mistimed ruse was to have to carry the platoon's 36lb Boys anti-tank rifle instead of his own 9lb Lee-Enfield.

It is probable that the battalion was meant to pick up requisitioned local transport at Mons-en-Pévèle, as were the 9th Foresters, but the civilian French drivers failed to show up. On the morning of 27 May, the battalion therefore had to march a further 5 miles to Avelin. During the march, Captain Armstrong went off ahead to reconnoitre on a bicycle he had acquired; he was not seen again until the battalion arrived in England. The men were exhausted from their exertions and the heat, and their feet blistered by marching, but with another senior officer gone, several of the junior officers rose to the occasion. Second Lieutenant John Kerly walked alongside his men, sharing tots of whisky from his hip flask and even carrying some of the weaker men's rifles. 'If I was hungry and I'd got nothing to eat, he would have given me his meals, he was as good as that,' recalled Corporal Victor Tupling.[1] Lieutenant Cecil Wall, the signals officer, was another whose exertions stood out. George Price, who had been spared the combat on the canal when Wall had sent him back to the Battalion HQ, remembered the lieutenant's hair turning from black to white during the campaign.

At Avelin, the battalion was finally able to pick up RASC motor transport, which carried it north-west though Seclin, Lille, Armentières and Bailleul, finally ending up for the night at the village of Steenvoorde, near the Belgian border some 20 miles south-west of Dunkirk. The BEF usually planned road movements on a basis of 12½ miles an hour by day and 10 miles by night, but it had taken most of the day to travel the 40 miles from Avelin to Steenvoorde at an average speed that barely exceeded walking pace. The convoy of vehicles had to contend with roads packed with refugees, as well as persistent German air attacks. Armentières was nothing but a heap of rubble following an air raid, severely restricting movement through the streets. Inmates from the local asylum, destroyed in the raid, lined the roads watching the passing vehicles.

The retreating Foresters had only just made it out of the Lille pocket. During the day, the panzers finally forced the La Bassée canal and Rommel's 7th Panzer Division cut the Lille–Armentières road behind them at Lomme. This trapped 35,000 men of the French First Army in Lille, including many of the North African troops that had fought alongside the Foresters on the canal around Oignies. The 46th Division's retreat also took it across the front of the enemy forces pushing west through Belgium, and it was only able to reach Dunkirk due to the resistance put up by I and II Corps of the BEF along the Ypres–Comines canal to the north. It was behind this screen (which included the regulars of the 2nd Foresters) that the Foresters' convoy got through to the town of Steenvoorde on the evening of 27 May.

Here, the bulk of the men went into billets, while Major Cooper headed off for a meeting at 8.30pm at 46th Division HQ, 3 miles further up the road in Winnezeele. There were reports of about forty German tanks in the area, so just after midnight a defensive *laager* for all-round defence against armoured attack was set up around Steenvoorde. The 2/5th formed a sausage-shaped perimeter surrounding half of 8 Anti-Tank Battery's guns to the west of the Steenvoorde–Winnezeele road; the 9th Foresters did the same to the east. But no enemy tanks appeared. To the south-west, around Cassel, III Corps of the BEF was also putting up a dogged resistance to the advancing panzers. Instead of pushing forward their valuable tanks, the German commanders decided to leave the destruction of the BEF mainly to the infantry forces approaching from Belgium and to the Luftwaffe. It gave the British a breathing space, of which they were to take full advantage.

From 7 to 9am on 28 May, Steenvoorde came under heavy dive-bombing attacks, which reduced the village to rubble. Later came a torrential downpour, the men sheltering beside a hedge and using their gas capes to protect them from the rain, a practice discouraged but widespread in the army. Despite the thunderstorm, many men fell asleep, among them Willis Dixon. He was woken by Lieutenant Williamson with the news that King Leopold of the Belgians had capitulated that morning. This left the BEF with a huge open flank to the north and meant a further withdrawal. Williamson, another one of those officers who looked after his men in adversity, was still awaiting orders from Battalion HQ, so he took Private Dixon and some others to a farm; Dixon recalled that they acquired some chickens and vegetables and 'made up a great stew and enjoyed our first decent meal since leaving Rennes'.[2]

The rain at least meant that the battalion escaped further air attacks that day as it completed its move into the Dunkirk perimeter. The 46th Division had been allocated to the defence of the westernmost sector of the British line, to the north and east of Bergues. This historic town, encircled by fortifications constructed by Vauban in the late seventeenth century, was held by yet another ad hoc formation. 'Usherforce', under Colonel Charles Milne Usher, consisted of about 1,000 men, mostly line-of-communications troops, stiffened by the regulars of C Company, 2nd Warwickshire Regiment, and stragglers from various units. West of the town, the perimeter defences were the responsibility of the French, whose 341st Infantry Regiment protected the immediate British flank. As on the Canal de la Haute Deule, there were also several French units already in the sector allocated to the division, in various states of disorganisation. Most important of these were some 500 engineers in Bergues and the 137th Infantry Regiment to the north-east of the town.

Past the road junction at Vyfweg, 10 miles south of Dunkirk, the 2/5th Foresters began to see the full enormity of the disaster that had befallen the BEF. The roadsides were full of abandoned transport vehicles; only fighting vehicles, ambulances and artillery were allowed to enter the perimeter. The 2/5th left their trucks to be set on fire or otherwise disabled along with the others and finished the journey on foot. Sergeant Frank Hession's typewriter went into a ditch along with all the other equipment except for the men's rifles and packs; written orders and neatly drawn-up lists of soldiers present had been early casualties of the retreat. Elsewhere, Hampton and Tomlinson, with the assistance of some helpful French officers and British military police, had also managed to find their way to Dunkirk with their truck full of rations. Although the food they carried would have been greatly appreciated by the men on the beaches (possibly excepting the beef, which by this time was smelling quite high), they were turned off the road into a field and told to abandon their vehicle, immobilise it and make their way into Dunkirk on foot.

The 2/5th Foresters took up a reserve position guarding six bridges on the Téteghem Canal, about 3 miles behind the front line and halfway between Bergues and Dunkirk, where they remained the following day. Lieutenant Doug Cousin, now in command of A Company, was tasked with the protection of some of the bridges. He posted one platoon under a sergeant to the bridge on his right flank, with another led by a corporal on the left. When Cousin returned later to inspect the position, he couldn't find the sergeant or his men. Arriving at the left flank, there was no sign of the corporal either. A staff captain with Cousin said, 'If you find him shoot him for desertion', but fortunately Cousin discovered that the corporal had been there all the time, under cover of the embankment.

Private Alan Orme, one of the six men posted with Sergeant John Creswick on the right-hand bridge, remembered the incident somewhat differently. According to him, they had been ordered to hold the bridge for six hours, but after twenty-four hours no relief had come. By this time they were also coming under enemy attack. Creswick told the men to conserve their ammunition, since they had just the fifty rounds each man could carry. Having exhausted this beating off German attacks, Creswick reluctantly decided to pull out, telling the platoon it was every man for himself and that they should make their way back to Dunkirk.

By the morning of 30 May, the Royal Navy had successfully lifted 126,606 troops from Dunkirk. Many of the first-line fighting formations that had protected the 46th Division as they had made their way north from the Lille pocket were scheduled to leave that night, and the 2/5th Foresters now took their turn in the defence of the perimeter. The war diarist of the 9th Foresters recorded that battalions waiting to embark handed over Bren guns and ammunition to them, making them better equipped than at any time in the campaign. It is probable the same was true of the 2/5th. For example, Willis Dixon was carrying 200 rounds of .303 ammunition—four times the usual allowance—when he left Dunkirk.

It was another grey, overcast day that gave some protection from the enemy's air power when the 2/5th moved up to the Bergues–Furnes Canal either side of the village of Hoymille, taking up strong positions to cover three bridges. To their left was the 1st East Lancashire Regiment, a regular battalion. Their right was anchored on Bergues, where the 1st Loyal Regiment had relieved Usherforce at midnight on 29 May, joining the Warwicks. This garrison now came under the command of General Curtis. North of Bergues, the 9th Foresters provided cover for the British flank should the French be driven back, while the 2/5th Leicesters, down to a mere seventy men, formed a meagre brigade reserve. The

16th Field Regiment was still in support in the Téteghem area. The regiment had only nineteen guns left as one of its troops had embarked for the UK in error, having disabled its guns, indicative of the confusion pervading the retreat. But it had taken under its wing an equal number of guns from a variety of other units. Four of these were deployed in an anti-tank role along with 8 Anti-Tank Battery, which still had eleven of its guns, deployed in ones or twos covering the bridges. Brigadier Chichester-Constable ordered posts of twenty men to support these guns, but the artillerymen were often better equipped with Bren guns than the infantry sent to defend them.

Bergues itself was being systematically destroyed by enemy bombing and shelling. The town was in flames and covered by a pall of black smoke so thick that despatch riders, dismounting to enter the ruined town, were forced to wrap handkerchiefs around their mouths to breath. A wood near the town caught fire, destroying the transport which had been earmarked to carry the garrison to the beaches. There was also heavy enemy shelling of the 2/5th Foresters positions at around 6pm that evening, but this was only a foretaste of much stronger enemy attacks the following day. At about 5pm on 31 May, the battalion came under heavy mortar bombardment from the German 20th Motorised Division. Two men were killed; they were buried by their comrades, but shortly afterwards the intense shelling blew them out of their graves.

All this was too much for some of the men, who withdrew from their positions. Where they were well led by experienced officers or NCOs, however, the raw soldiers of the 2/5th held their ground. During one skirmish, Private Sydney Cooper was manning a Bren gun in a ditch. Behind it was a line of trees, under which stood Doug Cousin, leaning on a walking stick. German bullets where whipping through the branches and leaves were dropping all around him, but Cousin refused to take cover. 'He was a cool customer alright,' remembered Cooper.[3] Sometimes the leadership was not from within the battalion. Sergeant Dooley of 8 Anti-Tank Battery rallied some of the Foresters around his gun, which was posted to cover one of the blown bridges along the canal. The position was restored until the battalion was relieved by the Warwicks from Bergues at 7pm.

When not manning the Bren gun, Cooper found himself by the road leading to Dunkirk, sitting on a pile of stones and sheltering from the rain under his gas cape. A staff car full of officers drew up and a hand appeared from the window and beckoned him to approach.

'Who are you?' asked the officer.

'2/5th Foresters.'

'Well done lads, we are going home if we can make it.'[4]

The officer was Lord Gort. He left Dunkirk at 6pm that evening, handing over command to Major General Harold Alexander, who would take command of I Corps, the last British rearguard. The 2/5th Foresters and the rest of 46th Division now came under I Corps.

Evacuation: Dunkirk, May–June 1940

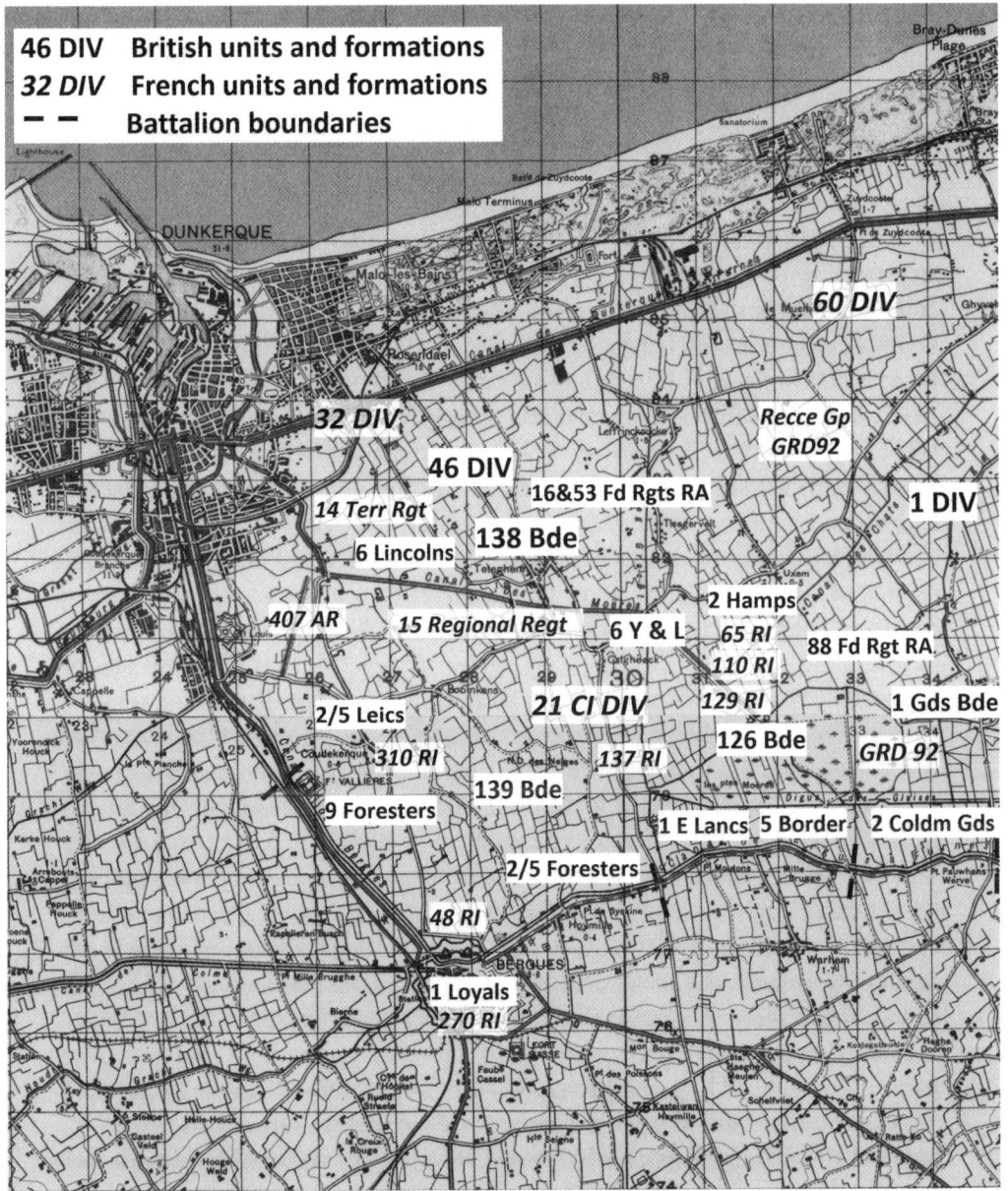

The Dunkirk Perimeter, 28 May–2 June 1940.

The Foresters were pulled back to their billets in Téteghem. Only some 20,000 British troops were now present in the Dunkirk perimeter, and it was clear that it could not be held much longer against determined German attacks. However, Alexander was determined that his new command would not surrender, and the final evacuation of the BEF was planned for the following night. The men of 46th Division received the order to prepare for evacuation at 10.30am on 1

June, and at 4.30pm the 2/5th Foresters received in turn orders from 139 Brigade to proceed to Malo-les-Bains, east of Dunkirk harbour, to await embarkation. By this stage of the evacuation, German air power was too strong to risk ships in the harbour during daylight, so they would have to wait until nightfall. In their rear, the Germans continued their heavy mortar and artillery bombardment, accompanied by air attacks. This was followed by a determined assault by the German 18th Infantry Division that penetrated the canal line, drove in the Warwicks and required counterattacks by the Loyals, supported by a squadron of light tanks from the 5th (Inniskilling) Dragoon Guards, to prevent the enemy breaking through. The Loyals were now in danger of being surrounded in Bergues, and supported by the Inniskillings they fell back to the Téteghem canal. Here they held of the German advance until 8pm, when they handed over to the French 137th Infantry Regiment and moved back to Dunkirk themselves.

Covered by this stubborn rearguard action, the 2/5th Foresters were able to march back from Téteghem to the beach. Although molested only by enemy bombing and shellfire, it was still a significant trial of their morale and discipline. Dunkirk itself was a terrible sight, albeit one no longer unfamiliar to them: 'Flattened buildings, debris of all description, cratered streets, dead oxen and bodies, in an intense summer heat, created that cloying putrid stink of death, once smelt never forgotten.'[5] Thick clouds of oily black smoke rose from bombed oil tanks in the harbour district. Lorries had been driven into the sea to act as artificial piers from which men could be ferried by the famous 'little ships' to destroyers and other larger craft offshore. The men rested in the dunes outside the town to wait their turn to be evacuated that night by the navy. Just inland from the beach, alongside the East Mole bastion, a French battery 'kept up a continuous ear shattering bombardment from its long-distance naval guns'.[6] The German artillery was trying to silence this battery, and the shells frequently overshot, falling among the men sheltering in the dunes or queuing at the mole. Unable to dig effective shelter in the sand, the men had to endure the bombardment until it was their time to leave.

During the hours of daylight, German fighters and bombers added to their misery, although the latter tended to target the ships rather than the infantry on the beaches. Both Alan Orme and George Price witnessed a hospital ship bombed, despite being clearly marked with the Red Cross. This was presumably HMHS *Worthing*, which was attacked and heavily damaged by twelve German bombers between 2.32 and 2.42pm on 1 June. In the dunes, bodies lay on stretchers, the blankets covering them riddled in holes from strafing. One enemy fighter was hit and the pilot seen to bail out. As he floated down on his parachute, he became the focus for all the pent-up hatred and anger that the men on the beach had accumulated during the last two weeks, and they let fly at the German with a hail of bullets from every rifle available.

The war diary describes the battalion embarking on 'various boats'; but the bulk of the men probably embarked, as did the majority of evacuees, from the mole at Dunkirk. This was in the early hours of 2 June. There were about 420 officers and men in the main party that had marched from Téteghem during the afternoon. Around midnight, an officer from a Scottish regiment told the men that if they could get to the mole they should be able to board a ship home. The mole was still being shelled, as well as having large holes in it from bombing, which the men had to cross on makeshift bridges made from planks or stretchers. A further obstacle was the French troops, who at this point in the evacuation were being taken off on a one-for-one basis with the British. Many of them carried huge bundles of personal possessions or loot, which they had to be persuaded to dump into the sea. Even when the men got to the ships, it was difficult to board them. Not only had the mole not been designed for ships to moor against to take on passengers, but many of the destroyers (which together were responsible for over 27 per cent of the evacuees) had suffered severe damage from earlier trips to the port, and several had huge parts of the ship missing. Jumping from shore to ship in full fighting gear, including rifle and ammunition, was not for the faint-hearted and could prove fatal: 'The soldier who had been Colonel Everard's batman, jumped for the ship and missed, and fell between the ship and the mole, and was drowned.'[7] The destroyers crammed aboard as many men as they could. HMS *Codrington*, on which Sergeant Jack Schofield, Sydney Cooper and probably many other Foresters were evacuated, arrived at Dover at 3.25am on 2 June with 878 men on board, in addition to its normal complement of 185 sailors. *Codrington* was so overladen that the soldiers were instructed to lie still on the decks, as any movement could destabilise the ship. Much to the dismay of many of the soldiers, to make space the sailors threw overboard the rifles which they had faithfully carried throughout the retreat.

Those men who had become separated from the battalion had a variety of experiences trying to get away from Dunkirk. Hampton and Tomlinson had been sheltering in a shed near St Malo le Bains, where they tried but failed to get some sleep, before making their way onto the mole, where they were lifted off by the SS *Tynewald*. Hampton slumped on deck, exhausted, and opened his iron rations, a slab of solid chocolate measuring 6 by 5 inches and an inch thick, but only managed to eat a quarter before falling so soundly asleep that he slept through an attack by enemy bombers the following morning. When he finally awoke, he was told it was 1 June. Private Albert Pegg, who had a nasty surprise when he found that the truck he had been sheltering under for the night was full of live artillery shells, was a 'true' Dunkirk evacuee, being lifted of the beach in one of the 'little ships' and taken back to Ramsgate.

Among the last away were Alan Orme and two of his mates. Upon reaching the beach, they had reported to one of the beach masters, officers who were trying to organise the men into units to send back home. When they told him they were Foresters, the officer said they had gone two days previously, and that they would have to wait until some more came. The resourceful Derbyshire men were not going to be denied the chance to get away, however. They had spotted some men from the Staffordshire Regiment going through, (probably the 1/6th South Staffordshires, who arrived at St Malo-les-Bains on 1 June), and they slipped further down the beach and spoke to another officer. This time they claimed that they were 'Staffies' and were allowed to join the queues of men holding hands in the sea in the hope of being picked up by from the beaches. Having tried this four times with no success, they decided to head into Dunkirk and try their luck there. Making their way down the mole, they saw a destroyer beginning to pull away, so they ran and jumped on, and were fortunate enough to be caught and pulled in by the sailors. They, together with some 460 other men, had managed to board HMS *Winchelsea*, which arrived in Dover at 5.45am on 2 June There were three other Foresters on board.

Most of the destroyers crossed the Channel back to Dover, the large passenger ships to Folkestone, while smaller vessels went to Ramsgate or Margate and hospital ships to Newhaven. These were the principle receiving ports for the evacuated BEF, and wherever the men landed they got a warm and sympathetic reception from the people of south-east England. Upon arrival at a British port, disembarkation took around ten to twenty minutes, and the exhausted and hungry soldiers were given tea and sandwiches by members of the Women's Voluntary Services (WVS), Salvation Army, Church Army or simply local volunteers. They were also given a postcard to send home to their families to tell them they were safe. But they did not stay long here. With so many soldiers being evacuated (26,256, including French troops, on the night of 1–2 June alone, and over 60,000 on each of the previous two nights), the priority was to get the men away from the docks for the next load to arrive. With formations broken up by the evacuation, basic administrative processes such as providing food, clothing, accommodation and pay had ceased to function. Where possible, fighting units were kept together, but otherwise the men were told to 'Get on any train', and the army would sort them into their units later. A train left Dover approximately every fifteen minutes, running non-stop either to Redhill in Surrey or Ashford in Kent. From these stations they were sent to reception areas in southern England, army bases where there was time to register who had survived and give them food, shelter and clothing. While they were in the reception areas, accommodation could be arranged in a redistribution area, where they would be re-formed into their units and formations.

The main body of the Foresters were sent to a reception area at Blackdown Camp in Camberley. Here, the men could get a hot meal and a bath, and were given a blanket, clean towel and shaving kit. They also got some beer money and were entertained by variety stars who came down from London. They stayed here for two days in tents before entraining at Blackwater Station for a move to Belle Vue, Manchester, where 46th Division would be re-formed. Those who had been separated from the battalion were scattered across the country. Alan Orme and his group ended up in Aldershot, which was where most of the 'stragglers' who had become separated from their unit were sent. But Sydney Cooper and Frank Hession were put up at Bordon, while Albert Pegg found himself in the Royal Welch Fusiliers' depot at Wrexham, North Wales. George Hampton, who had landed at Folkestone, was at the Lulworth Cove Tank Training Depot, Bovington Camp. Rather than getting any rest, he and the men with him were put on guard duty, as well as having to dig slit trenches to defend the camp; though they were given £1 apiece to go into town in the evenings. A lucky few, including Frank Offiler, who had finally got to fire his rifle for the first time while defending the Dunkirk perimeter, ended up in Derbyshire at Alfreton, where they took the opportunity for a few days' unofficial leave in Nottingham before going to Belle Vue.

*

It cannot be said that the 2/5th Foresters had covered themselves in glory during their time in France. Aside from the Mentions in Dispatches given to Hartigan and McCall, they received no gallantry awards. They had been seriously engaged in combat only twice, both times defending canal lines, at Oignies and Bergues. In the first engagement they had been pushed back and then ambushed, while on the second they had been shaken by enemy artillery and mortar fire. However, on neither occasion had the battalion completely broken; even though woefully under-equipped and largely composed of untrained recruits, they had put up a good fight. In the words of the regimental historian, 'They had displayed the staunchness which is customary in their regiment and played a worthy part in the withdrawal to and defence of Dunkirk.'[8] Sydney Cooper described the unit on its final march to the beaches as 'not a rabble like some units had become, but like a Battalion'.[9] While this is grossly unfair to the many other battalions evacuated from Dunkirk that had both suffered higher casualties and engaged in heavier fighting than the 2/5th Foresters, and whose disorder was therefore understandable, it does illustrate the sense of pride that the battalion had developed in its short time in combat. Others may have fought harder, but that cannot take away from the fact that these men, sent to France to perform pioneer duties and complete their training, were amongst the last to leave.

Individually, they were suffering from the mental strain of their first combat. Ernie Gibson recalled that 'it took a long while for us to stop diving for cover when we heard sudden noises, or aircraft overhead. I witnessed one or two punch ups because some practical joker had given a long whistle by mouth, or created some sudden bang!'[10] Many had lost good friends or respected officers. But rather than lowering their morale, this had the effect of hardening their attitude towards the Germans, as demonstrated by their action against the lone pilot on the beach at Dunkirk.

Most of them felt that they had been beaten by superior numbers and materiel—tanks, artillery and aircraft—and by better preparedness and tactics, rather than by any superiority in the enemy's fighting ability. General Curtis pointed to the successful counterattacks that had been made around Bergues (largely by regular troops, it must be said) as evidence that however potent their panzers had been, the German infantry were not as good as in the last war. This feeling that the Germans could be beaten was also felt lower down the ranks. They hadn't stood a chance being sent against panzers and Stukas with twenty-five-year-old rifles that they had hardly been trained to use, but give them a fair fight and they could win: 'The major portion of the force that was let of the hook, and got back to England, had received a very sudden, if unwelcome baptism of fire, and in approximately six weeks been transformed from wide-eyed recruits to quite a hard battle-conditioned force.'[11]

Eventually, the Germans would regret letting the BEF escape from Dunkirk. But for the men of the 2/5th re-forming in Manchester, thoughts of victory were a long way off. First, they would have to reorganise, re-equip and prepare to defend Britain itself from invasion.

5

Education: Scotland and England, June 1940–September 1942

On 5 June, the men at Blackdown Camp went to nearby Blackwater station and were put on the train to Manchester, where 46th Division was reforming. The people of the city welcomed them as heroes; they received free haircuts and cinema tickets, were bought free drinks in the pubs and were given free meals in the restaurant at the huge Lewis's department store. Encamped in Belle Vue Park, they were given civilian clothing in place of their dishevelled uniforms. Some men, including Jack Schofield, promoted to corporal for his actions in France, received a few days' leave and were able to visit their homes in Derbyshire.

The battalion did not stay long in Manchester. It was not considered a suitable place to re-form the unit, but whether due to the limited facilities of Belle Vue or concern over the effect of the temptations of the city on discipline is not clear. It was possibly the former, as Schofield wrote that the 'professional ladies of easy virtue' of Manchester, while engaging the interest of the men, did not attract them too much due to their limited funds. On 15 June, the troops were transferred to Rochdale, where they went into billets and the real work of rebuilding began. By now, many of those who had become separated from the battalion in France had rejoined, and in Rochdale a substantial new intake of men arrived from the ITC back in Derby. At Dunkirk on 1 June, the battalion had numbered fifteen officers and 411 other ranks, but by the end of the month the latter had grown to 903. This was substantially larger than its war establishment, and a new E Company had to be formed to accommodate the new recruits. Merely adding men was the easy part though, as the new intake had scarcely any training and hardly any equipment. The battalion did at least receive a batch of Canadian Ross rifles, though these were another First World War weapon and generally regarded as inferior replacements for the Lee-Enfields which the navy had thrown into the English Channel.

Equally significant was the lack of officers, of which there were still only twenty-six by the end of June to manage the oversize battalion. On 18 June, Major Cooper, who had shepherded it through the retreat from Oignies and evacuation at Dunkirk, handed over command to Major Jacob Hassell and resumed his previous post as adjutant. The new CO had no prior connection with the regiment, though at the start of the war he had been living in Basford. He had been a regular soldier before the First World War, been promoted from the ranks in 1915 to become an officer in the King's Own Yorkshire Light Infantry, won both the MC and the DSO on the Western Front, and then served in India post-war. His appointment reflected army preference for regular officers over territorial officers; they were considered better trained and therefore more competent. But he was fifty-two years old and had been retired since 1932, so it also reflected the dearth of capable battalion commanders available as the army expanded. Six more replacement officers arrived at the battalion in July, all new war commissions. By then the Foresters had left Rochdale and were accommodated in the Knox Institute school buildings in Haddington, East Lothian, where the 46th Division had been assigned to defend the area around Stirling and Edinburgh. The 139 Brigade HQ was set up in the centre of Haddington in Baillie's Gift Shop, whose owners, by coincidence, were associated with the construction company that was building the Ladybower Dam near Schofield's hometown of Hathersage.

*

Not all the Dunkirk survivors went to Haddington. John Creswick had avoided being shot by Doug Cousin at the bridge at Teteghem, but he still found himself up on a charge of quitting his post and was court-martialled on 27 June. He was defended by Lieutenant Geoffrey Laurence, another former private soldier in the Artists Rifles and a solicitor in civilian life, and Alan Orme gave evidence at the trial. They were both sure he would get off, and Orme was shocked when Creswick was found guilty and sentenced to three years in prison, later commuted to eighteen months' hard labour, as well as losing his sergeant's stripes. There must have been many men, not only private soldiers but also NCOs and even officers, who in the confusion of the Dunkirk bridgehead had decided that their best course of action was to escape to the coast and live to fight another day. Two privates in the 9th Foresters, tried earlier that month, had received a year's hard labour for quitting their posts, while a private in the 2/5th was tried in August for the even more serious offence of desertion (whether at Dunkirk or in Scotland is not clear), and he also got a year's hard labour.

Why was Creswick singled out for harsher treatment? The detailed court transcripts for Creswick's trial have not been retained, but his military record may provide a clue. Originally a miner by trade, he had enlisted in 1921 and attained the rank of corporal before being discharged in 1935. He had then re-enlisted in 1936 and been a recruiting sergeant in Derby in 1939. So Creswick was one of the few pre-war regulars in the battalion, and possibly its most experienced NCO. As such, his was a critical role as a mentor and source of discipline to the inexperienced young men around him. According to Orme, Creswick had also been asking questions of why his squad had not been relieved at the bridge. His important position in the battalion combined with his apparent challenging of his officer's authority probably told against him, with the tribunal deciding that an example had to be made in order to prevent further incidents of indiscipline. 'If that was army justice we knew we had to watch our step,' thought Orme.[1] But Reg Markham believed that Creswick was hard done by, and that Lieutenant Cousin had let his men down and got away with it. Creswick was immensely popular throughout the battalion, and the men held collections every payday, openly in front of the officers, to send to his wife and two children, who would have received no money from the army while he was in prison. Together with Arthur Barlow, who had also been at the bridge at Teteghem, Orme was assigned to escort Creswick to prison. En route, they lost him on a crowded bus in Edinburgh, eventually locating him in a pub on Princes Street calmly having a pint and waiting for them to find him. They bought him another drink before resuming their distasteful duty, pleased to have avoided a court martial themselves for letting him escape. Orme recalled seeing Creswick again in 1942 and that he had regained the rank of corporal, but he never returned to the battalion.

The posting of the 46th Division to defend Scotland, rather than to south-east England, where an invasion was most likely to occur, clearly reflected its second-line status and the beating that it had received in France. General Alan Brooke, who visited the division on 27 July as Commander in Chief Home Forces, declared it to be 'in a lamentably backward state of training, barely fit to do platoon training and deficient of officers'.[2] It also had a new commander. General Curtis had been assigned to command the 49th Division in Iceland, which has to be considered even more of a backwater than Scotland, and had been replaced on 8 July by Major General Desmond Anderson CB, CMG, DSO, previously commander of 45th Division and briefly the Assistant Chief of the Imperial General Staff. If Curtis' career was on a downward track, that of his former GSO1 (senior General Staff Officer), Chichester-Constable, was on the rise. The only part of the 46th Division to fight as a cohesive formation in France was 139 Brigade, and Chichester-Constable's handling of it had been singled out by Curtis for praise. On 1 July, he was awarded a bar to the DSO that he had won in the First World War. The citation highlighted the way in which with disregard for his own safety, he had carried out personal reconnaissance and consistently reported details of enemy movements. It also regarded as 'masterly' his handling of the situation and organisation of the counterattack when the perimeter was penetrated near Bergues on 1 June.

*

Many of the troops involved in that counterattack, and Chichester-Constable himself, were regulars, but nevertheless this citation to a small extent refutes the view that the second-line territorial brigades had no impact on the 1940 campaign. A report had appeared referring to the force left in Dunkirk on 31 May as being 1st, 42nd and 50th divisions, but at the bottom of the copy in the 46th Division war diary is a handwritten comment from Chichester-Constable: 'I must have been dreaming. I thought we were there.'[3] More significantly for the 2/5th Foresters, his DSO positioned Chichester-Constable and his brigade as the most experienced infantry in the division, and they would be assigned the most important defensive position, east of Edinburgh. In comparison to the infantry-only formation that had gone to France, supporting units would also be directly placed under Chichester-Constable, making 139 Brigade into something approaching an all-arms brigade group. Because Scotland was not seen as a likely point for invasion, any attacks in the area were expected to be diversionary, and 139 Brigade was warned that it could not expect much support from neighbouring formations. It would have to rely upon its own resources, which were still meagre at best.

The brigade's artillery support came in the form of 70th Field Regiment RA, armed with a mixture of old 18-pounder guns of First World War vintage, the slightly better 18/25-pounder conversions and some American 75mm guns. There was a section of two 6-inch guns at Dunbar and another overlooking the island of Fidra at the entrance to the Firth, but their role was to guard against seaborne invasion; they could not engage any airborne landings or troops that had managed to fight their way inshore. There was also an armoured train, stationed on the east coast rail line near the Longnidry golf course. The brigade had no other armoured support, although it did have attached 230 Anti-Tank Battery RA with five 2-pounder guns, as well as a machine-gun company from the 2/7th Middlesex Regiment. It was augmented, numerically at least, by several training units, including the Royal Scots ITC, Cavalry Training Regiment and 38th Signals Training Regiment, all stationed in Edinburgh; the 6th Field Training Regiment of the RA at Gosford; and the Dunbar Officer Corps Training Unit (OCTU). There were also some units of the Local Defence Volunteers—what would soon become the Home Guard. But at this stage of their development, these were virtually unarmed and lacked even uniforms, being distinguished from civilians only by their LDV armbands. They could not be considered of any fighting value. The defence plans called for them to be used to guard VPs and to act as observers and guides. With this ad hoc, under-equipped and under-trained force, 139 Brigade was responsible for about 36 miles of the East Lothian coast between Prestonpans in the west and Cockburnspath in the east. The infantry were posted in the standard deployment of two battalions forward and one in reserve. The 2/5th Leicesters covered the western sector, which stretched from Seton Sands to North Berwick. From there to Dunbar was the responsibility of the 9th Foresters. This still left the town of Dunbar itself and about 9 miles of coast to the south as far as the coastguard station at Reed Point, this sector being guarded by the trainees and instructors of the Dunbar OCTU. Detachments from the Royal Scots and the Cavalry Training Regiment were stationed at the local airstrips at Drem and Macmerry, which would be primary targets if the Germans were to attack the area.

Education: June 1940–September 1942

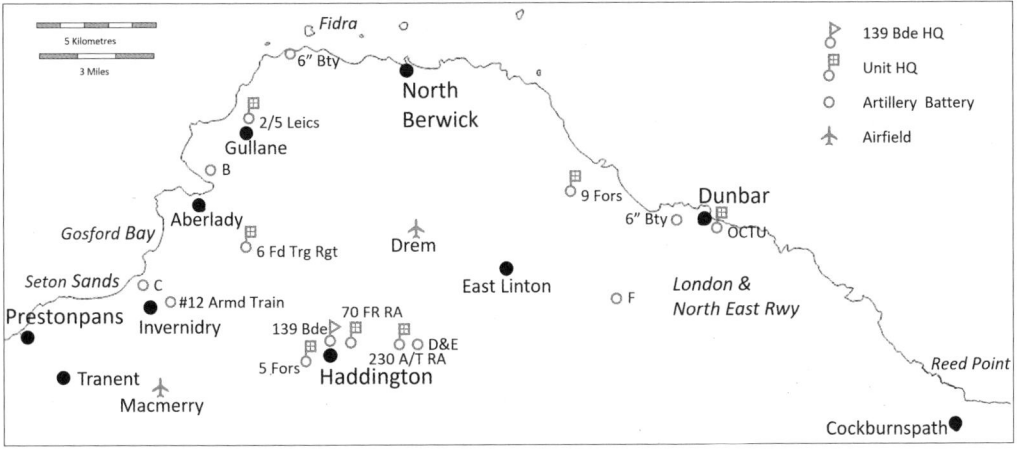

Scotland, winter 1940.

The infantry were organised into a number of small defensive localities to a depth of between 2 and 5 miles from the coast, with instructions to hold their positions as long as possible in the event of attack, and as large a mobile reserve as they could then manage. The key principle in the defensive plan was to be 'aggressive mobility', and the 2/5th Foresters were held in brigade reserve and allocated this counterattack role, along with the anti-tank guns, the machine-gun company and one-third of the artillery. It was a role to which the battalion responded with that mix of amateur enthusiasm and inspired improvisation which had always been part of the British volunteer tradition. The battalion now had its own carrier platoon, which would form the mainstay of any mobile column, as well as a pair of 3-inch mortars in a 3-ton lorry. There were not enough trucks for the rifle platoons, however, so they would be carried in thirty buses provided by local transport firms. Most innovative was the creation of an ad hoc motorcycle platoon, which was not part of the standard establishment. The officers commanding these new platoons were the young subalterns in the unit, men perhaps more receptive to the new mobile warfare seen in France than the veterans of 1914–18. Second Lieutenant Alaric Gordon Hine was appointed to command the carriers and Bryan Cowderoy the mortars; both were less than twenty-two years old and had been with the battalion barely a month. Hine, from Newark, wore very unmilitary-looking thick glasses, and Corporal Bill Sheppard and the other men transferred to the new platoon nicknamed him 'Spotlight'. Meanwhile, 2nd Lieutenant Christopher Perry, a comparative veteran at 25, commanded the motorcycle platoon, and in September three other junior officers were sent on motorcycle instruction courses. There was one further addition to the mobile column. In the aftermath of Dunkirk, the British Army had commissioned a report to look at what lessons should be learnt. As well as the mixed-arm brigade group, another of its recommendations was the importance of infantry formations having their own integral anti-tank capability. As a start to providing this, a brigade-level anti-tank company was created, equipped with 2-pounder guns. One of its platoons was formed from men of the 2/5th, with Doug Cousin as platoon commander. Although the threat of invasion in Scotland was low, these preparations made to counter the threat indicate that lessons were starting to be applied from the experience gained in France.

A rather less successful experiment to counter invasion was developed at 139 Brigade HQ, where Victor Tupling had been posted as transport corporal. The idea was to construct a sort of mobile pillbox by placing a square armoured box protected by ½-inch riveted metal plates on top of a reinforced lorry chassis. Six men occupied this 'turret', shooting rifles through slits or throwing grenades out of holes—there was no machine gun or heavier weapon—while the driver sat in front in an armoured cabin, together with a sergeant or corporal straining to see out of a tiny visor to command and direct the vehicle. Nicknamed the 'Armadillo', it was 'bloody awful' according to Tupling, and the section was fortunate never to have to go into action. Cumbersome and slow, the whole contraption was so top-heavy that the drivers, many of whom were newly taught, were scared to death of taking a corner at any speed lest it overturn, which some did. Tupling was laid low by one of these monstrosities in a less dramatic fashion. One day in October, he was inspecting one of the trucks in the rain when he slipped and fell, and was rushed to Peebles hospital with a fractured spine. This ended his time with the 2/5th Foresters, as after a long period in plaster he was medically downgraded and spent the rest of the war serving in Royal Electrical and Mechanical Engineer (REME) workshops.

Once the organisation and dispositions of the brigade and battalion were sorted, Chichester-Constable and Hassell could look at improving the training of their troops. Relieved of the need to provide VP guards or work details, and with the threat of invasion making the need to practice counter-measures vital, the 2/5th Foresters probably did more serious training between July and September 1940 than they had in the rest of the war to date. On 24 July, there was a practice for their role as mobile reserve, and the next day they participated in a brigade exercise—another first—with the theme of 'Mobile Reserve in Action against Parachute Troops'. Before they went to France, there is no evidence that they had ever trained with other arms, but in August they carried out practice operations with 275 Field Battery RA to respond to landings at different point on the coast from North Berwick to Cockburnspath. On 23 August, the Duke of Gloucester visited 139 Brigade to observe a joint exercise by the 2/5th Foresters and 2/5th Leicesters with both naval and air support. The training demonstrated the woeful shortage of signals equipment in the region—there were no radios, and messages had to be sent by runner, motorcycle, visually by morse or semaphore, or over local telephone lines where available. But at least it was a start. Battalion training was also becoming more realistic. On 11 September, there was an exercise specifically

Education: June 1940–September 1942

to learn and practice how to rapidly deploy the mobile column, including the employment of the Bren carriers and motorcycles. In addition to this were further brigade exercises, referred to as 'schemes', on 13 and 19 September with field and anti-tank batteries of the Royal Artillery. The second of these schemes was designed to focus on coordination of the different weapons, defence in depth, concealment, counterattack and patrolling. All of this was in addition to primary training of the new recruits in physical fitness, marching and weapons training.

Scotland may have been a relatively quiet sector, but the battalion was not entirely spared enemy action. The same day that it arrived in Haddington, there was an air raid nearby at noon that lasted half an hour. The very first German air raid on Britain had been an attack on the important naval installations in the Firth of Forth in October 1939, and the conquest of Norway meant that the Luftwaffe now had air bases much closer to Scottish targets than before. In 139 Brigade's area, these included not only the Forth, but also Edinburgh and its port of Leith, while there were a few incidents of bombs seemingly dropped at random in the countryside. Most of these raids were by lone raiders or small groups of aircraft, but reports of parachute bombs and downed aircraft still needed to be investigated. This was nothing compared to the intensity of the fighting taking place in the skies over southern England. On 17 August, during a week that saw '*Adler Tag*' (Eagle Day) and massed raids by the Luftwaffe to try to take out the RAF airfields in south-east England, the 2/5th Foresters were holding a sports day! On 7 September, however, the day on which the Luftwaffe first bombed London, the battalion—like every other unit in Britain—received the codeword 'Cromwell', indicating that invasion was thought to be imminent. At 2.20am, reports were even received at 139 Brigade HQ of enemy agents landing on the coast. Towards midnight, gunfire was reported in the Forth, and the Admiralty went so far as to order ports to be made ready for immobilisation. The orders to stand down from these false alarms did not arrive until 9.45am on 8 September.

With hindsight, it is clear that an invasion in the autumn of 1940 was unlikely in the face of the Royal Navy and RAF, and the threat to Scotland especially low. But how would the battalion have fared if Hitler's forces really had invaded on 7 September? One answer to that may be deduced from a battle practice that it took part in on 24 September, a report of which is contained in the battalion war diary and was published to all ranks. Following an inspection in camp, the men were marched to the rifle range at Dunbar, where they were inspected again and rested for ten minutes. Then each platoon commander was given a simple attack plan, which was executed on the range. Starting 400 yards from the butts, the men advanced to 350 yards, at which point standard bullseye targets appeared. They were then ordered to double to 300 yards and open fire. The targets then went down and the platoon advanced to a range of 250 yards, when snapshooting targets appeared for thirty seconds and they fired again. Each Bren gun was given fifteen rounds and each rifleman five rounds.

Turnout for the inspections was considered good, though some marks were deducted for ill-fitting kit and badly cleaned brasswork and bayonets. This could be dismissed as parade ground 'bull', though a little more worrying were poorly adjusted gas masks and capes and, in view of the accident to poor George Cripps in France, the fact that some safety catches were not applied. March discipline was described as 'on the whole excellent', though there was a tendency to press the pace—'rarely justified and in view of the consequent fatigue does not pay'. When it came to the battle exercise itself, however, there was 'a great deal of room for improvement'. Numbers 3, 5 and 16 Platoons were singled out as being well handled, but other platoon commanders were criticised for not retaining control of their men. Orders were described as 'frequently indistinct and incomplete, and sometimes considerably delayed'. The men themselves did not comply with basic fire discipline, such as taking up good positions and readjusting their sights before moving to the next firing point, and wasted ammunition by not ceasing fire immediately the targets disappeared. The handling of the Bren light machine guns was 'not good'; many guns never fired at all and gunners often didn't know how to clear a stoppage. But the worst comments are to be found in the shooting results: 'The number of hits on a large target under easy conditions were very disappointing. Many rounds were just blazed off unaimed. Examinations of the targets indicated that holding and aiming of the Brens was bad.' The report did not give the exact scores but commented that not less than 50 per cent of shots should have resulted in a hit. It can reasonably be assumed that the results fell well short of this.[4]

This was a damning first-term school report. Had German paratroopers actually landed in Scotland, either as a diversion or to seize a vulnerable point such as the Drem airfield, their performance in operations in Holland and Belgium suggests that they would have quickly overcome the isolated local detachments. The Foresters mobile column might well have reacted quickly, since they had practiced deploying to different threatened locations, and after debussing would probably have arrived at their attack line in good order, if a little fatigued. But they would probably have failed in any counterattack against a determined enemy holding good defensive positions.

Fortunately, this situation never arose, and the battalion was able to continue its training without any further major alarms. On 17 September, Hitler postponed the invasion of Britain, and on 7 October the Luftwaffe switched to the nightly bombing raids that would come to be known as the Blitz (four bombs fell on Edinburgh that night). The next day, the 2/5th repeated their battle practice at Dunbar; a report of the results for this second exercise has not survived, so it is impossible to tell whether their performance had improved. On 12 October, the invasion was further postponed until the following spring. Nobody could know it at the time, but this effectively meant it was permanently cancelled.

Battalion-level training and below was to be the focus over the winter, such as a night march and attack exercise on 1 November. Brigade- and divisional-level field exercises with all-arms combinations were suspended, although there was a divisional 'message-writing' exercise on the night of 11–12 November simulating a response to invasion, reflecting the previously poor signals capabilities within the division and the need to improve what would today be referred to as '3C'— command, control and communication. Training aimed at repelling an immediate invasion was now less urgent; in any case, opportunities were becoming more difficult as the long Scottish nights and harsh winter weather began to set in. From October onwards, officers at all levels from the CO down to the subalterns were being sent more frequently on a wide range of classroom courses at the Scottish Command Central School in Edinburgh. The increase in attendance on such courses was perhaps recognised by the appointment of former schoolteacher Charles Williamson as battalion education officer on 28 November. There were still serious expectations that gas would be used by both sides. Consequently, Lieutenant Colonel Hassell attended a week-long gas course at Tregantle Fort, Cornwall; MO Kenneth Bruce a course in Edinburgh; and Jack Schofield, now promoted to sergeant, a ten-day course at the chemical warfare establishment at Porton Down. Furthermore, a battalion gas officer was appointed.

*

Back in Derbyshire, the battalion's duties defending VPs had been taken over by the 10th (Home Defence) Battalion Sherwood Foresters. The nucleus of this unit was the pre-war National Defence Companies, to which had been added volunteers too young for normal military service and some 'militia' conscripts. Although this may seem to have parallels with the personnel now joining the new Home Guard, the battalion was quite separate from that force. Whereas the Home Guard units were volunteers and did not come under military discipline, the Home Defence battalions formed part of the army and were organised within the regimental system. Its officers, initially retired First World War veterans from the TA Reserve, were returned to the active list with an effective seniority date of 24 August 1939. At one notable church parade in Nottingham on 8 September 1940, the battalion's ranks contained no less than three Great War VCs. By then it numbered 1,027 'Old Soldiers', 942 'Young Soldiers' and seventy-six officers, organised in thirteen companies. According to its war diary, this was the largest battalion ever known in the British Army and far too unwieldy, so that September it was split into three. The older personnel were divided between a 1/10th comprised mostly of militia men and a 2/10th containing mostly veterans, while about 400 of the youngest personnel formed a new 70th, or 'Young Soldiers', Battalion.

Many of the infantry regiments in the army had formed these Young Soldiers battalions. They had a different establishment to normal infantry battalions, recognising their role as elementary training units rather than bodies that would ultimately be sent overseas to fight. They often had six rather than four companies, organised into five rather than four platoons, and with a much smaller ratio of senior officers to subalterns than normal battalions. They also had a minimal allocation of heavy weapons, with just one Bren gun and one anti-tank rifle per company, though each man could expect to be trained how to handle a rifle. Although the quality of many of the recruits was high, since they were voluntarily joining up before they were compelled to do so, battalions also attracted an element of what one official historian described as 'highly undesirable adolescents from the slums'.[5] Once army discipline had been imposed, however, the advantage of these units was that the recruits remained in the same platoons throughout their initial six-month training period, which greatly contributed to teambuilding and morale. Once trained and of an age to go overseas, they were transferred into the field battalions, and at least 100 officers and men who had served in the 70th Battalion would transfer to the 2/5th Battalion during 1942.

Frank Mardell might well have been one of those joining the 70th Battalion that the official historian categorised as 'highly undesirable', though had that been the case, events would have proven him wrong. Born in November 1924 in Netherfield, about 4 miles outside Nottingham, Mardell was the youngest of ten children, the son of a platelayer on the railway. By his own admission, the family was poor and he had a rough childhood. The hardships increased when his parents died within a few months of each other in early 1940, and the orphaned Frank found himself passed around other members of the family for his accommodation. But through his sister he had got a decent job in 1939 as a messenger at the area's largest employer, Boots the Chemist in Nottingham, where he now worked as a warehouseman. He had an elder brother who was both an ex-Grenadier Guardsman and a policeman, and an uncle in the territorials. This family support network kept him out of trouble.

The war would change Frank's life, but not in ways that he could have anticipated in the summer of 1940. He joined the local Home Guard in June, and while they might have been of limited fighting value, Frank enjoyed this first exposure to military life. He became proficient at rifle and Lewis gun drills and was appointed corporal of his platoon over men much his senior. In January 1942, still only just 17, he joined the real army, and since he did not express a preference for any unit he found himself a few days later reporting to the Sherwood Foresters at the Drill Hall in London Road, Nottingham. From there he ended up in Lincoln Barracks with the 70th Battalion. The drill was much tougher than in the Home Guard, but his previous experience with weapons stood him in good stead. Also, as an orphan, he was more used to fending for himself in matters such as cleaning and sewing than other recruits; and coming from a large family, the lack of privacy was something he could accept. The army gave Frank discipline and purpose, and he began to think that he might make it his career. By June 1942, when his company was split up and he was assigned to guard duties with IX Corps headquarters, he had already been appointed lance corporal.

*

The 2/5th Foresters had moved into winter accommodation in the Galashiels area during October, where it celebrated Christmas and New Year. But new orders had arrived for 46th Division to move to East Anglia, where it would come under II Corps. The new location was strategically more important than Scotland, and must be seen as a promotion for the formation as a whole and recognition of an improved level of efficiency. Anderson had also handed over command in December to 48-year old Major General Charles Edward Hudson, a native of Derby with a distinguished military record from the First World War, rising from 2nd lieutenant to lieutenant colonel of the 11th Foresters and earning five Mentions in Dispatches, the MC, DSO and Bar, and finally the VC on the Piave River in northern Italy in 1918. The 139 Brigade HQ was stationed at Kimberley Hall, with the 2/5th Foresters at East Dereham and the 2/5th Leicesters at Norwich. The 9th Foresters had not come south with its sibling. It had been earmarked for conversion to a motor battalion and replaced in the brigade by the 16th DLI (stationed at Thetford). This would remain the composition of the brigade until the end of the war. Although on occasion the brigade took up positions on the coast to relieve other formations, its main roles in the defensive plans were the protection of the many RAF airfields in the area from airborne landings, and to be part of a divisional- or corps-level counterattack in the event of seaborne invasion.

Just as the battalion's training in Scotland had reflected its mobile defence role, so the exercises in East Anglia reflected these new responsibilities. There was still a good deal of section-, platoon- and company-level training, including yet another battle practice in March 1941, but new elements such as cooperation with local RAF units began to appear. Responses to a seaborne landing were still prepared, but plans against airborne landings with names such as 'Aero' and 'Fighter' were put together and various exercises in defence of airfields practiced. Among these were one at RAF Swanton Morley on 13 May, and a field firing and 'mopping-up' of paratroopers at RAF Lakenheath on 2 July reviewed by the Duke of Gloucester. A further brigade exercise in September practiced communications between battalions, brigade HQ and the fighter aerodromes. As in Scotland, the defence of the Norfolk airfields was based upon rapid mobile deployment, in which the Foresters were the main brigade reserve. This relied upon a good deal of initiative by local commanders, Brigadier Chichester-Constable specifically stating that he would not 'lay down any hard and fast rules or issue rigid instructions in connection with the operational role of 139 Bde Gp'.[6]

The exercise of 13 May was also notable as the last to be overseen by Lieutenant Colonel Hassell, who had been posted to the ITC in Derby. His replacement was

Major Robert Edwin Hugh Stott, who arrived on the day of the exercise and took command on 21 May with the acting rank of lieutenant colonel. At 42, Stott was eleven years younger than his predecessor, and although a regular officer in the Foresters he also had territorial experience in the 1/6th Battalion in 1918 and with the 8th Battalion between the wars. He also had immediate wartime experience as commander of A Company in the 2nd Battalion in France in 1940. This background made him an ideal choice as commander for the 2/5th; he would stay in that post for the next two years, providing continuity in leadership during their period of training. Another regular soldier joining the battalion that month was Major Geoffrey Gofton-Salmond, posted in from No. 6 Commando and familiar to some of the men from their training at Egginton Hall.

Aside from increased engagement with the RAF, the other new feature of the training in East Anglia was a greater number of large-scale divisional and corps schemes to practice the counterattack role. These had begun almost as soon as the battalion arrived in East Anglia, with a divisional exercise in occupying its new defensive positions at the end of January 1941, followed by a corps exercise practicing a move to its 'harbouring' areas from 13–15 February. The training now took on a scale and frequency that the battalion had never before experienced. March saw a divisional signals exercise, battalion battle practice, a gas exercise and then a divisional scheme to practice an advance to the coast as part of its counterattack role. From 2–4 April, they participated in their first II Corps field exercise, in which 139 Brigade represented the 'enemy'. After a brigade-level scheme the following week which included a river-crossing with folding boats, there was a divisional exercise, 'Drake', from 22–25 April to practice the defence of the River Waveney against panzers. Immediately after an exercise in the defence of RAF Swanton Morley in early May, there was a two-day route march, then yet another divisional exercise ('Nelson') from 28–30 May and a battalion night attack practice on 13 June. The battalion was getting a good grounding in the practice of modern mobile warfare, although equipment was still in short supply. Buses were still being used to transport the men rather than the regulation trucks, though these were now under army command as the rather grandiosely named 17th Motor Coach Company.

On 22 June 1941, Hitler's real panzer divisions invaded the Soviet Union in Operation Barbarossa, the largest military operation yet seen in the war, and one which was to completely alter the course of the conflict. The men of the 2/5th Foresters probably did not pay too much attention to it at the time, as they were in the middle of their own 'large scale' operation, a second corps-level exercise, 'Bulldog', which took place between 20 and 25 June, with 46th Division opposed by 42nd and 45th divisions. The Foresters' role was the defence, together with anti-tank and field gun units, of the Lakenheath area, identified as particularly favourable ground for armoured fighting vehicles (AFVs). Their initial 'defence' was successful, but the brigade was then deemed to have been forced to retreat because

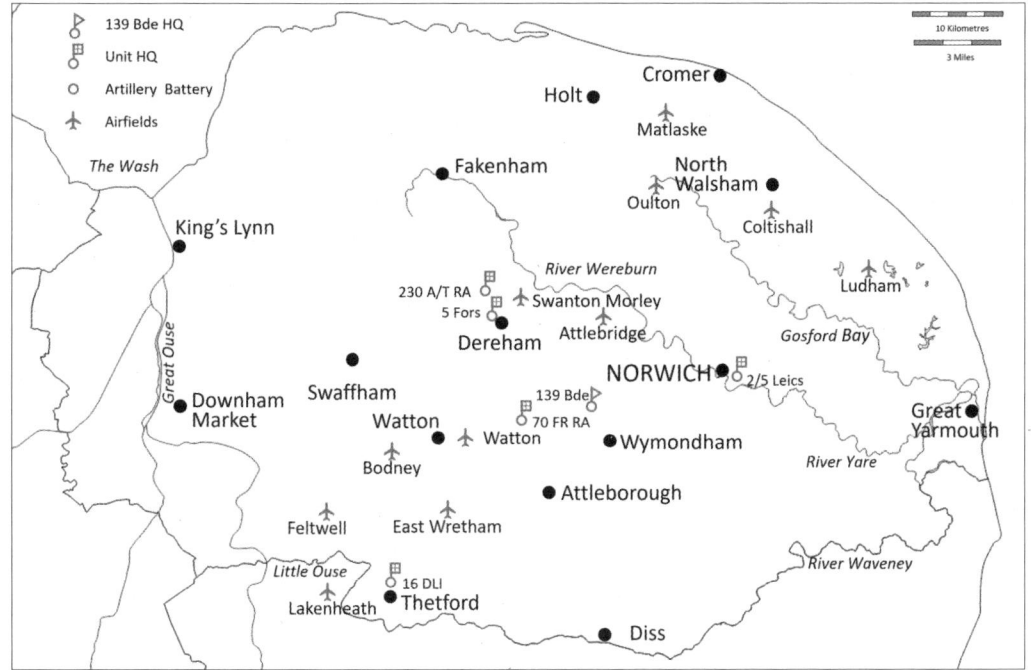

East Anglia, 1941.

of ground lost by battalions to their flank. This was followed by the battalion exercise at Lakenheath and then another on 4 July, when it conducted a practice river crossing by night across the Little Ouse. From 13 July to 18 August there was a break in training when the battalion was rotated into coast defence duties near Great Yarmouth, but John Watts Potter, now promoted to major and commander of HQ Company, led a group of officers sent as umpires to yet another divisional exercise during this period. Corps exercises were held roughly two months apart, so the battalion returned from the coast in time for 'Boxer', another simulated defence against tanks, in which 139 Brigade represented the flank guard of a German panzer advance through Stowmarket and was successful in holding off a British counterattack from the north along the line of the Little Ouse. Also representing German forces on this occasion were 268 Squadron RAF, newly equipped with American Tomahawk fighters. The 2/5th Battalion seems to have developed particular links with this squadron, as both Captain Charles Williamson and the battalion adjutant, Major Patrick Blandy, were sent on temporarily assignments to it during 1942. There were also temporary postings of RAF personnel in the other direction, though it is not clear whether from 268 Squadron.

From 27 September to 3 October, while the seemingly unstoppable German army was encircling Kiev and Leningrad, the battalion was involved in one of the largest British training exercises of the war. 'Bumper' was a massive scheme that involved over a quarter of a million troops, not only II Corps but also formations from other corps. It took place across a wide swathe of eastern England, encompassing much of Norfolk and extending into Cambridgeshire, Suffolk and Essex, with some troops travelling from as far as Berkshire to participate. Its aim was both to test the invasion defences and practice with the motorised and mechanised formations that would eventually comprise any expeditionary force to Europe. The exercise overall showed up many deficiencies in the handling of armour and artillery and in command and control, but the Foresters—once again cast in the role of the Germans, who 'won' the exercise—were positive about their performance. At its conclusion, Chichester-Constable issued a communication that praised 'the quick appreciation and capable leadership of Unit [sic] commanders, coupled with the resource and initiative of subordinate leaders and men', and complimented them on completing 'a really good job of work in a most soldierlike and efficient manner'.[7] Morale across the whole of the division was probably at its highest of the war to date.

'Bumper' was also the battalion's last operation in Norfolk. On 27 October, they received orders to move to south-east England, where they would join XII Corps and relieve the 2/7th Queen's Regiment defending Folkestone in Kent. At the same time, 46th Division got another new commander, its fourth within the year, Major General Harold Augustus Freeman-Atwood OBE, MC. Newly promoted, at 43 he was probably the youngest major general in the army. His record in the Great War included service with the 1st Royal Welch Fusiliers in France, Belgium and Italy, being wounded twice and awarded a Mention in Dispatches as well as his MC. After the war he had extensive service in India, the Sudan and Cyprus, and had been in France in 1940 with the 50th and 47th divisions. Most significantly, from 1932–34 he had served in the War Office with responsibility for the Officer Training Corps, and his keen interest in the training of his division in order both to prepare for combat and maintain morale is evident from his communications.

Although the division's primary role was now to defend the south-east coast, the area that represented the most direct and most likely invasion route, it was considered that any such attempt would not occur until the middle of April 1942. The priorities until then would be completing defensive preparations, preparing to move to summer quarters in May, when the men would be accommodated in tents or Nissen huts rather than billets, and yet more training. By 15 April, the Foresters had completed the first of these, and from then until the move to summer locations the focus would be on platoon and company training, especially on night action. The period after 25 April was designated 'Night Week', with all training to be done at night and all sleeping and recreational activities during the day. Training was often competitive, with 'tactical stakes' in which companies represented their battalions or brigades in trials of drill, fitness and shooting. Nor did the rear echelons escape attention, as it was suggested that motor transport rallies could be used to stimulate and improve the quality of vehicle maintenance. Freeman-Atwood called for officers at all levels to take responsibility for training, stressing that it was vital that each one 'should use his brains and his imagination in the organisation and execution of the training of his formation, unit or sub-unit'.[8]

One officer took these instructions about imaginative training to the extreme with Exercise 'Alert', three versions of which were held in May 1942, with the 2/5th Foresters taking part in the first. The background, or 'general idea', for the exercise told the story of a Balkan state called Kentia that in a post-war future had disintegrated into several factions fighting for supremacy. Each of the three brigades in the division put together a force built around one of its infantry battalions, adding a field gun battery, reconnaissance troop, machine-gun platoon and field ambulance section. Live ammunition and bayonets were not to be used, but 'pyrotechnics' were allowed, and there would be occasional air support. The 'Men of Kent' east of Stone Street (the modern B2068 north of Lympne) supported the royalist claimant to the throne, the 'Fair Maid of Kent', and were represented in the exercise by the 1/7th Duke of Wellington's (West Riding) Regiment (DWR) from 137 Brigade. A would-be dictator, 'Kraftyvitch', led the 'Kentish Men' to the west (the 6th Lincolns from 138 Brigade). The Foresters would play the independent-minded but generally republican-leaning 'Men of the Marshes', based in the Romney area under their leader 'Belch'. The 'specific idea' for the first version of the exercise was that a local scientist had been rumoured to have developed a 'death-ray', which each of the different factions desired to enable it to destroy their rivals. Each unit was then given secret instructions about plans to march to a location in the vicinity of the village of Kingsnorth to take possession of the weapon. The intended result was to pit the DWR and Foresters in separate and competing 'attacks' upon defensive positions hastily taken up by the Lincolns. The anonymous designer of the exercise must have had immense fun making all this up, and there were no doubt many obscure in-jokes among the names and narratives. Nonetheless, there were also a series of practical training objectives behind all this: to practice administration and command capability in twenty-four hours of independent operation by the battalion; to test its physical fitness; and to develop initiative in both officers and men. Other than pretending to be umpires, civilians or soldiers of one of the opposing factions, the teams were told that any subterfuge was permissible. The formation of the battalion groups also tested once again cooperation between different units and different arms.

The most significant feature of 'Alert', however, is that, like the battle training exercise in Scotland, the records contain a detailed analysis of the performance of the battalions. The report states that the administration for the operations was well managed, and although there is no direct comment on the fitness of the Foresters, the 1/7th DWR were singled out for praise in marching some 27 miles to the exercise area, a further 10 miles to conduct their mock attacks and then returning 15 miles to their camp. The expectation was set that a unit should be able to march some 50–60 miles in forty-eight hours and still be in a condition to fight at the end of it. The conduct of the 'battle' drew several criticisms. Both the DWR and the Foresters were criticised for attacking piecemeal upon their arrival, without taking the time to reconnoitre the positions held by the Lincolns. This temptation had effectively been written into the scenario, since both wanted to be first to capture the 'death-ray', but it was to be discouraged in real combat. 'Com[an]d[er]s must get sufficient information before launching their b[attalio]ns into attacks and must avoid frittering co[mpan]ys away one at a time with insufficient supporting fire,' the reported stated regarding the lessons learnt. When the mock attacks went in, the men advanced well until about 100 yards from the 'enemy' positions, but then had a tendency to stop and enter into a firefight at 50–25 yards. This was frowned upon: '[I]n actual war if men lie down at that distance they will take of lot of getting up again with bullets in the air.' The army's doctrine was that the last 100 yards had to be covered at pace and without stopping, to get in with the bayonet. This was particularly desirable at night or twilight, when it was expected that defensive fire would not be accurate. 'Officers and NCOs must lead their men as close as possible under cover and when they break cover must charge straight in to kill,' the report continued. This should not, however, be interpreted as a lack of appreciation of modern firepower or adoption of 'human wave' style attacks regardless of casualties. Also criticised as poor was the general standard of fieldcraft and the troops' use of cover for protection. The appraisal suggested further training in which companies would practice moving under cover for a distance of around 4 miles. Observers would deduct points if the troops moving were spotted. The mantra was to be the following: 'If I am seen I will be killed. If I am not seen I shall surprise and kill the enemy.' The final comment was that both officers and other ranks were not alert enough to danger. When halted, they did not make preparations against a surprise attack. 'Be prepared for attack from any direction at any time,' the advice stated.[9]

This appraisal shows both how far the battalion had developed since its time in Scotland and its ongoing weaknesses. The latter were principally the tendency to try to undertake actions too quickly and without proper reconnaissance; a lack of fieldcraft, which it was difficult to learn in simulated conditions; and the lack of experienced leadership amongst junior officers and NCOs.

Another new feature of training had been introduced following the move to Kent. XII Corps was in the forefront of an innovation called 'Battle School', and in December 1941 the 46th Division Battle School opened in Beachborough with a staff of thirty-five officers and thirty-five NCOs. The first commandant of the school was Major Alexander McKechnie, then 2iC of the 2/5th Foresters. Not every officer and soldier was expected to attend battle school; its role was to instruct key personnel so that they could go back and train others within their units. Although there are no explicit references to the divisional battle school in the 2/5th Battalion's records other than McKechnie's posting, it is almost certain that several men in the unit were trained there. The school was largely the brainchild of Captain Lionel

Wigram, who had won the support of the Commander in Chief Home Forces, General Sir Bernard Paget. It had three elements: live firing, vigorous physical training and 'battle drill' in which troops went through drills that aimed to simulate the tactics used in battle, such as using fire and movement to approach and assault an enemy position. All this was carried out in conditions simulating as closely as possible the conditions on the battlefield. The concept was hugely controversial. Its critics feared that it would introduce stereotyped tactics and suppress innovation and initiative in battle; its proponents held that it helped transform civilians with little knowledge of war into useful soldiers and avoided the need for detailed tactical orders. Both sides had some valid arguments. War and battle do not come naturally to most men. Military drill has always been about instilling into the soldier, especially new recruits, actions that they perform on the parade ground so that under the intense stress of battle they will perform those actions automatically, without thinking or questioning. The application of this principle to technical skills such as loading, firing or unjamming a weapon is clear, but what was more questionable was its relevance to tactical decision making. Wigram himself thought that initiative was better than drill, but that drill was better than nothing. The evidence from 46th Division is also that both were considered important. Drill may not have been ideal, but it was absolutely necessary in order to quickly turn large numbers of civilians into competent soldiers, especially given the wide variation in the experience levels of men within units such as the 2/5th Foresters.

A report prepared for General Paget towards the end of April 1942 concluded that there were only three infantry divisions in the UK that were ready for combat, all of them in XII Corps, and not including the 46th. The division had, however, clearly made significant progress since General Alan Brooke had been so dismissive of its condition nearly two years earlier. The report's comment was that it required 'collective training' but was expected to be battle-ready by 1 July, the main reason for its 'backwardness' being given as a lack of suitable transport.

*

The move to south-east England meant that the Nottinghamshire and Derbyshire men who still made up the majority of the battalion were more distant from their homes, but many of the newer officers and men in the ranks were from the south-east. Amongst them was one of the most unlikely but also one of the most colourful characters in the battalion, Private Gerald Summers. The son of a high-ranking Indian Army officer and colonial governor, Summers had become a regular officer in the 1st Green Howards (a Yorkshire regiment) before the war when he was only 18, but he had then resigned his commission. When a friend later joined the Sherwood Foresters, Summers enlisted with him as a private soldier. Since he was young and fit, already familiar with the weapons drill and could handle a rifle and a Bren gun, the only thing Summers found difficult was the level of profanity in the ranks. After training at Egginton Hall like many others, Summers was posted to B Company of the 2/5th Foresters at Folkestone in March 1942, and then moved with them to the camp at Camber Sands near Rye at the end of the month. There, he recalled, discipline was not oppressive, and he was able to regularly visit his family home 25 miles away at Horam in Sussex, provided that he turned out for inspections, church parades and guard duty. While walking one morning on the beach at Camber, Summers found a wounded kestrel, which he took back to camp and nursed back to health. The bird, which he named Cressida, became a sort of mascot within Summers' platoon and would accompany him when the battalion left England to go to war.

In July, the Foresters took part in their first corps-level exercise in the south-east, a scheme codenamed 'Harold' in which 46th Division was opposed by the 3rd Canadian Division and an army tank brigade. The battalion engaged in continuous battle simulations and marching for six days, during which they covered 148 miles on limited rations. The following month, the battalion went into bivouac on the South Downs north of Brighton for an exercise using live ammunition. The live firing area on the South Downs had only been set up that year, in order to enable 'a proper battle to be staged, living dangerously and abolishing all unnecessary safety-first precautions'.[10] There was nothing especially unusual about training with live ammunition—Summers recalled that the French-Canadians in particular were in the habit of using live rounds. There were two variants: 'field firing', where live ammunition was fired by the trainees, and 'battle inoculation', where the instructors did the firing, generally a few inches above the men's heads. There was a certain amount of danger involved; at least three men in the battalion had suffered gunshot wounds earlier in the year, and officers in the brigade and divisional HQs had also suffered injuries during demonstrations, but the level of casualties was considered acceptable. The battalion had done field firings in the past, but this was the first time that its war diary mentioned battle inoculation, although battle schools frequently used this practice. It seems possible that it was part of the final programme of training before 46th Division was to be sent overseas. The exercise would last for three days from 15–17 August, and would end in tragedy.

On the final day of the exercise, the battalion was practicing an attack supported by the 3-inch mortars, commanded by Sergeant George Stokes. Several companies were to advance across a valley to attack the 'enemy' on a wooded ridge opposite the mortars' position. The bombardment should have stopped before the men advanced into the wood, but either the shells fell short or the umpires with the men failed to stop their advance in front of where the mortar bombs were falling. To the horror of Sydney Cooper, now serving in the mortar platoon, the infantry just kept going and he saw some of the men fall. There was frantic waving from the valley floor and Stokes stopped the firing, ordered Cooper and the rest of his men into the platoon's two carriers, and they dashed off down the slope to do what they could for the casualties.

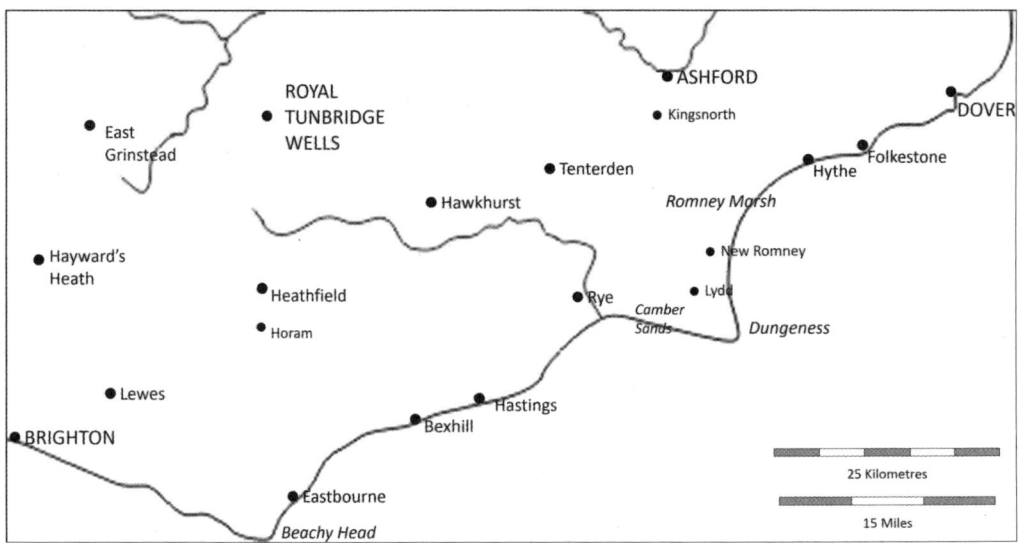

South-east England, 1942.

Frank Offiler was already on the scene helping the wounded. After Dunkirk, he had been posted to the battalion's medical section as a stretcher-bearer, partly because he had pre-war first aid experience in the Boy Scouts and the St John's Ambulance Brigade, and partly because this was the traditional role in battle for the battalion band of which he was a member. Although it was normal on exercises for a detachment from an RAMC Field Ambulance to participate, for some reason none was available on this occasion. Medical assistance was limited to the battalion's own medical team, which had supplies of bandages but had to improvise other medical equipment such as using rifles for splints. They were supported by the Assistant Director Medical Services for the division, who helped triage the casualties. Offiler remembered five or six men being killed and taken to the mortuary in Lewes, while twenty-eight were wounded.

The official records give four men from the Foresters fatally injured by the mortar fire and an officer and two other privates wounded, along with two men who appear to have been Foresters attached to the brigade HQ and may have been part of the umpire group. Some of the other injuries may have been considered minor and not formally recorded as casualties. The brigade war diary indicates that a court of inquiry took place the following week, but the findings of that inquiry and whether any disciplinary action was taken were not included. The men who died were not new inexperienced recruits. They included Corporal Louis Boulton from Summers' platoon, who had been one of the umpires, Lance Sergeant Ernest Harris and Corporal Thomas Barradell from D Company, who was a veteran of Dunkirk and well known in the battalion as an excellent sportsman. The fourth man, Private John Walker, a 21-year-old plumber and decorator from Brailsford, Derbyshire, had been married less than four months earlier and had lost a brother at Dunkirk. It was the battalion's greatest loss in a single day since their action at Oignies. It may also have contributed to the new MO, Lieutenant Murray, suffering a nervous breakdown; he was fresh out of medical school and had been in the post only four months. He was replaced at the beginning of September by Lieutenant Julius Cowen, a 32-year-old Glaswegian who had worked as a GP in Newcastle pre-war and in Tottenham during the Blitz before being called up to serve in the RAMC.

Alan Orme's platoon had escaped any casualties, but Orme recalled that there was none of the usual raucous singing as the men marched back to their barracks that evening: 'Everyone was thinking it could have been him.'[11] However, there is nothing to suggest any more serious loss of morale or permanent change in the mood of the battalion, which had been buoyant since 'Harold'. At the start of 1942, morale had been a particular concern of the division's CO, Major General Harold Freeman-Attwood, and indeed throughout the army high command. The move to Kent meant that 46th Division's role had changed from one of mobility and counterattack to the less glamorous one of relatively static defence. After more than two years of conflict and few signs that Britain was anywhere closer to victory, war-weariness was a significant worry, particularly as the conflict in the first half of 1942 had gone badly for Britain and its allies, with a string of defeats in the Far East and North Africa and a renewed German offensive in Russia. The most important factor within the unit itself was that throughout 1941 and 1942, there continued to be a series of comings and goings of both officers and men. Rather than the battalion going overseas as a whole, experienced personnel were posted as drafts to other units, including Dunkirk veterans such as Doug Cousin and Cedric Colver, who had both gone to East Africa. Over the course of 1942, about 700 men were transferred out to other units, back to the ITCs or into overseas drafts, almost the equivalent of the entire battalion. In their place arrived nearly 800 new men, around a quarter of them inexperienced direct intakes, another fifth from the ITCs, 100 from other regiments and the remainder—a little under half the total—from other Forester battalions. This must have had a negative effect on the cohesion of the battalion, just as it had in 1939 and 1940.

Although by August the battalion was in the final stages of training before being sent overseas itself, this still did not reduce the turnover in men. In just eight days, from 16–23 September, 158 men left the unit in drafts, while 125 men joined from outside the battalion. Fifty-five of these were Foresters, from the 70th Young Soldiers Battalion. Another forty were from the York and Lancs and thirty were from the Lincolns, regiments which since August 1941 shared a common ITC with the Foresters in Lincoln Barracks. Nineteen-year-old Private Fred Hirst from Bentley in West Yorkshire was one of these who joined from the York and Lancs, being posted to B Company. His recollections indicate that the battalion had retained much of its TA nature in the relationship between officers and men. Hirst thought the behaviour of the officers in the 2/5th Foresters, many of whom were also new to the unit, very different from the petty 'bull' of the ITC. The NCOs too 'were not forever nagging and criticising unnecessarily'. Hirst found the training hard, but there was now a purpose to it which raised his spirits: 'Regimental pride became uppermost in my mind, and I really began to believe that I was in the best battalion in the British Army and that we were the toughest soldiers in the whole Division.' Hirst went on to say that in the ITC he had always been on the defensive, guarding against the whims of his immediate officers and NCOs, whereas with the Foresters '[w]e were treated like sensible young men rather than rebellious imbeciles'.[12] By contrast, Private Patrick O'Sullivan, a former steelworker from Scunthorpe who had joined Alan Orme's platoon from the 6th Lincolns in August, was more scathing, considering that both in fitness and fieldcraft the Foresters were inferior to his old unit. Nevertheless, he resigned himself to the new posting. The incorporation of new men like Hirst and O'Sullivan represented quite an achievement on the part of Lieutenant Colonel Stott and his officers. The relationship between the junior officers, NCOs and their men was one that was critical in maintaining the morale of a unit. The feeling of pride in the unit that had been seen in the aftermath of Dunkirk persisted.

There were, however, a few contradictory signs that all was not well. Judged by entries in the Courts Martial register, the 2/5th had a good disciplinary record in the first three years of war, but in June 1942 two privates were court-martialled for desertion after they had received orders to form part of a draft to be sent abroad. There were further cases after the division was declared fully mobilised to go overseas as a formation. On 17 October, Captain Geoffrey Sutcliffe, a pre-war territorial officer in the 2/5th Foresters with the temporary rank and post of brigade major, was given a 'detached command for disciplinary purposes', indicating that absenteeism and desertion was becoming a serious concern within 139 Brigade as a whole. One deserter from the 2/5th Foresters was caught in Belfast in October, and on 5 November another was tried by court martial, found guilty and given two years' detention. The last trial of a member of the battalion in England took place on 26 November; the accused was found not guilty of desertion but given thirty-five days' detention for being AWOL. In a battalion of over 800 men, these were relatively few cases of serious indiscipline, but indicate the stress and apprehension felt by some at the prospect of being sent to fight.

Desertion was only one possible reaction to overseas posting, and in an even smaller number of cases there were more serious consequences. Ernest Shaw had been a promising footballer for Chesterfield before the war, as an amateur since his father would not let him turn professional, while also working as a plumber, which was a reserved occupation until mid-1941. With his trade he had hoped to join the Royal Engineers when called up in October that year, but ended up in the Foresters, which initially made him very depressed. Shaw was one of 200 men drafted as an experiment directly into the battalion, without previous training. One of the men in Shaw's intake went AWOL, while another, a cockney called Tattersall, tried to shoot himself in the foot. Shaw resigned himself to the infantry and become good friends with Private Joe King from Tapton near Sheffield, an unlikely friendship as King was of small stature and not very athletic. Both men were given leave in autumn 1942, which was rumoured to be prior to shipping abroad. Shaw's leave was cancelled so that he could take part in a football match—still an important part of battalion life. King never returned from his. Ernest was told that Joe had taken his own life when he discovered that he was to go overseas. Shaw put in a request to leave the battalion and was posted to Lincoln Barracks, though he was later sent overseas himself and served with the York and Lancs in Italy.

*

On 23 August, Freeman-Attwood had received instructions to prepare 46th Division to be sent overseas by the following month. In a training communique on 24 October, he told his senior officers that mobilisation had completed, and that although they did not know where they were going to be sent, they would be going to war in a month to six weeks. How well had the training that the 2/5th Foresters received in the previous two-and-a-half years prepared them for war? British training usually comes in for criticism on four main grounds: that it took second place to defensive construction work and other activities; that it did not prepare men adequately for modern combat conditions; that it lacked a cohesive doctrine, especially at a tactical level; and that it lacked realism. The first criticism cannot reasonably be made of the Foresters' training activities. In Scotland, training was an integral part of and indistinguishable from the battalion's operational defensive deployment, which admittedly had the benefit of being in an extremely quiet area. In Norfolk, the battalion had only once been deployed into coastal defence positions, and then to free up another unit for training. In the south-east, although defensive considerations were more important, every effort was made to complete construction work before the weather conditions improved to allow extensive training. The battalion was perhaps fortunate that by the beginning of 1942, with Hitler's legions halted by the Red Army at the gates of Moscow, the threat of immediate invasion from the continent was becoming remote, allowing regular training exercises even in more front-line locations. It was also never required to take on agricultural work, as some units were (a company of the 2/5th Leicesters suffered this chore during the 1941 harvest). The seasons and weather, and considerations of access to private farmland, did play a major part in determining what training could be done. The instructions for 'Nelson' in the late spring of 1941 prohibited the driving of vehicles over sown fields, for example. But given the pressing need for Britain to produce as much food as possible from its own farmland, this was an understandable constraint that had to be planned around. More significant, perhaps, was the restricted

Education: June 1940–September 1942

availability of petrol, one of the key factors limiting large-scale corps exercises to one or two a year.

Nor can the battalion be accused of planning for the last war. Before Dunkirk, it was certainly the case that a lot of British army training anticipated the forming in France of static lines that would be overcome by the set-piece offensives seen in the First World War. But from the earliest days after Dunkirk, the training emphasis for the 2/5th Foresters was not on the defence of fixed positions but in mobility and counterattack, whether small mobile columns to pick off paratroopers in Scotland, retaking airfields in East Anglia or the larger mobile exercises of 'Bumper' or 'Harold'. Artillery cooperation and anti-tank operations were all practiced, and within the army at least there was an increasing awareness of the need for cooperation with the RAF following the example of the *blitzkrieg*. This leads into the question of doctrine, and here the record is not so good. Although there were exercises with armoured formations, these were limited, and by late 1942 the army had still not produced a single effective doctrine for the support of infantry by tanks and vice versa. Freeman-Attwood's communique singled out anti-tank operations as an area that needed 'a lot of tidy[ing] up', despite a three-day exercise, 'Ante', in October 1942, particularly in the use of non-battalion resources such as artillery and light anti-aircraft guns in anti-tank roles. Even basic infantry tactics were still a matter of debate, as shown by the controversy over battle drill. The biggest problem was that the basic training received by both officers and men before joining their units was both limited and highly variable. Remedial instruction on fieldcraft, and on individual and section training, was often needed before men progressed to platoon or company tactics, and there was always a shortage of competent instructors within units, particularly at company level. As the company commanders did not know the tactics, they could not teach their subordinates, who in turn could not teach their men. The commentaries on exercises indicate that officers were well prepared to get their men to the battlefield, but less well versed in the tactics that they would need to use or the orders that they would need to give to achieve their objectives once there.

The final question is one of realism. This is extremely hard to fully realise in military training—though a dozen or more casualties sustained by the battalion over the period indicates that the element of danger was neither totally lacking nor unacceptable to the authorities. Thunderflashes, blank ammunition and 'pyrotechnics' were not always available to replace live rounds. The alternative simulation of enemy or even friendly forces, particularly tanks, artillery and other supporting units, by flags, skeleton teams or similar devices, did not accustom men to the noise and confusion of battle. The preparation of NCOs and private soldiers was particularly difficult, especially as the continuous drafting of men to go overseas disrupted sections and teams and replaced many of the most experienced men with newly trained intakes. For the officers, classroom training, administrative exercises and TEWTs, though all vital as a basis for command, could also only go so far to prepare them for combat. Another criticism that is made concerns the nature and quality of umpiring, for example that the umpires were often less competent officers that units wanted out of the way, who rigidly applied predetermined outcomes, and perhaps prejudiced views, to the results of particular actions. There seems to be no evidence that when the Foresters provided umpires they were of poor quality; they included, for example, both Major Potter and Lieutenant Colonel Stott. A pre-planned script was perhaps a necessary evil to ensure that a training exercise covered all the lessons intended. But Freeman-Attwood criticised umpires for ruling that a unit was pinned down and could not move on the grounds that movement was always possible, albeit with risk of casualties. Freeman-Attwood did not regard the division's training as complete. He highlighted several areas that needed further work, in particular individual training, teamwork, speed and cooperation. His very last paragraph set out what remained to be learnt.

> Above all, from now on let all our training be permeated with REALISM. Let nothing which would fail in war go unchecked. Introduce into all training a sense of urgency. Encourage initiative. Condemn as unforgiveable sins any lack of decision, any tendency to sit down and do nothing, any failure to appreciate the value of time.[13]

The battalion's time in Britain was now nearly over. At the beginning of December, most men were given ten days' embarkation leave. While Gerald Summers took his at the family home in Sussex, the battalion moved to Camberley, where they were billeted in private houses. Here, on 18 December, it was inspected by King George VI. Five days later, it moved by train to Liverpool, where the men would embark for overseas. There was a light fall of snow, and the dockers were singing Irving Berlin's latest hit song from America, 'White Christmas'. The men were given cups of tea on the docks by women from the WVS. For veterans of 1940, it perhaps brought back memories of the return from Dunkirk. Now they were to be given the chance to fight the enemy on more even terms.

6

Deaths in the Family: Norway, North Africa and the Far East, April 1940–July 1942

Although this is a battalion and not a regimental history, just as the activities of family members affect the life of an individual, the activities of other Forester battalions during the war impacted the lives of the men of the 2/5th. The overarching theme of the regiment's history in the Second World War is one of bad luck, as it had the misfortune to be involved, through no fault of its own, in four of the British Army's most ignominious defeats: Norway and France in 1940, and Singapore and Tobruk in 1942. So before following the 2/5th Battalion overseas to its second meeting with the enemy, it is necessary to briefly relate the experiences of the rest of the regiment to this point.

First to see combat were the 8th Foresters, the first-line Nottinghamshire territorials. The battalion had been assigned on 6 April 1940 as part of 148 Brigade to the forces planned to occupy Norway. It left Scotland on 17 April and landed together with the 1/5th Leicesters at two locations in south-central Norway: Molde and Andalsnes. The two battalions joined and came under the command of the Norwegian 2nd Division, 10 miles south of Lillehammer. With the Germans pressing northwards from their initial landings in Oslo, the Norwegians withdrew, covered by the British. A stand was made by two companies of the Foresters and one from the Leicesters at the village of Tretten on 23 April. The British, who had lost most of their transport and heavy weapons to a U-boat during the voyage to Norway, were completely outclassed by the superior training and equipment of their enemy. They had no answer to the German aircraft, artillery and mortars, or to their use of tanks and ski troops. The under-equipped territorials were also cold, tired and hungry, not being prepared for the semi-arctic weather and having had little food or sleep for two days. By midday, their positions had been overrun and the Foresters' CO and 2iC captured, along with many other officers and men. The Leicesters had suffered a similar fate and the two battalions were no longer an effective force. Together with other British troops in the area, they re-embarked at Andalsnes on 30 April and arrived back at Scapa Flow on 2 May. Out of an initial force of 656 Foresters, only nine officers and 368 men eventually got back to Britain. Sixty-nine men managed to escape to neutral Sweden, where they were interned, while 185 were taken prisoner and twenty-five killed. The latter included 26-year-old Lewis Mellors from the town of Arnold in Nottinghamshire, who died at Tretten. His younger brother, Harold, who was also serving in the battalion, in the contingent that had landed at Molde, escaped unscathed.

Not every Forester who failed to retire from Tretten was captured. For instance, 2nd Lieutenant Richard Garrett, together with his company commander, two other subalterns and a dozen other ranks, had managed to evade the German forces and found a barn in which to shelter. The farmer's wife gave them some food and they headed into the mountains, evading German patrols before coming upon a Norwegian detachment in a small winter-sports resort. The Norwegian commander advised them that there was no hope of rejoining their battalion and offered them a local guide to help them cover the 300 miles to the coast on the Sognefjord. The route took them across the Jotenheim, the highest mountain range in Norway. They travelled by night, using snowshoes and skis, and rested by day in small shepherd huts. The weather was fortunately kind to them, but it was an arduous journey and it was not until 12 May that they reached a village on the southern shore of the Sognefjord, where the locals again gave them food and shelter. They then learnt of more German patrols, clearly making it impossible to leave the country from any of the larger fjords, so they decided to head northwest to the Eikefjord, which it was considered might be small enough to have escaped enemy attention. It meant another challenging trip, this time across the Jostedalsbreen glacier. Once again they were given a guide who led them over the mountains. When they arrived at Eikefjord, they managed to find a fishing boat, whose captain and mate agreed to take them back to Britain. A few days later, they arrived at Lerwick in the Shetlands, and their odyssey finally ended on 13 June when they rejoined the 8th Battalion in Renfrewshire, where it was regrouping and re-forming as part of 148 Independent Brigade Group.

The battalion had to be all but rebuilt. Among the young 2nd lieutenants joining it at this time were pre-war regulars Hector Tulloch and Peter Litton, along with newly commissioned Tony Lord, all of whom would later serve in the 2/5th, as would Garrett and another Norway veteran, Mike Kirk. More than 550 ORs were posted in from holding battalions and training centres. After a month recovering in Scotland, the battalion was sent to Northern Ireland in July 1940. It returned to England in April 1942, but soon ceased to have an operational role. In June it became part of 148 Training Brigade in Kent, where its function was to prepare candidates for officer training. The chief significance for the 2/5th of the effective disbanding of the 8th Battalion was that 212 men, including Corporal Harold Mellors, were transferred into its Derbyshire sibling on 20 July 1942.

*

Deaths in the Family: April 1940–July 1942

The training and *esprit de corps* of the second-line Nottinghamshire territorials, the 9th Foresters, had hardly been tested during the 1940 campaign in France. In December 1940, the unit was transferred out of 139 Brigade to become the infantry battalion of 1st Armoured Division, with its own integral motor transport. Much to its disgust, the battalion did not accompany the division to North Africa in August 1941. Instead, along with several other infantry battalions, it was converted to an armoured car unit, as the 112th Regiment Royal Armoured Corps in 42nd Armoured Division. It later became the armoured car regiment for XII Corps, but was replaced in this role by the Royals in February 1944. Thus, it once again missed out on seeing combat, becoming merely a draft unit for the armoured car regiments fighting in Normandy before being disbanded in October 1944.

*

The regular soldiers of the 2nd Battalion had advanced into Belgium in 1940 as part of the BEF to take up defensive positions on the River Dyle, then found themselves having to retire in confusion to Dunkirk, making brief stands on a series of temporary defence lines as they fell back. Companies were cut off, broke out, retired and regrouped, the CO was wounded and the adjutant killed. Eventually, on 28 May, a mere sixteen officers and 140 ORs arrived at Hoogstade, where they were placed in reserve behind troops holding the River Yser. Pulled back into the Dunkirk perimeter proper, they were evacuated on 31 May, and like the 2/5th served the next eighteen months in Home Defence.

Until the spring of 1942, the 1st Battalion had experienced a much quieter war. In Palestine at the start of the conflict, they moved to Cyprus in July 1940. This was not an entirely safe location, as there were occasional Italian air raids which resulted in some casualties, and individuals and detachments from the battalion saw service in Eritrea and Syria. But apart from a small and abortive naval sortie in February 1941 against the island of Castelorizo, south of Turkey in the Italian Dodecanese islands, the bulk of the battalion remained inactive in Cyprus until they were sent to Egypt in December 1941. Here, they were converted into a motor battalion, a more mobile version of the standard infantry battalion with only three rifle companies, the fourth being replaced by a company of sixteen of the new 6-pounder anti-tank guns. Well provided with Bren carriers and trucks, they were designed to operate in the desert with armoured formations. The British were preparing for an attack on Rommel's German–Italian army south of Gazala.

In the event, the planned British offensive was forestalled by Rommel's own plans. On 26 May 1942, his panzers swept round the southern flank of the British defences and threatened their rear. The 1st Foresters were hastily despatched from Cairo to the fortress port of Tobruk, where they arrived on 3 June. The battalion was split into three. Two companies went to an area known as Knightsbridge, where 201 Guards Brigade had a defensive 'box' protecting the lines of communication. The third company held Raml Ridge to the north, while two platoons of anti-tank guns were placed on Aslag Ridge a few miles to the south. On 5 June, when Rommel turned his attention to the Knightsbridge box, the anti-tank gunners were the first into action, claiming eleven German tanks knocked out, but losing seven of their eight guns and forty-seven men. By 14 June, the battle at Knightsbridge had been lost and the rest of the 1st Foresters retired in confusion, first to Acroma, where Stuka dive-bombers destroyed over twenty vehicles, and then to Tobruk itself, 20 miles to the north-east. Half the battalion was already missing. At sunrise on 20 June, the Germans began their attack on the famous fortress, overrunning the troops holding the front line. The Foresters were meant to be part of a mobile armoured reserve to counterattack any break-in. But the only tanks which appeared were German ones, and by late afternoon the battalion was surrounded. Morale had already been low, and in fixed positions they could not take advantage of their mobility. Pounded by enemy artillery and airpower, the battalion disintegrated. Almost all its personnel were either killed or taken prisoner, and only about forty men managed to escape.

Deleting a senior regular battalion from the Army List was unthinkable, and a new 1st Battalion was reconstituted in Britain the following September by the simple expedient of renaming the 16th Battalion (formerly the 70th Battalion and then serving in East Anglia), but it would remain in the UK for the remainder of the war.

*

When it came to bad luck, however, the story of the 1/5th Foresters eclipsed all others. In 1940, it had been amongst the line-of-communication troops in Britany when the Germans attacked, and therefore avoided being surrounded and evacuated with the three Forester battalions in the north. But the Dunkirk evacuation was not the end of the campaign in France. On 5 June, the Germans turned south and attacked the French lines along the River Somme. The 1/5th Battalion, which had spent six months guarding No. 1 Base Ammunition and Base Petrol Dump at Nozay near Rennes, was scarcely better trained or equipped than the 2/5th, but with two other similar units it was constituted as 'A' Infantry Brigade and placed under command of 51st (Highland) Division on the River Bresle. On 7 June, A Company of the 1/5th, which was attached to the 4th Battalion Borders Regiment, made a counterattack at Inchville, near the mouth of the Somme. Artillery support failed to materialise and the company took heavy casualties, including 2nd Lieutenant Percival Cripps, who outlived his elder brother by just a few weeks. The survivors were captured while retiring. This was the only action the battalion saw in France, the remainder being evacuated from Le Havre on 12 June aboard the SS *Canterbury*.

There remained many Foresters in France who were to fare much worse. Twenty-one-year-old Harry Higton had been called up just a few days into the war. Identified as a likely NCO, he had been posted as lance corporal to the 2nd Battalion in February, not to the fighting unit but as one of about 300 men left at the vast No. 1 Infantry Base Depot (IBD) in Rouen. After Dunkirk, the detachment moved south to Evreux, where they were joined by several stragglers from 1/5th Battalion, among them Arthur Castellette from Nottingham, whom Higton took under his wing. From here they were marched to Le Mans, covering 100 miles in three days in sweltering heat. They were in a shocking state when they reached there, but could not afford more than a single day's rest before they set off on a further march westward, reaching the coast at the little fishing village of Pornichet at the southern base of the Brittany peninsula, near St Nazaire. They collapsed in the dunes, taking what shelter they could from enemy aircraft. Out in the bay was a large ocean liner, the RMS *Lancastria*.

On the morning of 17 June, the Foresters were ferried out to the ship. Its pre-war passenger capacity had been 1,300, but by the time Higton and the others got on board it was packed with at least 6,000 British soldiers and civilians; some estimates put the number as high as 9,000. Harry and Arthur were starving and fought their way through the crowds to the galley down below, where they got a mess tin full of soup and another filled with tea. It was chaotic below decks, and the two men made their way back to the top decks near the stern. It was another hot summer say, and they hung their legs over the side and enjoyed the sunshine. Then the Luftwaffe arrived.

It was a little after 3pm, with clear skies and bright blue sea. A Junkers bomber swooped in, and a huge spout of water shot up in front of the two Foresters. Another appeared on the opposite side of the *Lancastria* as the bombs straddled the liner. The German plane turned for a second run. The only anti-aircraft fire came from a solitary soldier with a Bren gun somewhere above them, who defiantly but futilely blazed away at the Junkers. Higton saw the next bomb fall and then disappear. By chance it had gone down the ship's funnel, detonating in the engine room. The subsequent internal explosions tore the ship apart. *Lancastria* rapidly took on a list. Harry and Arthur quickly realised that the ship was going to sink, and that they had to get off fast. They took off their jackets and boots, that would weigh them down in the water, then slid down the ship's side into the sea.

Higton plunged deep into the water of the bay, his uniform still weighing him down. Fortunately, he had a pocket knife attached to a lanyard, which he used to cut off the remainder of his clothing. After what seemed an age, he emerged on the surface covered in oil and gasping for air, wearing nothing but his wristwatch. Arthur had disappeared, and Harry would never see him again. From the sinking ship he could hear men singing: first 'Roll out the Barrel', then the more sombre 'Abide with Me'. These were the non-swimmers or men trapped below decks on the stricken *Lancastria*. After a few minutes, the singing stopped. About 5,000 people went down with the ship, including thirty-nine Foresters. The sea was warm but choppy, and although there were still some 2,000 men in the water, Harry could only see one other survivor, who swam away from the sinking ship and advised him to do the same. Another German plane was strafing the water and Harry feared that it was trying to set the oil alight. Although not a strong swimmer, he used a mixture of backstroke and dog-paddle to escape the slick. For the next two hours he was alone, clinging to a foot-square piece of wreckage to keep him afloat. Then a small French rowing boat appeared and its occupants pulled Higton aboard, which was not easy as they kept losing their grip on his oily body and Harry was too exhausted to assist. There were another ten survivors in the tiny vessel, and he was given a sack to cover his modesty. The Frenchmen transferred him to a British trawler, coincidentally named *Derbyshire*, to take him back to Britain. It arrived at Falmouth the following evening. Still wearing nothing but a sack, Harry was not allowed to go ashore until after nightfall. The British government wanted no news of the disaster to leak to the press.

After recovering back in England, Higton was posted to the 1/5th Foresters. They were now in 55 Brigade, part of the 18th Division. In October 1941, the division sailed for the Middle East by way of Halifax, Nova Scotia, where it was transferred onto American transports. Since transit of the Mediterranean had become impossible by this point in the war, the convoy went by way of Trinidad to Cape Town, where it arrived on 13 December. By then, the strategic situation had been dramatically altered following the Japanese attacks on US forces at Pearl Harbor and on British possessions in Hong Kong and Malaya, and the convoy was diverted to the Far East. The Foresters first went to Bombay, where they disembarked on 27 December, and then on 19 January 1942 boarded transports once again to go as reinforcements to the British naval base at Singapore. They landed there on 29 January, three months after leaving Britain, just as the last British forces retired from the Malayan peninsula onto Singapore Island. The 18th Division was allocated to guard the eastern sector of the Johore Strait between the mainland and the island, and the Foresters formed the reserve for 55 Brigade. On 8 February, the Japanese attacked across the Strait, not in the east but against the weaker western defences, which were quickly overwhelmed. The battalion took up defensive positions about 4 miles west of Singapore City, as part of another ad hoc brigade-strength formation named 'Tom Force'. This made an unsuccessful counterattack on 12 February in which the battalion finally saw action before retiring back to the defensive perimeter. Elsewhere, the vital fresh water supply to the city had been captured by the Japanese, and the British commander decided there was no option but to surrender. On 15 February, barely two weeks after arriving on the island, and still confident in their ability to hold their defensive positions, the Foresters went into captivity along with around

70,000 British, Indian, Australian and other Imperial troops. It was the worst defeat ever suffered by the British Army.

In human terms, the true disaster was yet to come. The battalion had already suffered sixty-three fatalities by the time Singapore fell. The rest were taken captive and initially held on Changi air base along with other PoWs, where they were organised into working parties to clean up the damage in Singapore. After six months, the prisoners began to be moved by train to Ban Pong near Bangkok and set to work on the infamous Burma–Siam railway. The story of the appalling conditions on the railway and the brutality of the Japanese towards the PoWs has been told many times. For the 1/5th Foresters, the toll from three-and-a-half years' captivity was heavy; around 450 officers and men never returned. One of those was Arthur Castellette, who unbeknown to Harry Higton had been rescued after the *Lancastria* sinking and rejoined the battalion. He also survived the ordeal on the railway, only to drown when the ship taking him to Japan was sunk by a US submarine on 12 September 1944. Due to the hardships suffered by the captives, the Foresters were given the battle honour 'Singapore Island', even though their part in its defence had been limited.

Two other battalions, the 12th and the 13th—new battalions raised for the duration of the war in a similar fashion to the service battalions of 1914–18—followed the 1/5th east of Suez. Both had been formed in July 1940 and initially served in coastal defence roles in East Anglia. They were sent to India in 1942, where the 13th Foresters were briefly converted, like the 9th, to an armoured car unit. Restored as infantry, they were later employed on internal security and training duties until disbanded in September 1945, while the 12th Foresters ended up in Delwari Camp in Bhopal province as a training unit for jungle warfare. This did not mean that those who went to India with these units had a 'cushy' posting. Large numbers of the men who passed through their ranks were assigned to front-line battalions, and were subsequently wounded, captured or killed serving in the jungles of Burma.

*

While geographically remote, the disaster that befell the 1/5th Battalion and the subsequent despatch of two more battalions to India had an impact on the men in the 2/5th. Having narrowly escaped death on board the *Lancastria*, Harry Higton's run of luck had continued. He had been wounded during rifle training in 1941 when a bullet had ricocheted off a target support and into his right arm, so was in hospital when the 1/5th shipped out to Singapore. After he had recovered, he joined the 2/5th Battalion in Kent as an instructor. Others less fortunate than Higton had been transferred in the other direction. Because the two battalions recruited in the same areas and there were frequent transfers and drafts between them, many in the 2/5th had a relative or friend who had been killed or captured at Singapore. CQMS Reg Markham had a friend in Burma who eventually joined the Chindits. Reg, who had recently married, had heard of the cruelty of the Japanese and like everyone else dreaded a Far East posting.

By the middle of 1942, as a result of these various conversions, operations and disasters, there were only three field battalions of the Sherwood Foresters still available to be sent overseas: the 2nd (regulars), 2/5th (territorials) and 14th (formed in the summer of 1940 as another hostilities-only battalion). Although the most junior of the three, the 14th Battalion was the first to go. On 8 May 1942, it left Britain as part of a convoy to Egypt. After a ten-week voyage via Durban and Bombay, it finally disembarked in Suez on 18 July. It was immediately ordered to reorganise as a motor battalion, and once re-equipped and retrained it was assigned to 9 Armoured Brigade. Here, it finally broke the regiment's run of bad luck and defeats by participation in the British victory at the Battle of El Alamein. On 1–2 November 1942, 9 Armoured Brigade was the leading armoured formation in Operation Supercharge, the breakthrough phase of the battle. The 14th Foresters were fighting not as a single unit but split up between the armoured formations. Coming up against the veteran anti-tank gunners of the 15th Panzer Division, the inexperienced brigade took heavy casualties before the British 1st Armoured Division came up in support to finally break the enemy. The Foresters themselves were reduced in strength from four to two companies. As a result, they did not take part in the pursuit of the broken German army after the battle; along with the rest of the brigade, they were sent back to refit in the Nile Delta.

The 2/5th Battalion would also soon be sent to the North African theatre.

7

Leaving Home: Tunisia, January–February 1943

The North African campaign has a special place in the British narrative of the Second World War. For nearly three years, from the fall of France in July 1940 to the fall of Tunis in May 1943, Africa was almost the only theatre of war in which the British Army fought and on occasion got the better of the German Wehrmacht. Most of the fighting took place in the Western Desert, between Libya and Egypt. Here, the war took on a particular character, governed by the special geographic and geopolitical considerations of the theatre. The strategic imperative for the British was to protect both the oil reserves of the Middle East and the shortest sea route to India via the Suez Canal. These were both threatened in July 1940 when Italian dictator Benito Mussolini opportunistically declared war on Britain and France. Italian armies advanced a few miles into Egypt, but then the British seized the initiative and in a lightning campaign drove the Italians out of Cyrenaica (modern-day eastern Libya) in the winter of 1940–41. At this point, three things occurred which set the pattern for operations in the Western Desert for the next two years. First, the logistical difficulties of operations in the desert appeared. As the British pushed west, their supply lines grew ever longer, those of the retreating Italians shorter. The convoys of trucks carrying supplies to the British front line along the desert tracks eventually consumed more fuel and water in their journey than they delivered to the fighting units. Secondly, although now seen as a pivotal theatre of operations, at the time Africa was continually downgraded in strategic importance. Troops that could have successfully closed out the campaign were diverted to Greece and elsewhere, giving the enemy time to recover. And lastly, there arrived in North Africa a then relatively obscure German general who would become the most famous, respected and feared of all Britain's opponents: Erwin Rommel.

Rommel's individualistic and aggressive style of warfare had bought him success in France. He now took advantage of British weakness to launch his own offensive in March 1941 with his Afrika Korps, driving his opponents back to the Egyptian frontier. But here the same logic that had stopped the British halted the Germans. It was now Rommel who faced long supply lines and a lack of reinforcements as Hitler committed the vast majority of German forces to the invasion of Russia. Stalemate set in and was not broken until November 1941, by which time the British had built up their forces in Egypt, now designated the Eighth Army, to numbers strong enough to beat Rommel and drive him out of Cyrenaica. Then the inexorable logic of North Africa set in again. Rommel fell back on his bases; the British outran their supply lines. The theatre once again became secondary when the Japanese attacked British territories in the Far East, diverting troops originally intended for Africa to Singapore. Rommel counterattacked again, inflicting a further devastating defeat on the Eighth Army in May 1942, capturing their forward base at Tobruk and leading to the loss of 30,000 British and Commonwealth troops, including the 1st Foresters. Eighth Army retreated all the way to a small railway halt only 70 miles from Cairo; a place named El Alamein. Here, the seemingly endless cycle of victory and defeat continued. At the end of a thousand-mile supply line, Rommel was down to a few dozen tanks and reinforcements were not forthcoming, German attention once again focused upon Russia. In the first week of July 1942, Rommel was stopped at El Alamein. Both the Eighth Army and the Afrika Korps then dug in, laid defensive minefields and waited until one of them had received enough new men and equipment to take the offensive again.

The Allied cause seemed at its lowest ebb, but before the year was out that tide would turn in dramatic fashion. President Franklin D. Roosevelt and Prime Minister Winston Churchill had agreed upon a strategy of 'Germany First', and the commitment of American forces to the European theatre had begun to ramp up. American armaments began to flow to the Eighth Army in substantial numbers. In comparison, the operations in Russia at Stalingrad were beginning to bleed the German armed forces white, and Rommel's men were well down the priority list for receiving new equipment. The Eighth Army now had its own charismatic leader in the form of Lieutenant General Bernard Montgomery. Methodical where Rommel was intuitive, Montgomery built up his army to a point where it outnumbered Rommel by two to one. The British offensive at El Alamein between 23 October and 11 November 1942 overwhelmed the German and Italian defenders, finally breaking the two-year cycle of victory and defeat. Montgomery's men pushed Rommel's shattered army not only out of Cyrenaica, but further along the Libyan coast towards Tripoli.

While El Alamein was still in progress, a second operation further transformed the strategic situation in North Africa. Although America and Britain had agreed on 'Germany First', they were not aligned on where the fighting should take place. American strategists wanted a direct assault on France and Western Europe as soon as possible. The British high command felt differently, for a variety of reasons. They were wary of suffering losses of the scale of the Great War, were more realistic in their appreciation of the German military machine

Leaving Home: Tunisia, January–February 1943

and also had one eye on Imperial interests. Due to a combination of these concerns, they pressed for a strategy of clearing the North African coast before tackling mainland Europe. It was claimed this would free up shipping and make a subsequent cross-Channel invasion viable. It was also important to get American troops into combat somewhere, and the only place practical to land them was not German or Italian territory, but the French colonies of Morocco and Algeria. The landings on 8 November 1942, codenamed Operation Torch, were mostly an American affair, Anglo-French relations having been strained by events in 1940, when the British had fired on French naval forces at Mers el Kébir and Dakar to prevent them falling into Nazi hands. While the Americans landed in Morocco, British forces kept a low profile when they came ashore in central and eastern Algeria. This was a new army, consisting of troops who, like the 2/5th Foresters, had spent the last two years training in Britain, but few of whom who had ever been in combat. Not only was it low on experience, as it pushed eastwards to try to seize the vital ports of Bizerte and Tunis it was desperately short on both numbers and transport. Nominally the British First Army, in December 1942 it consisted of a single corps (V Corps), which in turn consisted of a single infantry division (the 78th), formed from disparate formations that had never trained or operated together, and the 6th Armoured Division.

Torch initially took the Axis forces in the Mediterranean by surprise, but they were quick to recover their composure and swiftly set about countering the threat to Rommel's battered troops. Key to this was control of the Tunisian ports of Bizerte and Tunis, long coveted by both Germans and Italians for their strategic value, but inviolate while controlled by the Vichy French regime. Within twenty-four hours, German airborne troops (Fallschirmjager) had landed and seized the main airfields at the two ports, presenting the French with a *fait accompli*. Possession of the airfields allowed the Axis to transport yet more troops by both air and sea. By the end of November 1942, there were some 15,500 German and Italian troops in Tunisia, and over 1,000 more arriving each day. These came to comprise the Fifth Panzer Army, under General Hans-Jürgen von Arnim, a veteran of the campaigns in Poland, France and Russia. In comparison, while there were some 200,000 American troops occupying Morocco and western Algeria, the number of Allied troops pushing towards Tunis in late November was very limited, consisting of a mere two infantry brigades of 78th Division, a few elements of 6th British Armoured Division and Combat Command B of the US 1st Armored Division. As a result, the fate of the 2/5th Foresters back in England suddenly became an issue at the very highest level of the Allied command.

Winston Churchill was not one to accept large numbers of men lying idle when there was fighting to be done. It was not just that by his estimation there were less than 15,000 Allied troops actually in contact with the enemy in Tunisia, out of about 250,000 men landed. The latest convoys being sent to North Africa were also, in Churchill's view, scheduled to carry far too few front-line troops and far too many rear-echelon personnel. The 46th Division, including 139 Brigade containing the 2/5th Foresters, was due to sail to North Africa in convoy KM.7 on 3 January 1943. In a memo dated 13 December 1942, Churchill urged the War Office to find a way to expedite getting a brigade group of 46th Division to sail on the preceding convoy KM.6, scheduled to leave Britain at Christmas. In his eyes, the army lacked 'teeth': the support train might be first class, but 'there must always somewhere up front be a certain number of people who are actually engaged on trying to kill the enemy with the weapons which they hold'.[1]

Such a memo from Churchill necessitated a prompt response, particularly given the short timescale, and within two days the War Office had managed to find the shipping to accommodate the prime minister's request and determined that 139 Brigade, plus supporting artillery and engineers, could be sent in KM.6. However, it meant leaving behind about half of the brigade's transport, and the extra eight ships would exceed what the Royal Navy normally deemed an acceptable size for a convoy. The decision needed the approval of the Expeditionary Force in Algiers and its overall commander, Major General Dwight D. Eisenhower. Eisenhower told Churchill on 16 December, followed up with an official response the following day to the War Office, that there was no possibility of accommodating the additional shipping in North Africa. Churchill, not prepared to leave it there, insisted on an explanation. Eisenhower's staff then performed a U-turn, explaining that their previous reply only related to the ports at Bone, Phillipeville and Algiers. Eisenhower himself now expressed enthusiasm for the move, agreeing that the situation called for the maximum number of troops in the theatre as early as possible. The men of 139 Brigade were urgently needed, the extra ships could be accommodated and means would be found to move it by road and rail to the front.

*

So it was that on 23 December 1942, the men of the 2/5th Foresters arrived by train at Liverpool docks and filed up the gangways onto the troopship that would take them to North Africa, the aptly named SS *Derbyshire*. Built in 1935, the 11,660-GRT liner had served on the Rangoon and Colombo routes pre-war. This was its second trip to North Africa, having carried American troops from Liverpool during the initial invasion. The men were mostly accommodated deep in the bowels of the ship, below the waterline, where hammocks had been slung for them to sleep in. The accommodation was far from comfortable, being crowded and poorly ventilated. In the morning, many decided to get some air on the main deck, where they watched the mostly lascar crew get the vessel ready to sail. Eventually, the ship cast of from the dock, but only to move as far as the middle of the Mersey, where it anchored for the night. Private Fred Hirst assumed that this might be to make it more difficult for would-be deserters to jump ship.

It was around 11am on Christmas Day when the convoy finally left Britain. For most of the men, this would be their first ocean voyage, and the majority still had no idea where they were going. Out in the Atlantic, the German U-boats and Allied navies were still locked in deadly combat for the sea-lanes that were vital to Britain's survival and war effort. It was therefore a mixed blessing when a series of Atlantic storms set in, lowering the threat of submarine attack but heightening the discomfort of the voyage itself, as many of the landlubber soldiers became seasick. At night, the portholes were closed and covered with blackout curtains, making the atmosphere even more stifling, not to mention the smell from the hundreds of closely packed bodies. Some men preferred to take their groundsheets and sit on the open deck.

New Year's Day saw the convoy passing through the Strait of Gibraltar, and the men were informed of their destination: Algiers. The dangers from enemy action were far from over; submarines were still a potent threat, as were enemy aircraft flying from Sicily and Tunisia. The convoy escort thus received powerful reinforcements in the form of the battleships *Nelson* and *Rodney* and two aircraft carriers. The passage through the western Mediterranean went without incident, however, and at 3pm on 3 January 1942, the *Derbyshire* berthed in Algiers harbour. From the sea, Algiers struck many of the men as picturesque, with white colonial houses dotted around a green hillside and the Atlas Mountains forming a thin purple ridge on the landward horizon. The sun was shining, and the blue sky was reflected in the even deeper blue sea. As the men disembarked at around 6pm, a refreshing breeze blew in from the Mediterranean. It was not a bad start to a war.

After ten days cooped up in the confines of the troopship, Hirst and the others were glad to stretch their legs and get some air. Cranes were busy unloading stores from the holds of the ship, and the heavy baggage was left on board while the men's kit bags were stored in a shed on the docks. The battalion transport would not arrive in Algiers for another six days, so after about two hours the men started marching, with rifles and small packs, to their accommodation for the night: an old brick factory at Gué de Constantine, south of Algiers. The initial glamour of the city quickly wore off as the column passed from the affluent French area of town into the rundown brown and grey buildings of the Arab suburbs. Beggars appeared on the streets, the tarmacked road turned into a dirt track stinking of sewage and it began to rain heavily. The men had yet to recover their land legs, and for Fred it was the worst march that he had ever experienced; 10 or 12 miles in the dark, with only a half-hour rest. It was early morning when they arrived at the brickyard, were issued the portable spirit-fuelled stoves known as 'tommy-cookers' and in typical British fashion began to brew tea. The only other occupants of the factory were a bunch of American signallers.

Life at the brickworks was mostly very dull. After morning roll call and rifle inspections, training consisted primarily of route marches to get the men's fitness back, and they were then largely restricted to barracks when off duty. Although Algiers was only 10 miles away, there were strict regulations limiting which clubs, bars, restaurants and cinemas were open to British and American servicemen. The army was concerned about drunkenness; the sale of spirits had been banned and warnings were given about the strength of the local wines. Those bars that could be visited were only open from noon–2pm and 5–7pm. There was an 8.30pm curfew to be back in barracks, and although the camp was sited close to a railway station, the use of local transport other than trolley buses was forbidden. Another danger was the Luftwaffe, which bombed the city almost every night from their air bases in Sicily. This meant that visiting the city was both unattractive and difficult, but not impossible, particularly to officers. Lieutenant Denys Crews set out to Algiers one evening with two other lieutenants, Richard Garrett and Bob Berkeley-Schultz, to have dinner with the proprietors of a local tavern with whom they had made friends, a former French Army sergeant and his wife. After a pleasant meal in a restaurant, and much good wine and liqueurs, an argument arose with some French officers at the table next to them, whom the ex-sergeant accused of having Vichy tendencies. A scuffle broke out and Crews' party beat a hasty retreat when the local gendarmerie arrived. By then, however, the young officers had missed the bus back to Gué de Constantine, so they ended up sleeping off the evening's entertainment in a flat overlooking the harbour owned by their French friends. At five in the morning, they caught the local Arab bus out of town, and three hours later climbed over the back wall into the brickworks. Fortunately, nobody seemed to have noticed they had been away!

Much closer, about 3 miles away, was the town of Maison Carrée (now the Algiers suburb of El Harrach). One of the main attractions of the town was the local brothel, which had been inspected by the American medical authorities and passed as 'OK' to be used by the troops. Fred Hirst and his best mate, John Sissons, took the opportunity to investigate this curiosity when a group of Foresters was taken into town for a much-needed and well-received shower and then told to make their own way back to their billets at the brick factory. Walking through the door of the brothel led to a mixture of shock and disappointment as a buxom lady approached the two young and sexually naïve soldiers, offering her services in the crudest possible fashion. Hirst and Sissons left in a hurry, consoling themselves with the fact that they could not have afforded the prices even if they had been interested, and that at least they would not contract a sexually transmitted disease. The older and more-worldly soldiers in the battalion would go to Maison Carrée at daybreak to get a good place in the queue, which was still considerable at that time. But even they were put off by the sordidness of the bordello and the elderly, over-painted madams, few visited more than once.

The troops' initial contact with the Arab population had not been one to generate trust. Private Eric Morral's first memory of North Africa was buying fresh fruit on the Algiers dock. A French paratrooper asked the British lads what they had paid. When they told him, the paratrooper struck the Arab, overturned his stall and told the Tommies, 'Help yourselves—he was over-charging you.' Prices in Algiers were officially controlled by the French authorities, but this did not stop the Arab traders from inflating their prices when they could. Indeed, oranges in Algiers could fetch five times the price that they did on the Tunisian border. Theft of supplies was also endemic. Maison Carrée, wrote Gerald Summers, had 'an atmosphere of evil'.[2] There were rumours in the local *estaminets* (cafes) that several American soldiers had disappeared, and that unarmed soldiers had been beaten to death in the alleyways for their cigarettes or even their battledress.

*

On 9 January, the battalion motor transport arrived in Algiers and the 2/5th Foresters began to prepare to go to the front line. Although it may seem somewhat excessive to delve into the minutiae of road and railway timetables, it is worth describing the battalion's journey to the front to understand the logistical problems faced by First Army. It is very easy eighty years later to sit as an armchair general and criticise the operations in the winter of 1942–43, and to argue that with a bit more audacity the Allies could have taken Tunis before the Germans had fully built up their forces in Tunisia. Operations on the ground were much more difficult than might appear from the map. The movement orders for 139 Brigade simply to travel from Algiers to the Tunisian border included instructions for five road convoys and three rail movements. The Foresters had men and equipment that would travel in four separate groups before they could be reconstituted as a fighting formation.

First to move at 6.30am on 13 January was an advanced party consisting mostly of senior officers from each of the brigade's units. They were to contact the battalions in the front line who they were to replace, make themselves familiar with the ground and make arrangements for the relief of the existing troops. Leading this column of nearly 200 vehicles, in front of the scout cars and armoured cars of C Squadron, 46th Recce Regiment, was the Forester's CO, Lieutenant Colonel Stott. Also in this party were the IO, Geoffrey Laurence, now a captain, and the five company commanders. Spread out at 120yd intervals, the whole convoy took up about 15 miles of road, and it took an hour to pass each checkpoint along the way. It was three days to the frontier and a gruelling driving schedule. The vehicles would be on the road from 7am until 6pm each day, with just an hour's halt at noon and a further ten-minute break every other hour.

Next to leave were the tracked vehicles—the carrier platoons and mortar platoons with their Bren carriers, and the anti-tank guns, which were towed by the very similar Carden-Lloyd carrier. These set off in brigade convoy from Maison Carrée at 2pm the following day. There were some thirty vehicles from each infantry battalion, another thirty from the 46th Recce and around twenty others. Commanding and physically leading the column was 'Spotlight' Hine, also promoted to captain. To save wear on the tracks, the maximum speed allowed for was significantly less than the wheeled vehicles of the advanced column, only 10mph by day and 7½mph by night. The carriers had fuel capacity for 160 miles at best, so had to make frequent refuelling stops, and they also had to wait at various intervals to allow faster convoys of trucks to overtake. On one day, the plan was to drive until 11pm, quite a challenge on the rough Algerian roads. It had originally been planned for the carriers to be transported by rail; the road schedule of 500 miles in three days was far too ambitious, and the need for ongoing maintenance to the vehicles en route slowed the convoy down.

The main road party consisted of about 150 wheeled vehicles, of which thirty belonged to the Foresters under MTO Dick Newell. It included the brigade HQ, the rest of the Recce squadron and the motor transport of the three infantry battalions; the artillery and medical units within the brigade had their own separate convoys. The trucks were expected to travel somewhat faster than the tracked vehicles, 15mph, and the Foresters' party left Maison Carrée on 14 January at 6.30am. The convoy route went south-west to Sidi Embarek, where it stopped for the night. The following night's stop was Aine Abid, and on 16 January it arrived at Souk Ahras. About 40 miles further on was the Tunisian border and the town of Ghardimou, 139 Brigade's concentration area, where it would regroup before advancing further.

Less than one-third of the battalion travelled by road. Even in North Africa, rail transport was still vital when transporting men, vehicles and supplies long distances. The majority of the men (twenty-two officers and 591 ORs) left the brick factory at 11.30am on 14 January and marched to Maison Carrée railway station, where they entrained at around 1.15pm and left around 5pm. The men were in the familiar *40 Hommes 8 Chevaux* cattle wagons, twenty or thirty to the truck, while the officers were slightly better accommodated in third-class wooden seating compartments. A company of French colonial troops shared the train. But there the similarities with 1940 ended. The capacity of the North African railway network was nothing like that in France. At best, only half a dozen trains could negotiate the single-track line from Algiers to Tunisia each day. The route climbed up vertiginous mountainsides, across rickety bridges hundreds of feet above the rivers below and through numerous tunnels. The landscape was not desert, but a mix of cork trees and cactus scrub, the Tunisian mountains receiving substantial rainfall in the winter months. The speed of the trains varied between 'slow, very slow, and stop'.[3] Men needing to relieve themselves would jump off the train, perform the necessary functions, and then catch the train up again at a gentle trot. Rations had been provided for seven days, consisting mainly of tinned food and hard tack biscuits. Whenever the trains stopped at a station, the men would get off to stretch their legs, buy fresh food from local Arab traders and, of course, brew up tea on their spirit stoves or, scrounging some petrol, in makeshift holes in the sand. At night, to offset the cold, they would even burn fires in the wagons themselves. It was not until the evening of 16 January that they reached the railhead at Ghardimou. It was still another 100 miles by truck to the front line.

On 5 January 1943, 36 Brigade had tried and failed to break through to Mateur and Bizerte in northern Tunisia. It was intended that 139 Brigade should now relieve 36 Brigade in this sector of the front, and at 6pm on 17 January the now reunited battalion left Ghardimou under the command of the adjutant, Captain Bryan Keith-Lucas, travelling past the supply dump and airfield at Souk el Arba, near the Algerian border, and on to Beja. The road then split, one branch going east to Oued Zarga and Medjez-el-Bab, the other north to Djebel Abiod (the 'Hill of the Devil'), where at a steep rock defile it met a road coming from the coast and the harbour of Tabarka. The battalion went north through Djebel Abiod to the mining settlement of Tamera, where a harbouring area had been set up for units to rest up as they travelled to the front. The following day, they would relieve the men of the 6th Royal West Kents east of another mining town called Sedjenane. From Ghardimou onwards, all movement had to be made at night, as the Germans had total air superiority by day over this region of Tunisia, which was nicknamed 'Messerschmitt Alley'. Flying from a base at Mateur only 20 miles away, two German fighter planes appeared regularly each morning along the Sedjenane valley, called 'Gert and Daisy' by the troops after a popular female comedy duo back in Britain.

*

In organisation and equipment, the battalion as it moved up to the front line in January 1943 was not much different from that which had left Dunkirk in 1940. The establishment of rifle sections had nominally been increased to ten men, but this was to maintain a front-line strength of eight men in the case of absentees off sick or on leave. The men had received substantially more training than the raw recruits of 1940. The two best shots in each section, such as Eric Morral and Gerald Summers, had been given extra rifle training and were designated snipers. Some NCOs had acquired American .45-calibre Thompson sub-machine guns, popularly known as the tommy gun. Its limited accurate range (about 150 yards) was offset by its rate of fire of 600rpm, making it a potent close combat weapon akin to the German Schmeisser machine pistol. An alternative was the British 9mm Sten machine carbine, with a rate of fire of 500rpm, a shorter range and less accurate than the Thompson, and an unhappy tendency to jam. Otherwise, the rifle companies had not changed much.

The HQ Company had been given two new support platoons that greatly increased its capability. The first was a medium machine-gun (MMG) platoon of four Vickers .303 machine guns. At 500–600rpm, this First World War design lacked the rate of fire of the more modern German weapons and the punch of a true .50-calibre heavy machine gun such as those used by the Americans, but it had the advantage of reliability. It could provide fire support at a longer range than the light Bren gun, out to 2,000 yards. In 1940, these weapons had been concentrated in specialised machine-gun battalions organised at brigade or even divisional level; their addition to standard infantry battalions boosted their firepower and capability of independent action.[4] A similar lesson had been learnt with regards to anti-tank weapons. The battalion now had its own anti-tank platoon of six guns. The tactical benefit was offset by the fact that these were the pre-war 2-pounder gun, effective against 1940-vintage German armour but almost useless against most tanks in North Africa at the end of 1942. There were also rumours of a new German tank, a 60-ton monster armed with the deadly 88mm gun, which had been photographed by the German press, reportedly in Tunis. British intelligence was sceptical as to why the enemy would forfeit the element of surprise by releasing such photographs, but within a month this new Mark VI 'Tiger' tank would become the most feared weapon in the enemy's arsenal. The battalion's 2-pounders and obsolete Boys anti-tank rifles were impotent against them.

In total, the battalion had left the UK with thirty-eight officers and 879 other ranks. This significantly exceeded its war establishment of thirty-two officers and 753 men. Upon arrival in Algiers, five officers were posted to the IBD there, and on 9 January there were 753 ORs present, in line with establishment. The remainder who had arrived in Algiers presumably also stayed at the IBD as first reinforcements. It is difficult to assess exactly how many of the men who had landed in North Africa had any battle experience, but it was certainly limited. Perhaps one in four had participated in the three weeks of retreat in France in 1940, while others had transferred in from the 8th Battalion and had fought in Norway. These men at least had some idea of what it was like to be under attack by aircraft, artillery and machine guns. Some of them, such as Alan Orme, had been promoted to corporal or sergeant and could pass on what experience they had to the newer members of their sections and platoons. But the majority of the private soldiers had either been conscripted or had volunteered after the outbreak of the war. Many of these had come through the 70th Battalion, so had built up friendships with other men in their platoons and sections, and with some of the officers such as 2nd Lieutenant John Stanley ('Ginger') Martin, who had also served in the 70th Battalion. The battalion was undeniably more combat-ready and the average soldier better trained than in the spring of 1940, but how they would bear up under battle conditions was still unknown.

One major factor in how they would cope would be their leaders. The make-up of the battalion's officers had changed substantially in the two-and-a-half years since Dunkirk. Gone were the pre-war territorials and veterans of the Great War who had made up the senior command in 1940. Aged over 40, these were now considered too old to cope with the mental, physical and tactical demands of the modern battlefield. Out of the thirty-three officers who arrived on the front line in January, only the battalion commander, Lieutenant Colonel Stott, held a commission dating from 1918. C Company was under Captain Frank Holbrook from Wollaton in Nottingham, another pre-war regular who like Stott had been at Dunkirk with the 2nd Battalion. There were nine other officers with territorial or wartime commissions who had also been with the 2/5th Battalion in France. Many of these now constituted the senior leadership of the unit. The ex-schoolmaster Charles Williamson took over as 2iC from 'Ginger' McKechnie on 17 January 1943, with the temporary rank of major, while Captain Cecil Wall commanded HQ Company. Captain Geoffrey Laurence was the IO. Keith Davenport, whose death at Oignies had been misreported, commanded A Company; John Kerly who had shepherded his men in the retreat to the coast was his 2iC. Captain Roger Newton and Captain Philip Claud Palmer commanded B and D companies respectively. In the B Echelon—the motor transport, cooks, clerks and stores—MTO Dick Newell and QM Dick Hammond completed the list of Dunkirk veterans.

A second group had joined after Dunkirk in 1940–41, so although they had no combat experience they did have over a year's continual service in the battalion. These twelve officers included the adjutant, Bryan Keith-Lucas, who had served in the ranks of the Buffs before being commissioned into the Foresters. It also included the leaders of the various support weapons platoons: 'Spotlight' Hine in charge of the carriers, Captain Eric Lloyd ('Dolly') Armitage the mortars and Lieutenant John Norman ('Johnny') Walker the anti-tank guns. The continuity of command in these technical roles, even if not accompanied by battle experience, meant that they had been with their platoons throughout their training and knew their men well.

Next, there was a group of six officers who had only been transferred into the battalion in August and September 1942, just as preparations were made to send it overseas. Only one had seen any fighting: Lieutenant Richard Garrett, in Norway with the 8th Battalion. Lieutenant Denys Crews was a pre-war territorial who had been commissioned into the 5th Battalion on 1 June 1938, but he had not been posted to any of the Forester battalions at the outbreak of hostilities. Crews, like Charles Williamson, had been a schoolmaster and instructor in the OTC before the war, at St Peter's School, York, and had initially been employed at 164 OCTU at Colchester and later Barmouth. Garrett and Crews commanded two of the three platoons in B Company. The third was under Lieutenant Bob Berkeley-Schultz, a Canadian who had been an actor in London in civilian life but had taken a wartime commission and ended up in the 70th Battalion. All three officers had joined the 2/5th Battalion at the same time. Twenty-three-year-old Captain Robert Anthony ('Bobby') Case and 20-year-old 'Ginger' Martin, who both commanded platoons in C Company, were also wartime commissions. The last of the group, Lieutenant Wilfred Stuart Jackson, was significantly older than the average platoon commander. Fred Hirst, who remembered 35-year-old Jackson giving a lecture on 'Social Matters' at Iden Green in Kent, had the impression that he would be more at home behind a desk.

The five remaining officers were distinguished by the fact that they were not members of the Sherwood Foresters regiment at all. Four had transferred from the 7th Battalion East Yorkshire Regiment and one from the 5th King's Regiment

(Liverpool), all at the beginning of September 1942. Together with seventy privates from the Lincolns and the York and Lancs transferred into the battalion as it prepared for overseas service, this had begun to dilute the original county identity of the battalion. The 46th Division had also lost its regional character somewhat. Although 138 Brigade was constituted as it had been in 1940 — the 6th Lincolns, 6th York and Lancs and 2/4th King's Own Yorkshire Light Infantry — 137 Brigade had been converted to an armoured formation and replaced by 128 Brigade, consisting of three territorial battalions of the Hampshire Regiment, and in 139 Brigade the 9th Foresters had been replaced by the 16th DLI.

On 17 January, the main body of 46th Division was only just arriving in Algiers, and when Churchill had got 139 Brigade sent to North Africa in advance it had gone as a brigade group, with supporting arms attached at brigade level. Thus on 19 January, Brigadier Chichester-Constable had under his direct command in the Tamera area not only his three infantry battalions, but also two field artillery batteries of 25-pounders (a total of sixteen guns), a medium battery of eight 5.5-inch guns, an anti-aircraft battery of twelve 40mm Bofors guns and an anti-tank troop armed with four of the new 6-pounder guns—a much more potent weapon than the 2-pounders in the infantry battalions. Finally, two British commando units and a company of the Corps Franc d'Afrique (CFA), which had been in the area before the brigade's arrival, were also placed under the brigadier. In theory, this transformed the original infantry brigade into an independent, all-arms formation. In practice, the command organisation in Tunisia was continually changing throughout January and February. As a result, the precise units under 139 Brigade at any point in time also varied, meaning that its component units were not always familiar with working together. Major General Harold Freeman-Attwood had left England determined that his division would fight as a compact formation, taking advantage of the fifteen months of combined-arms training that they had received back home. Once he had his division concentrated in the northern sector of the front, he envisaged a coordinated attack with all his forces. Events on the ground were already undermining this desire.

The geography of northern Tunisia in the sector where 46th Division was assigned to operate can perhaps best be visualised as an upturned left hand with its wrist in the central Mediterranean. In the palm sit two great salt lakes, the Garaet Achkel and Lac de Bizerte. The port of Bizerte sits on the north-east corner of the latter. South of the Garaet Achkel is the town of Mateur, a major rail and road junction and the gateway to Bizerte. The fingers of the hand are a series of low but steep mountain ranges running roughly parallel to each other in a south-westerly direction. An elongated little finger represents the coastal range, which stretches from north of Bizerte as far as Cap Serrat in the west. Between this and the ring finger is the valley of the Oued Sedjenane, which has its source in a marshy area at the head of the valley and its mouth in the Garaet Achkel. Between the ring and middle fingers lies the next valley, along which ran the main road and railway line between Djebel Abiod and Mateur. This was the most direct overland route to Bizerte from the Algerian coastal ports, and it was here that 139 Brigade took up its positions. At the top of this valley is the town of Sedjenane itself, while slightly further to the west, at the end of the middle finger, is the town of Tamera. The next valley to the south, between middle and index fingers, is that of the rivers Joumine and Bou Dissa. The road connecting Beja to Mateur runs across the hills represented by the index finger and then turns back into the valley. Below the index finger is the River Tine, and then, starting east of Mateur and running roughly south-east, is the thumb of the hand, which stretches down to the peaks north of Medjez-El-Bab. South of these peaks, the character of the terrain changes into the wide valley of the River Medjerda, the most fertile agricultural land and the best tank country in Tunisia. It is also the most direct route to Tunis. This route is nevertheless dominated by the ridge to the north, notably a relatively low hill nicknamed 'Longstop' by the British, which the Guards Brigade had attacked and briefly captured on 24 December but could not hold. At the end of January, the British front line ran roughly north by north-east across this series of mountains and valleys, from Medjez-El-Bab on the Medjerda to Cap Serrat on the coast. The length of this line direct across the mountains was about 45 miles.

Stott and three of his senior officers arrived at the front line at 3pm on 16 January to reconnoitre the position that the battalion was to take over from the West Kents, who had been there for seven weeks. The following day, Stott and his officers came under enemy shellfire for ten minutes. The West Kents' war diarist recorded that this was due to them over-exposing themselves, adding that the new arrivals 'have yet to learn'.[5] The handover itself started at 8pm the following night, which was clear with a full moon, and it went smoothly enough. The Foresters marched up the side of the road in single file as the muddy and exhausted men of the West Kents pulled out in silence, and by 2am they had taken over responsibility for the line.

When the sun rose on 19 January, the Foresters were able to better understand the positions that they had taken up. The Brigade held the valley between Tamera and Mateur, with the front situated just west of the rural railway halt of Jefna. North of the road and railway, where they passed the station, was the Djebel el Azzag. Covered with abundant low-lying scrub, this was nicknamed 'Green Hill' by the British troops. To the south of the railway lay the Djebel Ajred, whose rocky summit emerged from the scrub on its lower slopes like a monk's tonsured scalp. This inevitably became known as 'Baldy'. This was where 36 Brigade had been brought to a halt in November, with the Germans holding both hills and therefore dominating the valley between. Their positions on the tops and reverse slopes of the hills were about 1,000–2,000 yards in front of the British lines and held by veteran Fallschirmjager engineers, who could be heard blasting with explosives to improve their dugouts and defences. Halfway across no man's land were the wrecks

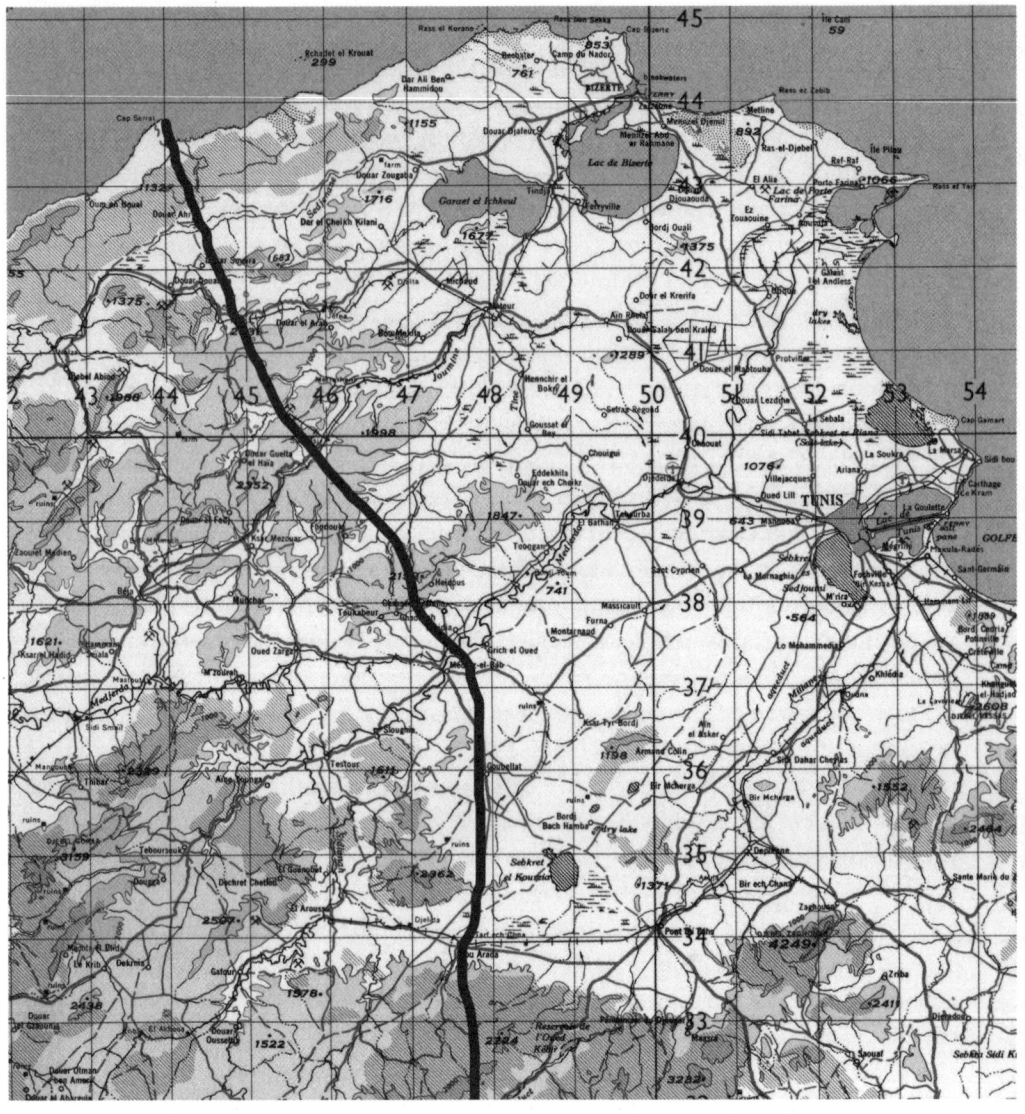

Northern Tunisa, approximate front line as of 26 January 1943.

of several Bren gun carriers, perfectly spaced as on a march, but manned only by corpses on which the occasional vulture would still swoop to feed. These bodies were men of the 8th Argyll and Sutherland Highlanders killed on 28 November. It had been impossible to recover their remains because the area was under constant observation, and a British minefield had since been laid across the valley. The British positions rested on a series of lower hills to the west of the German lines, with the DLI to the south of the road and the Foresters to the north. North-east of Djebel el Azzag was a lower ridge nicknamed 'Brown Hill', and to its north-west the confusingly named Djebel Azag, which from its distinctive pointed shape

Training with a Bren gun at Belper, 1939. (*Nottinghamshire Archives (NCA) DD/SF/5/2*)

The first death, grave of Private Ernest Hill, Chinley Chapelyard.

Regimental War Memorial, Crich.

Officers of the 2/5th Battalion *circa* September 1939. (*Museum of the Mercian Regiment, image from Bill Newton*)

...EGIMENT (SHERWOOD FORESTERS)

...B. Jackson, C. Bethell; (middle row) 2nd Lieut. C. Wall, Lieut. J.
..., G. S. Sutcliffe, D. H. Cousin, C. H. Perry, W. G. Yeomans;
...M., T.D., Major A. S. Giles, O.B.E., M.C., Lieut.-Colonel H. B. Everard,
...H. McCall, V. H. Ward, J. W. Jackson

Right: The 'Clive' telegram received on 1 September 1939 at the Derby Depot. (*ITC War Diary*)

```
APPENDIX 8.
                    Copy of telegram.

        336   2.0   York G  O H M S.
                Depot Sherwood Foresters Derby.
                        Clive
                              Area York.

                received 1925   1/9/39.
```

2nd Lieutenant George Cripps … (*Cripps family*)

… and his grave at Lapugny War Cemetery.

Memorial to the civilian and military dead at Oignies Municipal Cemetery.

Above left: The Haute Deule Canal today, near the Pont du Batterie.

Above right: Captain John Wyndham Hartigan, killed in action at Oignies, 26 May 1940.

Below: Commonwealth War Graves of men of the 2/5th Foresters in Oignies Municipal Cemetery.

Above: The Villa Floralies at Oignies, site of the alleged burning to death of a British officer by the Germans.

Below: The Foresters' HQ during the action at Oignies, the old brewery at Evin Malmaison.

Above: Troops return to Dover from Dunkirk on the deck of HMS *Codrington*. (© *National Museum of the Royal Navy RNM 1984/640/360*)

Below: On manoeuvres in East Anglia, 1941. On the far right is Lieutenant Colonel Hassell, and the officer third from right writing in his notebook is Bryan Keith-Lucas. (*2/5th Foresters' War Diary*)

'R' Company of new recruits, Lydd, 1942. (*Bill Newton*)

Above and opposite: On manoeuvres in East Anglia, 1941. (*2/5th Foresters' War Diary*)

2/5th Foresters inspected by HM King George VI before embarking for North Africa, 1942. (*NCA, DD/SF/5/6, uncatalogued item from IWM*)

HMT *Derbyshire* in 1943. (© *National Museum of the Royal Navy RMM 2003/252/7*)

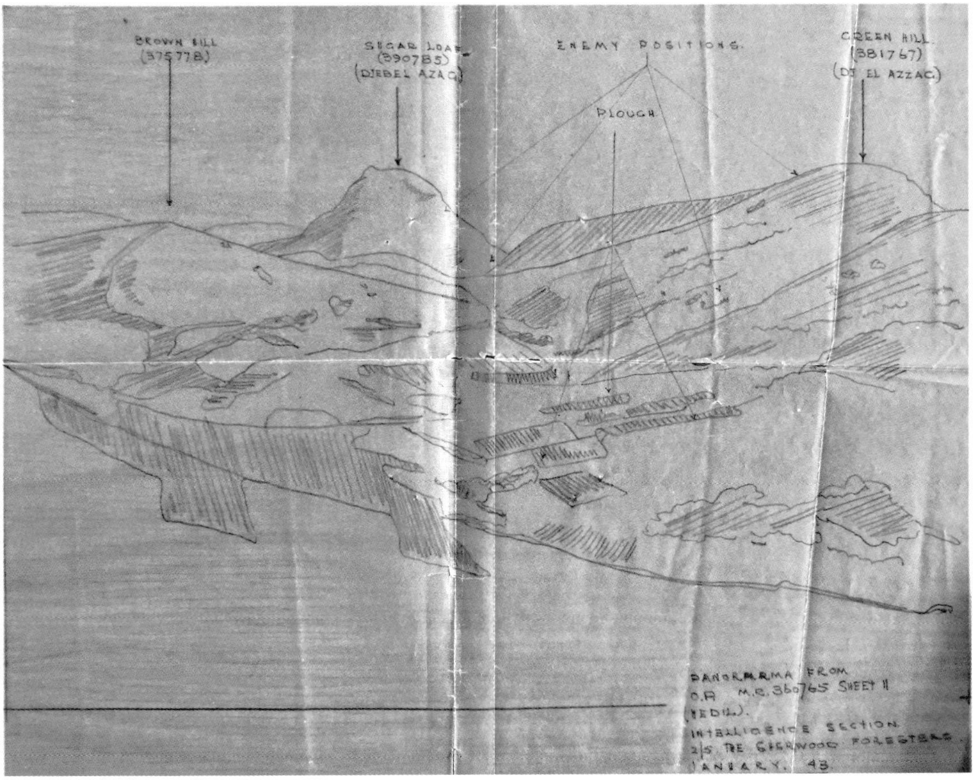

Above: Sketch of Green Hill. (*2/5th Foresters' War Diary*)

Right: Reverend Harold Barratt. (*Barratt family*)

Above and below: 2/5th Foresters' front lines facing Green Hill, positions on rear slope. (© *IWM NA795 and NA786, images from Museum of the Mercian Regiment/Memories of Sedjenane*)

Sedjenane. The bare hill in the background is where Captain John Kerly was killed leading A Company in a bayonet charge. (*NCA, DD/SF/5/7, photographer probably Wally Binch*)

D Company position at Sedjenane viewed from B Company. The road to the right is where the enemy AFV was knocked out by Sergeant Jack Bland with his Bofors gun. (*NCA, DD/SF/5/7, photographer probably Wally Binch*)

Above left: Evacuation of B Echelon from Sedjenane, March 1943. (*NCA, DD/SF/5/7, uncatalogued image from IWM*)

Above right: Lieutenant 'Jacko' Jackson, killed in action 13 March 1943. (*Mary Jackson*)

Below: Djebel Bel March, Tamera. (*Memories of Sedjenane, photographer unknown*)

Above: Victory parade in Tunis. (© *IWM NA 3049*)

Right: Officers of the 5th Foresters relaxing after the fall of Tunis. (NCA, DD/SF/5/2)

 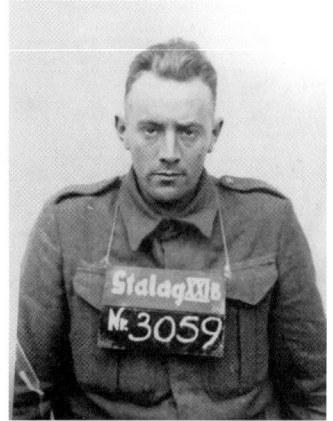 

George Burgess, George Sharpe and Noel Deall as prisoners of war. (*The National Archive, Kew, from German records*)

US LCIs in Bizerta harbour, July 1943. (*US Naval History and Heritage Command*)

was known as 'Sugar Loaf'. In the rear of the German positions, a rough track ran north-west into the Oued Sedjenane valley. Patrols from both sides would scout the rough terrain in this region, but the area was not strongly held by either, so it became known as the 'Buckshee Road', after the army slang for 'free'. From the Allied point of view, this sector was mostly covered by the *goums* of the French CFA; fierce Moroccan hillmen in many ways ideally suited to the task of scouting in the trackless hills, but lightly armed and lacking almost any semblance of military discipline. The opposition here were mainly Italian light infantry units.

During the day, the battalion occupied a warren of trenches and dugouts that had been built by the British or French troops who had previously occupied the lines. During the night, two men from each section were sent forward with a Bren gun to occupy slit trenches on the forward slopes. They would stand-to thirty minutes before dawn to guard against an enemy attack, and then retire to their daytime positions behind the hill. The men quickly learnt that exposing themselves on the skyline in daylight would immediately result in enemy fire from snipers, mortars or artillery. However, the steep slopes meant that even though overlooked, the trenches themselves were relatively secure from artillery fire, which would usually overshoot them and fall in the valley beyond. After a few weeks, even those who had never been in the front line before became slightly oblivious to the danger. Occasionally, men would fall asleep while on watch in the trenches through exhaustion. Fred Hirst did so on one occasion and was lucky that his platoon sergeant let off him and his companion for their first offence; an order was issued by Chichester-Constable on 31 January saying that two other incidents had been reported to brigade HQ, and reminding all ranks that sleeping on post was a court-martial offence carrying the death penalty. The order stated that several such sentences had been imposed, though none were actually carried out.

Once shelter had been established, food was next on the men's minds. Rations came in the form of 'compo' boxes, each one containing rations for fourteen men for one day—an inconvenient number, as it did not quite match the size of a section. There were seven different 'menus' (the 'A' box was considered to be the best because it included steak and kidney pie and fruit), mostly comprising different tinned foods sufficient to provide three meals a day—breakfast, dinner and supper—as well as tea, sugar, milk powder, biscuits, margarine, boiled sweets, cigarettes (unless these had been stolen in transit by troops in the rear) and, perhaps most essential, forty-two sheets of toilet paper. The regimental quartermaster sergeant (RQMS) divided the battalion rations between companies, and the company quartermaster sergeants (CQMS) such as Reg Markham allocated them to sections. Then George Hampton and other dedicated cooks back in the battalion rear area—B Echelon—opened the boxes and divided the tins to send forward in 15cwt trucks to the companies overnight; it was too dangerous to send vehicles forward by day. The tins were steamed and placed in insulated boxes, surrounded by hot water to keep the food warm. A lot of the cooking, however, was done within the company or section by amateur chefs such as 'Tinker' Taylor, whose own brand of rissoles (presumably manufactured from the corned beef rations) became a staple in Lieutenant Willoughby Gilliver's 9 Platoon. To avoid detection, the cooks on the front line used petrol or charcoal for fuel, as it did not produce smoke that would give away their positions to the enemy. If fuel was not available, as was often the case, the rations were designed to be eaten cold if necessary. On special occasions, such as the day that Stalingrad fell to the Russians, the men got bottles of beer, and in early February a small supply of rum became available. Water was more of a problem. There was a stream at the bottom of the hill in which men could have a wash or shave (in cold water), but it was unfit for drinking because it ran through a local cemetery. When possible, compo rations were supplemented by dates, oranges and *oeufs* (eggs) purchased from the local Arabs, or even the occasional wild pig shot with a .303 rifle. Signaller Fred Hutt recalled that Lieutenant Colonel Stott was offered one such animal but ordered it to be taken away and buried, as wild meat was possibly dangerous for human consumption. Undeterred, one of the other signallers exhumed the carcass and it was cut up and added to the Signal Platoon's compo rations. When some men in B Company killed another pig, their officers were not so adverse to taking their share. It was cut up by Private Kia Hunt, a butcher from Ripley in civilian life.

After use, the wooden compo boxes themselves were put to good use as building material to shore up the trench and dugout walls, or as covers for the latrines to keep out flies. Gas-capes and groundsheets were also used to make the dugouts a little more comfortable and weatherproof. Showing a light at night was clearly risky. While some opted to sit in darkness, another more dangerous option was to cover the trench or dugout with a groundsheet. Illumination could then be provided in the form of an empty fifty-cigarette tin filled with petrol, with a piece of string or wood as a wick. While a degree of comfort could be obtained, as in the First World War the dugouts were lousy and infested with rats, with scorpions adding a novel variation to the menagerie of vermin. Furthermore, from the day after the Foresters arrived in the line, the weather soon became more of an ordeal for the men than enemy action, the winter sunshine that had greeted them at Algiers giving way to a steady rain which turned the fine Tunisian soil into a quagmire equal to those experienced by their fathers in 1914–18. Temperatures in the mountains were also much lower than on the coast, and the worst downpours would cause trenches and dugouts to fill with ice-cold water up to the waist, or even to collapse completely. Daytime was taken up with catching up on lost sleep, picking lice out of clothes and drying them if the weather allowed, writing home or repairing or deepening the trenches. Army 'bull' also reared its head even here. Eric Morral remembered having to clean and blanco his mud-encrusted webbing for inspection; against orders, he also dropped his rifle in a nearby stream to wash off the sludge.

Leaving Home: Tunisia, January–February 1943

B Echelon was set up in some woods west of Sedjenane, 15 miles behind the front-line dugouts in front of Green Hill and Baldy, well outside the range of the enemy's artillery. Here, the motor transport was parked in camouflaged positions in the nearby woods and fuel and rations were stored. The RQMS and CQMS were responsible for keeping the front-line troops supplied with water, rations, ammunition, mail and other essential needs. Storemen were also assigned by each company. During the day, working parties fetched supplies from central supply dumps in the wood and carried it to the trucks. The journey to the front line itself was always by night to avoid air attack. Also established at Sedjenane was the main dressing station (MDS), staffed by the RAMC personnel of 183 Field Ambulance. Advanced dressing stations (ADS) were positioned closer to the trenches, where the railway line passed through a tunnel, for the immediate treatment of casualties at the front. The administrative brigade HQ was in the damaged French colonial post office in Sedjenane, still occupied by the postmaster and his heavily pregnant wife, with a forward tactical HQ in front of Green Hill.

Troops were sent back to the rear area for between twenty-four and forty-eight hours every week or two to rest and clean up. Compared to the mud of the front line it was luxury, with mats to sit on, mugs of tea and hot food. Men could change their underclothes and have a shower using a perforated biscuit tin or a 'bath', also out of a biscuit tin; first washing the top, followed by the legs, then sitting in the tin to wash the rest. Alternatively, they could choose a communal bath, taken in a large hole in the ground covered with a tarpaulin. Water was heated up using petrol blowers, and after several dozen men had been through the bathing hole the scum would be skimmed off and the water topped up. There was a de-infestation unit to get rid of the lice, but best of all was the opportunity to get a good night's sleep away from enemy gunfire. Nevertheless, not everyone found the rear area relaxing. Fred Hirst only went back there once, and never volunteered again. He found it more stressful than the positions in front of Green Hill, where the dangers were relatively well known and could be minimised by keeping low in the trenches. In the rear echelon, the risk of air attack was always present.

On 29 January, about four dozen men, including Alan Orme and Fred Hutt, had gone back to the rest camp. The weather that morning was bright and clear, when at 11.08am enemy fighter planes—four Focke-Wulf 190s and four Messerschmitt 109s—attacked Sedjenane. The aircraft came in low, at between 1,000 and 2,000 feet, in line astern. There was no warning until men heard the drone of their engines close overhead. Some of the guards in the camp, seeing the concern on the faces of men who were settling down to eat, said not to worry as the planes were friendly. The next instant, cannon shells were ripping through the tin roof and ricocheting off the concrete walls of the hospital building. Five minutes later, the attack was over, having inflicted twenty-one casualties, fifteen of them Foresters.

Private Robert Lyon, in civilian life a plumber's assistant from Nottingham, lost his life that day, not in the front line but in the supposedly safer rest area. He was the battalion's first fatality of the campaign. Another four men from the battalion were seriously wounded, requiring operations, and ten received lighter wounds.

On 4 February, another group of Foresters were at Sedjenane on sick parade when at around 9.20am twelve enemy aircraft again attacked the MDS from about 1,000 feet, this time with both bombs and cannons. Of the eight bombs dropped, three failed to explode, but one scored a direct hit on the hospital building, which was completely destroyed. Lance Corporal Arthur Bull, who looked after the petrol and oil stores for the battalion, was amongst the ten killed, as well as three of the medical staff. Arthur Soulter and Dennis Willett from the transport section looked for his body, but found nothing but his torn and twisted tin hat. They also found in a crater the remains of a bomb casing with '2/5 SF' marked upon it—a remarkable coincidence, or perhaps evidence of the quality of German intelligence.

In Tunisia, the more affluent, political class of Arabs in the cities—from the national leader, the Bey of Tunis, down—were pro-Axis, mainly on the 'enemy of my enemy' principle that they were anti-French, though a few also supported antisemitic German activities against Tunisia's small Jewish population. In the countryside, it is unlikely that the Arab population had any strong political leanings towards either side. It mostly consisted either of labourers on the French colonial estates or independent subsistence farmers trying to eke out a living in the hills. Within the immediate vicinity of the front line, normal economic activity broke down and the local Arabs made up for lost income by selling their eggs, dates and oranges to both sides. The British were happy to buy their goods, but were always suspicious of them, and not just over the price or hygiene concerns (the oranges were dropped into Jeyes Fluid to disinfect them). A commodity much more valuable than farm produce was information, and since it was impossible to control the movement of the local Arabs across the front line, they could obtain plenty of that to sell to either side. One Arab was arrested in no man's land by Lieutenant Keith Cowie on 26 January, following an assertion from two others that he had been carrying information to the Germans. A few days later, a French commando officer was attached to the battalion to act as liaison with the local population. What happened to Cowie's prisoner after he had been sent back for interrogation is not known, but on at least one occasion the French were seen to shoot an Arab for assisting the Germans. The British troops were generally told to leave them alone, as their information could be useful to the Allied intelligence officers as well. Untrustworthy though they might be, the British Tommy could also have some sympathy with the Arabs in their plight. The local population had to try to survive in the middle of someone else's war, often continuing to plough their fields while the troops around them traded bullets and shells instead of eggs and oranges.

Once shelter, defence and food were arranged, attention could be turned to more active military pursuits. Small infantry patrols went out most nights, except when there was torrential rain, which made the hilly slopes too treacherous underfoot. As in the First World War, patrols were considered useful combat training and kept the men active. More importantly, they supplemented the intelligence gained from the local population, identifying the precise location of enemy positions and, if lucky enough to capture prisoners, the enemy units occupying the opposing trenches. Patrols almost invariably set out at midnight and returned at dawn. They would operate in two groups: a small reconnaissance party consisting of an officer with a Thompson or Sten sub-machine gun and two privates with rifles, and a larger group led by a senior NCO, armed with a Bren gun, rifles and occasionally a 2-inch or 3-inch mortar. As the patrol neared the enemy lines, the latter group was set up in a suitable position to provide covering fire in the event of the patrol being discovered, and then the smaller team of men moved forward to inspect the enemy lines.

As well as patrols, the batteries of 70th Field Regiment RA kept up a constant but low volume shelling of the enemy positions, to which their German counterparts responded rather less frequently, indicating either that they had less ammunition or were conserving it. Artillery observers would occasionally go out with a radio set to identify and engage targets, with a protective patrol provided by the Foresters or one of the other infantry units. Trying to locate and silence the German artillery and mortars sited on the reverse slopes of the hills was, however, incredibly difficult. On 3 February, the regiment received a novel form of ammunition: seven smoke shells, from which the smoke canisters had been removed and leaflets stuffed inside. On the leaflets was a message to the enemy troops telling them how hopeless their position was, and how they could go about surrendering. That night, a single 25-pounder of 279 Field Battery became the first gun to try out this new ammunition, dropping leaflets onto German positions up to 2,000 yards beyond Green Hill. Corporal Bert Pinnock, a signaller attached to B Company of the Foresters, was returning from a bathing party back at B Echelon, and as he approached the company positions in the dark got the fright of his life as the gun went off close by. One of the gunners said to him that there might be some retaliation in the morning. The air attack on Sedjenane on 4 February was possibly one such reprisal, for as well as hitting the MDS it came within 50 yards of hitting the artillery HQ. But more was to come.

Few officers had served longer in the 2/5th Foresters than 32-year-old Reverend Harold Norman Barratt, Chaplain (4th Class). Before the war he had been a curate in the parish of Acomb outside York, where he had been a stalwart of the local scouting movement, and he had been ordained a priest at York Minster in 1938. In the lead up to war, Barratt had joined the Royal Army Chaplaincy Department on 24 May 1939, and he was posted to the battalion on 19 March 1940. For nearly three years he had administered to the spiritual, moral and emotional needs of the battalion. He had seen them through the trauma of Dunkirk, and had won the love and respect of officers and men. Former guardsman RSM Patrick 'Tara' Hennessy told one group of men constructing dugouts in front of Green Hill, 'this is for the padre, let's make it a bit special', and upon its completion placed a wooden sign marked 'THE RECTORY' above the entrance. Barratt had baptised Alan Orme in Kent during the previous summer, and officiated at the wedding of bandsman and stretcher-bearer Bob Fellows. He also helped men out on practical matters, such as arranging for the battalion adjutant (and peacetime lawyer) Bryan Keith-Lucas to draw up a will for Frank Offiler. On the battalion's last Sunday at Maison Carrée, there had been a service in the brick factory. Although voluntary, unlike many church parades, the service was attended by most of the battalion, with some watching the proceedings from the gantry. Both religious and non-religious alike found the service very moving, and it would remain in their memory.

Barratt had married in October 1939, and back at their home in Edinburgh, his Scottish wife, Katherine, was expecting their second child.

Barratt's routine was to alternate weeks spent in the front line with a week seeing to the needs of the wounded and sick in the MDS at Sedjenane. On 4 February, he was at the front, and Barratt travelled from Battalion HQ to the forward trenches to conduct Holy Communion. It was a Thursday, so his congregation that day was small: only four men. Second Lieutenant 'Ginger' Martin had just returned from thirty-six hours' leave in the rear depot and had persuaded Barratt to hold a service and his platoon sergeant, Maurice Enser, to go with him. It was contrary to regulations for both the platoon officer and platoon sergeant to be away from their men at the same time, but it would only be for half an hour. The group was completed by Bert Pinnock and Private John Blake; Barratt had also asked Bob Fellows to join them, but he was doing guard duty. Barratt selected for his chapel a small hut belonging to one of the local Arab villagers, which sat on top of a hill about 150 yards in front of the slit trenches held by A Company, and not far from the Argylls' burnt-out carriers. Willoughby Gilliver advised him against holding the service in such an exposed position, but the padre insisted. The hut was made of mud, with branches supporting a roughly thatched roof. He laid out some ration boxes for a communion table and started the service.

At 10.30am, the enemy began to shell the Foresters' positions. For a few minutes, Barratt tried to continue with the devotions, but the noise of the crashing shells became too great and he told everyone to take cover. Then a shell smashed into the little hut, and the air was filled with smoke, fumes and dust. Enser and Pinnock had dived for cover in one corner, and emerging unharmed from the rubble their first impression was that miraculously nobody had been hurt. Enser got up and went to remove some of the debris from Martin, but as he turned over the unconscious body, the young officer died. Blake had also been killed instantly in the explosion; like Martin, he was only twenty years old. The padre had been partly protected by the makeshift altar, but was badly wounded, with both his legs shattered. Stretcher-bearers hurried forward to the hut, and Enser helped them put Barratt onto one to carry him down the hill, while dispatch rider Steve Loach was sent back to B Echelon to get an ambulance. German shells continued to fall around Loach's motorcycle on the way there, but having fired fifty-two shells, including the one that had hit the hut, the guns fell silent as he and the ambulance wound their way back up the valley. The medics were too late. Reverend Barratt died of his wounds two hours after being hit.

For the first time in the war, Sergeant Enser had the duty of reporting casualties to his company commander. Captain Frank Holbrook told him to take command of the platoon, after which Enser returned to the platoon's command dugout and got drunk on the contents of a bottle of Ginger Martin's whisky. The loss of the popular padre was a great blow to morale and brought home to those still untested in a real battle just how dangerous life at the front was. Not even a man of God was safe.

*

Aside from the almost nightly patrols and almost daily artillery duels, there was only one significant operation carried out on the Foresters' front in the month after they arrived. This was Operation Scorch, an enlarged patrol-like engagement undertaken on 10–11 February to ascertain the enemy's positions and intentions in the wild hill region north of 139 Brigade's main positions, and to drive the enemy in this region, believed to be mostly Italian, from their forward positions. The forces used for this operation were primarily small teams from No. 1 Commando, whose training and familiarity with the terrain made them most suited to the task. Also involved was a company from the 2/5th Leicesters, previously in reserve, while a detachment of Royal Engineers was instructed to lay a defensive minefield. The Foresters' involvement, rather unimaginatively code-named Ram, was for an officer and twenty men to occupy an observation post (OP) on a hill to the left (north) of their positions in front of Green Hill, to monitor enemy movements during the main operation. The OP was established in the early hours of 10 February. Their only interaction with the enemy was on 11 February, when an Arab led a small enemy patrol up to the OP and enquired whether they were English or *Americano*, from which it was deduced that the patrol was Italian. Corporal Andrew was interrogating the Arab when he was shot at, and the Foresters replied with rifle fire. In the evening, after the Foresters had retired, the enemy retook the position. The Foresters took no casualties during Scorch, but the Leicesters lost four killed, five wounded and six missing. A couple of days later, on 13 February, a British soldier with his arm in plaster approached the Foresters' lines under a white flag. It was Private Cresswell, one of the missing Leicesters, and he carried a letter from the local German commander asking about the whereabouts of a German officer, Oberleutnant Goerke, who had been captured during Scorch, with the intention of exchanging prisoners. Goerke, it appears, was the commander's son and, given later events, it is possible that Goerke possessed information that the Germans were keen should not be extracted by British intelligence officers. His father's request was ignored and the young Oberleutnant was hurriedly sent back for interrogation.

By the beginning of February, the German army had proved itself to be expert at defensive warfare in the Tunisian hills, and together with the weather this had put an end to the Allies' advance. The British and American commanders now determined to sit it out in their existing positions until the weather improved in the spring and the ground dried, allowing them to use their tanks to better effect. But standing on the defensive awaiting attack was not the preferred German way of warfare. It was definitely not part of the military psyche of Erwin Rommel, who on 13 January had arrived in Tunisia with the lead formations of his retreating Afrika Korps and been given command of all the enemy troops there. He had made his reputation in both world wars by daring thrusts through and round enemy lines, and his instinct was to take the offensive. The result of the so-called 'Race for Tunis' on the Allied side had been to leave them with an extended front line, where British, French and American troops were interspersed, with individual units often in tactically inferior positions—like the Foresters at Green Hill—but with orders not to give ground. Rommel planned to attack the exposed Allied right flank, held mostly by raw American and poorly equipped French troops, and to drive north as far as Beja and beyond. This was a variant on the enveloping flank attack that he had used so often in the desert; by threatening the enemy rear, he would force them to choose between a strategic withdrawal or annihilation of their army.

The German counter-offensive began with an attack not by Rommel's Afrika Korps but by von Arnim's Fifth Panzer Army. On 14 February, two *Kampfgruppen* (Battle Groups) from 10th and 21st panzer divisions attacked American troops at the town of Sidi Bou Zid, 150 miles south of Sedjenane. The 10th Panzer had fought on the Russian Front, and in a classic envelopment battle it surrounded and all but annihilated the inexperienced Allied force as an effective unit. A few days later, Rommel's 21st Panzer Division struck another American formation 25 miles to the north-west at Sbeitla. The outcome was much the same, with the untested GIs outmanoeuvred and outfought by the desert veterans, who drove them back through the Kasserine Pass. Rommel's arrival in the Tunisian theatre, and the apparent ease with which he had bested the Allied forces that opposed him, threw the outcome of the campaign into doubt. It also put a severe strain on Anglo-American relations, with the British regarding the American troops as inadequately trained, while the Americans blamed the British commanders for faulty dispositions. Meanwhile, at First Army HQ, the familiar response of creating ad hoc formations from any available reserves and throwing them in to hold the lines was taking place. As in France three years earlier, there was little or no alternative.

One unit drawn into the battle was the 2/5th Leicesters, the same battalion whose first encounter with the enemy back at Oignies in 1940 had ended in disaster. If the Foresters can be considered an unlucky regiment during the war, the 2/5th Leicesters must surely be considered an unlucky battalion. On 18 February, they were withdrawn from their positions in the north and placed under the command of 26 Brigade in 6th Armoured Division. On 20 February, they formed part of 'Nick Force', an ad hoc formation created under Brigadier Cameron Nicholson to defend a gap through the hills at Thala, about 20 miles north of the Kasserine Pass. Its loss would have turned the right flank of the British 78th Division. The Leicesters spent the day digging in, deployed in two lines each two companies wide astride the road. On a ridge behind them were several artillery batteries, two companies of the Rifle Brigade and some anti-tank guns. Tanks of the 17th/21st Lancers retired through the battalion during the day, so there was little possibility of laying defensive minefields. As evening fell, another column of about nine retiring tanks appeared. The column passed down the road, then some of the vehicles turned to each side between the two lines of Leicesters. Panzer grenadiers jumped off the tanks, revealing them to be German, and opened fire. In the words of an officer in one of the artillery batteries posted behind them, 'the Leicesters disintegrated'.[6] Taken by surprise and under fire from all sides, the inexperienced battalion could hardly have done otherwise, losing over 300 men in just a few minutes. Fortunately, the Leicesters were well supported by artillery and tanks. Brigadier Nicholson refused to surrender and organised a counterattack during the night, in which some of the Leicesters took part. A mere forty of the battalion finally withdrew to Thala the following morning, though more would rejoin over the following days. But after five days of German success, Rommel's advance had been held, and the Desert Fox called off his offensive. He was running low on fuel, Allied opposition was strengthening and Montgomery's Eighth Army was arriving in eastern Tunisia to threaten his rearguard.

As early as 16 February, it had been decided that an army reserve was needed to avoid continually having to produce ad hoc responses to the enemy attacks, but the troops selected, from 6th Armoured Division, had been sucked in to meet these new threats. V Corps determined that as the next best solution, 139 Brigade Group should be pulled out of the front line and form part of a corps reserve based around Beja. The 46th Division issued an order on 22 February to put this into effect, including moving the 2/5th Leicesters north to come back under its control. In itself, this was a sound military decision; it would provide a mobile formation to respond to further enemy counterattacks, should they arise. It also made some sense for the troops providing the reserve to come from the northern part of the front, which did not have much strategic importance compared to the south. The area in front of Green Hill had been relatively quiet since

January and had been defensively mined, while still further north the terrain was unsuited to large-scale operations and intelligence indicated that it was lightly held by both sides. This apparently safe sector from Jefna to the coast could be held by the French CFA, No. 1 Commando and the 6th Lincolns (detached from 138 Brigade). On the morning of 22 February, officers of the Lincolns arrived at the Foresters' area to inspect the positions, and that afternoon orders were received from brigade to hand over the positions that night to the commandos. At 11pm, the battalion set off to march 10 miles back towards Sedjenane. Less than an hour after they left, a German patrol was discovered by the commandos, who killed eight and captured one of the enemy.

The Foresters spent two days digging trenches in their new positions to the rear, just east of Sedjenane. Then on 26 February, they were told to move south to take up their new role as corps reserve. At 7pm, they fell back to their transport in the woods north-west of Sedjenane and drove overnight to Beja. This was a good location for a reserve, roughly equidistant from Djebel Abiod and Medjez-el-Bab, with a railway line also running through the town. Arriving at 7am, Stott went to 46th Division HQ and was told to recce a defensive position on the River Beja. Then at 4.30pm came an order for the whole battalion to get back in their transports and go back to Sedjenane. Their role as corps reserve would be taken over by the 8th Argyll and Sutherland Highlanders. In pouring rain and a thunderstorm, the Foresters made their way back to their old transport lines, where they arrived at 4am on 28 February. That night, the men left their vehicles and made their way on foot back into the lines that they had vacated less than forty-eight hours earlier, or as near as they could find them in the dark after hacking their way with bayonet and machete through thick cork forests and cactus scrub.

On 1 March, the 2/5th Battalion officially changed its designation to '5th Battalion The Sherwood Foresters (Nottinghamshire and Derbyshire Regiment)', and it was as the 5th Battalion that it now prepared to face its toughest test to date.

8

Examinations: Tunisia, March 1943

'Order, counter-order, disorder' is a well-worn military maxim, but one which aptly fits the Foresters' abortive race to Beja and back. The concept of the corps reserve was a good one, but unfortunately nobody had told the Germans that Sedjenane was a quiet sector. After the abandonment of Rommel's Kasserine offensive, Field Marshal von Arnim had set in train his own plans for an attack. Von Arnim was less ambitious than Rommel, and it had the limited objective of pushing back the Allies' starting line for their expected spring offensive. This would buy time to allow the Germans to withdraw the Afrika Korps from the south and strengthen their defence in depth. It fitted in with the overall German and Italian strategy to prolong the Tunisia campaign until the end of 1943, or at least late enough to prevent any Allied offensive action against Italy itself that year. Von Arnim's plan was codenamed *Ochsenkopf* (Oxhead), and its focus was a three-point attack that would strike across the divisional boundary between the British 46th and 78th divisions. One attack would be down the road from Mateur to Beja via Sidi Nsir; the second across the mountains to envelop the British at Medjez-El-Bab; and the third in the Bou Arada valley, towards El Aroussa. In addition to these, a diversionary operation codenamed *Ausladung* (Disembarkation) would first take Sedjenane, then continue along the road and railway line to Djebel Abiod, from where it could threaten Beja.

This diversionary German attack would be made by an ad hoc formation of their own, Division von Manteuffel, named after its commander, Colonel Hasso von Manteuffel, who would later command the Fifth Panzer Army in the Ardennes offensive of December 1944. The division was spilt into semi-independent and largely self-contained *Kampfgruppen*. Two of these would advance on Sedjenane from the north: *Kampfgruppe Latini*, formed around *Tunis-Feld-Bataillone* (Tunis Field Battalion) *T4*, and *Kampfgruppe Witzig*, which consisted of two companies from the 11th Parachute Engineer Battalion and *Marsch-bataillone A30*. A *Marsch-bataillone* (march battalion) was the term used in the German Army for rear-echelon formations on their way to the front to provide replacements for losses in front-line units. There was often a core of veterans returning from injury or leave, who would then train the rest of the unit, which consisted of new recruits. They were mostly equipped with small arms and were administrative organisations, not intended for front-line combat. The original personnel of the *A30* battalion had been young men taken from anti-aircraft units. The field battalions had been formed and air-lifted to Tunisia after Operation Torch by the simple expedient of renaming five of the existing *Marsch-bataillone* intended to replace losses amongst Rommel's Afrika Korps. The *T4* battalion was relatively untried in combat, but had arrived in Tunisia on 27 November. So the troops knew the ground on which they would fight, and had been bought up to something approaching a standard battalion establishment with regards to heavy weapons, though not transport, which was in short supply in Tunisia. The battalion had at least twelve heavy machine guns and six heavy mortars; it may have had up to twice this. *Kampfgruppe Witzig* was named after its commander, Major Rudolf Witzig, already a famous war hero though only twenty-six years old. He had led his airborne engineers in the assault on the supposedly impregnable fortress of Eban Emael in May 1940 that had opened up Belgium to the German invasion. He then served as adjutant to Reichsmarschall Hermann Goering and led a battalion in the airborne invasion of Crete in 1941. Sent to Tunisia in November 1942, his 11th Parachute Engineer Battalion had first stopped the British advance at Green Hill and then used their engineering skills to turn it into a fortress.

Two further *kampfgruppen* were in these positions around Green Hill. *Kampfgruppe Jefna* was based around the T3 Field Battalion, commanded by Hauptmann (Captain) Michael Burgermeister. At the end of January, he had described the battalion as good regarding its morale, but deficient in all other aspects: 'The level of training of the rank and file of the battalion is insufficient, as [it] has had no chance at all since its establishment to conduct any kind of comprehensive weapons practice.'[1] Many of its men were non-combat personnel, others new recruits and some even prisoners convicted of minor offences and assigned to front-line service for punishment duty. Even the core of veterans did not have the familiarity with their comrades that makes an experienced unit effective in battle. The same could not be said of the second formation, which consisted primarily of the Luftwaffe Regiment Barenthin, named after its commander, Colonel Walter Barenthin. This was a powerful unit of about 2,500 men, containing two infantry battalions and an anti-tank battalion— the last of these possibly split up between the different *kampfgruppen* for this operation. Formed in November 1942 using personnel drawn from the parachute schools and rushed to Tunisia, the regiment had been one of the key elements holding the British advance. Their morale was high, and they were described by Field Marshal Harold Alexander, Commander of the Allied 18th Army Group, as 'perhaps the best German troops in Africa'.[2]

Kampfgruppe Latini formed up in the Oued Sedjenane valley and advanced westwards on 26 February on each side of the river. Its task was to turn the Allies' northern flank, destroy the light forces on the road between Cap Serrat and Sedjenane, then swing south to capture the village and ultimately cut the Allied supply lines at Djebel Abiod. Advancing alongside it to the north were some 3,000 men of the Italian 10th Bersaglieri Regiment, which had arrived in Tunisia in January. Several deserters had been taken prisoner from this regiment and indicated its morale was poor. On 26 February, the French CFA encountered the Italians in the mountains north of the Sedjenane valley, claiming 230 prisoners, but two companies of French were later surrounded and the rest fell back under enemy pressure. The anti-tank section of C Squadron, 46th Recce Regiment, was supporting the French and was overrun, losing all its guns. But the number of enemy troops reported by the French was low and since the 16th DLI were still in their transport area west of Sedjenane, they were ordered to move north the following day and retake the ground lost.

The DLI had not followed the Foresters to Beja on 26 February, but when they tried to carry out their orders they found that the enemy did not consist of a weak Italian force in the Oued Sedjenane valley but German troops in considerable strength, holding a series of hills about 3 miles north of Sedjenane, particularly the Djebel Guerba. To the DLI's left, two troops of No. 1 Commando secured a position on Djebel Guerba which allowed one company of the DLI to take and hold a spur in front of this dominating feature, but under fire from their right flank, the DLI had to fall back. The next day, 28 February, was spent reorganising and preparing for a more substantial attack to retake the hill on 1 March.

The German advance from the east had been due to start on 28 February with a double envelopment of the 6th Lincolns and supporting units in front of Green Hill. *Kampfgruppe Jefna* would advance through the hills to the north of the British positions, the Barenthin Regiment to the south. Fortunately for the Lincolns, intelligence gathered by the commandos had anticipated the attack and the decision had already been made to pull them back. They had been under increasingly heavy mortar and artillery fire since 26 February, and overnight on 28 February–1 March they retired back through the newly arrived Foresters, who now became the forward line defending Sedjenane from the east. The Lincolns had left their transport in the rear due to the enemy fire, so much of their equipment had to be left behind. The bad weather that had made the Foresters' journey back north so miserable also meant that 277 Field Battery RA, which had been supporting them in the front line, had to destroy all but one of their guns because transport could not be brought forward to pull them out. These would be sorely missed in the next few days.

The defence line occupied by the 5th Foresters had originally been intended to be held by an entire brigade, but was now held by a single battalion almost

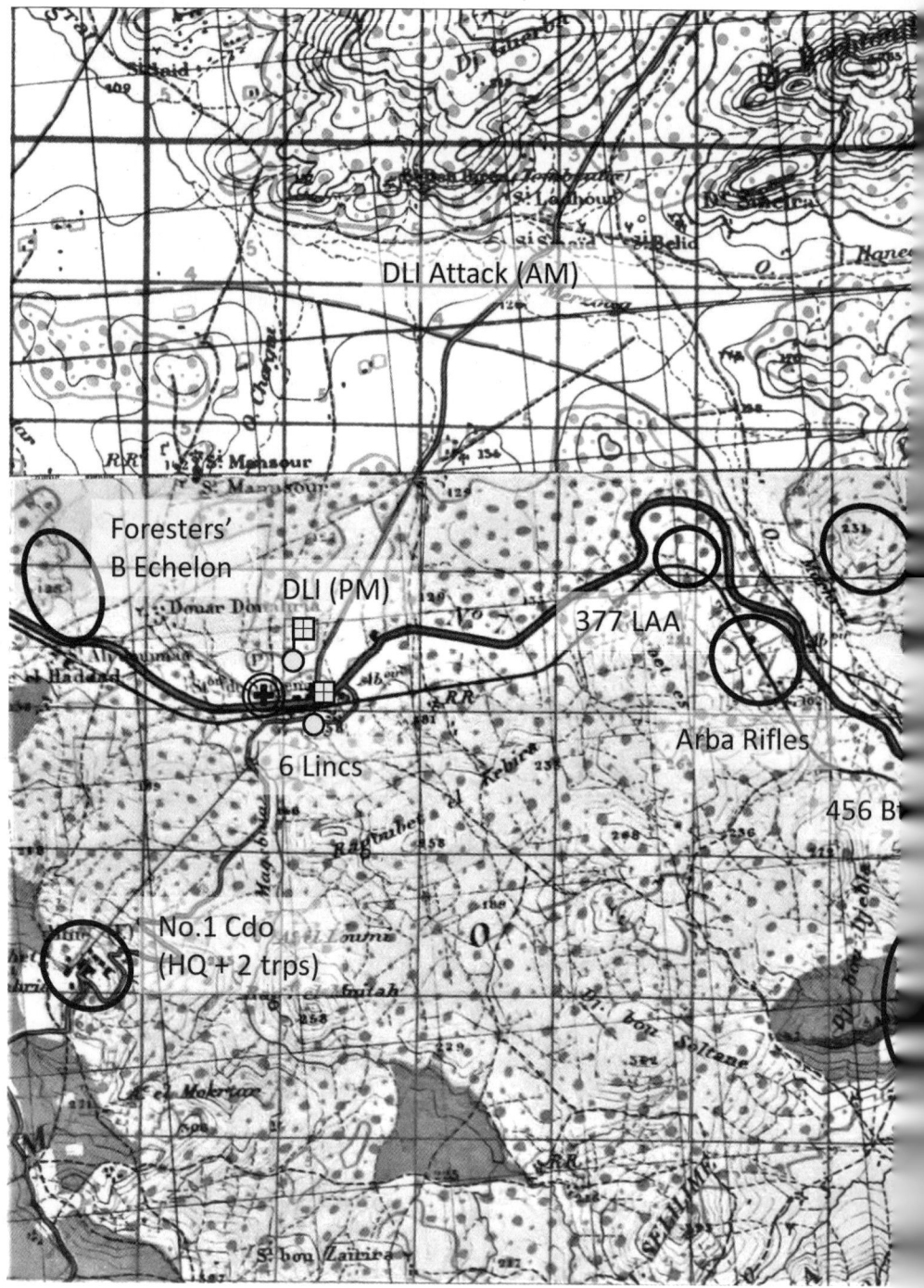

Sedjenane, 2 March 1943.

Examinations: Tunisia, March 1943

unsupported. The main position was about 5 miles east of Sedjenane, north of the road and railway, along a low line of hills. On the left was B Company under Roger Newton. To their right was Frank Holbrook's C Company, with the Battalion HQ and most of the mortar platoon behind them on the rear slope of the hill. A mile to the south-west, on the Djebel Bou Djeblar, Philip Palmer and D Company held another group of positions that had been taken over from the Lincolns. A mile-and-a-half in front of this main line was an advanced group that consisted of Captain Keith Davenport's A Company, the carrier platoon (less its carriers) under its second in command, Lieutenant Horace Leaver, and three anti-tank guns. The road had been mined by the Royal Engineers at this point, which had caused some delay to the Lincolns' withdrawal when the Foresters closed the final gaps in the minefield the night they arrived. Roughly midway between the two positions was a small Arab settlement and railway station named Sidi Abdallah Ben Saiden.

The 16th DLI were due to renew their counterattack north of Sedjenane on the morning of 2 March, supported by D Company of the Lincolns. The rest of the Lincolns had been pulled back into the town itself, which they would prepare as a base in case the DLI's attack failed. Of the four artillery batteries in 139 Brigade Group, 449 Field Battery, one troop of 279 Field Battery and half of 15/17 Medium Battery had been assigned to support the attack. This left 456 Light Battery, C Troop of 279 Battery and one troop of 15/17 Battery to support the Foresters—a total of twelve 25-pounders and four 5½-inch guns. Number 456 Battery was positioned on the road to the rear of the battalion, but 279 Battery was much further north, around an area known as Sapper's Corner, 2 miles east of Sedjenane, where there was a hairpin bend in the road. The mediums, with their longer range, were about a mile west of the town. Although 456 and 279 batteries had both been ordered to send OPs up to the Foresters' front, on the morning of 2 March Major Arthur Blaxland, assigned as senior artillery liaison officer to the Foresters, was still in Sedjenane. Air defence for the artillery was provided by a troop from 379 Light Anti-Aircraft Battery. Protecting the guns from attack on the ground, on a hill known only by its height in metres as Hill 231, were four troops of No. 1 Commando—as tough a bunch of fighters as could be found in Tunisia but numbering in total only around 250 men. The rest of the commando, another two troops and the HQ, were in reserve at a mine 2 miles south-east of Sedjenane. The line of hills that ran parallel to the road between Hill 231 and the rear of B Company of the Foresters had been held on 1 March by a single company of the Arba Rifles, a French Algerian unit, but on the morning of 2 March it appears that they had retired to the west of the road, taking up positions near the British artillery. This meant the left flank of B Company was completely exposed. The same was true of both flanks of A Company and the carriers.

The DLI's counterattack went in before dawn at 6am, just after the first shells of the supporting artillery barrage came down. Keeping close to the barrage, B and D companies on the left assaulted the Djebel Guerba and managed to advance to within 25 yards of the German positions before the enemy opened fire. By this time it was daylight, and the superior training of the Germans became apparent. The attack faltered, and although at 8am the Lincolns began to move up to support, the DLI's commander decided that the enemy's position was much too strong to be taken by a single company and sensibly recalled them. Of the two companies of the DLI, only one officer and sixty ORs out of about 200 men made it back to their starting lines. By noon, all those who had survived the attack had been sent back to the transport lines in Sedjenane to regroup, leaving only the Battalion HQ, the carrier platoon and the company of Lincolns north of the town.

The sounds of the DLI's attack 5 miles away could clearly be heard from the Foresters' lines, but otherwise the day had opened quietly. At Battalion HQ, the adjutant, Bryan Keith-Lucas, together with the new chaplain, Reverend Paul Guinness, wandered up the hill to a small mosque. The padre read a few chapters from the Bible and then the two men walked back. The peace and calm of the morning were gradually disturbed by mortar and machine-gun fire from the east. While *Kampfgruppe Latini* was holding off the DLI's attack to the north, the main German effort was being made by the Barenthin Regiment astride the Jefna–Sedjenane road, supported by around fifteen AFVs—fortunately these were light armoured cars and tanks from the 10th Panzer Division reconnaissance battalion, and not the massive Tigers. The Luftwaffe troops would come up against the positions held by A Company and the carrier platoon. To their right, the troops of *Kampfgruppe Jefna* would work their way through the hills north of the road and then swing south. The target for both arms of this pincer movement was the settlement of Sidi Abdallah Ben Saiden.

Despatch rider Stanley Storey had just got back to the carrier platoon early that morning from the Algerian port of Bone, from where he had directed a convoy transporting new 6-pounder anti-tank guns for the battalion. The guns were still in the rear, but Storey had been sent to relieve some men in the front-line trenches while they got some food. He was still there when the Germans began their attack, but was so exhausted that during a lull in the fighting he dozed off! He awoke to find 'what appeared to be the whole German army, swarming like ants, coming towards me with machine gun fire forcing me to keep my head down as they circled to my left'. The enemy kept up a constant stream of fire; all Storey had was a revolver which was quite useless against such an attack: 'Although one of our corporals had managed to get back to a tree behind me, we had no option but to surrender or be killed.'[3] It was about 1.30pm and the heavily outnumbered carrier platoon was rapidly being overrun by the Barenthin Regiment's attack.

Down the hill from the carrier platoon was one of the battalion's old 2-pounder anti-tank guns under the command of Lance Sergeant Bernard ('Lucky') Jewkes. Amongst the crew were Wally Binch and his pal Eddie Hallett. They were the same age (19), had joined the Young Soldiers Battalion together and became close friends. They both fancied themselves as entertainers, Wally playing his ukulele while Eddie would write parodies of army life to the tune of well-known songs as they developed their own comedy routines. That afternoon the war stopped being a joke and became deadly serious. Their gun was sited in a gully to the left of the road, positioned to fire on any enemy coming from El Aouana. As the enemy shelling intensified, the men kept their eyes peeled down the road. Then they realised that the bullets hitting the ground around them were coming not from in front but from behind them, up the hill, where the carrier platoon should have been, and from no more than 100 yards away. With their gun pointing the wrong way and lacking even a rifle, which had gone back to B Echelon with their transport, Binch removed the breech block from the gun and they then crawled through a drainage sewer under the road and began to run back across the fields to the main battalion position.

In a small quarry across the road from Wally Binch's gun, Sergeant Pat McKay had finished digging in another anti-tank gun around midday. He was happy with the position; it had a good field of fire up the road, was well camouflaged, and although there was a bit of enemy shelling it was not too bad and had not stopped his preparations. But then McKay's position also came under fire from the higher ground to their rear. Somehow, at around 2.30, a DR managed to get word to McKay to 'spike' (disable) his gun and to fall back on Battalion HQ. McKay's method of doing so was more drastic than Binch's—one shell in the barrel, one in the breech, then tie a lanyard to the trigger and retire well back into a slit trench. The barrel of the gun 'split like the petals of a flower', while at the same time the whole piece flew into the air and landed in clear view of the road. As McKay and his crew prepared to leave, a group of enemy armoured cars appeared on the road in front of them and began to spray them with machine-gun fire. Cursing their bad luck and timing in destroying their gun minutes before a target appeared, they could do nothing but hug the bottom of the trench. Eventually the armoured car must have decided that they were all dead and continued on down the road. It was now about 3.30pm, and McKay and his party began to follow Binch and the others west towards Battalion HQ.

The reason for the order to McKay to retire was that by 2pm, A Company's position was also surrounded. Even before the serious fighting began, the company had become the victim of bad luck. Keith Davenport had only recently taken command when the battalion had returned to Sedjenane from Beja. During the morning, Davenport had identified some enemy activity to their front, and while trying to investigate he was wounded and evacuated to the rear. Command now devolved onto Captain John Kerly. By all accounts, Kerly was a capable, courageous and respected officer, who cared for his men but did not suffer fools gladly. One young officer who had failed to check that all his men had returned from a patrol had found himself promptly sent off on a training course, leaving Sergeant Alan Orme in command of 7 Platoon that morning, alongside lieutenants Charles Barker (8 Platoon) and Willoughby Gilliver (9 Platoon).

Kerly was familiar with the ground that the company now occupied, having performed a recce of it when the battalion had been at Green Hill—presumably as a potential fall-back line. But as an advanced position it was, in Davenport's words, 'perilously exposed', and Kerly cannot have been happy with the situation he inherited.[4] The top of the hill was bare rock, the ground difficult to dig in. There was plenty of surrounding cactus scrub which afforded some concealment, though no protection from bullets; conversely, it prevented the company's own mortars firing in support, both because they could not locate targets and for fear of hitting their own men. It also allowed the enemy to approach up the lower slopes of the hill unseen until they were in close range. The main positions were on the front slope of the hill, with the Company HQ on the reverse slope.

Alan Orme and his men were just about to brew some tea when they first spotted Germans about half a mile away and received orders to stand-to. Under a growing hail of mortar bombs and machine-gun bullets, and with hundreds of Germans advancing up the hill all around, Orme told his platoon to hold their fire until the enemy was close. Then a solitary Bren gun opened up on the right, which was taken as a signal for everyone to start shooting. The Foresters fired furiously at anything that moved, but before long their ammunition began to run low. In their forward positions there had been no time to bring up reserves of ammunition from the main line further back, and it was now impossible to do so as the Germans enveloped the hill. Unable to communicate with Company HQ to the rear due to the noise of battle, Orme crawled back to try to get more ammunition. Kerly informed him that there was none, and told him to pull his platoon back. Orme set off to do so, but as he got nearer the platoon he heard German voices. They had infiltrated the Foresters' positions, and with A Company spread so thinly they were able to outflank and surround platoons, sections and even individual trenches. The experience of Dunkirk veteran Fred Jeffery that day was typical. He was manning a forward position when he spotted a few Germans to his left and gave them two bursts from his tommy gun. At that point an Unteroffizier (NCO) and a Feldwebel (CSM) appeared behind him from the right. Fred thought his time had come, but they stood him up and one covered him with his rifle while the other took away his weapons and kit.

Most of A Company had now been overrun and taken prisoner like Jeffery. Orme once more crawled back over the hill to the Company HQ, where Kerly was still determined not to give up the position. Although there were barely a dozen men with him, he declared, 'We'll soon get them off our hill.' He then gave the order 'Fix bayonets' and led the charge up the rocky slope, armed with nothing but a revolver. Like other survivors of that day, Orme felt no sense of fear at the time, though later admitted that 'when thinking about it I get a shiver through my body'.[5] Caught in the open, the Germans fired a few shots then turned and ran back into the shallow slit trenches that the Foresters had previously occupied. Then their machine guns opened fire again from only a few yards away. Kerly, who was not wearing a helmet, was shot through the forehead and killed instantly. For a brief few minutes the Foresters' counterattack held the top of the hill, but now they were the ones in the open on the rocky ground, and it was untenable in the face of enemy mortar and machine-gun fire. Willoughby Gilliver, the only officer left in the tiny group, gave the order to retire back into the cactus, which would at least obscure them from sight and perhaps allow the opportunity to escape as night fell.

While the Barenthin Regiment was surrounding and eliminating A Company, no assistance could be given from the rest of the battalion because a separate German attack by *Kampfgruppe Jefna* was outflanking the main position from the north. B Company had arrived in these positions during the night, and like Kerly's men had found that the rocky hilltops made it hard to dig in. On the extreme left flank was Denys Crews' 11 Platoon, spread out with a good field of fire over the flat plain to the east towards Green Hill. But Crews had no idea where Roger Newton's Company HQ was located, or even where Richard Garrett was with 10 Platoon to his right. Aside from the sounds of gunfire to the north-west, where the DLI were attacking, the morning had passed without incident. At around midday, the men were stood down to have lunch, when a large number of Germans were seen emerging from some trees about 700–1,000 yards away in open order. Crews shouted 'Stand-to', and mugs of tea and tins of meat stew were discarded as the men took up positions in the rocky ground. Like Orme, Crews told his men to wait until the enemy were close before opening fire. Although this was the first time that they had been in close action with the enemy, the fire discipline of the platoon seems to have been reasonably good. According to Willis Dixon, many of the less experienced young British lads wanted to fire at around 500 yards, but they held on, waiting silently as the tension mounted. After what seemed an age, and with the Germans beginning to approach the cover of some thick trees and scrub at the foot of the Foresters' hill, Crews finally gave the order to open fire. The range was somewhere between 200 and 400 yards. Dixon, whose position was on the right of the platoon where the terrain was more open, still felt that the decision was premature, a view shared by Fred Hirst, though Denys Crews thought that it made little difference to the outcome of the day. As on the A Company hill, all hell broke loose, with rifle and machine-gun fire coming from all directions. The initial German attack was stopped; the grey-clad figures disappeared and seemed to be working their way round through the wooded area to the left. As the fight went on, however, Crews and his men also found that the firing to their right began to intensify and they were becoming surrounded. It appears that the Germans had used a gully to infiltrate between Crews' and Garrett's platoons. Gerald Summers later recorded how Garrett's men held off the enemy's attack, but with heavy casualties. Summers engaged a German light machine gun section before being wounded in the right shoulder. Garrett, Sergeant Fred Coxon and Lieutenant Charles Morris, who was 2iC of the company, managed to make their way over to him and bandage his wound, and told him to report to Battalion HQ and the regimental aid post (RAP).

C Company further south also came under attack. Here, the ground in front was more open, and rather than holding their fire until the enemy was close, the British engaged them with long-range Bren-gun fire. The Foresters' positions were then heavily mortared. Sergeant Maurice Enser commanded twenty men in 14 Platoon on the forward slope overlooking the road, to the right of the company position. Enser could not see the rest of the company, nor many other troops of the battalion. Private Paxton of his platoon was killed and Private Neild wounded. Then the fighting got closer and more casualties were incurred from grenades. Harold Lambert, who had the 2-inch mortar, was killed and a Private Cooper had his foot blown off. Further up the hill, 15 Platoon was overrun and the platoon sergeant wounded, but despite this, C Company was able to hold its positions until dusk.

Away on the right with D Company, Eric Morral was also experiencing his first contact with the enemy. He and another sniper named Macpherson had taken up a position behind a low stone wall to the south of the road when they saw the enemy. Morral fired and missed, but this enabled Macpherson to determine the range. As a bunch of Germans crossed the road, they employed a First World War sniper technique of aiming at the second soldier in line and then firing on the third. Morral did not say whether they hit them or not, but shortly after they fired at a German staff car coming down the road at a distance of about 1,000 yards, which promptly reversed out of sight behind a bend. Private Ernie Boultby, manning a Bren gun nearby, was not quite so cool in his first contact with the enemy. With a clear view of the Germans in front of him as he fired, he could not believe that they kept on coming, apparently without casualties. After raising the gun and then raising the elevation of the barrel, he still could not understand why the bullets were falling short. Later, it came to him that he had the sights set to 200 yards when the actual range was four or five times that. Doubtless he was not the only man that day who panicked a little in his first time in action, of which the more experienced German troops took full advantage.

Boultby gave the time of the first attack on D Company as 1.30pm, but it seems likely that they did not come under serious pressure until mid-afternoon, after the companies to the left of the road had been partly overrun. This is inferred by the account of signaller George Price, who was attached to the company and recalled everything being quiet until suddenly 'all hell was let loose'. Price then tried to get instructions from Battalion HQ on his wireless, but only got through to fellow signaller Lance Corporal Geoff Booth, who told him that they were surrounded by Germans. Price was wounded trying to move downhill with the wireless set and eventually taken prisoner. Whatever time the attack occurred, the results were much the same as elsewhere. The positions D Company had taken over during the night had previously been held by three companies of the Lincolns, and they were once again too thinly spread out to prevent the Germans infiltrating them and taking out sections piecemeal. The only advantage they had was that they did get some support from the 3-inch mortar platoon behind Battalion HQ, which fired onto the Germans' right flank. After around two hours, the pressure from the enemy, who attacked in two lines on both flanks, became too great and they were ordered to pull back up the hill. Boultby and his number two on the Bren gun, a lad called Johnson, took up position in a wooded area under the command of Corporal Reg Roome. From here they were able to inflict some casualties, but as elsewhere they again began to run short of ammunition. Roome sent Johnson back to get more ammunition from the platoon HQ. He returned not only without any ammo, but with the news that there was no longer a platoon HQ. It had been captured, and the remains of D Company were in retreat back to Sedjenane, leaving the three men alone on the hill. The Germans were so close in the gathering darkness that their officers could clearly be heard giving out orders, but the Foresters had no ammunition left between them.

While the rifle platoons were being engaged all along the Foresters' line, Binch and Hallett were making their way back towards rest of the battalion. The road was raised above the level of the field, which gave them some concealment from the enemy, and once out of range they headed north, crossed the road, and reported to the anti-tank platoon commander, Lieutenant 'Johnny' Walker. Walker had the last of the battalion's 2-pounder guns positioned behind a hedge, covering the road, about 50–100 yards from the Battalion HQ. At around 3pm, an armoured car came up the road. Walker ordered the crew to man the gun, but either they did not move out of their trench or did so too slowly for Walker. Walker manned the gun himself; Binch grabbed a shell and rammed it in the breech, and Walker fired. The gun recoiled back into the cactus scrub and the vehicle carried on up the road. Walker took out his hip flask, took a good slug of whisky, then held it out.

'Would you like a drink, Binch?' 'No thanks, Sir', replied Wally. 'If I'm going to die, I'd rather die sober.'[6]

Two more armoured cars appeared, and this time they were better prepared. The first vehicle was about 100 yards away to their right when they hit it, and Binch could see the crew abandon the vehicle. As the second came up on the left, Binch loaded again and Walker fired: again the gun recoiled back into the cactus, and again they had scored a hit. Two kills out of three was not a bad result for their first time shooting at the enemy. The one armoured car that had got through, however, inflicted casualties on the Battalion HQ to the rear, including Private Romeo 'Dogger' White, who was killed instantly, before it continued on down the road towards Sedjenane.

Directly behind the Foresters' lines were the 25-pounder guns of 456 Light Battery RA. These were the only artillery actively supporting the Foresters at this time, firing onto the ridge to the north. According to their war diary, at 2.30pm (it must actually have been later) four enemy armoured cars came down the road, and two of the battery's four guns were manhandled into position to fire upon them. Three of them broke through, but the fourth was knocked out, with three of the crew taken prisoner. The distraction caused by the armoured cars meant that the enemy were able to push forward on the ridge to the north, and it was this movement that threatened the left flank of B Company. By 5pm, the gunners' own flank was being turned, and at 6.30pm the position became critical, with the guns firing over open sights within machine-gun range of the enemy. Having done all they could to support the beleaguered Foresters, the battery fired off its last few rounds and the gunners made their way towards Sedjenane, blowing up their guns or removing the breeches and howitzer nuts to make them inoperable. Keith Madden, a 20-year-old lieutenant with the battery, was seen to rally some retiring Foresters from 12 Platoon and lead them in a charge to cover the withdrawal of the battery. Madden, who was believed to have been taken prisoner, received the Military Cross (MC) for his actions that day. He was later declared killed in action. Amazingly, the battery lost only one other man.

Still further up road were the two batteries of 70th Field Regiment RA, which were now threatened. At least six AFVs were reported to have broken through. At around 4pm, three of these arrived at Sapper's Corner, where one of the Bofors guns of 379 Light Anti-Aircraft Battery, under Sergeant Jack Bland, was sited to protect the artillery from air attack. Two of them were moving too fast to be engaged; the third called out *Finis Kamerad* for the gunners to surrender, then opened fire. The rest of the gun crew took cover, but Bland swung the gun around and pumped seven 40mm shells into the armoured car from around 30 yards, and it burst into flames. Bland then took a sub-machine gun, and with another gunner went into the scrub to try to find any survivors from the crew. The gunner was mortally wounded, and under sniper fire the detachment were forced to destroy their gun and withdraw. Bland received a Military Medal (MM) for his actions that day. Walker and Binch were not even mentioned in dispatches; they were just doing their job.

The 5th Battalion war diary for 2 March reported that:

At 1430 hrs, 15 A.F.Vs were reported on the road followed by motorised Infantry and at 1500 hrs, 5 of these armoured cars had broken through our positions, 2 being destroyed by our Anti-Tank guns, 1 by Light Battery, 1 by the 379 A/A Battery with a Bofors Gun, and one by 279 Battery.[7]

Wally Binch, writing forty years later about his experiences that day, was adamant that only three AFVs came up the road, and that this was backed up by the recollections of other Foresters and of Lieutenant Walker in particular. The answer may be found in the 70th Field Regiment war diary. Immediately south of A Company's position, the road and railway line through the valley ran closely together. Just past their hill, the railway line took a wide bend to the south, rejoining the road again immediately to the rear of the Foresters' main position, roughly where the Battalion HQ was sited. The diary says that 'information from 456 Light Battery stated that 9 Tanks [sic] were moving *up the Railway line* [author's emphasis] and that large bodies of men were visible in numerous areas'.[8] Since movement off-road both in the waterlogged fields and on the rocky hills was almost impossible to the tanks and armoured cars then being operated by the Germans, it seems probable that they split into two; one group moving up the road and a somewhat larger group moving up the railway line to the point where it rejoined the road. Wally Binch, manning his gun on the other side of the road to the railway line, fully focussed on preventing any further AFVs from passing that way, and in the noise and smoke of the battle would have been unaware of this outflanking force. Another reason this makes sense is that the road had been mined where A Company were positioned. While reports state that the Germans cleared these, this would have delayed the German advance, and it may be that the railway line was either not mined or easier to clear. If progress down the railway line was faster, this could also explain why the attack on the Foresters' anti-tank gun seems to have happened later than that on 456 Light Battery to their rear. Moreover, Major Blaxland had set out that that afternoon to make contact with the Foresters and arrange artillery support. After rounding a bend near 449 Battery's position, he ran into an enemy AFV, which forced his car off the road. Blaxland emptied his tommy gun into the AFV, to no effect, and its return fire mortally wounded the major. Several enemy AFVs had definitely broken through, and four or five of them were knocked out, which tallies with the Foresters' diary. What happened to the others is not clear.

Blaxland's death was a major contribution to the disaster that befell the Foresters that day. Two forward observation officers (FOOs) from 279 Battery who tried to contact the battalion also went missing. The brigade's artillery resources had already been split between two fronts, and now any liaison between the rear batteries and the Foresters was lost, leaving only 456 Light Battery and the battalion's own mortar platoon to provide support. The commander of the mortar platoon, 'Dolly' Armitage, was in a forward OP using sound-ranging equipment to identify possible targets, while Sergeant George Stokes and the mortars themselves were in a gully about 100 yards from Battalion HQ. Stokes recalled that they started to fire on the advancing enemy around noon, but like the rifle platoons the mortars had no ammunition reserves, and after firing about sixty bombs apiece their ammunition was exhausted. Stokes moved his position a little closer to Battalion HQ, from where he could see both C Company on the hill and Walker and Binch where they manned the anti-tank gun on the road. With no ammunition and no more orders forthcoming, he ordered one of his men to make tea and a rice pudding! Up the hill, they could see some of C Company starting to surrender.

Battalion HQ was situated on the reverse slope of the hill. Early in the action, Lieutenant Colonel Stott decided to move forward into a slit trench on the forward slope to see what was going on. From here he had a good view of A Company's predicament, and of the enemy armoured vehicles and infantry advancing past them up the road. While demonstrating Stott's personal courage, the decision was a mistake in the opinion of Bryan Keith-Lucas because when the trenches came under enemy fire it meant that Stott effectively lost control of the battalion. There was perhaps little that the senior officers could do in any case. The initial positions had been too widely spread out to provide mutual support, and there was no company in reserve that could be used in a counterattack to help A Company or any of the others as they were surrounded and overrun in detail. Wireless communications also seem to have broken down. The battalion 2iC, Major Charles Williamson, sent for Sam Fullwood, one of the DRs, and told him that he had to get through to Brigadier Chichester-Constable back in Sedjenane to inform him of the situation. With German troops advancing on all sides, Williamson thought Fullwood's chances of getting through were slim, and did not give him a written message in case he was captured. The roads in the valley were all raised above the plain, and Sam recalled that he was 'a sitting duck, all hell broke loose, it seemed that everyone was using me for target practise'. A few hundred yards back from the HQ was a small bridge, and a German machine gun was firing along it on a fixed line. Sheltering beneath it as Fullwood sped across was a group of signallers, to whom the 'tracer bullets appeared to be going through me, and not over or round me'.⁹ He made it through and reported to the brigadier. Chichester-Constable told Fullwood that everything was under control, as armoured support was moving up. But he would not let him return, saying that it was now impossible to get back to the battalion positions. Somehow—it is not clear by what means—the message did get to the battalion to pull out back to Sedjenane.

By dusk, the 5th Foresters had been reduced to many small groups of men fighting and making their way back as best they could. A Company had almost ceased to exist. Only Gilliver, Orme and four other men remained uninjured. Lieutenant Gilliver had tried to get his party away, but as they moved along a gully, hoping to escape under cover of darkness, they chanced upon a German patrol moving up to the front, who pointed their guns at them and told them to surrender. Without a round of ammunition left, the Foresters had no choice. A similar fate befell Maurice Enser's men who were making their way back up the road to Sedjenane. Enser split the platoon into two, one under himself and the other under Corporal Jack Kidger. Enser's section was making its way through some scrub when they ran into a German patrol and 'went into the bag'. Kidger was more fortunate; his group evaded the enemy for three days until they finally met up with friendly troops.

Private Frank Lees was with the Battalion HQ when orders were given to withdraw, and with others made it to the cover of a small stream at the foot of the hill, about a foot deep, shaded by overhanging bushes. Here, they hoped to hide until dark before making their way back to British lines, but a German armed with a Schmeisser appeared and called out, 'Come out Englander or I will fire', followed by an immediate machine-gun burst. One of the group broke cover with his hands on his head, and many of the men in the HQ were taken prisoner here. When George Stokes tried to get orders from RSM Hennessy, he was told to 'Stand and fight to the last man or bullet'. Hennessy was taken prisoner, but Stokes chose to live to fight another day. After hiding the 3-inch mortars, he made his way to a river which ran alongside the road, where he found that his mortar section of eight had swollen to eighteen men. They made their way back to Sedjenane, where they bedded down for the night. Stokes had even acquired four German PoWs during his journey, possibly from the commandos, who had taken six prisoners that day.

The retirement of Denys Crews' platoon seems to have been a little more organised. Crews give his men the order to retire down the hill as the light began to fail, then rallied them at the bottom and led them through the thick woods to the road. But even Crews discovered that many of his men were missing and would later be found to have become PoWs. In the darkness, Crews fell in with other Foresters, who told him that the Battalion HQ was surrounded and that they had orders to retire on Tamera—the next mining settlement west of Sedjenane. A lucky few like Fred Hirst managed to get lifts on the artillery transport. It was Crews' twenty-ninth birthday.

Back in Sedjenane, the men in B Echelon had heard the artillery barrage preceding the DLI's counterattack, and then a gradual crescendo of rifle and artillery fire. In the afternoon, reports started to come through of the German breakthrough, which gave rise to a minor panic. Captain Hammond was forward at Battalion HQ, leaving RQMS Sydney Flude in command. Initial orders were that everyone should grab their rifles and be prepared to put up a last-ditch resistance. Then at around 4pm, the woods where the transports were stationed began to be shelled and Flude gave instructions to evacuate to another wood 5 miles to the west. The cooks had just got the petrol blowers going to prepare the evening food, and while not quite panic the resulting scene was chaotic. The lorries never usually moved during daylight, but now they were hurriedly loaded up and made off as fast as possible down the road, with backboards down and camouflage netting flapping out of the back.

There were a few attempts to set up further organised resistance, including by Stott himself, having crawled back from the exposed slit trench. He gave instructions to his senior officers that they would rendezvous on a tall hill about half a mile behind Battalion HQ. Eric Morral's party fell in with Stott and a section of HQ Company, and after learning that some German parachutists were holding a hill to the right (probably along the ridge between B Company's original position and the commandos on Hill 231), one group made a bayonet charge to clear it. They were almost wiped out by machine-gun fire. Some of the retiring Foresters joined with the men of No. 1 Commando, whose positions had come under attack at 3pm. Bert Saxby, one of the few who had managed to escape from A Company, met a group of them protecting one of the AA guns around Sapper's Corner. Although the commandos had lost one sub-section (roughly equivalent to an infantry section) to an enemy ambush earlier in the day, the rest of them had held their position throughout the afternoon, covering the Foresters' withdrawal before themselves retiring to their HQ at the mine south-west of Sedjenane. Roger Newton and around twenty men from B Company fell in with the carrier platoon of the 16th DLI, who were holding an unnamed Arab village about a mile north of Sedjenane.

The final example of resistance comes from D Company. As Ernie Boultby retreated up the hill, he passed Corporal Bill Pidgeon, one of the section leaders, firing his Bren gun at the enemy infiltrating their positions. After inflicting considerable losses on the German attackers, like all the other platoons Pidgeon's was gradually surrounded, and the platoon sergeant gave him orders to retire. While doing so, Bill was wounded in the shoulder, but continued to lead the section until he had successfully extricated his men. For his 'outstanding determination and cool leadership throughout the action', Pidgeon won the battalion's first MM.[10]

Despite the personal bravery and determination shown by Pidgeon and others, the day was without doubt the worst that the battalion experienced in its short existence. As night fell, it was almost impossible to know the full extent of the disaster, but the total losses of the day in killed, wounded and taken prisoner amounted to at least nine officers and 337 ORs.[11] This was over 50 per cent of the fighting strength of the battalion. At the time, with stragglers like Ernie Boultby's party still making their way back across country, the losses appeared even greater. Eventually fifteen men, in addition to Captain Kerly, would be identified as killed in action or dying of wounds. The number wounded is harder to assess. It appears it was only possible to evacuate two officers — Keith Davenport, whose injury occurred early in the day, and 'Dolly' Armitage, who had been spotting for the mortars near the Battalion HQ — and four other ranks, including Pidgeon. The remainder of those listed as wounded in the fighting were taken prisoner— fifteen of them, including Gerald Summers and Sergeant McCallun, the platoon sergeant of 15 Platoon. This is a very low proportion of wounded to killed in action, and almost certainly understates the number of wounded taken prisoner by the Germans. For example, Maurice Enser related that after being captured, he and three other men were allowed back to search for Private Cooper, who had lost his foot. They had just put him on a stretcher when a German ambulance travelling to the front stopped, turned around and took him to the rear along with Private Neild. But while Neild appears in the official casualty lists as a wounded PoW, Cooper's serious injury was not recorded. The German medics treated the wounded prisoners as well as their own casualties, and the worst cases were dealt with first, irrespective of nationality. Among the British prisoners was the Foresters' MO, Julius Cowen, who worked alongside the German medical staff treating casualties from both sides. The fate of many of the wounded came through information received from Reverend Paul Guinness, who along with Cowen had gone into captivity in order to tend to the wounded. That of others recorded missing, including John Kerly, would remain unknown for many months.

Even if the number of wounded was two or three times the figure officially indicated, the majority of the losses on 2 March—four officers and around 300 other ranks—were taken prisoner. This raises the question of whether the battalion had put up as good a fight as it could have. Some evidence suggests not. Although the battalion's own war diary and most of the personal accounts of the action stress that their positions were not abandoned until dusk, and the 70th Field Regiment diary says that they continued to fight to the last though completely surrounded, that of the 6th Lincolns says that a report was received at 2pm that the Foresters' positions (probably those of A Company) had been overrun—a time when the Foresters' account says that the carrier platoon was only 'partly overrun'. The anti-tank gunners near the carriers' positions were clearly taken by surprise when they found they had enemy to their rear, indicating that the platoon may have crumbled without warning. Alan Orme was also somewhat shocked to see his men surrendering when he crawled back with news from the Company HQ, and several accounts report some lack of fire discipline. It would be naïve to suggest that there were none in the battalion whose nerves went when faced with their first experience of combat. German sources state that *Kampfgruppe Jefna* took about 150 prisoners, indicating that 150 were taken by the Barenthin Regiment—roughly the whole strength of A Company and the carrier platoon. But when men are surrounded and nearly out of ammunition, as was certainly the case with the carriers and A Company, it is hard to criticise them for surrendering rather than pointlessly dying to the last man.

Like the wounded, the prisoners were mostly well treated by their captors. Sergeant Stephen Wallhead from the carrier platoon was shot while trying to escape, but this appears to be an isolated incident. A few were immediately put to work on the unpleasant task of burying the dead of both sides. The rest were assembled and marched to the rear under their own NCOs, RSM Hennessy being particularly determined to maintain discipline amongst the captives. They were questioned about where stores were to be found, especially alcohol, which seemed to be in short supply amongst the Germans. However, there was little looting of personal possessions—that would only come later, from the German rear echelon troops. The prisoners were put into a field of long tents, with no other bedding than straw on the ground, where they were given food which Hennessy dismissed as 'bloody camel meat' and refused to eat. Later, they were put on trucks to Tunis and handed over to the Italians, who by agreement with their allies were responsible for all prisoners taken in North Africa—a sensible arrangement as it freed up German manpower for the more important business of fighting. Officers were interrogated, just as a German prisoner would have been by a British intelligence officer, but there was no mistreatment. Lieutenant Richard Garrett was questioned in the town of Mateur by an immaculately dressed officer who turned out to have been a travel agent in London before the war. After Garrett offered his name, rank and serial number, the German smiled and proceeded to tell him the number of the platoon he commanded, the company, battalion and brigade to which it belonged, and even the name of Garrett's girlfriend! Garrett surmised that the Germans must have captured a British mail shipment to have acquired this level of information, but in general the Germans had always shown that they were remarkably well informed about the British units facing them. Some of this no doubt came from the local Arabs. Willoughby Gilliver remembered that after being taken prisoner, a tall Arab called out to him from a crowd of Germans, 'How do you like your *oeufs* now soldier?'

*

The morning of 3 March found what remained of the 5th Foresters west of Sedjenane, while most of the DLI had been sent back to new lines beyond Djebel Abiod. Adjutant Bryan Keith-Lucas had gathered together a group of men from Battalion HQ and retired through the hills south of Sedjenane. En route he had met up with Charles Williamson. Pushing through the undergrowth, they eventually heard voices, but did not know whether they were friend or foe. A few Anglo-Saxon expletives from a sentry confirmed that they were English. Keith-Lucas was told to report to the Brigade HQ, where he informed the brigadier of what little he knew of the situation. Here too the quartermaster sergeant of the Lincolns offered Keith-Lucas the use of his razor and a brand-new battledress. Now immaculately attired, in contrast to his bedraggled appearance only a few hours earlier, he chanced to run into Howard Marshall, a BBC reporter who was doing his daily report. Marshall was duly impressed, as he later wrote in his memoir of the campaign *Over to Tunis*:

> A little further down the road we came upon the adjutant of a Midland Battalion which had been fighting to hold a hill overlooking Sedjenane Plain. It was a fight against the odds. There could be only one end to it. The Battalion had pulled out when human courage and endurance could do no more. The adjutant had reached our lines at dawn that morning. He had been without sleep or rest for forty-eight hours. He was shaved and clean, as spruce and spick-and-span as if he were just going on to a ceremonial parade.[12]

That morning, at 10am, Chichester-Constable handed over command of 139 Brigade to Brigadier Bernard Howlett, previously commanding officer of the 6th Royal West Kents and then of 36 Brigade, and generally acknowledged to be one of the best brigadier generals to serve in Tunisia. There was not much of a brigade left to take over. The defence of Sedjenane was now in the hands of the 6th Lincolns. They were exhausted by the constant bombardments and moves of the last five days, but were at least near full strength, having only suffered around forty casualties since the Axis offensive started. They had been reinforced with four 6-pounder anti-tank guns the previous evening. Even more welcome was the armoured support that Chichester-Constable had told Sam Fullwood about, which had arrived in the form of ten Churchill tanks of C Squadron, North Irish Horse (NIH). These tanks had been designed specifically for infantry support, with a top speed of only 15mph, but they were heavily armoured and carried a 6-pounder gun as well as two machine guns. At 39 tons, they were not quite as formidable as a Tiger, but more than a match for most of the enemy armour in Tunisia. The presence of these tanks at Sedjenane helped stem the flood of the enemy's advance. In the morning, there was an attack on the Lincolns east of the village, which was held off by artillery, mortar and machine-gun fire, and the assistance of three Churchills. During the rest of the morning, the Germans probed forward from the north-east road and railway line, and succeeded in placing an infantry gun at the edge of some scrub less than 800 yards from Sedjenane. The much-depleted DLI still held the Arab village and the woods to the north, where they experienced some shelling during the afternoon. The CO of the DLI put his men under the command of the Lincolns. It was not until 4.45pm that two companies of enemy troops were seen advancing from the north, where they came under fire from tanks of the NIH stationed on the high ground west of the village. This halted the right company of the German attack, while the carrier platoon of the DLI held off the attack of the other company for two hours before both sides retired. The DLI reported Roger Newton and about twenty other Foresters supported the defence, but there are no details of whether or when they withdrew during the day to join the rest of their battalion. At about the same time as the attack developed from the north, the assault from the east against the Lincolns was resumed, but again with the support of tanks and Bren gun carriers this was driven off.

The relatively low level of German activity on the morning of 3 March is strange given the extent and success of the actions on the previous day against the Foresters. The unexpected presence of the tanks may have contributed, but it could also be that the Foresters, together with the DLI and the commandos, had inflicted significant casualties on the enemy, requiring them to regroup before assaulting Sedjenane itself. The limited German casualty records make it difficult to know, but clearly they did not feel that a quick assault on Sedjenane would succeed. For most of 3 March they restricted themselves to company-size probing attacks, while bringing up mortars, artillery, anti-tank guns and infantry guns (light, manhandled artillery pieces) to support a coordinated assault. During the day, the Lincolns lost only one killed and ten wounded, while the DLI account gives two wounded and two missing. The commandos had been withdrawn to the mine south of Sedjenane, where they prepared to defend against enemy attack from the Barenthin Regiment. They did not come under attack on the 3rd, but Ernie Boultby and the two other Foresters with him joined a group of twenty-seven commandos and fought with them the following day before retiring.

The Foresters' position on 3 March was a wood some 2 miles west of Sedjenane and north of the road. There were trenches here that had previously been dug by the DLI. The Foresters were still close enough to the enemy to come under fire, both from mortars and artillery (possibly from a troop of 15cm guns which the Germans had bought up into position behind the hills to the north). The Division von Manteuffel war diary suggests that the main enemy in this area may have been *Marsch-bataillone A30* under Witzig's command, which it says was attacking across the Cap Serrat–Sedjenane road in support of the main assault on the village. Before noon, a shell wounded both Captain Cecil Wall, the former signals officer now commanding HQ Company, and 'Spotlight' Hine, the carrier OC. George Stokes was near to where the two officers were hit and put a first aid dressing on Wall, while Sergeant Harry Rider did the same for Hine. Several eyewitnesses remembered that Hine kept on shouting out 'I won't die, I won't die', while the more seriously injured Wall remained silent. Both men were loaded onto one of the battalion's Bren gun carriers driven by Sergeant Jeff Mathers, who evacuated them back to the ADS at Tamera and from there to the MDS, which on the evening of 2 March had relocated by rail to the port of Tabarka on the coast. Hine did survive, although he was critically ill for many days. Wall died of his wounds five days later. The battalion war diary states that there were others wounded in the ranks that day, and total casualties were similar to those suffered by the Lincolns and DLI who were the subject of direct attacks. By the evening, the battalion had pulled out. Fred Hirst recalled that as they did so, they passed Lieutenant Colonel Stott, leaning on his walking stick, who called out, 'Well done boys, and keep going.'

The attack on Sedjenane continued through the night—a relatively rare tactic for the Germans, possibly indicating that the troops involved were the veteran paratroopers rather than the inexperienced field battalions. By 5am, they had taken possession of the slag heap from the mine and a gantry which meant that they could overlook the British positions. A counterattack at first light by the Lincolns supported by tanks was unable to dislodge them. As another Churchill was knocked out and snipers began to take their toll of the infantry, 139 Brigade HQ gave the Lincolns' commander permission to withdraw, so critical was the situation that he took the risk of evacuating the village during the afternoon rather than waiting until dark. Over the three days, the Lincolns had suffered casualties of eleven officers and 154 ORs killed, wounded or missing. German casualties are again not known, but they must have been significant. The Division von Manteuffel's orders for 5 March refer to 'eight days of hard fighting and heavy losses' over bad terrain and in appalling weather. Although they had captured over 1,000 prisoners, Manteuffel also recognised that they had faced 'a determined and stubborn enemy ... the division has decided to go into a defensive role to consolidate the position it has won'.[13]

9

Graduation: Tunisia, March–May 1943

The resistance put up by the Foresters and the rest of 139 Brigade at Sedjenane, like other rearguard actions during Oxhead, bought the British time to rush reinforcements to the threatened portion of the front. The first of these was the 2nd Battalion Coldstream Guards, who took up position on 4 March west of Sedjenane and covered the withdrawal of 139 Brigade. The Foresters reorganised behind the guardsmen at the next stop along the railway, Tamera station, and then pulled back to Djebel Abiod with the DLI. Between 6 and 7 March, the single battalion of Guards was relieved by the three battalions of 1 Parachute Brigade under Brigadier Edwin Flavell, to which the battered 2/5th Leicesters had also been attached. Their arrival was just in time, as on the following day the enemy resumed their advance towards Djebel Abiod with an attack involving elements of at least four battalions. By 10 March, with fresh enemy troops from I/47th Infantry Regiment and III/756th Mountain Regiment now identified as being engaged, Flavell decided to go to 46th Division HQ in person to explain the seriousness of the situation. All the parachute battalions were below strength, as were the Leicesters. Furthermore, the remains of the French CFA were, by the admission of their own commander, not in much state to offer further resistance, and the enemy had begun to infiltrate the British positions. They had also succeeded in placing OPs on a substantial formation of hills to the east of the settlement called the Djebel Bel March. These overlooked both the British infantry on the lower slopes—which earned the unenviable nickname of Death Ridge—and artillery positions further down the valley. The slightest movement in the British lines could bring down a barrage of German shells.

As a result of his visit, Flavell was placed in command of the whole sector, with all the units of 139 Brigade under his orders. Heavy rain on 11 and 12 March resulted in a lull in the fighting, but the situation remained serious. On 12 March, Lieutenant General Charles Allfrey, commander of V Corps, visited 1 Parachute Brigade HQ. Allfrey and Flavell decided that it was necessary to clear the enemy positions on Djebel Bel March the following day, and that the 5th Foresters would be used to do this, supported by the 1st Parachute Battalion. The Foresters would come under the direct command of 1 Parachute Brigade for the attack. At 8pm, Stott and Lieutenant Colonel Alistair Pearson, commander of 1st Parachute Battalion, arrived at the Brigade HQ to discuss the plan of attack. No written order for the operation appears in the battalion or brigade war diaries, indicating that given the short notice only verbal orders were issued to the units participating. Nobody knew how strong the enemy were.

*

Since 4 March, the Foresters had been in a reserve position around the town of Djebel Abiod, 8 miles south, together with about 200 French troops of the CFA, where they had re-formed into companies and received reinforcements. Some were men who had arrived on the *Derbyshire* but had been left behind in Algiers as first reinforcements. Others had been sent out later from the UK—at least one of these, Private Len Major, was only 17. These were not enough to make good the losses, so other reinforcements were provided from the Norfolk Regiment, the Royal West Kents and the Buffs. By 13 March, the battalion numbered twenty-eight officers and 650 men, not far from establishment strength. But this concealed the fact that many of these men had not fought or even served together before. A Company suffered the most from this. It had mustered a mere eleven men when it began re-forming at Djebel Abiod, so only the other three rifle companies would participate in the attack. While the Foresters were to attack from the south-west, two companies of 3rd Parachute Battalion, which had been attached to the 1st Battalion, would carry out a diversion against a feature called Commando Hill further north. Meanwhile, 279 Battery was assigned to support the Foresters, but with a secondary role of aiding the Paras' diversionary attack. This was a very weak allocation of artillery to a battalion-scale assault. The Foresters were also assigned an OP from 449 Battery, but that unit's main role remained to provide defensive support to the 2/5th Leicesters. Although 1 Parachute Brigade had two troops of C Squadron, North Irish Horse under command, no armoured support was allocated because the slopes of the djebel were too steep and wooded for tanks.

Confusion seems to have reigned from the very start of the operation. Allfrey and Flavell's original intent was for the Foresters to make the main assault. This is clear from the war diary of 1 Parachute Brigade, supported by that of 70th Field Regiment, which contains instructions dated 12 March stating that they were informed that '2/5 [sic] SF would move up during the night and in the early hours of the morning will attack the high ground D[jebel] B[el] M[arch] area ... with the intention of seizing and holding this feature'.[1] There are further discrepancies across different diaries as to exactly where on the massif the enemy positions, and therefore the Foresters' objectives, were. Not knowing the enemy's location or strength was asking for trouble. Compounding the problem was the impression conveyed to the men of the Foresters that it was the paratroopers who were the assaulting troops, and that their role was along the lines of a 'mopping-up' operation, with an expectation of limited opposition. The Paras duly attacked and carried Commando Hill on schedule at 9am, but with just a single company rather than the two originally planned. The 5th Foresters had arrived only five hours previously, having travelled overnight from Djebel Abiod, and were lying up in an area between Tamera station and the paratroopers' positions. They only began to move forward towards their start line at 10am, in line with the idea that this was a mopping-up operation. At this point, the last fatal weaknesses in the plan and preparations for the attack appeared. The djebel was not a single hill but a series of connected peaks and ravines, covered with heavy scrub and thick cork forest. Having only arrived that morning, the assaulting troops had no time to familiarise themselves with the details of the terrain. The only way to transport heavy equipment up the mountain was by mule. George Stokes had loaded his six mortars and their ammunition on to a dozen mules that morning, but after trying for over an hour to get the beasts to move forward up the steep slope, the mules bolted, leaving him with only a single mortar. Four mules had also been provided to carry the heavy radio sets for the two artillery FOOs, and in view of subsequent events it seems likely that they too were unable to climb the hill. The infantry went forward, with B Company on the left, C Company on the right and D Company following up as a reserve. They struggled up the steep slopes, sometimes having to pull themselves up using the roots and branches of the thick vegetation, until eventually they arrived at a slightly more level piece of ground where the exhausted men briefly halted to catch their breath and form up. Then the British artillery opened up.

It was standard practice for infantry to advance behind a creeping barrage, a technique perfected in the First World War. A wall of artillery shells was put down in front of the advancing infantry, and its placement slowly moved forward as the infantry advanced, forcing the enemy to stay in their dugouts and trenches rather than firing on the attacking troops. The closer that the infantry could keep to the barrage, the less time there was for the enemy to man his machine guns when it passed over. But it could also be dangerous. Fred Hirst in 10 Platoon saw one of the first shells land about 30 yards in front of them. The next two landed directly on their position. There was a shout by someone to stop firing—possibly one of the artillery observers, though this is not certain, given the problems they must have had bringing forward their radio sets—and further disaster was only prevented by the NCOs in the platoons, who got the men to move back down the slope. Three shells also landed amongst 11 Platoon, where Willis Dixon counted thirteen casualties. George Stokes reckoned that there were six dead and about twice as many wounded around his position, for which he organised stretcher parties. When they ran out of stretchers, gas capes were used to carry the wounded. A young soldier named Bennett, with his right trouser leg torn off, thought that he had soiled himself through fright. Stokes gave him a cigarette and then examined him: the top of his right buttock had been sliced off by shrapnel. C Company did not escape either, their wounded including 20-year-old Dennis Upchurch. Like Bennett, he was stretchered down the hill but would die a few days later.

The incident delayed but did not stop the advance. The 1st Parachute Battalion war diary says that at noon the Foresters were observed on a hill called Sala, about a mile south of Commando Hill and one of their assigned objectives. But 1 Parachute Brigade's dairy states that, lost in the scrub, the Foresters went up Commando Hill rather than leaving it to their left. It seems possible that B Company on the left strayed across Commando Hill, while C Company took the intended route up Sala. This diversion of routes, plus the difficulty of scaling the precipitous slopes, would explain why it was not until 2pm that the battalion was finally organised on the start line and 3.30pm before the attack on the summit began. Down on Commando Hill, the paratroopers heard the rattle of the Foresters' Bren guns as they approached the top of the djebel. After a tremendous final volley of gunfire, there was a load burst of cheering. This was taken to mean that the Foresters had taken the hill—after all, there were not supposed to be any Germans there.

In fact, the Djebel Bel March was held by a fresh enemy battalion, later identified as the newly arrived I/69th Panzer Grenadier Regiment (PGR). They held their fire until the last minute and then opened up with devastating mortar and machine-gun fire and hand grenades. A few of the Foresters did get close enough to lob grenades back, and Lieutenant 'Bobby' Case led 13 Platoon of C Company in a bayonet charge that temporarily took some enemy machine-gun positions. But outnumbered, surprised and caught in a crossfire, the Foresters' assault could not possibly succeed. As usual, the Germans first held the British advance and then put in a counterattack from the reverse slopes, which drove the exhausted Foresters back from those positions they had captured. It was the panzer grenadiers' shouts of success that the Paras had heard. Lieutenant Sydney Stansfield, who had just rejoined the battalion from Algiers two days earlier, tried to rally the men in C Company, but to no avail. In B Company, Roger Newton, who had earlier been wounded in the stomach, shouted orders to withdraw above the clatter of machine-gun fire. Willis Dixon, whose corporal had been wounded in the head and had told him to take over the section, had just ordered a local counterattack of their own and was incredulous—'What, and have to do it all again tomorrow?' But while Dixon's reaction may be understandable, withdrawal was essential and saved B Company from even worse disaster. Sergeant Stan Knight timed the withdrawal at 4.30pm, while George Stokes, finding himself alone with his solitary mortar, decided to pull out at 5pm. By 6pm, both the Foresters and the Paras had been forced to retire to their starting positions. Brigadier Flavell met with Stott and the two parachute battalion commanders at the Foresters' HQ, and it was agreed that the Foresters would remain in the area to guard the road north. D Company, who had not suffered heavily in the attack, were attached as a reserve to the 3rd Parachute Battalion, which took over the front line.

There were no witnesses to the fate of Lieutenant Wilfred Stuart Jackson, the officer who Fred Hirst thought looked as though he would have been happier behind a desk, who had been leading 11 Platoon. Denys Crews was still on the battalion's list of officers on 13 March, but he had orders to report to the 18th Army Group Battle School, where his experience both from the OCTU and the front line would be put to use training American officers new to the theatre. Jackson had replaced him, and in his short time had done his best to keep up morale and look after the physical wellbeing of Hirst and others. Jackson could probably have kept a safe desk job back in the UK, but had volunteered to serve overseas, perhaps because while he had enjoyed temporary promotions in England they had not resulted in a change to his substantive rank. When the roll call was made back in Tamera that night, the 35-year-old father of two from Sherwood, Nottinghamshire, was the only officer missing. His body was never found, and it was over a year later that he was finally declared to be believed killed in action by the army authorities. His widow Elsie refused to accept his death for many years after that.[2]

Also missing after the attack, but with a happier outcome to their story, were Lance Corporal Stan Corby and one of the Bren gunners from C Company, Private Tommy Kingdon, who had been shot in the ankle and could not walk. As the rest of the company retreated, they had found themselves surrounded by the Germans. Not willing to surrender, they made their way slowly down the steep hillside on hands and knees, with Stan dragging or pushing Tommy through the undergrowth of cactus bushes. They were fired at sporadically by the Germans, and once were nearly hit by their own artillery again. Eventually, after two days, they found an old farmhouse, where they spent the night. The following morning, 16 March, Stan went on alone to find the British lines. He walked right into his own company, who told him it was a good thing that he had not arrived the previous night as they had orders to fire on anything that moved. Kingdon was taken to the RAP, where the new MO, Captain McKerrigan, saw to his wounds. He was then evacuated by ambulance, while Corby rejoined the platoon.

The 46th Division war diary for 14 March 1943 contained the entry: 'Yesterday's attack by 2/5 [sic] For[ester]s NOT completely successful & they withdrew to former positions.'[3] Written some miles away in Beja, this was something of an understatement. The action of 13 March was the first time that the battalion had undertaken a major attack, and it had suffered heavily. As well as Jackson, twenty-three other men had been killed and two more would die of wounds at the MDS in Tabarka over the next two days, nearly twice as many deaths as on 2 March. Roger Newton and at least thirty-one others were wounded. A further seven men, two of them wounded, were taken prisoner on the hill.[4]

The Foresters' war diary was in no doubt that the attack failed because of insufficient preparation: particularly the lack of intelligence about the enemy, the failure of the artillery support and the difficult terrain limiting the supply of mortar ammunition. No blame seemed to attach itself to Lieutenant Colonel Stott for the defeats at either Sedjenane or Tamera. On 14 March, Brigadier Howlett went back to 36 Brigade and Stott was put in charge of 139 Brigade—although this was for now largely an administrative post, as operational command of the units in the front line remained with Flavell and 1 Parachute Brigade. Major Eric Alfred Hefford, previously 2iC of the 6th Lincolns, took over the 5th Foresters. Aged 29, Hefford was much younger than Stott and one of the new generation of officers now being appointed to senior regimental commands. He had been commissioned into the Lincolns in 1935 and served with them in the pre-war regular army in Palestine, and was wounded in the leg during the retreat to Dunkirk. He was a firm disciplinarian—there is a story that Montgomery dismissed him as adjutant for being over-zealous—and a good soldier. The new CO addressed the battalion and likened them to a boxer who had lost two or three rounds but would win the next. The battalion's morale had suffered from a second heavy defeat within a fortnight. Meanwhile, a truce had been agreed with the Germans to allow the dead left on the hill to be collected and buried, but Fred Hirst, badly shaken by the friendly-fire incident, could not bring himself to volunteer. Others did form a party to carry out the unpleasant task, and within a few days Hirst found his spirits were back to normal and that the experience had even hardened him somewhat.

*

Another period of atrocious weather stopped serious fighting for a few days, but the Allied positions in the Tamera area were becoming perilously exposed. The Foresters were ordered to send another company up to support 3rd Parachute Battalion. In pouring rain on 15 March, the newly re-formed A Company moved forward, and then the next day the rest of the battalion relieved the Paras. The 1st and 3rd Parachute Battalions, which had been in near constant action for a fortnight, were then withdrawn south of Djebel Abiod to rest. This left five understrength battalions of Allied troops facing perhaps eight enemy battalions, albeit similarly understrength. To the north of the Sedjenane-Djebel Abiod road was a battalion of the French CFA, bolstered by two troops of British commandos, holding a hill called Djebel Aziz. Facing off against these troops were Witzig's paratrooper engineers, possibly with a platoon of motorised infantry attached. Further to the north were the Italian Bersaglieri, though nothing had been heard or seen of them for over a week. The road itself was blocked by A Company of the 5th Foresters, with the Battalion HQ in a small farmhouse nearby, while B, C and D companies held the trenches on the lower slopes of the Djebel Bel March massif previously occupied by the British paratroopers. Opposite them were I/69th PGR. E Company of the DLI was about a mile-and-a-half to the rear of these forward positions at Tamera station and placed under command of the Foresters to provide defence in depth. Not far from the station, west of the road, was the 2/5th Leicesters' HQ. Like the Foresters after Sedjenane, the

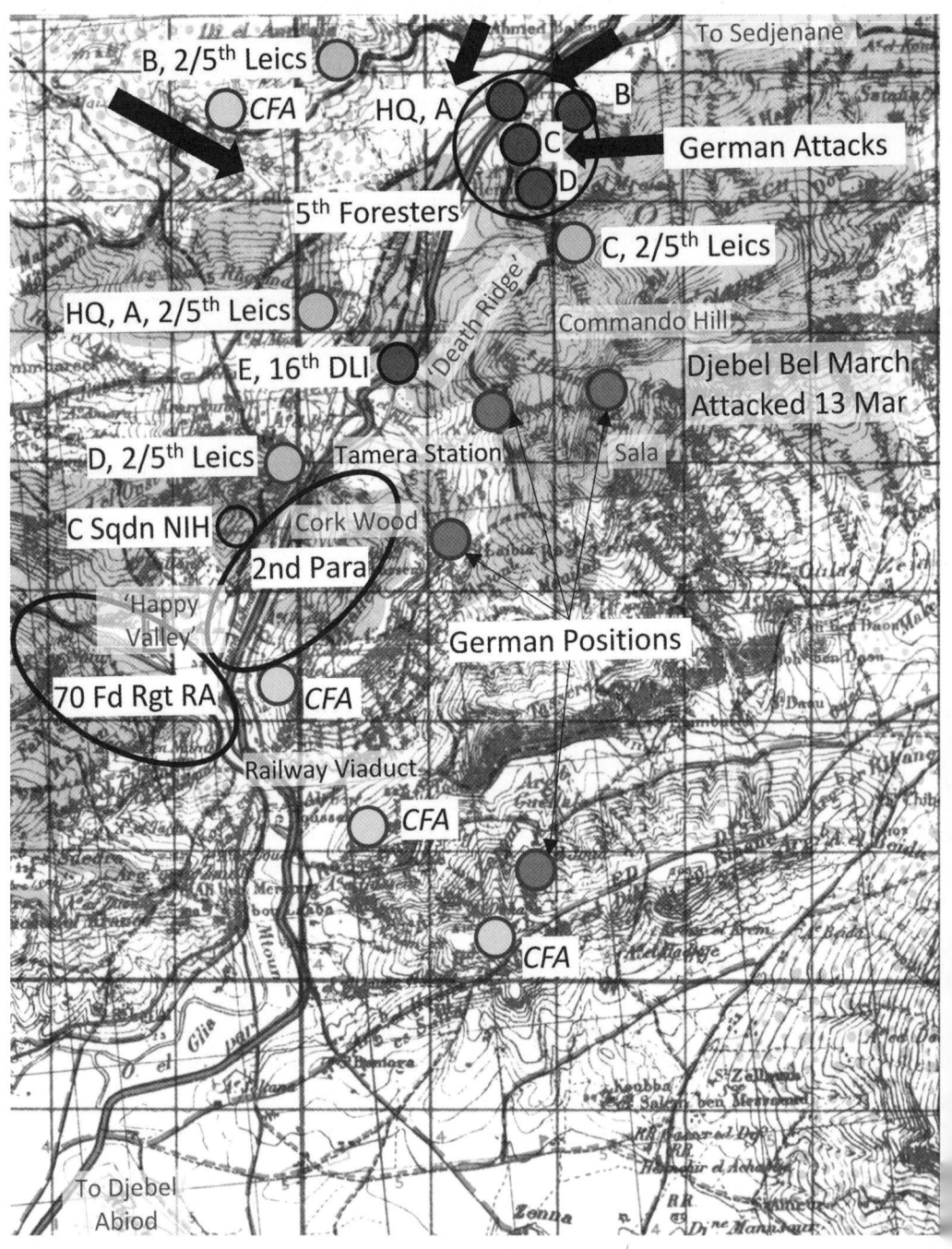

Tamera, 17 March 1943.

Leicesters had received reinforcements, which had bought them up to a strength of twenty-six officers and about 500 ORs. Their rifle companies were widely separated though: one company was north-west of the Foresters, linking their positions with the French, a second company was on the Foresters' right and a third in reserve south of Tamera. The 2nd Parachute Battalion held a ridge of high ground east of the road and about 3 miles south of the Foresters' position, where it was opposed by the T3 Field Battalion. They were protecting the forward artillery positions, which contained 279 and 449 field batteries, 457 Light Battery and 229 Anti-Tank Battery. A second CFA battalion extended the protection for this gun line to the south-east, along a line of hills into which the T4 Field Battalion had been infiltrating. The medium guns and a further field battery were another 3 miles south at Djebel Abiod, together with the Lincolns and the DLI. A single troop of the NIH just south of Tamera provided some armour support.

At around 6.30am on 17 March, heavy shelling and mortaring of D Company's positions began. This included bombardments from a new German weapon, the six-barrelled *Nebelwerfer* mortar, which would become known to the troops as the 'Moaning Minnie' due to the peculiar sound of its bombs as they fell. As well as attacks on the front line, the artillery positions in the rear and those of 2nd Parachute Battalion nearby were not only shelled but between 8.10 and 8.30am also came under air attack from Stuka dive-bombers. These air attacks continued during the day, indicating that the enemy was making a major effort, but requests by 1 Parachute Brigade for its own air support were denied. The casualties that morning included one of the battalion's most experienced officers, Captain Frank Holbrook, who was killed by a mortar bomb only a few minutes after leaving the Battalion HQ. The effect of the bombardment on morale was mixed. Those new to the battalion—and these constituted about half of the men under fire—were unnerved by its intensity. In contrast, the older hands who had been under fire in the trenches before Sedjenane were relatively sanguine about it, able to tell from the sounds of the explosions whether or not they were being targeted directly. One of Stan Corby's gripes was having to eat cold soya sausage-links out of the compo rations for breakfast, since it was impossible to bring food up to the exposed front-line positions. They were also short on rations in 11 Platoon, then the ration corporal appeared and told Fred Hirst's section leader to send two men back 50 yards to the nearest ration dump to pick up supplies. When the section leader asked for volunteers, none of the new men put their hands up, so Hirst and another 'veteran' volunteered. They went back and found the supply dump, but no corporal. They gathered as much food as they could and began to make their way back to the section. Then the bombardment stopped and they heard small-arms fire.

It must have been sometime about 9.30am when Hirst and his mate picked up the supplies. At 9am, the French in the north had reported that they were being heavily attacked, and half an hour later this had extended to involve B Company of the 2/5th Leicesters to the 5th Foresters' left rear. Brigade HQ decided that the only way to restore the situation was to counterattack towards the Djebel Aziz and allocated 1st Parachute Battalion to do this, but it was too far south to be immediately available. A single company was rushed to the front to replace the Leicesters, who were meanwhile ordered to counterattack alone. Scarcely had this decision been made than the Foresters reported that B Company, occupying the lower slopes of the hill closest to the road, was under attack; then at 10.20am that the enemy were also passing along the ridge to their rear held by the Leicesters. The enemy started to infiltrate between B Company and C Company to its immediate right, through the thickly wooded terrain. Fred Hirst, trying to make his way back to his section with their rations, found himself on his own with machine-pistol and rifle bullets crackling overhead and German voices in the shrub calling on the British to surrender. Hirst crouched down low in a trench. Then there was a lull in the fighting and he decided to peek out. A few yards away were three soldiers in desert uniforms, who pointed their weapons at him and delivered a line straight out of a classic war movie—'Hands up Tommy. For you the war is over!' B Company was getting overrun, and the situation was starting to look like Sedjenane, with the Foresters being surrounded and defeated in detail.

There were some differences, however. Unlike on 2 March, the Foresters' positions, though somewhat exposed with regards to support from the rest of the brigade, were close enough to allow support between companies. Stan Corby's platoon in C Company was one of those that counterattacked that morning, crossing a patch of open ground under machine-gun fire and then climbing up a small but steep hill to their front and pushing the enemy back. About half-a-dozen men reached the summit, from where Corby could see panzer grenadiers debussing from vehicles on the road below. With so few men, they could not hope to hold the hill for long, so the lieutenant in charge decided to fall back. Nevertheless, the Foresters' counterattack had driven off the enemy, and by midday Hefford was able to report back to brigade that they had held the attack. They had even taken thirteen prisoners of their own. Private Joe Barnes, also serving in C Company, remembered one big blond grenadier arrogantly telling them as he was taken into captivity, 'I won't be here long'.

The German had some reason to be confident. While the Foresters had held the initial attack, the Leicesters on each flank were coming under pressure as the panzer grenadiers worked their way through the undergrowth and around their flanks. The company of paratroopers that had come forward had to be used to deal with this. Neither the Leicesters' own counterattack nor another by the French to the north had succeeded, and at around 4pm the enemy began to mass troops slightly to the north of the Foresters' positions around a small mosque. Artillery fire was called down to break up the concentration, but the pressure continued to build, with constant shelling and the gradual withdrawal of troops each side of the Foresters. One of the key elements holding the battalion together in this situation was the coolness displayed by several of the senior sergeants. George Stokes and his mortars kept up a constant fire on the enemy, even though under mortar attack themselves. Stokes fired 300 rounds from his mortar alone in support of the Leicesters, and the platoon's fire also destroyed three German infantry guns that had been brought forward to give close support to the panzer grenadiers. When not directing the mortars, Stokes assisted with the wounded, as he had on previous occasions, including Fred Hutt. For 'coolness, cheerfulness and devotion to duty' that day, Stokes was awarded the MM.[5] Reg Markham, temporarily the CSM for C Company as well as its CQMS, manned a Bren gun at Tamera. The battalion officers were also leading by example. Hefford himself visited the forward slit trenches to encourage the troops to hold on. Others singled out were Lieutenant Morris, who tended to Fred Hutt along with Stokes and was later seen to be suffering from shock, and Bob Berkeley-Schultz and Keith Cowie, described by Steve Loach as 'two very tenacious and gallant officers'.[6] But the most exceptional example of leadership was Captain Philip Palmer of A Company, which on 17 March consisted largely of reinforcements from many different regiments who had only joined the battalion in the last four days. Conscious of their potentially brittle morale, Palmer tirelessly went around his platoon positions under heavy mortar fire, encouraging the new men. Twice the position was attacked, and twice Palmer organised a successful counterattack. He was awarded the MC.

The resistance could not last indefinitely. By dusk, the French had been forced back and the Foresters' positions were being infiltrated everywhere and surrounded on two sides, completely overlooked from the high ground both to the east and west. The weather added to their discomfort once again, with a heavy thunderstorm that bought torrential rain and hail—but no respite from the enemy, who continued to attack throughout and even managed to call in an attack by Stukas. At 6.30pm, Hefford told brigade that due to increasing casualties they could not hold out much longer. Fifteen minutes later, radio communications went dead, probably due to the weather conditions, and a message was sent by runner asking permission to withdraw. A counterattack by E Company of the DLI was also attempted, but officers from that company who went forward to try to get orders found the enemy between their own positions in Tamara and the Foresters. Meanwhile, the 5th Foresters were ordered to pull back into a smaller perimeter around the Battalion HQ. Here, the men took up positions in the farm outbuildings and livestock pens and mostly tried to keep their heads down under the steady machine-gun, sniper and mortar fire, returning fire when they could. Nightfall brought the occasional lull, in which some of the exhausted men found it difficult not to fall asleep. In the darkness they could hear German trucks being bought forward in expectation of bagging most of the battalion as prisoners. The Foresters had other ideas and withdrew during the night to a position west of Tamera. At least one heavily laden Bren-gun carrier made a dash down the road, but most of the men made their way out on foot. George Stokes left shortly after midnight under a full moon, while others like Stan Corby waited until near dawn when the moon had set. Several wounded men had to be left behind in a cow shed. Reluctantly, the Foresters also had to abandon their prisoners. The big blond panzer grenadier had been proven right.

*

Corporal Les Fletcher had just joined the mortar platoon, and as they retired they passed some men of 2nd Parachute Battalion, who had been posted as guides to direct them back to their re-forming area. 'They weren't very pleased with us, as they had held the Jerries, and then after all those hours we had let them through.'[7] The Parachute Regiment proudly and rightfully records Tamera as a battle honour, as 1 Parachute Brigade was the mainstay of the defence. But more than half the infantry that fought at Tamera, not to mention the artillery and tank crews, were not paratroopers but men from ordinary territorial battalions, who fought hard and suffered equally. The Foresters' casualty toll in the defence of Tamera on 17 March was similar to that in the attack four days earlier, with around seventy killed, wounded and missing. Among the officers, Frank Holbrook had been killed and Bobby Case wounded. Nine other ranks had died in action, and there were at least thirty-eight wounded, three of whom would later die of their wounds. During the withdrawal there were twenty-five officers and men taken prisoner, including nine wounded, amongst which Keith Cowie and three privates would die of their injuries within a few days. The cumulative losses at Sedjenane and then Tamera had left the battalion critically short of experienced junior officers and NCOs, in no state to participate in the new defence line that was being hastily formed south of Tamera. It was ordered to retire further to the transport lines south-east of Djebel Abiod to concentrate. Here, on 20 March, it counted twenty officers and 483 men.

Before following the 5th Foresters south, it is appropriate to briefly finish the story of the British operations around Sedjenane. Operation Disembarkation had pushed the Allied troops back a distance of 20 miles, but now the logic of North Africa operations reasserted itself in microcosm. The British had withdrawn towards their supply bases and were working on internal lines of communication, allowing them to switch their limited reserves to where they were most needed. By contrast, the German supply lines were extending, and each extra mile stretched their limited motor transport resources. Fighting along the valleys, with steep trackless ranges of hills separating their columns, they could not easily switch their focus of attack. While 1 Parachute Brigade, 139 Brigade and their French allies had suffered significantly, Manteuffel's division had also taken severe losses, estimated as at least 2,000 men—German PoWs indicated that *Marsch-Bataillone A30* had been disbanded to fill the depleted ranks of other units. The growing strength of Allied air and sea power meant that Axis reinforcements from Italy had all but stopped, whereas Allied numbers in Tunisia continued to increase. The last line of defence north of Djebel Abiod held firm, and Von Arnim's offensive failed even in its limited objective of delaying a spring offensive by the Allies. Shortly after the Foresters were pulled out, 46th Division issued orders on 25 March for a counter-offensive to retake Sedjenane. This was undertaken by 1 Parachute Brigade, 138 Brigade and 36 Brigade from 78th Division, supported again by the North Irish Horse, and began on 26 March. These fresh forces were too strong for Manteuffel's exhausted battalions, and by 4 April the British were back in possession of the ground the Foresters had given up on 2 March. However, a patrol from 3rd Parachute Battalion reported that Green Hill was still held by the enemy, and the advance went no further. On 15 April, they handed over responsibility for the sector to the US 9th Infantry Division, part of a general reorganisation of the Allied dispositions in which 46th Division was replaced by the entire US II Corps—further indication of the growing Allied superiority in numbers and material.

Meanwhile, the 5th Foresters had temporarily been placed under the command of 1st Division in the Beja area. There were a few spells in the front line, but mostly the battalion spent the next three weeks, from 26 March until 14 April, carrying out training. In part this was to redress deficiencies found and assimilate lessons learnt in the actions of the previous month. One particular cause of the recent defeats was the tendency of most troops, not just the Foresters at Sedjenane and Tamera, to sit in static positions in defence. This allowed the Germans to move round and surround them using their infiltration tactics, and contrasted with the more fluid and flexible defensive tactics of the British paratroopers, who went out to meet the enemy with aggressive counterattacks. Another key new tactical element of the training was cooperation with tanks, as the battalion was to form part of a mixed-arms counterattacking force. Basic physical training was introduced to harden the men's feet and improve their stamina in the difficult terrain. But the main objective was to integrate the many different groups of reinforcements that had joined the battalion since Sedjenane.

During March, the unit had suffered around 500 casualties, equivalent to the entire strength of its four rifle companies, and the men who had trained together in England and arrived in Tunisia in January were now in a minority. Those who had been held back in Algiers as first reinforcements perhaps integrated easily. Then there were ninety men who had come from the Buffs, and a similar number from the Norfolks and other regiments. These had been rushed into the battle on 17 March after only a few days in the battalion, without the time to get to know their officers, NCOs and comrades in arms. Finally, there was a further intake to replace the losses taken at Tamera, which must have numbered over 150 men. Some of these came from a group of about sixty Foresters who had served in the 70th Battalion and arrived at Tamera just after the battle there. Half of these were posted to the 5th Foresters, including Frank Mardell, who had left England on 5 January 1943, exactly one year from the day he volunteered. The rest were assigned to the 6th Lincolns. It seems possible that others were drafted from rear echelon troops, as there is an observation in the war diary that many of them were very badly trained, some not knowing basic skills such as how to fire a Bren gun. With only half the establishment number of junior officers available, and a similar proportion of sergeants and corporals, training and integration was both essential and prolonged. Another deficiency was in trained medical staff. After Tamera, the medical section had been reduced to Captain McKerrigan and his batman. Recruits had to be found from elsewhere in the unit, and one of the few with any first-aid knowledge was Ted Hotching from C Company, who persuaded Stan Corby to volunteer as well. Both were appointed lance corporals and Hotching was quickly made up to sergeant. Many others were trained as stretcher-bearers. At last, on 15 April, the battalion was considered ready to return to the front line.

By mid-April, the Allied forces in Tunisia were poised to inflict upon the enemy a series of separate but loosely coordinated blows, with the overall intention of overwhelming his defensive positions. In the south, Montgomery's Eighth Army would attack the strongly held enemy lines at Enfidaville, assisted to the west by a French corps infiltrating through the mountains. In the north, the US II Corps would drive towards Mateur and Bizerte. The biggest prize, Tunis, was the target of the British First Army. The main drive would be by V Corps up the Medjerda valley to break through and drive on to the city, while IX Corps would attack further south on the Goubellat Plain. The 46th Division would break into the enemy positions to the east of the town of Bou Arada, allowing 6th Armoured Division and 1st Armoured Division (transferred from Eighth Army for the offensive) to exploit the breakthrough to the north-east. This was largely a diversionary operation, intended to draw the German armour into battle and hold down their reserves so they could not interfere with V Corps' attack, so it would be the first assault to go in, on 22 April. With 139 Brigade remaining in reserve, the initial infantry advance would be made by the other two brigades of the division, supported by infantry tanks.

The Foresters left their training area on 15 April and made their way south to Gafour, where 139 Brigade was regrouping. Together with two squadrons of Churchill tanks from 48th Royal Tank Regiment, they formed a mobile brigade reserve, while the 2/5th Leicesters and 16th DLI occupied the front line. Over the next few days, elements of 1st Armoured Division began to arrive, and these movements appeared to be successful in drawing some of the enemy's attention. Both the Leicesters and the DLI were shelled, and there were reports that 69th PGR—their old enemy from Tamera—had arrived in the area, together with 86th PGR. The weather was hot, with the occasional thunderstorm. On the night of 21–22 April, the Foresters moved forward to relieve the 16th DLI (who had been attached to 128 Brigade for the attack), and therefore had a grandstand view of proceedings the next day.

The artillery barrage began at 3.30am and was the heaviest that the battalion had yet seen. The ground shook from the blast of nine field and horse artillery regiments and two medium batteries—about 224 guns. The noise was so deafening that Eric Morral, on AA duty at the Battalion HQ, found that even when shouting as loud as he could it was impossible to speak to the person next to him. The guns fired for half an hour slow rate, half-an-hour normal rate and then fifteen minutes of rapid fire. Following behind this fearsome barrage, the infantry, who had moved to their starting lines an hour earlier, still made slow progress and were not able to take all their objectives that day. However, by 5.30am the following morning sufficient ground had been taken for 6th Armoured Division to begin their advance. The 46th Division declared its objectives secure at 9am, and 1st Armoured Division then added its weight to the attack, although they were held by a hastily organised but determined defence by 10th Panzer Division, including three Tiger tanks. Meanwhile, 46th Division was left to consolidate as the armour pressed forward, and on the morning of 24 April it was found that the enemy were starting to withdraw. The DLI, however, saw enemy movement on the Djebel Bessioud, a feature dominating the north side of the road between Bou Arada and the town of Pont du Fah, which French troops were about to attack. The 46th Recce Regiment probed towards the hill, supported by the guns of 172nd Field Regiment, but after temporarily gaining a foothold they were forced off. A more serious effort to take the feature was needed, and 139 Brigade was on hand to be given the task. The attack would take place overnight on 24–25 April and was to be made silently. The Djebel Bessioud comprised two peaks roughly a mile apart; the 2/5th Leicesters were assigned the southernmost of these, while the 5th Foresters would take the one to the north. A regiment of field artillery was assigned to support and a FOO attached to each battalion, but this was only intended to be used after first light to break up enemy counterattacks and follow up their retreat. Two squadrons of Churchills were also allocated to support at daybreak.

This was a strong force to take against what was believed to be only around 100 men on the objective, and it is not surprising that the brigade and divisional records reported that the start line was crossed at 2am and that by 9am the operation was completely successful. The Foresters' diary is similarly positive. The Leicesters' account of the night reveals that things did not go entirely smoothly, however. It appears their CO was originally opposed to the night attack and wanted to postpone the operation until the following day, but that Major General Freeman-Attwood at 46th Division insisted it should go ahead as planned. The Leicesters moved up, but they were unable to locate their guide from the recce regiment and became lost. They did, however, meet up with Eric Hefford and his IO, who according to the Leicesters also appeared lost. In the dark, the disoriented Leicesters moved up through some cornfields but discovered that they had strayed into the Foresters' forming up area, and they then had to veer to the right and south to line up against their own objective. The attack, originally due to start at midnight, was significantly delayed by the confusion. According to the Leicesters, at around 3am they heard a German call out, and they then moved up the hill in two lines. In a cactus grove at the bottom of the slope, about twenty Germans fired a few shots and then most of them surrendered. Reaching the top of the hill to find the enemy gone, the Leicesters heard machine-gun fire directed against the Foresters and the chatter of Bren guns in reply. The Foresters had started their attack a little later, at 4.25am, but by 5am they had also reached their objective and were consolidating. The Germans had abandoned their positions so rapidly that they had left behind much of their equipment and even their breakfast. Willis Dixon and his section found two plates of porridge, still hot! They also liberated some ham and a 7lb tin of Danish butter, which was like a can of oil. That night, they filled two sandbags with beans from one of the local farmers' fields and supplemented their compo rations with fried beans. At daybreak, around 250 enemy motorised infantry were seen to be preparing a counterattack from the south-east. The Churchill tanks that had been assigned to support the infantry moved around the right flank of the Leicesters and opened fire with their machine guns, and the Germans beat a hasty retreat behind a smokescreen. The artillery communications broke down yet again, however, and their withdrawal could not be followed up.

The Foresters took twenty-four prisoners from the Hermann Goering Division, the Leicesters eighteen. British casualties were very light: Private James Hayes of the Foresters was killed and five Foresters and three Leicesters were wounded. Twenty-six-year-old Hayes came from Leytonstone in what was then Essex and had originally been in the Royal West Kent Regiment. He was one of the replacements sent to the battalion after Sedjenane and had previously been wounded at Tamera. Over the next two days, the battalion set up defences, cleared booby-traps and identified minefields in the area—one single minefield was reported to contain 1,700 anti-tank mines. On 28 April, they handed over their positions to French colonial troops of the Régiment Tirailleurs Sénégalais.

The taking of the Djebel Bessioud was not much of a battle, even in its own right. The British had overwhelming numbers, artillery and tank support, and while their opposition was an elite regiment, its morale was almost certainly in decline by this time in the campaign. The seizure of the hill had secured the right flank of the British advance to the north, and the left flank of a French offensive that had begun the same night. But in the overall history of the North Africa campaign, the assault on Tunis, even the operations of IX Corps that week in April; it does not even warrant a footnote. For the 5th Foresters, though, it was a milestone in their development. For the first time, they had achieved a clear-cut victory over the enemy. Major Hefford's boxer had finally won its first round.

The Tunisian terrain remained almost as much a problem as the enemy; in combination they could still prove dangerous in many ways. The battalion went north in a series of moves to provide cover to the right flank of the 1st Armoured

Division. On 29 April, the battalion left its lying-up area at 7.30pm, travelling about 6 miles overnight to take up the positions then held by 138 Brigade. In the dark, and crossing deep wadis, several parties lost their way and wandered off the tracks into enemy minefields, resulting in seven casualties. Two days later they went north again, in a move described by the war diary as the most difficult yet encountered. The tracks were once again intersected by deep wadis, making them almost impassable to vehicles, and the battalion pioneers had to work all night improving the route, while the carriers had to tow the other vehicles up the steep slopes. The new positions, when reached, were as bad as any at Sedjenane, on high rocky ground in which it was difficult to dig trenches and with the enemy well dug-in less than 2,000 yards away. The enemy minefields and anti-tank guns had brought the 1st Armoured Division to a stop. For a few days, the battalion settled into a routine not unlike life in front of Green Hill three months earlier, although the weather was now hot rather than wet and cold. Patrols were sent out nightly, most notably a sixty-man 'fighting patrol' on the night of 5 May. Although this engaged the enemy, there were no casualties and they failed to capture any prisoners. The following day, the positions were found to be empty, with scattered enemy equipment left behind indicating the speed of their retreat. On 7 May, 1st Armoured Division was able to advance again, and the battalion went back into reserve. That evening it was learnt that British troops, spearheaded by the Derbyshire Yeomanry, had entered Tunis, and that First and Eighth Armies had met up near Gafsa in south-west Tunisia. Although mopping-up operations would continue for another five days, for the 5th Foresters the North African campaign was over.

How should the battalion be judged following its first serious trial? It had gone to North Africa much better equipped and trained than two years earlier, but still lacking in experience of what it meant to fight a modern war. The same was of course true of most of the units in the First Army, and there were many territorial units that rose to the occasion and whose achievements in Tunisia surpassed those of the 5th Foresters, either in the solidity of their defence or the effectiveness of their attacks. Three defeats at Sedjenane, Djebel Bel March and Tamera may not seem to constitute a record to compare to the 5th Hampshires at Sidi Nsir, or the 8th Argyll and Sutherland Highlanders at Longstop. The enormous losses suffered by the Foresters in March meant that there had to be a rapid replacement of men, meaning troops were often fighting under unfamiliar officers and NCOs, alongside unfamiliar companions. But other units had also suffered heavy casualties and gone on to famous victories. What mitigates the defeats somewhat is that in none of them had the Foresters been masters of their own fate. In every one they had gone into action in positions that they had occupied only hours before, with poorly constituted or non-existent plans and without adequate artillery or armoured support. Many of these problems were endemic in the early battles fought by First Army, but the

5th Foresters seem to have been particularly unfortunate in their experience of them. CQMS Jack Schofield, still serving in 139 Brigade HQ, felt that they had been given an impossible task:

> I am almost certain in my own mind that 139 Brigade, with its battalions of Leicesters, Foresters and Durham Light Infantry, in company with certain other accompanying formations, was tactically ordered, and to a large extent sacrificed, to a monumental task, which resulted in almost decimating it, and certainly lessened its high effectiveness, having to take on impossible odds, in respect of the enemy's immense superiority in troops and fire-power, and control over the air-space at the time.[8]

It may be added that except for the minor action at Djebel Bessioud, 139 Brigade and the 5th Foresters never reaped the benefits of experience and material superiority that other battalions later did during the final advance on Tunis. And while they may not have faced Rommel's elite panzer divisions or Tiger tanks, Witzig's men and the paratroopers of the Barenthin Regiment were as tough opponents as any to be found in the theatre. It had been a gruelling examination, but one they had ultimately survived and passed.

One other characteristic seen after Dunkirk also persisted. On 20 May, there was a victory parade organised in Tunis. Each unit was to be represented, and four officers and 150 other ranks from the 5th Foresters were to march in a composite battalion along with men from the Leicesters, DLI and Hampshires. Eric Morral was amongst the 'old sweats' chosen to represent the Foresters in the victory parade. The military bands were too far away to be used for keeping step, but the RSM gave the order, 'Take your step from me', which they did. 'Every time the parade halted,' recalled Morral, 'all the other units sounded like the patter of machine gun fire. But when the "Notts and Jocks" halted; CRACK! it sounded like one man! and there were loud cheers from the onlookers.'[9] Through all the defeats, disappointments and deaths, the men's pride in their battalion was still strong.

10

Captives: Germany and Italy, June 1940–August 1943

Typically, regimental histories omit the fate of those captured, and there is always a faint suspicion of cowardice hanging over them, that surrender implied dishonour. The exceptions are the accounts of the horrific treatment of those like the men of the 1/5th Foresters captured in the Far East by the Japanese, whose sufferings take on a heroic aspect. The public perception of PoW life in Germany is largely driven by books and films such as *The Colditz Story*, *The Wooden Horse* and *The Great Escape* (or even, since the Foresters captured in Tunisia were initially imprisoned in Italy, the fictional *Von Ryan's Express*), which focus on brave deeds of defiance and escape. The facts of PoW existence for most men could not have been more different; at best it was a life of tedious monotony, at worst a struggle for life itself. If the young soldiers of the 2/5th Foresters were ill-prepared for war in 1940, they were even less prepared for captivity. But over the next five years they would experience the Nazi and fascist regimes more directly than their fellow Foresters fighting the Wehrmacht in the front line. To fully understand the experiences of the battalion, the story of these prisoners needs to be told. At least 606 men serving with the 2/5th Foresters (eighteen officers and 588 ORs) were taken prisoner by German forces between 1940 and 1944, roughly the entire strength of an infantry battalion once B Echelon personnel such as drivers and cooks are excluded.[1] Their experiences of PoW life were very varied.

Twenty-eight men were captured in 1940, a remarkably small number given the scale of the debacle in France and the inexperience of the troops, although they did include the CO, Henry Everard, and his 2iC, Eric Deall. It shows that much of the battalion was able to withdraw with a semblance of good order, while many of those initially thought missing and captured were nevertheless able to use their initiative to get away from the Dunkirk beaches. Only a handful were taken around Dunkirk itself, the majority surrendering during the fighting near Oignies. None of them have left a detailed account of their experiences, but other tales of the defeat describe long marches from Dunkirk to railheads near the German border, with casual brutality along the way from German guards who treated the surrendered Tommies with contempt. There were reported atrocities in the aftermath of the Oignies action, but with these one or two exceptions the treatment of the Foresters does not seem to have been bad. Eight of them were wounded and were passed rapidly into the German army medical system, the most serious cases to a military hospital (*Gefahr Lazarett 60*) at Ghent in Belgium. Since Oignies was much further east than Dunkirk, the unwounded Foresters' march into captivity was probably shorter than that for most PoWs. At least one of them, Private George Thompson, was initially processed at a temporary camp (*Front-Stalag 101*) near Cambrai, about 30 miles to the south-east of Oignies. From here or other railheads, they were placed in the now-familiar *40 Hommes 8 Chevaux* railway trucks for transportation to Germany.

Everard and Deall were probably given more comfortable transport. They were both processed at *Dulag XII* (*Durchgangslager*, or transit camp) at Mainz, where they would have been interrogated before being sent on to *Oflag VII-C* (*Offizierslager*, or officers' camp). Most camps were identified by the military district in which they were located and an identification letter: *Oflag VII-C* was in Laufen Castle in south-east Bavaria. A few private soldiers were placed in *Oflags* to act as batmen to senior officers. Everard certainly would have had such an orderly, but if so he was not selected from the other Foresters taken prisoner. Amongst the other inmates at *Oflag VII-C* was Captain Pat Reid, captured at Cassel on 27 May 1940, the day after Everard had been taken at Oignies, and who only seven weeks after arrival tried to escape with five other officers. All six ended up at *Oflag IV-C* in Colditz castle when the attempt failed. At 43, Everard would not have participated in Reid's plan, and Reid later wrote that senior British officers were not aware of the attempt.

The other ranks, including NCOs, were sent to *Stalags* (*Stammlager*, literally, a 'main camp'). The two-dozen Foresters were split up and placed in several different *Stalags*. These already held many Polish soldiers taken prisoner in September 1939, but the success of the *blitzkrieg* in France had surprised the Germans almost as much as their opponents; accommodating nearly two million French and over 40,000 British prisoners (as well as Belgians, Dutch and Norwegians) taken in such a small space of time put a huge strain on the system. Locations that the Foresters were sent to included *Stalag VIII-B* at Lamsdorf (now Łambinowice) in Silesia, which had a long history as a PoW camp dating back to the Franco-Prussian War of 1870–71. The wooden barracks there had been constructed during the Great War, and it would eventually house 64,000 prisoners, about a fifth of them British. Nearly 300 miles away in north-east Poland was *Stalag XX-A* at Thorn (now Toruń). Before the First World War, this had been German territory, surrounded by a complex of nineteenth-century forts that had guarded the eastern border. Some of these had been used to house Polish prisoners in 1939, and more were now added and converted to accommodate around 5,000 British troops.

Under the Geneva Convention, it was legitimate for physically fit PoWs to be put to work, provided it was not dangerous, unhealthy or directly contributing to the war effort. Officers were exempt from this, while warrant officers (WOs) and NCOs could only be used in supervisory roles. Some of those captured were put on work details very soon after capture, in particular to repair damage to transport networks in France, which delayed their arrival in the camps. Once in a *Stalag*, they were sometimes quickly sent out to sub-camps for work. The men who had been seriously wounded did not enter the *Stalag* system until much later, and for some reason most were sent to *Stalag IX-B* at Bad Orb in Hesse, which was primarily a French (and later Russian) camp and never contained many British PoWs. In the First World War, the spa resort of Bad Orb had been a hospital town, so it may have resumed this function.

Germany was obliged under the Geneva Convention to provide information about the capture and location of prisoners of war through Switzerland and the International Red Cross Committee (IRCC). This did not usually happen until they reached a permanent camp, and it was not for several months—early 1941 in a few cases—that news of their fate reached their families back in England. Joan Burgess must have been especially anxious to receive news of her husband, George. The two had met while working in the Players cigarette factory in Nottingham, and after 22-year-old George had been called up they got married in April 1940 only days before he went to France. The young couple would not see each other again for over five years. Dora Sharpe, a hosiery worker from Newton near Alfreton, had also married in early 1940. Her husband, George, had been a labourer at the local coal mine. The news that he was a prisoner in *Stalag XXI-B* at Wortelager near Poznan in Poland must have come as a relief, since he had originally been reported killed in action. Like Joan, she did not see him again until the war ended in 1945. There was some comfort in the fact that the army continued to pay family allowances and dependents allowances for men who had been captured, as well as basic pay, part of which could be sent to dependents by the army paymasters. Men put to work by the Germans were also entitled to be paid for this, though this was often subject to arbitrary deductions and paid in *lagergeld*, script notes that could only be spent in camp canteens.

Not all those Foresters taken prisoner in 1940 ended up spending the rest of the war in captivity. The Geneva Convention allowed for the seriously ill and wounded to be repatriated, usually in exchange for sick or wounded German prisoners held in Britain. However, for a long time the PoWs were pawns in drawn-out negotiations as diplomats of the two countries vied for concessions, and the first exchange of around 4,000 prisoners did not take place until October 1943. Candidates for release were selected within the camps, then examined by a Mixed Medical Commission of three doctors (two Swiss and one German), who decided eligibility. Those fortunate enough to be selected for the first exchange included six Foresters, two of whom were amputees, so surely an obvious decision for the commission. They were taken to a *Heimatlager* (homeland camp) at Montwy in Poland, then to the island of Rugen in the Baltic, where they were put on board a Swedish ship, the *Drottingholm*, which carried them through the Skagerrak and across the North Sea to Scotland. Another three exchanges would follow in 1944. The most unusual case amongst those repatriated was Eric Deall. He had a long history of bronchial illness, dating back at least to 1916, although this had not stopped him serving at the front in two world wars. Incarcerated in *Oflag IX-A* at Spangenburg Castle, the British MO advised Deall to smoke heavily to exacerbate his condition. This dubiously ethical advice got him judged physically unfit by the Mixed Medical Commission and he was repatriated in September 1944.[2]

*

Just as the first prisoners from 1940 were starting to be repatriated, a new group of prisoners from the 2/5th Foresters began to arrive in Germany. These were men who had been captured in Tunisia and there were many more of them; no less than seven officers and 375 ORs had been surrounded at Sedjenane and in the operations around Tamera. Captured by the Germans, they had not immediately been sent to Hitler's Reich, but in common with all prisoners taken in North Africa had been the unwilling guests of Mussolini's fascist regime in Italy. Their German captors had treated the prisoners well on the battlefield, caring for the wounded, organising working parties to bury the dead and respecting personal property. The men were interrogated, but not beaten or abused. When they arrived in Bizerte, they were handed over to the Italians; smart officers dressed in pale blue, rather untidy-looking soldiers in blue-grey uniforms with baggy trousers. These new guards treated the Foresters not as respected foes but as pathetic losers. They were made to sleep on their groundsheets in open fields without shelter, and jewellery, watches and other valuables were demanded in payment for water or food.

The prisoners were marched into the Bizerte docks and loaded onto a variety of transports. Privates Lew Booker and Cyril Pearson ended up ankle-deep in coal dust in the hold of an old collier. On Fred Hirst's ship, the officers and WOs got accommodation in deckhouses, but the ordinary soldiers were prodded down ladders into the hold, where they were locked in. Hirst found himself in a dark smelly space with a bare floor to sleep on, a couple of oil lamps for light and two large 8-foot-diameter containers to be used as toilets. On Alan Orme's boat there were no facilities at all in the hold, just a single toilet and a single tap up on the deck, and the men were let out in pairs to relieve themselves and wash clothes. Orme teamed up with another sergeant of the 2/5th, Bill Wainwright from Ambergate, near the Crich memorial, and they managed to stay together through several camps until the end of the war. With 240 prisoners on board, there was a permanent queue for the toilet, it was also impossible to keep clean and lice quickly became a problem. Food was in short supply everywhere. Hirst's daily ration consisted of a tin of watery meat and a

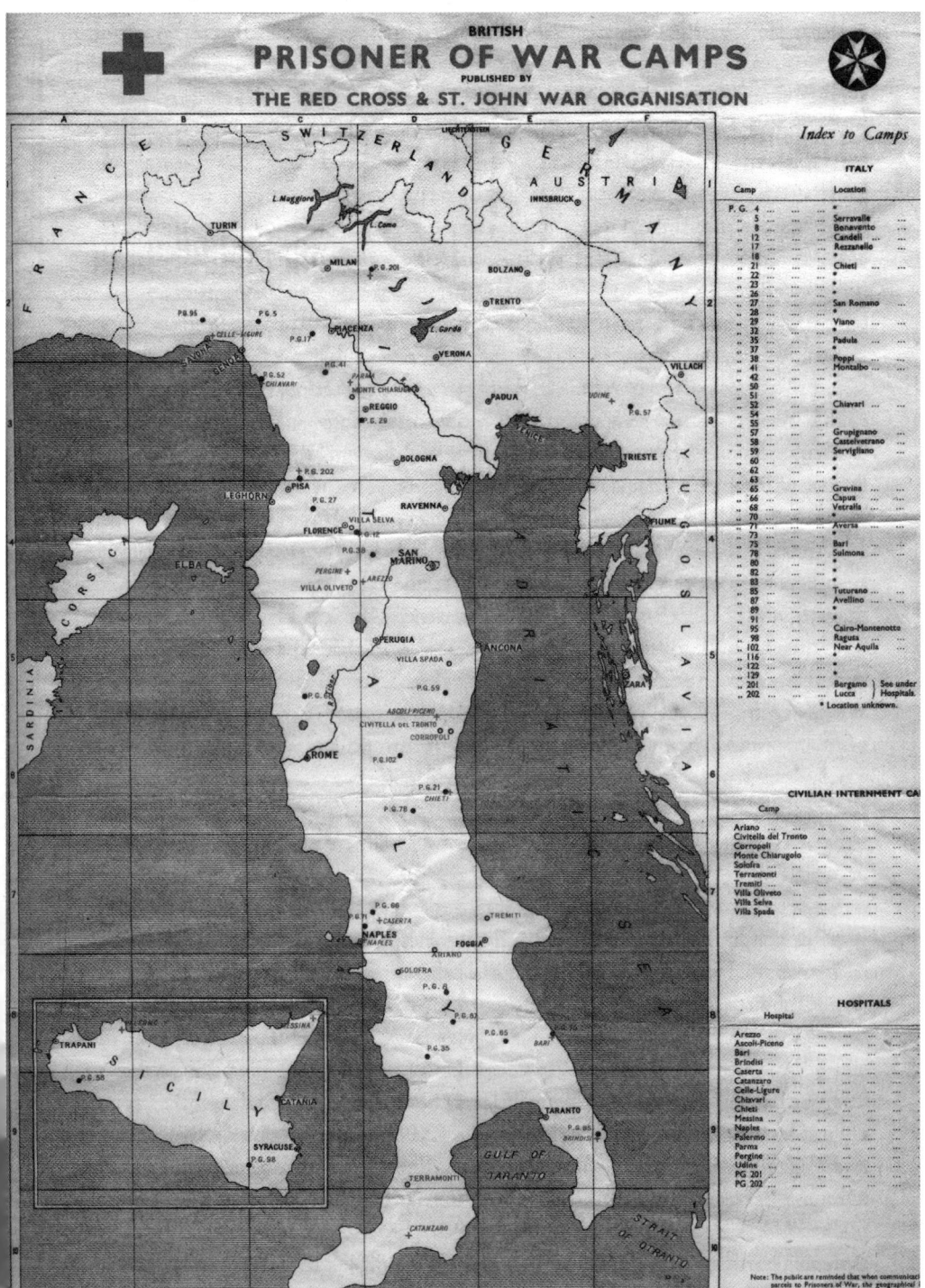

PoW camps in Italy, 1943. (*Red Cross*)

3-inch square hard-tack biscuit mostly covered in mould. If men had so far managed to keep their valuables, they were now so hungry that they would exchange them for a small cob (bread roll). A sergeant major of the Lincolns thought to relieve the men's hunger by getting the hatch opened and throwing down to them raw cabbage stalks that the crew were going to throw overboard; the result was a mad scramble and fights to catch these pathetic scraps of 'nourishment'.

Their sufferings intensified when the transports cast off but then anchored out in the harbour for several days. Not only were they starving, but everyone feared being killed in a friendly air raid. The anxiety did not subside when the vessels finally put to sea. The straits between Tunisia and Sicily were now hotly contested between the rival navies and air forces. Three days into the voyage, Hirst was startled by a terrific explosion from outside the ship. It could have been a near miss from an Allied bomb or a depth-charge from an Italian escort hunting a British submarine; there was no way of knowing. Some of the men panicked and began banging on the hatches to be released. Hirst decided to stay put. Battened down below decks, he was under no illusion what would happen if the ship was hit; they would either be killed in the explosion or drowned like rats, as there was little chance that the crew would take the time to free the PoWs before they abandoned ship. Miraculously, not only Hirst but every one of the Foresters taken captive in North Africa was fortunate enough to avoid death on these perilous journeys across the Mediterranean, and they were eventually landed at different Italian ports, including Palermo, Livorno and Naples. From here they were taken to various *Campo Concentromento Prigioniero di Guerra* (*PG*), as the Italians termed their PoW camps.

Food was still their main concern. The basic fare was a thin vegetable soup with macaroni, described by Hirst as 'poor quality and small quantity'.[3] Very infrequently, the soup would contain some meat of dubious origin. Each hut collected the soup from a communal cookhouse in a metal pot about 18 inches square, and the senior NCO would share it out to the men. The first helping was usually little more than vegetable stock, whereas the last had a decent amount of macaroni in it, so to ensure equal treatment each man was given a number and the first man in the queue was rotated each day. The men detailed to carry the pot were also rotated, as they got the scrapings after the contents had been shared out. Two or three times a week, they also received a supply of cobs, often containing what appeared to be bits of straw; these varied greatly in size, so again each man took their turn having first choice. Once a week, there was a bulk issue of cheese, shared out in 1oz portions. The Geneva Convention required that PoWs should get the same rations as depot troops of the holding power, and IRCC inspectors usually reported that the Italians were fulfilling these obligations. In some aspects they were indeed most diligent—in *PG47* near Modena, primarily for officers, the prisoners received a tobacco ration of cigarettes or cigars each day and there was even a wine ration, though it was of such rough quality that Julius Cowen recalled it burning through a metal hip flask. But from other accounts there is no question that the food received by the British prisoners from the Italians was insufficient. Thirty-year-old Cyril Pearson, a stretcher-bearer in C Company, fainted from lack of food in *PG98*, a holding camp in Sicily similar in purpose to a German *Dulag* but much more primitive. When transferred to *PG53* at Sforzacosta near Macerata, he described the men there who had been taken prisoner earlier in the war as 'just walking skeletons'.[4] Many would have suffered severe malnutrition if it had not been for a reasonably regular supply of Red Cross parcels to supplement Italian rations. Others resorted to more desperate means to relieve their hunger. At one camp, the *Comandante* owned a small dog—a dachshund by one account, a corgi by another—which was enticed away from its master, butchered and eaten by the prisoners.[5]

Parcels originated from the Red Cross organisation in the prisoner's home country, and in the case of British parcels consisted of a cardboard box weighing about 10lb. Standard contents included 2oz of tea, 2oz of sugar, a tin of condensed milk and a 4oz block of chocolate, together with twenty cigarettes and a bar of soap. Then there were various combinations of tinned goods—usually including cheese, meat, fish, vegetables, fruit and puddings—and also biscuits, jam and margarine. Most men teamed up with a buddy to share their parcels, in part to increase the variety but also because they were often issued one between two or more. There also grew up a substantial trade in the various goods. Cigarettes became the standard currency in the camps, and these could be exchanged for other items. Some men sold their entire Red Cross parcel for cigarettes, then used them to purchase from other soldiers food which they preferred or were in greater need of. Canny entrepreneurs would play the market as prices for different goods changed according to availability. There was also a limited amount of bartering with the guards, most often for bread. Cigarettes, soap and tea were the main commodities exchanged—the last of these consisting of used leaves dried out and repackaged, which the Italians seemed to prefer to the stronger fresh tea! Italy was economically the poorest of the major powers fighting in Europe, and by 1943 its own population was suffering substantial deprivation. When Alan Orme caught one guard stealing powdered milk from the Red Cross stores, the man broke down sobbing that it was for his *bambino*. Orme took back the milk but had pity on the poor guard and did not report him. He was, after all, only trying to do the best for his family.

Red Cross parcels did not just provide food and cigarettes; both the contents and the packaging could be used to manufacture a wide range of home comforts. Most ubiquitous was the 'blower', a cooking contraption made from the metal tins. Each one was unique, but they were big enough to hold a mess tin and had a fan turned by hand, for example using a piece of string and a milk tin lid, which forced air over a few slivers of wood. The heat was sufficient to cook food or, more importantly, boil water for tea. Tin plates were relatively easy to fashion, but the men's ingenuity knew no bounds. In *PG66* near Capua, some navy men built a radio, while an electrician in *Stalag IV-B* in Germany made an immersion heater. In *PG53*, one man even made a grandfather clock! Tins containing 'KLIM' (an American brand of powdered milk) were particularly useful, as a pair of them could be fitted together to make a primitive insulated cup or jug. Harry Higton (captured at Sedjenane) made sets of dominoes and cards from cigarette packets, and string from the parcels could be knotted together to form hammocks, to avoid bedbugs in the straw mattresses. Butter and condensed milk were blended to make cream; and cocoa, milk and butter to make chocolate spread. Margarine was used to fuel lamps, while raisins or other fruit could be fermented to make alcohol.

PoWs suffered from the cold in winter, but as temperatures rose the opposite problem arose for the new prisoners. The men who had been in the Italian camps when the Foresters arrived had been taken in Libya and Egypt, and they still had their desert-issue kit. In the Tunisian mountains, it had been far too cold to wear khaki drill, and the Foresters had been captured wearing full battledress, much too warm for an Italian summer. The men either cut the legs off their battledress trousers or simply wore their underpants as shorts. Sometimes they could borrow a spare shirt from one of the older inmates, but more often they went around bare-chested, especially when on working details. In Italy, the main forms of labour were roadbuilding, agricultural work or the construction of facilities in the camps themselves. Although hard physical work, it relieved the boredom of the camp, and particularly for those working on farms the food was considerably better than in the main camp, with bread and coffee supplied by the farmers. Some men became friendly with the local people, many of whom had relatives who were prisoners in Britain, taken in the Western Desert or Tunisia.

Another feature of life in the camps was that men who had mostly never been out of England before their war service encountered troops from other countries in the British Empire. The senior British officer (SBO) or the 'man of confidence' (a title given to NCOs appointed to represent the prisoners) could often be South African, Australian or, later in Germany, Canadian. There were also Indian and African troops in the camps. Although protected by the Geneva Convention, these generally suffered more in captivity than white troops—no doubt in part due to racism, but also because of practical difficulties with regards to diet, supply of Red Cross parcels, climate and communication with their families. They had their own senior officer or man of confidence, who represented their particular religious and physical needs, and they were usually held in separate compounds. This did not stop some of the Foresters from mixing, making friends and learning about their cultures. At *PG98*, English soldiers were treated by an Indian doctor, probably a first for most of them. When Maurice Enser arrived at *PG66*, he was desperate for a smoke, and a generous black soldier threw him a packet of cigarettes across the wire fence dividing the white and black compounds. The man was from Tanganyika Territory (now Tanzania) and had been captured while serving in a South African labour battalion. Before this he had spoken no English, but was now teaching himself from a Bible, and he persuaded Enser to visit him in the other compound.

Out of 'sheer cussedness because of the segregation', Enser accepted the invitation, though it meant risking being spotted and shot by the Italian sentries.[6]

The only shared activity between the compounds in *PG66* took place on Sundays, when an army padre had a rostrum erected straddling the wire and held a joint service. For many men, continuance of their religious obligations was extremely important, and it also provided structure to the week and an opportunity to socialise. In Italy, Roman Catholics were most easily served, as the local priest would come into the camp and celebrate the mass in Latin, sometimes to a mixed congregation of prisoners and guards. At his work camp, Fred Hirst attended Catholic services with the local civilians. In addition to two Catholic priests, the camp where Frank Offiler was held was fortunate enough to have both an Anglican and a Baptist minister, but elsewhere they had to be shared between several camps. Later, in Germany, Maurice Enser attended inter-denominational services in the camp theatre once a month, but religious duties sometimes had to be taken on by lay preachers. In one work camp in Germany, three or four prisoners set up a rota between themselves to give a service each Sunday.[7]

Technically, neither chaplains nor medical personnel were prisoners of war. Under the Geneva Convention, they were classified as 'protected personnel', free to move about and with an entitlement to food and accommodation equivalent to officers in the Italian or German armed forces. It was also expected that efforts would be made to repatriate them, and requests for such were often raised with Red Cross representatives. In practice, the need to tend to prisoners' medical and spiritual needs meant that many of these protected personnel remained in PoW camps until the end of the war, including two chaplains and two doctors taken prisoner while attached to the 5th Foresters. Reverend Paul Guinness and MO Julius Cowen were both captured at Sedjenane, placed in *PG47*, and after Italy surrendered in 1943 were transferred to *Oflag V-A* near the small village of Weinburg outside Stuttgart. In officers' camps there were usually more doctors than needed (sixteen in *Oflag V-A*), and they were assigned to *Stalags*, sometimes alongside civilian doctors. MO Thomas Munro Park, captured in Italy in October 1943, went to *Stalag 357* at Fallingbostel about 30 miles north of Hanover, where he was one of seven commissioned officers and around sixty other medical personnel. Towards the end of the war, Cowen was moved to an internment camp for Channel Islanders near Württemberg, where in March and April 1945 he also treated a group of seventy Dutch Jews who were sent to the camp from Belsen and had formerly been at Auschwitz. Despite this, and the fact that Cowen observed substantial weight loss among prisoners, his view was that the Germans mostly kept to the Geneva Convention with regards to medical treatment. This view would probably not have been shared by the average prisoner, who regarded their medical treatment as poorly as they did their food, whatever Red Cross inspections may have said. Some dedicated medical facilities were reported by inspectors to be excellent—such as the Italian military hospital

H206 in Naples, where most of those Foresters wounded and taken prisoner in Tunisia were treated. But most camps were short of equipment and medicines, and once again relied on Red Cross supplies. In Germany, prisoners assigned to work camps often received inadequate protection from German doctors, who under pressure from military authorities or civilian owners refused to excuse them work or assign them to lighter duties, even when seriously ill. Epidemics of typhus and other contagious diseases were another constant threat. In German camps, these often originated among Russian PoWs.

The protected personnel status was not always applied to other RAP members, although they had medical training and could and did perform valuable work in camp hospitals. Cyril Pearson was later put to work down a coal mine at *Stalag IV-C* at Brüx, because his Red Cross credentials had been taken by the Italians. Frank Offiler, captured in the RAP at Sedjenane together with Cowen and Guinness, eventually got a Red Cross ID card in Germany and was assigned as a medical orderly at a sub-camp at a copper mine. The medical staff there consisted of a French doctor, Offiler and four other orderlies: one French, two Russian and a South African. Men going on sick parade had to walk 2 miles to a station, take a half-hour train journey, then walk another mile to the hospital. Only a temperature or obvious wound were accepted as reasons for going sick. Surprisingly, Offiler remembered few actual casualties, though there were several psychiatric cases.

Capture and internment could lead to depression. When Patrick O'Sullivan, captured at Sedjenane with A Company, was moved from Sicily to *PG59* at Servigliano, he took to his bunk and did not move for weeks. He was eventually snapped out of his torpor by an SAS sergeant who forced him to go out into the exercise yard. Survival in the camps meant staying active both mentally and physically. Escape attempts were one means to this end, but not only were the majority of these unsuccessful, they were also dangerous. At *PG66* in January 1943, before Orme and the other Foresters arrived, about thirty men had tried to escape through a sewer; several were shot, others bayonetted or clubbed by the guards, and none escaped. Some SBOs actively discouraged escaping because it brought down reprisals on the entire prisoner community. Sport was an obvious distraction, and the prisoners organised football leagues between the huts and rugby and cricket 'test matches' between the different nationalities, although these could be restricted by lack of facilities and equipment or simply fatigue due to the poor rations. Concerts and theatre productions were staged in most camps. At *PG66*, there was an entertainments officer nicknamed 'Uncle Harry' who organised activities almost along the lines of a Butlin's holiday camp. There was even a camp song with a verse about the attempted escape through the sewer.

Educational activities were popular and easier to arrange. The prisoners themselves gave lectures around the huts on an extraordinary range of subjects, based upon their personal experiences and interests. Books were received from the Red Cross or from families back home, and the larger camps developed substantial libraries. One of the most frequent complaints to Red Cross inspectors was poor lighting in the prisoners' huts, which restricted their ability to read. After being transferred to *Stalag IV-B* in Germany, Harry Higton made the most of these opportunities: he took classes in French and psychology, read extensively from the camp library and took up weightlifting, as well as playing football and swimming in a pool the prisoners had built themselves. Those less inclined towards intellectual pursuits could gamble, playing Crown and Anchor dice games for cigarettes.

*

By far the strangest story of those captured at Sedjenane has to be that of Gerald Summers, who initially managed to evade capture when B Company's position had fallen. He still had with him Cressida the kestrel, also wounded when Summers stumbled and bruised her wing, but his captors did not bother to search him terribly well and he arrived at Bizerte still carrying the bird within the tunic of his battledress. He was taken into the office of a German medical officer and ordered to remove his tunic. When he claimed he could not because of his injuries, the orderlies cut it off and pulled it over his head, revealing Cressida to the amazed onlookers. The German MO just stared and exclaimed, '*Ah, ein Turmfalke*' ('Ah, a kestrel'). Summers had the good fortune to meet possibly the only German officer in North Africa who was also a keen amateur falconer. He was allowed to keep his kestrel when he was moved into the hospital ward, and the doctor even brought him a box of mice to feed her.

As it happened, Summers' wounds proved to be a blessing in disguise, because he was held in a German hospital for several weeks before being put onto a transport aircraft that took him to Sicily. He and the other wounded therefore avoided the appalling conditions suffered on the sea voyage across the Mediterranean, though flying to Italy in a slow-moving transport with RAF fighters from Tunisia and Malta contesting the skies was not without danger. Arriving in Sicily, he was sent to *PG98*. High up in the mountains south of Palermo, remote from any habitation, it comprised a large compound surrounded by a 10-foot-high barbed wire fence, lit up at night and with towers at intervals all around. Accommodation was in tents and marquees, and there was a hut for cooking and another for prisoners placed in solitary confinement. The camp sick bay was another tent. Dysentery was rife, but food and conditions in the sick bay were so bad that many who came down with it refused to go sick, treating themselves by only drinking water until they recovered.

Patrick O'Sullivan, also initially held in *PG98*, did not think much of Summers as a soldier. Although he had become a sniper, so must have been proficient with his rifle, according to O'Sullivan he was slovenly and ill-disciplined, often getting the rest of his section and company into trouble on parade. This independent streak had perhaps contributed to Summers resigning his pre-war commission, as well as the strange business with the kestrel. But the same freedom-loving traits that made him a bad soldier also made him a likely escapee. Indeed, Summers was no more inclined to stay cooped up than Cressida was. In *PG98*, he met up with Tom Cosgrave, another Forester with freedom in mind. Cosgrave was an Irishman from County Dublin who had volunteered to fight with the British Army. He had qualified as a glider tug pilot in the Army Air Corps (AAC) but had celebrated a bit too hard, and the following day had crashed his plane, for which he was dismissed from the AAC and sent back to the Foresters. There was no way that he was going to spend the rest of the war languishing in an Italian PoW camp. He had been a salesman in civilian life and had the gift of the blarney, and also proved to be an exceptional thief, liberating cheese and wine from the Italian stores. Both were valuable assets in captivity. With April came warmer weather, Red Cross parcels that lifted spirits and filled stomachs, and news of Allied successes in Tunisia. Several groups of prisoners began to be moved north to Italy, there were growing expectations that the invasion of Sicily would follow soon, and Cosgrave and Summers turned their thoughts to escape. The plan was to get out through the wire, make for the coast, steal a fishing boat and sail to North Africa.

The first step was to make a store of food from the Red Cross parcels, which was not easy as the Italians deliberately punctured all tinned food to ensure that the contents had to be eaten at once. Groups of six people would pool their food resources to save some food for escape. Alan Orme and Bill Wainwright were also in Cosgrave and Summers' group. As NCOs, Orme and Wainwright were not obliged to go out on working parties, but Cosgrave and Summers did so every day on a road-building detail, and one evening Cosgrave came back with a pair of wire-cutters concealed under his greatcoat that he had 'liberated' from a storeroom. Four American GIs, including an Italian-American who would be valuable as an interpreter, were also brought into their plans. Meanwhile, Orme and Wainwright walked around the camp and threw stones at the lights that illuminated the wire. By the Easter weekend, they had managed to knock out six lamps in a row.

Early on 25 April, Easter Sunday, Orme was awoken by the sound of machine-gun fire. Everyone dived for cover as stray bullets tore through the tents, and then the guards came and lined them up in the glare of the floodlights to be counted. Cosgrave, together with Summers and the Americans, had jumped the gun and decided to go that night, leaving a note for Orme saying, 'My need is greater than thine'.[8] The six men got together just before midnight, shared out the rations that they had managed to save and covered their boots in rags to muffle any noise. Then Cosgrave crawled out and cut a 6-foot hole in the wire.

Here, the stories told by the would-be escapers diverge substantially. Orme says that Summers failed to get out when the guards opened fire. This matches Cosgrave's recollection of the escape attempt, which states that only he and one of the Americans made it out, and that they were on the run for six days before being captured by a searchlight battery near Borgetto. Both men were sick with dysentery when apprehended, but they were denied medical treatment or even access to the latrines. They were handcuffed and left out in the sun for six days to discourage further escape attempts. In his version of events, Summers says that both he and Cosgrave escaped, as well as three Americans. He adds that they were on the run for several days, hiding out in caves, supplied with food by Sicilian peasant farmers, before being captured by a German patrol. This appears to be pure fabrication on Summers' part, though perhaps based upon information told to him by Cosgrave. He also gives a different date for the escape, saying it was 13 May, his birthday, and makes no mention of any punishment.[9]

What both accounts show is that getting out of the PoW camp was the relatively easy part. Staying out was much more difficult, and getting away nearly impossible. Sicily was a poor land, the support of the local population could not be relied upon (the locals in Palermo had spat at the prisoners arriving by sea) and escapees could not carry food for a long trek. In northern Europe by this time, there were established resistance groups and escape routes, largely set up to support shot-down RAF aircrew. RAF personnel were also given instructions, training and escape materials such as compasses and maps to help evade capture. None of this existed in Sicily, where RAF operations were minimal, and British privates and American GIs were relying purely on their own initiative. Add to this a lack of knowledge of the local geography and language (the Italian-speaking American was one of those unable to escape), and the chances of reaching the coast were small, those of finding a boat to get away even less.

After his escape, Cosgrave was moved to *PG78* at Sulmona, south-west of Pescara, but Summers remained in *PG98* until June. When North Africa fell, the Italians expected Sicily to be invaded soon, and one day the inmates were told to collect their meagre possessions and marched to the station, where they boarded a train north. By now all the guards were used to this mad Englishman with his pet falcon, and Cressida perched in clear view on Summers' knee or on the rails of the train ferry that took them across the Strait of Messina. After a time at *PG66*, Summers was moved north to a camp near Bologna. In September 1943, the Germans took over the camp and Summers was transported across the Alps to *Stalag IV-B* at Mühlberg. Here, a couple of South African officers decided that there was an opportunity to escape, but to do so they needed to pass themselves off as ordinary private soldiers, for reasons not made known to Summers but probably to do with being sent on a work detail. To even up the counts at rollcall, in return they needed two privates to pose as officers. Summers was given the fastest field-promotion in history, jumping from private to 2nd lieutenant in the blink of an eye. Deceiving the Germans was no problem, since he had previously held a real commission. He continued to pass himself off as an officer until the end of the war, finally being liberated by troops of the US Ninth Army at *Oflag 79* in Braunschweig (Brunswick) on 9 April 1945. Summers was repatriated to England—along with Cressida, who he had managed to keep by his side all through his captivity.

11

Time Out: North Africa, June–August 1943

Back in Tunisia, with the end of hostilities, the 5th Foresters' activities had turned to the more mundane tasks of processing PoWs, clearing the battlefield of the debris left by the fighting, guard duties and training. A quarter of a million German and Italian soldiers had been taken prisoner and were now being placed in PoW 'cages'. The battalion's share of these numbered 605 officers and ninety-seven other ranks by the end of May, after which the captives were sent to camps in Algeria prior to being sent back to captivity in Britain or the United States.

Battlefield clearance included the unpleasant task of burying bodies, both friend and foe, but mainly the salvage of arms, ammunition, clothing and other equipment from both sides. This was taken to divisional salvage dumps, staffed in 46th Division's case by the 2/5th Leicesters. It could be dangerous work, and the men engaged had to be wary of both minefields and booby traps. Nevertheless, no serious casualties were incurred by the Foresters. The list of items to be collected shows not only the need to reuse and refurbish valuable war materiel, but also an intelligence-gathering aspect. It also highlights the types of equipment in short supply in the army. The top priority was not weapons but jerricans and other fuel items. Then came communications equipment and optical instruments, such as compasses. Amongst the captured equipment, the items of most interest were artillery sights and fire control instruments, as well as telephones and even signal wire, German wire being much more robust and effective than British wire. Mine detectors were also valuable, as the Allied armies were under-equipped with these. Automatic pistols and sub-machine guns completed the high-priority list. Lower priorities included water containers, small arms and all forms of ammunition, both enemy and friendly. The salvage work was mainly done in the Medjez-el-Bab region, but George Stokes and others did return to the Sedjenane battlefield, where Stokes recovered his hidden mortars.

On most days, only one company of the battalion would be engaged in salvage. The rest would be training or, if lucky, partaking in some rest and recuperation. On 13 May, many had their first bath in weeks at a mobile bath unit at Oued

Zarga. Later, the battalion was moved to the coastal town of Hamman Lif, south of Tunis, where sea bathing was possible and sports events were organised. As part of the Brigade HQ, Jack Schofield was lucky enough to be accommodated in comfortable rooms in a hotel on the beach. Trips to Tunis had been banned while at Oued Zarga, although Schofield, and probably many others, had found ways to get round both this and the alcohol bans in the local cafes. At Hamman Lif, the restrictions were relaxed and some visits to the city were allowed. On 2 June, the battalion lined the roadside in Tunis to cheer a visit by Winston Churchill, and over the next few days provided guards to VPs in the Tunis area.

Once again there were huge influxes of new men to fill up the ranks, with no less than five officers and 277 ORs on 19 June alone. Some were Foresters, but there were also men from the Welch, Border and Essex regiments, all needing to be integrated into the battalion. Unlike previous replacements, many of these had already seen active service, mostly in Tunisia, though some came from India, distinguishable by the different toe-caps on their boots. Few came from Derbyshire or Nottinghamshire, but Schofield relates that they were all relatively quickly absorbed into their new unit. Deficiencies in training identified during the Tunisian campaign could begin to be seriously addressed. It was hardly surprising that training carried out in East Anglia or south-east England had not really prepared men for either the terrain or weather conditions associated with mountain warfare in Tunisia. Hefford, an ex-regular and determined to make his still somewhat demoralised battalion the best in the army, decided that the immediate priority was to toughen it up. Training started at 6.30am, there was a break for breakfast from 7.30–8.30am, then it continued until 11.30am daily. The afternoon, when the temperature was at its height, was mostly left free. From the end of June, more intensive training in mountain warfare began; this now took place from 6am to noon, then resumed at 5pm when the heat had become more bearable. It was physically hard work. Typical exercises involved treks of 20 miles or more across the mountainous terrain, initially 'dog and stick' marches without equipment, then progressing through 'light arms' when the men carried their rifles and ammunition, and finally to marches in full kit, albeit sometimes with an overnight rest. It seemed to Sergeant Phil Plowright, one of the men recently arrived from England, that Hefford thought that 'to make us efficient he had to kill us', and for some this was literally the case.[1] There were three deaths from heatstroke and dehydration, and many other men ended up in hospital. Reg Markham considered Hefford 'a sod' and a 'medal-hunter', though grudgingly admitting that the harsh training 'might have been a good thing in the long run'.[2] As the summer wore on, there was more and more discussion of seaborne assault from landing craft. All of this naturally led to speculation about the battalion's next objective.

*

Even before the Tunisian campaign had ended, the Allies had been planning their next move, but the British and Americans did not see eye-to-eye on this. The British general staff saw the conquest of North Africa as only partly completing the job. In their opinion, the logical next step to reap the benefits of victory in Tunisia was to seize the island of Sicily. This would allow convoys to travel safely through from Gibraltar in the west to Suez in the east, freeing up valuable shipping that currently had to travel all around Africa via the Cape. The Americans, however, were suspicious that the real objective of the British Mediterranean strategy was to dominate post-war Southern Europe, particularly the Balkans. American planners saw the Mediterranean as a mere sideshow. The defeat of Germany was paramount, and to achieve this they wanted to shift resources as soon as possible to Britain to take part in a cross-Channel invasion of north-west Europe. There simply were not enough landing craft in 1943 to support both strategies. The respective staffs, as well as Prime Minister Winston Churchill and President Franklin D. Roosevelt, had met at Casablanca in Morocco in mid-January to thrash out the arguments. The British view prevailed. The next target for the Allies would be Sicily in a joint invasion by both British and American troops, codenamed Husky.

The 46th Division would take no part in the Sicily campaign. Montgomery's Eighth Army veterans were to be the British component, while General George Patton's US Seventh Army would form the American contingent. But the 5th Foresters did have one significant role to play in the operation. On 13 June, the battalion set off on a five-day journey to the town of Blida, south-west of Algiers. Blida was a relatively modern settlement with a large French residential suburb as well as an Arab quarter, but the battalion was accommodated out of town, where it was put up in tents in a pre-prepared encampment. They were to form part of the defending force for Exercise 'Conqueror', a practice for the Husky landings. This was also to be a joint Anglo-American exercise, the first time that the battalion had cooperated with American troops to any large extent. The invading 'enemy' for 'Conqueror' would be the US 1st Infantry Division (known from its divisional symbol as 'The Big Red One') plus a battalion of US rangers (the equivalent of British commandos), together with tanks, airborne troops and aircraft. On the defending side were 46th Division, the 102nd US Mechanised Cavalry Regiment as a mobile reserve, a squadron of RAF Beaufort bombers representing the Luftwaffe and some French coastal batteries. The practice landing beaches, extended from Sidi Ferruch (now Sidi Fredj) in the north to Fouka in the south, representing the Big Red One's intended landing zone at Gela in Sicily. It was a soft, sandy beach (now the site of a popular holiday resort) with a belt of fine gravel backed by sand-dunes, some of which the French colonial farmers had reclaimed by planting vines. The important airfields a short way inland from the real beaches—a key objective for the first day of the landings—were represented by taped areas.

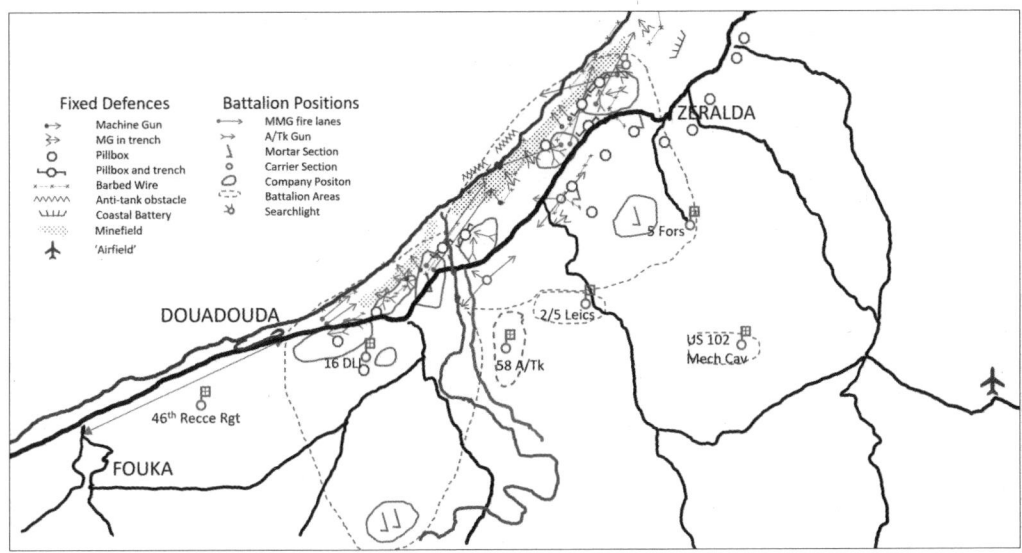

Exercise 'Conqueror', June 1943.

The defences were laid out in a combination of standard British practice and expectations of enemy preparations. In its sector, 139 Brigade set up with the 5th Foresters on the right, the 16th DLI in the centre and 46th Recce Regiment on the left, with the 2/5th Leicesters held as a reserve for counterattack. There were pillboxes and wire on the beaches. Representing German practice, at battalion level the forward defensive line consisted of machine-gun posts, with the bulk of the infantry held back for counterattack. One company was withheld as a battalion reserve. The 6-pounder anti-tank guns of the infantry battalions covered the exits from the beaches, while the divisional anti-tank regiment was held in reserve. Dummy positions were made to look as though they were occupied, and lights would be used to confuse the attackers. There were two artillery FOOs with each battalion, communicating with three regiments of the Royal Artillery. The 270 Field Company RE laid mixed anti-tank and anti-personnel minefields in the scrub behind the beaches and on the exit roads, and had prepared bridges to the rear for demolition. Other men, three per infantry battalion—including one from the intelligence section and another from the pioneer platoon—were given the role of 'saboteurs' to delay the American advance. Although no live ammunition or bayonets were to be used, the assaulting US troops would use live bangalore torpedoes (explosive charges placed on long metal tubes) to clear the wire and other obstacles.

The set-up for 'Conqueror' was thus a realistic training exercise for defender and attacker alike. In practice, the Foresters were unimpressed with the American handling of the operation, which certainly seems to have failed Freeman-Attwood's requirements for realism:

The landing itself is carried out well, but subsequently the US troops lose all sense of tactical considerations. They ignore 'heavy machine gun' fire directed against them and refuse to countenance any counterattack, but quickly form up in threes and march to their objective. The 'fighting' is over by 1700 hrs and our troops are not 'bothered' by American troops for the rest of the day. The Americans land transport and tanks on the bridgehead which they do not hold and quickly bring the exercise to a successful conclusion.[3]

It is unlikely that this critique went much further than the Foresters' war diary. Earlier in the year, a British corps commander, Lieutenant General John Crocker, had caused embarrassment when well-intentioned but frank criticism of US troops' performance in Tunisia had leaked to the press. Undoubtedly, the Foresters' comments would not have gone down well immediately prior to Husky. When the Big Red One landed for real in Sicily on 10 July, there was initially some confusion on the beaches due to poor weather and unexpected enemy minefields. Fortunately, the beach defences consisted largely of second-line Italian formations; poorly equipped, badly trained and low in morale, they put up scarcely more resistance than what the US troops came across in the training exercise. This allowed the Americans to consolidate their beachhead before they encountered much stiffer resistance from better-quality German and Italian forces that had been held back inland to counterattack the invasion. Naval gunfire helped break up these attacks, and the American landings were successful, although it was another five weeks before Sicily was cleared of the enemy.

The day after 'Conqueror', the Foresters filled in the trenches and took up the wire defences before returning to the camp at Blida. On 28 June, along with other infantry battalions, they implemented a significant organisational change in which HQ Company was split into two. The changes largely reflected the way in which the company was already working in practice. Remaining in the original company were the administrative and signals platoons. The combat platoons—the mortars, carriers, anti-tank guns and medium machine guns—were formed into a Support (S) Company. Also in this new company was the pioneer platoon. This reflected a change in the pioneers' role from one of specialist labour to something more akin to the combat engineers of other armies, skilled in mine-clearing, demolition and field engineering. Eric Morral was one of those who transferred from the rifle companies to this new role and received training in handling explosives.

By the end of June, the reorganised battalion was up to strength in other ranks but still woefully short of officers, even though Keith Davenport and Roger Newton, wounded in the March fighting, had rejoined the unit. Three other valuable returnees were Major Geoffrey Gofton-Salmond, who had left in 1941 to join the Parachute Regiment but was now posted as 2iC; Captain Denys Crews, released from training US officers; and Lieutenant John Walter Peacock, who had recovered from a gunshot wound received during training in England.

But the main influx of officers over the summer were about a dozen new and inexperienced lieutenants and 2nd lieutenants from the reinforcement depots, a mix of Foresters and men from other regiments. Among the 2nd lieutenants were Johnny Wright and 'Paddy' Bolton of the Royal Irish Fusiliers, posted—somewhat to their disgust—to the Foresters in March. Wright, in civilian life a manager at the Daventry Co-op, did not have deep Irish roots, but two years serving in Northern Ireland with the Inniskilling Fusiliers and then the Royal Irish Fusiliers (RIF) had instilled him with a strong sense of attachment to his adopted regiment. Wright had further reasons to feel an outsider. Aged 30, he was substantially older than the other newcomers, and he had also been promoted from the ranks. A significant proportion of the officers in the battalion were still pre-war TA men from Derbyshire, and this clique looked down on men like Wright, who in turn regarded those who had not gone through training at an OCTU or battle school as 'PSA' ('pleasant Sunday afternoon') soldiers. Nevertheless, even when Bolton was posted back to the RIF, Wright decided to stick it out with the Foresters rather than ask for a transfer. Such was the shortage of officers that three sergeants were given emergency commissions in August.

*

Captain John McKerrigan of the RAMC, attached to the 5th Foresters since Sedjenane as their MO, may not have had to deal with battle casualties, but he was still very busy during the summer of 1943. One aspect of this was the building up and training of the battalion's medical section. By the time of 'Conqueror', his new team had become reasonably proficient, as well as acquiring two 15cwt trucks and drivers to carry men to and from hospital. Lance Corporal Stan Corby had been appointed as McKerrigan's clerk and was responsible for making sure people attended appointments, usually accompanying them into Algiers. Corby also kept the daily medical returns. In the war diary, one aspect of the weekly returns was a list of officers and men absent from the battalion 'whose return to the unit is particularly requested'. By mid-June, the list of men in field ambulances, hospitals or convalescing included nine officers and over forty other ranks. This was around 7 per cent of the battalion's strength, and there may have been more who were not seen as critical to the battalion's effectiveness. Only a dozen of these were recovering battle casualties, the rest receiving medical attention for illness. Some had succumbed to Hefford's rigorous training regime, some were just random chance—for example, Johnny Wright came down with appendicitis shortly after his arrival at the battalion and ended up in hospital at Algiers. Others were the result of the unfamiliar Tunisian climate and environment. Large numbers of men suffered from 'Tunisian tummy', the symptoms of which were excessive vomiting and almost complete loss of control of the bowels. This probably resulted from a combination of dehydration due to the intense heat, unusual diet and poor food hygiene. Although the men were explicitly told not to eat the local food or drink the local water, this was difficult to enforce. Unripe or unwashed fruit purchased from locals, a popular means of supplementing army rations, constituted a particular hazard, and McKerrigan's warnings against eating the wild boar due to parasites were also often ignored.

While it was extremely unpleasant and completely incapacitated its victim, an attack of Tunisian tummy usually only lasted a few days. More seriously, malaria was endemic in the region, the marshy river valleys and the coastal lagoons being perfect breeding grounds for mosquitoes. The army issued mepacrine tablets, mosquito cream and mosquito nets, but since few of the troops had ever been out of the UK and had no experience of exotic diseases, observing the necessary precautions had to be drilled into them. The responsibility for ensuring that they took the unpleasant-tasting medication fell on already overworked junior officers, while the men had to be warned that the nets had to be hung well clear of all exposed parts of body to prevent the mosquitoes biting through them. Several officers came down with yellow jaundice, an indication of hepatitis, which aside from the obvious change in colour also made men unable to eat and led to dehydration and loss of weight. Jaundice was much less prevalent amongst the ranks. The officers had set up a formal mess for dining, and the disease's spread was probably attributable to these different eating arrangements. The officers shared cutlery and plates; the NCOs and privates, using their own mess tins, did not succumb as readily to the disease.

Private F. Ellis was among those identified as being in hospital and whose return was particularly requested. Ellis was back with the unit on 31 May, when he was one of three Foresters up before a court martial, in his case for 'misbehaving before the enemy in such a manner as to show cowardice'. The two other prisoners were charged with being AWOL. These tribunals were of a consistent format: the judiciary panel comprised a major, a captain and a subaltern from across the brigade, while a prosecuting officer (usually of captain rank) and a defending officer were normally appointed from the accused's own unit. No records survive of the actual proceedings or the details of the incident for which he was tried, but Ellis received a sentence of two years' imprisonment. There were nine other men in the battalion tried for serious offences that summer, the heaviest sentences being imposed on two men charged and found guilty of desertion, who both received ten years' penal servitude, later remitted to five years.

*

The Sicilian campaign had not been concluded before plans began to be put together for the next advance, and once again the target caused dissension between the Allies. The British saw an opportunity to separate Hitler from his most significant ally, Mussolini's Italy. After a year of unmitigated defeats, the Italians were anxious to be rid of their dictator and out of the war. The Americans continued to mistrust British intentions and wanted to shift the focus

Time Out: North Africa, June–August 1943

of the European war to France, but the attraction of the opportunity to break up the Axis was too great. With Montgomery and Patton still embroiled in Sicily, the forces allocated to the invasion of the Italian mainland would be the US VI Corps and British X Corps, together constituting the US Fifth Army under Lieutenant General Mark Clark. The 46th Division was assigned to X Corps under Lieutenant General Brian Horrocks, and from 23 July the staff of 139 Brigade started planning in support of the corps staff. Options being considered included Operation Buttress, an invasion in the Gulf of Gioia, north of Reggio, and Avalanche, a landing near Naples in the Gulf of Salerno. On 1 August, Horrocks addressed the officers and NCOs of 139 Brigade, indicating that they would soon be fighting in mainland Europe, but not revealing the actual objective.

Between 8 and 13 August, the 5th Foresters moved back to Tunisia, where they encamped near Bizerte in the shade of some olive groves near the sea. The location was not quite as idyllic as this description implies, as the water supply was limited to 1½ gallons per man per day and they used the sea for bathing. Training began almost immediately on embarking and disembarking from various landing craft, the main one being the Landing Craft Infantry (LCI). Much larger than the Landing Craft Assault (LCA) familiar from images of the Normandy landings, these grounded on the beach and then lowered ramps on each side of the bow, down which the men ran. Once their occupants had disembarked, the LCIs pulled themselves back off the beach using their rear anchor chains.

With four divisions allocated to the initial landings, the harbour and lake at Bizerte were crammed with shipping, and the surrounding land was full of encampments, ammunition dumps and vehicle parks. It was impossible to hide these from the enemy. Allied air superiority protected these preparations during the day, but throughout August there were regular nightly raids by large formations of between seventy and 100 aircraft. One occurred on the night of 17–18 August. It was a beautiful clear, starlit night, and the defending anti-aircraft batteries and naval ships in the bay put up a hail of flak against the enemy bombers. Several of the battalion watched the breathtaking spectacle from the hills overlooking the town. Perhaps the men had become rather nonchalant after being out of the front line, as some did not put on their helmets. While the Foresters were not the bombers' target, falling shrapnel and spent tracer bullets from the barrage began to cascade down amongst the spectators, who dived for cover under trucks. Three men were wounded and DR Stanley Waine, who had crashed his motorbike back in September 1939, was killed.[4] He was given a military funeral the next day, the last battalion casualty in North Africa.

This unfortunate incident gave Stan Corby and the medical team some practical experience, but John McKerrigan was not there to see how they coped. The previous day, he had himself been admitted sick to the 56th US Evacuation Hospital. Although he was back within a week, it seems his health was still poor, as he was replaced by Lieutenant Thomas Munro Park, RAMC, on 2 September.

This was Park's first experience as a regimental MO, and he would only have two or three days to settle in with the unit before it embarked for Italy.

Although the 5th Foresters were not assigned to the first assault wave, they were equipped for the invasion at assault levels of equipment. For the HQ and Support companies, this meant a much-reduced scale of transport, embarked on 2 September on two Landing Ships Tank (LST) of the US Navy, each carrying twelve motorcycles, one jeep, seven 15cwt and two 30cwt lorries and eight or nine Bren carriers, plus three of the battalion's 6-pounder anti-tank guns pulled by American General Motors trucks. The bulk of B Echelon would follow on some days later, and as the battalion had never undergone assault training, the equipment scale probably reflects the shortage of shipping rather than any tactical considerations. One day's worth of compo rations per man was carried on the company transport, and another in the battalion transport, while the water allowance was 2 gallons per man, in 2-gallon cans. Other spare kit carried on the battalion transport included mosquito veils and gauntlets to be issued to all ranks once ashore.

The infantry platoons embarked on three LCIs, also of the US Navy, each one carrying 183 men and under the supervision of one of the senior officers in the battalion. Denys Crews, whose work with the battle school had led to him being promoted acting major over the heads of more senior and longer-serving captains, was allocated to LCI-140, which would transport his own A Company. Acting Major Roger Newton had LCI-141 carrying B Company, and Major Charles Williamson LCI-142 and C Company. D Company was split between the three vessels.[5] Every man was given an embarkation card, which they were specifically ordered not to lose or destroy, and which they were to hand over to the major responsible for the LCI only when they were actually on board, to ensure that all men were properly accounted for. Each man would land in field service marching order, with equipment which weighed around 60–65lb. On top of this he carried his anti-gas cape (tied on his belt), a light assault respirator and a sandfly-proof bush net. He had a haversack which contained his cap comforter, a cardigan, towel, holdall, spare pair of socks, pair of canvas shoes and his mess tin. It also contained a forty-eight-hour ration pack, one emergency ration and a further ration bag comprising a tin of meat and one packet of biscuits. Thus equipped, the soldier was prepared for two days of independent action after landing. Bulkier or less-essential equipment, such as his greatcoat, groundsheet, a change of underwear, and spare boots, shorts and shirts, were in a larger pack on the company transports.

The battalion still had many men in the hospital with malaria and jaundice, but one of them, Lieutenant Bert Verity, who had joined the 5th Foresters on 27 April after the bulk of the fighting in Tunisia was over, was determined not to miss the action this time. Commissioned into the West Yorkshire Regiment the previous December and nicknamed 'Tich' due to his small stature, Verity had been assigned to A Company under Denys Crews, who connived with the 'tough, loyal, good-natured and outspoken Yorkshireman' to get him on board the landing craft.[6] Crews took a jeep and drove to the hospital in Bizerte, where Verity was waiting in the latrine, wearing a greatcoat over his hospital pyjamas. Bundling Verity into the jeep, they set off at high speed to the harbour, where although clearly still not well, Tich managed to embark with the rest of the company.

The series of Luftwaffe raids that had killed Stan Waine had also resulted in a more senior casualty. General Horrocks had been wounded in a strafing attack, and his place as X Corps commander taken by Lieutenant General Richard McCreery. Another general who would be missing the show was 46th Division CO Harold Freeman-Attwood. He had received the DSO for the division's operations around Djebel Abiod, but then, in an extraordinary breach of security, he had revealed in a letter home to his wife that the division was bound for Italy. Freeman-Attwood was promptly court-martialled, removed from his command and retired from the army. He was replaced by 50-year-old Major General John Ledlie Inglis Hawkesworth. The new CO's career was typical of senior British commanders. He had served on the Western Front with the 1st Battalion East Yorkshire Regiment throughout the First World War, including on the first day of the Somme, and in the UK and Palestine between the wars. From 1939–40 he had commanded a brigade in France, then had been Director of Military Training in the UK during 1941. Assigned to command the 4th Division, he had led it in action during the closing battles of the 1943 campaign. Hawkesworth took over command of 46th Division on 28 August, addressing the men of the 5th Foresters the same day. Only three days later, he and his headquarters boarded the USS *Biscayne*, flagship of Vice Admiral Richard L. Connolly, USN, who would command the naval assault force assigned to the British invasion beaches.

Hawkesworth's address would not have included specifics about where the battalion was to land or the plans for the operation; these details were only revealed to battalion and company officers by Brigadier Stott on 30 August. The men began the move to their assembly area the following day. On 4 September, they were entertained by a concert party from the cruiser HMS *Aurora*, and the next morning they boarded their respective landing craft, which sailed into Bizerte Lake. Here, on 6 September, they were subjected to another air raid, which fortunately caused no damage or casualties. At midday the next day, the invasion fleet set sail and the men of the battalion were finally briefed on their task. They were to land at Salerno, capture the town and then advance north to Naples.

Extract from Volume 2

Later that day, B Company was ordered to take Il Telegrafo. It was desperately short of officers: of those who had landed with it on 10 September, Roger Newton was lying fatally wounded in hospital in Algiers, Captain Sullivan had also been wounded, Captain Charles Morris had suffered a motorcycle accident and Willie Naylor had been killed. This left Lieutenant Johnny Wright as the senior officer. He now carried out a recce with 2nd Lieutenant Reginald Oliver, who like Ronald Stroud had been promoted from sergeant with an emergency commission in August. Their patrol discovered that the enemy was still on the hill in some force, but in doing so Oliver received a bad wound to the head. The two men made their back to Battalion HQ at the castle some 2 miles to the south, where Oliver was treated at the RAP. Stan Corby heard Oliver refuse to take the MO's advice to be evacuated, insisting on rejoining his platoon at the earliest possible moment, but the severity of the wound was such that this would not be for another six weeks. Wright, who had only been in the army a little over three years and commissioned less than ten months, was now the only officer left in the company. Hefford did, however, arrange for artillery support for the attack on Il Telegrafo, which went ahead at 6pm with Wright in command. During the attack, some of the 25-pounder shells fell short, hitting Wright's HQ and causing some casualties, but eventually the Foresters were established on the hill. The top of the mountain was very exposed and the enemy's shellfire was lethal amongst the rocks, sending up fragments of stone that forced a retirement to safer positions further down the slopes. Denys Crews' A Company, now reconstituted after its ordeal around Ponte Fratte, was sent through B Company to consolidate.

The advance through the mountains continued, but much slower than anticipated by divisional HQ. Crews' company took over the lead, advancing with one section up front followed by the Company HQ and then by the rest of the unit. In the mountainous terrain, communications even within the company were difficult and contact with the Battalion HQ broke down almost completely. The relentless shelling and mortaring of the previous week was now thankfully a thing of the past, but there was still what British intelligence reports termed 'small party' resistance. Usually the enemy tactics were to withdraw by night and then hold their positions during the day in these small groups. On 25 September, Crews' men entered a village high up in the hills unopposed. The villagers welcomed them in; a nun rushed up to Crews and embraced him, pressing a crucifix into his hand to give him her blessing. The Foresters were crossing the village square when a shot rang out and the man at the rear of the column was hit. The area was searched to no avail, but the men learnt to be more alert in future.

On 25 September, for the first time in three days, Crews had been in radio contact with the Battalion HQ. He was not even sure of which village he was in—when he reported what he believed to be his position, he was told that it was not possible. Also on this day, C Company occupied the village of Pregiato, which had a commanding view of Highway 18 below, taking five German prisoners. The battalion engaged in patrols and skirmishes over the next few days, assisting the KOYLI in bringing in another thirty-five PoWs. The main offensive down the Vietri–Cava road had also broken through, and on 26 September some of the battalion transport managed to make its way up the main road, now congested with the vehicles from two divisions, to relieve the struggling human supply line a little. On 28 September, 7th Armoured Division passed through 46th Division to break out to Naples, and the Foresters' role in the Salerno campaign ended. Consolidating and reorganising in the recently taken villages, most of the battalion slept under a solid roof for the first time since landing. They set to washing their clothes and other domestic tasks—Crews visited a mobile dentist unit to have a troublesome tooth seen to. It was exactly twenty-five years since their Great War predecessors had broken the Hindenburg Line.

Notes

Chapter 1: Heritage

1 Colonel Philip Hugh Dalbiac, *History of the 45th: 1st Nottinghamshire Regiment (Sherwood Foresters)* (London: Swan Sonnenschein, 1902), pp. 12–13.
2 Anon, *The Sherwood Foresters (Nottinghamshire and Derby Regiment): A Brief History* (Derby: English Life Publications, 1980), p. 3.
3 Ibid., p. 7.
4 Brigadier C. N. Barclay, *The History of the Sherwood Foresters (Nottinghamshire & Derby Regiment) 1919–1957* (London: William Clowes and Sons, 1959), p. 25.

Chapter 2: Birth

1 Modern values from <https://www.bankofengland.co.uk/monetary-policy/inflation/inflation-calculator> and <https://www.ons.gov.uk/employmentandlabourmarket/peopleinwork/earningsandworkinghours/datasets/earningstimeseriesofmeangrossweeklyearningsfrom1938to2022>, all sites accessed 16 June 2024.
2 *Derby Evening Telegraph*, 1 April 1939, p. 5.
3 *Derby Evening Telegraph*, 28 April 1939, p. 7.
4 £298 in 1939 would be more than £16,000 in 2025.
5 WO 166/998, 139 Bde WD, Nov. 1939, Appendix 16: Report by Lt.-Col. Lancaster dated 24 Nov. 1939.
6 WO 166/998, 139 Bde WD, Oct. 1939, '139 Inf. Bde Sub-Area, Civil Defence Scheme 1939', p. 9.
7 Crewdson quote from WO 166/998, 139 Bde WD, Oct. 1939.
8 WO 166/998, 139 Bde WD, Sept. 1939, 'Manning of V.P.s & tng of V.P. gds'.
9 WO 166/998, 139 Bde WD, Feb. 1940.

Chapter 3: First Steps

1 Transport records in WO 277/17, *Movements, Control and Planning 1939–1945*, Appendix C show a net 288,007 men landed in France between Sept. 1939 and March 1940. Front-line troops based upon a theoretical infantry division establishment of 13,863 men in 1939. The establishment strength of the initial six infantry and one cavalry divisions in the BEF in 1914 was around 118,000.

2 Sydney Cooper, in Wally Binch (ed.), *On Active Service* (2nd ed.) (unpublished, c. 1990), pp. 20–21, hereafter *OAS*.
3 WO 167/825, 2/5th SF WD, May 1940.
4 Cooper, in *OAS*, p. 20.
5 WO 167/731, 9th Foresters WD, 18 May 1940.
6 WO 167/395, 138 Brigade WD, 21 May 1940.
7 WO 167/472, 16th Fld Rgt WD, 25 May 1940.
8 Willis Dixon, in *OAS*, p. 19.
9 WO 167/825, 2/5th SF WD, May 1940.
10 Gregory Blaxland, *Destination Dunkirk: The Story of Gort's Army* (London: William Kimber, 1973), p. 255.
11 Quoted in Richard Garrett, *None but the Brave* (unpublished regimental history), p. 65, the original source is Anon, *Oignies, Première Cité Martyre de la Campagne de France* (n. l.: n. p. 1947), p. 4, trans. by T. & I. Lariviere, 1990, p. 10.

Chapter 4: Evacuation

1 IWM #16086, Victor Tupling interview with Peter Hart (1995), Reel 2.
2 Dixon, in *OAS*, p. 18.
3 Cooper, ibid., p. 22.
4 Ibid.
5 Jack Schofield, 'Recollections of an Infantryman in World War II' (unpublished MS in Museum of the Mercian Regiment, n. d.), p. 24.
6 Cooper, in *OAS*, p. 22.
7 Fred Jeffery, ibid., p. 16.
8 Barclay, *Sherwood Foresters*, p. 46.
9 Cooper, in *OAS*, p. 22.
10 Ernie Gibson, ibid., p. 29.
11 Schofield MS, p. 27.

Chapter 5: Education

1 NCA, DD/SF/3/12, Alan Orme, 'Some Experiences of War' (unpublished memoir, n. d.), p. 6.
2 Field Marshal Lord Alan Brooke, *War Diaries 1939–45* (London: Weidenfeld and Nicholson, 2001), entry for 27 July 1940, p. 95.
3 WO 167/286, 46th Div. WD, May 1940 [*sic*], 'Summary of Events: Flanders Campaign 10 May–3 June 1940'.
4 WO 166/4665, 2/5th SF WD, Sept. 1940.
5 WO 277/36, Lieutenant-Colonel J. W. Gibb, *The Second World War 1939–1945: Training in the Army* (1961), p. 310.
6 WO 166/998, 139 Bde WD, Operational Instruction No. 9, 9 July 1941.
7 WO 166/999, 139 Bde WD, Oct. 1941, Brigadier R. C. Chichester-Constable, Special Brigade Order #55, 4 Oct. 1941.
8 WO 166/6288, 46th Div. WD, Mar. 1942, Appx. A.
9 All quotes from WO 166/6288, 46th Div. WD, May 1942, Appx D.
10 WO 205/1C, Minutes, 17 Mar. 1942, quoted in David French, *Raising Churchill's Army: The British Army and the War Against Germany, 1919–1945* (Oxford: OUP, 2000), p. 199.
11 Orme, 'Some Experiences', p. 10.

12 All quotes from NCA DD/SF/3/20, Fred Hirst, *A Sherwood Foresters' Story of World War II* (Poynton, Cheshire: n. p., 1997), pp. 8–9.
13 WO 166/6288, 46th Div. WD, Oct. 1942. Original capitalisation.

Chapter 7: Leaving Home

1 WO 216, PM Minute M 604/2 dated 13 Dec. 1942.
2 Gerald Summers, *The Lure of the Falcon* (London: Fontana, 1976, first published by Collins, 1972), p. 112.
3 Hirst, *Sherwood Foresters' Story*, p. 15.
4 Ian Mitchell, *The Battle of the Peaks and Longstop Hill* (Warwick: Helion, 2019), p. 61, says First Army battalions left their machine-gun platoons in the UK, but Fred Gamble in *MSFM*, p. 101, says the 2/5th Foresters MMG Platoon was on board the *Derbyshire* when it left England.
5 WO 175/509, 6th Royal West Kent's WD, Jan. 1943.
6 Quoted in Kenneth Macksey, *Crucible of Power: The Fight for Tunisia 1942–1943* (London: Hutchinson, 1969), p. 168, original source not given.

Chapter 8: Examinations

1 Quoted in Douglas E. Nash, 'Rommel's Lost Battalions', *Army History* 84 (2012), pp. 6–24 (p. 21).
2 Field Marshal Viscount Alexander of Tunis, 'The African Campaign from El Alamein to Tunis from 10th August 1942 to 13th May 1943', *Supplement to The London Gazette*, 5 Feb. 1948 (London: The London Gazette, 1948), pp. 839–87 (p. 881).
3 Stanley Storey, in Wally Binch (ed.), *Memories of Sedjenane* (2nd Edn) (1998, first published 1986) p. 55, hereafter *MoS*.
4 Keith Davenport, ibid., p. 65.
5 Orme, ibid., p. 109.
6 Wally Binch, ibid., p. 46.
7 WO 175/552, 5th SF WD, Mar. 1943.
8 WO 175/332, 70th Fld Rgt WD, Mar. 1943.
9 Sam Fullwood, in *MoS*, p. 54.
10 WO 373/1/149, MM citation for William Pidgeon.
11 Author's calculations from official War Office casualty lists in WO 417.
12 Howard Marshall, *Over to Tunis* (London: Eyre and Spottiswoode, 1943), quoted in Garrett, *None But The Brave*, p. 136.
13 Translation of Division Manteuffel War Diary by Ken Clark of 6th Lincolns, in *MoS*, p. 12.

Chapter 9: Graduation

1 WO 175/332 70th Fld Rgt WD, Mar. 1943.
2 Information about Wilfred Jackson provided to the author by his daughter-in-law Mary Jackson.
3 WO 175/157, 46 Div WD, Mar. 1943.
4 Author's calculations from WO 417; the number wounded is probably understated, e.g. Bennett does not appear.
5 WO 372/2, MM citation for George Stokes.
6 Steve Loach, in *MoS*, p. 59.

7 Les Fletcher, ibid., p. 35.
8 Schofield MS, p. 50.
9 Eric Morral, in *MoS*, p. 94.

Chapter 10: Captives

1 Author's calculation from WO 417, including officers of other regiments, MOs and chaplains serving with the unit.
2 WO 416/92/249, PoW record for Eric Deall. Smoking anecdote told to author by Major John Cotterill. Deall died in May 1975, aged 78.
3 Hirst, *Sherwood Foresters' Story*, p. 34.
4 DD/SF/3/23 Pearson diary, undated note, also entry for 29 Mar. 1943.
5 Orme, 'Some Exeriences', p. 18, and IWM #20789 Patrick O'Sullivan interview with Thomas Tunney (2001), Reel 15. There are such significant discrepancies between the two accounts that one or both may be based on hearsay rather than actual experience, but are probably based upon a real event.
6 Maurice Enser, 'The Story of Sgt Maurice Enser, Taken Prisoner March 2nd 1943' (n. d.), pp. 5–6.
7 NCA DDSF/3/24, G.F. Warsop 'In God's Pocket: A Personal Diary of Events During the Second World War' (n. d.), pp. 184–85.
8 Cosgrave's original note is in NCA DD/SF/2/8.
9 WO 208, Cosgrave escape report; Orme, 'Some Experiences', p. 18, and IWM #21600, Alan Orme interview with Tom Tunney, (n. d.), Reels 14–15; Summers, *Lure of the Falcon*, pp. 148–60.

Chapter 11: Time Out

1 IWM #15590, Phil Plowright interview with Peter Hart (n. d.), Reel 7.
2 IWM #13561, Reg Markham interview with Peter Hart, (n. d.), Reel 10.
3 WO 175/552, 5th SF WD, 24 June 1943.
4 See p. 36. In 1939 Stanley had enlisted as Stanley Waine Darwent, his stepfather's surname. His death was recorded under his original birth surname, Waine.
5 Probably temporary designations, as there were no USN vessels with these numbers.
6 NCA DDSF/3/5, Denys Crews manuscript 'First Meeting With "Tich" Verity'.

Bibliography

Unpublished Sources

MUSEUM OF THE MERCIAN REGIMENT, NOTTINGHAM (MMR)

The Regimental Archive contains the battalion war diaries, as well as a database of men known to have served with the regiment though this is not directly accessible to the public. There are also several personal accounts, some of which are also in the Nottinghamshire Archives, including:

Binch, Wally (ed.), *On Active Service* (1st Edn, n. d (c. 1990))
Binch, Wally (ed.), *More Sherwood Forester Memories* (1998)
Schofield, Jack 'Recollections of an Infantryman in World War II' (n. d.)
Schofield, CQMS J[ack] Untitled typescript [Operations of 46th Div. 10 August–12 December 1944] (1944–45)

NOTTINGHAMSHIRE ARCHIVES, NOTTINGHAM (NCA)

The County Archives contains the records of the 2/5 Sherwood Foresters Battalion Association, deposited by Wally Binch. The most important of the materials consulted are listed here.

DD/SF/3/4	Coombs, Geoffrey, 'Personal Account, Tunisia 1943' (n. d.)
DD/SF/3/5	Crews, Denys, personal accounts (n. d.)
DD/SF/3/6	Enser, Maurice, 'The Story of Sgt Maurice Enser, Taken Prisoner March 2nd 1943' (n. d.)
DD/SF/3/12	Orme, Alan, 'Some Experiences of War' (n. d.)
DD/SF/3/14	Schofield, Sergeant Jack, 'Recollections of an Infantryman' (n. d. [c 1970])
DD/SF/3/15	Stonier, Edmund, 'Extracts from Personal Diary' (Dec 1942–July 1945)
DD/SF/3/19	Garrett, Richard, 'What Did You Do in the War Grandad' (c. 1990)
DD/SF/3/20	Hirst, Fred, 'A Sherwood Forester's Story of World War II' (Poynton, Cheshire: n. p., 1997), published as *A Green Hill Far Away: by an Infantry Soldier* (n. l.: Lane Publishers, 1998)
DD/SF/3/22	Mellors, Harold, '[extracts from personal] Diary' (Jan 1943–May 1945) (full diary also made available by Tony Mellors)
DD/SF/3/23	Pearson, Cyril, 'War Diaries and Documents' (1943–45)

Bibliography

DD/SF/3/24 — Warsop, G. F., 'In God's Pocket: A Personal Diary of Events During the Second World War' (n. d.)
DD/SF/3/29 — Binch, Wally (ed.), *More Sherwood Forester Memories* (1998)
DD/SF/3/30 — Binch, Wally (ed.), *Memories of Sedjenane* (2nd Edn) (1998, first published 1986)
DD/SF/3/31 — Binch, Wally (ed.), *On Active Service* (2nd Edn) (1998, first published c. 1990)
DD/SF/5 — Photographic Archive; includes wartime images, association reunions and members' visits to Tunisia

Imperial War Museum (IWM)

IWM #16596, Harry Higton Papers. The IWM's sound archive contains many interviews with veterans of the battalion; these are listed here with catalogue references.

Binch, Wally #12941
Booker, Lewis Charles #15591
Coombs, Geoffrey Kendall #22080
Cowen, Julius #19628
Crews, Denys Kingwell #19987
Hampton, George Arthur #13260
Hession, Francis Burnett #13457
Higton, Harry #18618
Knowles, Joe #13347
Lord, Charles Anthony #18257
Mardell, Frank William #16400
Markham, Reginald Charles #13561
Offiler, Frank Edward #16352
Orme, Allan #21600
O'Sullivan, Patrick #20789
Plowright, Phil #15590
Shaw, Ernest Walter #15556
Sheppard, William #13455
Tupling, Victor #16086
Willett, Denis Vincent #13346
Wright, John #19079

The National Archives, Kew (TNA)

War Diaries: The National Archives contains copies of the war diaries for the Sherwood Foresters as well as those of other regiments and battalions and those of higher formations. Around 100 have been consulted for this volume; the most important are listed here.

WO 166: UK Home Forces
WO 166/552 46th Div. Sep. 1939–Mar. 1940 and July 1940–Dec. 1941
WO 166/6288 46th Div. 1942
WO 166/998 139 Bde Sep. 1939–Mar. 1940 and July–Dec. 1940
WO 166/999 139 Bde 1941
WO 166/6604 139 Bde 1942
WO 166/4666 2/5th Foresters Sep. 1939–Apr. 1940, July–Dec. 1940, Jan.–Dec. 1941
WO 166/8955 2/5th Foresters Jan.– Nov. 1942

WO 167: France 1940
WO 167/286 46th Div. Apr.–June 1940
WO 167/396 139 Bde Apr.–June 1940
WO 167/731 9th Foresters Apr.–June 1940
WO 167/785 2/5th Leicesters Apr.–June 1940
WO 167/824 1/5th Foresters Aug. 1939–June 1940
WO 167/825 2/5th Foresters Apr.–June 1940

WO 175: North Africa (Tunisia)
WO 175/157 46th Div. Dec. 1942–June 1943
WO 175/225 139 Bde Jan.–June 1943
WO 175/498 16th DLI Jan.–June 1943
WO 175/513 2/5th Leicesters Dec. 1942–June 1943
WO 175/522 2/5th (later 5th) Foresters Dec. 1942–June 1943

OTHER WAR OFFICE SERIES

WO 24 series specifies the official war establishments for different types of unit
WO 208 series are the records of the Directorate of Military Operations and Intelligence files, including both PoW escape reports and prison camp histories
WO 213 series contains records of field general courts martial and military courts
WO 224 series contains reports of PoW camp inspections in Italy and Germany by the Red Cross used to identify the locations of PoWs and the conditions in which they were held
WO 373 series contains details and citations of awards for gallantry or distinguished service
WO 391/1, WO 391/11 and **WO 392/21** contain lists of PoWs held in German and Italian camps
WO 416 series contains personal records for individual PoWs
WO 417 series contains lists of casualties sustained by the British Army during the Second World War.

OTHER UNPUBLISHED WORKS

Anon, *Oignies 28 Mai 1940, Entre Memoire et Histoire*, unpublished booklet by ONYACUM (Oignies historical society) (n. d.)
Drewienkiewicz, Brigadier K. J., 'Examine the Build-Up Early Training and Employment of the Territorial Army in the Lead-up to and the Early Days of The Second World War', paper submitted to the Royal College of Defence Studies (1992)
Garrett, Richard, *None But The Brave*, unpublished regimental history lent to the author by Major J. Cotterill (also held in the IWM)

Published Sources

There are few published sources that directly tell the story of the 2/5th Foresters, and relatively few that cover to any significant extent the operations and battles in which they participated. The following is a selection of secondary sources that have been consulted.

FORMATION, REGIMENTAL AND BATTALION HISTORIES

'A. H. W.', *The History of the Sixth Battalion the Lincolnshire Regt.* (Uckfield: Naval and Military Press, n.d., originally published 1946)
Anon, *The Sherwood Foresters (Nottinghamshire and Derby Regiment): A Brief History* (Derby: English Life Publications, 1980)
Anon, *The Story of the 46th Infantry Division*, (Graz: n. p., 1946)
Barclay, Brigadier C. N., *The History of the Sherwood Foresters (Nottinghamshire & Derby Regiment) 1919–1957* (London: William Clowes and Sons, 1959)
Dalbiac, Col Philip Hugh, *History of the 45th: 1st Nottinghamshire Regiment (Sherwood Foresters)* (London: Swan Sonnenschein, 1902)
Hart, Peter, *The Heat of Battle: 16th Bn, Durham Light Infantry 1943–45* (Barnsley: Pen & Sword, 1999)
Housley, Cliff, *'First Contact': a History of the 8th Battalion the Sherwood Foresters, 1939–1945* (Nottingham: Millquest Publications, [1997?])
Housley, Cliff, *First In Last Out: A History of 1/5th Territorial Battalion the Sherwood Foresters 1939–1946* (Long Eaton: n. p., 1995)
Stringer, Lawrence, *The History of the Sixteenth Battalion Durham Light Infantry* (Graz: n. p., 1946)

Personal Memoirs

Guinness, Paul, *We Pledge Our Lives: A Post-War Manifesto from a War-Time Prison* (London: Hodder & Stoughton, 1945)

Stainforth, Peter, *Wings of the Wind* (London: Falcon Press, 1952)

Summers, Gerald, *The Lure of the Falcon* (London: Fontana, 1976, first published 1972)

General Histories and Reference

Bull, Stephen and Gordon L. Rottman, *Infantry Tactics of the Second World War* (Oxford: Osprey, 2008)

Dennis, Peter, *The Territorial Army 1906–1940* (Woodbridge: Boydell, 1987)

Ellis, Chris and Peter Chamberlain (ed.), *Handbook on the British Army 1943* (London: Purnell Military Book Society Edition, 1975, first published 1943)

Ellis, John, *The Sharp End of War: The Fighting Man in World War II* (Newton Abbot: David & Charles, 1980)

Fraser, David, *And We Shall Shock Them: The British Army in the Second World War* (London: Hodder and Stoughton, 1983)

French, David, *Raising Churchill's Army: The British Army and the War Against Germany, 1919–1945* (Oxford: OUP, 2000)

Harrison-Place, Timothy, *Military Training in the British Army 1940–1944: From Dunkirk to D-Day* (London and Portland: Frank Cass, 2000)

Hockley, Anthony Farrar, *Infantry Tactics 1939–45* (London: Almark, 1976)

Joslen, Lieutenant Colonel H. F., *Orders of Battle United Kingdom and Colonial Formations and Units in the Second World War, 1939–45*, 2 vols (London: H. M. S. O., 1960)

France 1940

Anon, *Oignies, Première Cité Martyre de la Campagne de France* (n. l.: n. p., 1947), available online at www. wikipasdecalais.fr (accessed 19 June 2019), unpublished English translation by T. & I. Lariviere, 1990

Blaxland, Gregory, *Destination Dunkirk: The Story of Gort's Army* (London: William Kimber, 1973)

Karslake, Basil, *1940 The Last Act: The Story of the British Forces in France After Dunkirk* (London: Leo Cooper, 1979)

Lynch, Tim, *Dunkirk 1940, 'Whereabouts Unknown': How Untrained Troops of the Labour Divisions were Sacrificed to Save an Army* (Stroud: Spellmount, 2010)

Richardson, Matthew, *Tigers at Dunkirk* (Barnsley: Pen & Sword, 2010)

Tatlow, Peter, *Return From Dunkirk: Railways to the Rescue, Operation Dynamo (1940)* (Usk, Gwent: Oakwood Press, 2010)

Winser, John de S., *BEF Ships Before, At and After Dunkirk* (Gravesend: World Ship Society, 1999)

Wynn, Stephen, *The Lancastria Tragedy, Sinking and Cover Up: June 1940* (Barnsley: Pen & Sword, 2020)

Tunisia 1943

Alexander, Harold Field Marshal, 'The African Campaign from El Alamein to Tunis from 10th August 1942 to 13th May 1943', in *Supplement to The London Gazette*, 5 February 1948 (London: The London Gazette, 1948)

Anderson, Lieutenant General K. A. N., 'Operations in North West Africa from 8th November 1942 to 13th May 1943', in *Supplement to The London Gazette*, 6 November 1946 (London: The London Gazette, 1946)

Atkinson, Rick, *An Army at Dawn: The War in North Africa 1942–1943* (New York: Henry Holt, 2002)

Austin, A. B., *Birth of an Army* (London: Gollancz, 1943)

Blaxland, Gregory, *The Plain Cook and the Showman: The First and Eighth Armies in North Africa* (London: William Kimber, 1977)

Macksey, Kenneth, *Crucible of Power: The Fight for Tunisia 1942–1943* (London: Hutchinson, 1969)

Mitchell, Ian, *The Battle of the Peaks and Longstop Hill* (Warwick: Helion, 2019)

Nash, Douglas E., 'Rommel's Lost Battalions', in *Army History* 84 (2012), pp. 6–24

Playfair, Major General I. S. O. and Brigadier C. J. C. Moloney, *The Mediterranean and the Middle East: Vol IV, The Destruction of the Axis Forces in Africa* (London: H. M. S. O., 1966)

Villahermosa, Gilberto, *Hitler's Paratrooper: The Life and Battles of Rudolf Witzig* (Barnsley: Frontline, 2010)

Prisoners of War

Anon, *A Handbook for the Information for Relatives and Friends of Prisoners of War* (London: H.M.S.O., 1943)

Longden, Sean, *Hitler's British Slaves: British and Commonwealth POWs in German Industry 1939–45* (Moreton-in-Marsh: Arris Books, 2005)

Richards, Anthony, *Guests of the Third Reich* (London: Imperial War Museum, 2019)

Rolf, David, *Prisoners of the Reich: Germany's Captives 1939–45* (London: Coronet, 1989, first published 1988)

Online Sources

General sites

The following have been accessed multiple times for information and reference.

<ancestry.co.uk> for personal background information

Anon, 'Army Military Abbreviations Acronyms Slang Words' <https://www.qaranc.co.uk/armyabbreviations.php>

British Newspaper Archive, <britishnewspaperarchive.co.uk>. Newspapers consulted include *Derby Evening Telegraph*, *Derbyshire Times and Chesterfield Herald*, *Nottingham Journal*, *Ripley and Heanor News and Ilkeston Div. Free Press*, and *Sheffield Telegraph and Independent*

Commonwealth War Graves Commission, <cwgc.org>

<Crich-memorial. org.uk/obituries/obituries.html> for obituaries of battalion members (accessed 6 January 2020 and 3 December 2022; the site is no longer available)

<findmypast.co.uk> for personal background information, and casualty and PoW records

<fold3.com> for Army Lists

London Gazette, <thegazette.co.uk> for details of commissions and awards

Index

Note: page numbers in *italics* refer to images or maps.

Abbeville, 59
Acomb, 133
'Aero', Exercise, 93
Aine Abid, 122
Aire, Canal d', 61
Albert Canal, 53
Aldershot, 80
'Alert', Exercise, 97-98
Alexander, Field Marshal Harold, 76-77, 140
Alfreton, 76, 170
Algeria, 117, 190
Algiers, 118, 119, 120, 121, 122, 124, 126, 130, 161, 163, 171, 192, 195
Allennes, 58
Allestree Hall, 38
Allfrey, Lt Gen. Charles, 160, 161
Alma, 17
Alps, 22, 189
Alsace, 24
Altmayer, Gen. René, 61
Alvaston, 36
Ambergate, 180
Amiens, 44, 58
Andalsnes, 107
Anderson, Maj. Gen. Desmond, 85, 93
Andrew, Cpl, 135
'Ante', Exercise, 105
Ardennes, 54, 139
Armentières, 66, 73
Armitage, Capt. Eric Lloyd ('Dolly'), 125, 152, 155

Armstrong, Capt. Phillip ('Dolly'), 47, 49, 52, 68, 72
Arnim, Field Marshal Hans-Jürgen von, 117, 139, 170
Arnold (Notts.), 108
Arras, 44, 58, 59, 60, 62, 63, 69
Ashford (Kent), 80
Ath, 55, 56
Atlas Mountains, 119
Attiches, 69
Auby, 59, 62
Auschwitz, 185
Ausladung (Disembarkation), Operation, 139
Austria, 25
Avalanche, Operation, 197
Avelin, 63, 72, 73
Aylesbury, 15

Bad Orb, 179
Badajoz, 16
Bailleul, 73
Baisieux, 58
Baldy Hill, 127, 131
Bamford, 32
Ban Pong, 113
Barbarossa, Operation, 94
Barenthin, Col Walter, 140
Barker, Lt Charles, 146
Barlow, Pte Arthur, 85
Barmouth, 125
Barnes, Pte Joe, 168
Barradell, Cpl Thomas, 101
Barratt, Revd Harold Norman, 49, 133-135

Basford, 46, 84
Bavaria, 178
Beachborough, 98
Beaurevoir-Fonsomme, 21
Beauvin, 61, 66
Bee, Capt. J. W., 39
Beja, 123, 127, 136, 137, 138, 139, 141, 146, 164, 171
Belfast, 103
Belgian army, 53, 55
Belgium, 44, 53, 54-58, 56, 61, 68, 73, 74, 90, 109, 140, 178
Belle Vue Park, 80, 81, 83
Belper, 26, 27, 31, 38, 68
Belsen, 185
Bennett, Pte, 162-63, 204n
Bentley (Yorks.), 102
Bergues, 74, 75, 76, 78, 81, 82
Bergues–Furnes Canal, 75
Berkeley-Schultz, Lt Bob, 120, 125, 169
Berkshire, 96
Bersaglieri Regiment, 10th (Italian), 141, 165
Berwick, 86, 88
Bey of Tunis, 132
Bhopal, 113
Binch, Pte Wally, *11,* 145-46, 150-52
Birmingham, 38
Biscayne, USS, 199
Bizerte, 117, 123, 126-27, 172, 180, 187, 197, 199
Blackdown Camp, 80, 83
Blake, Pte John, 134
Blanchard, Gen. George, 69
Bland, Sgt Jack, 151
Blandy, Maj. Patrick, 95
Blaxland, Maj. Arthur, 144, 152
Blida, 192, 194
Bologna, 189
Bolton, 2nd Lt 'Paddy', 195
Bombay, 17, 112, 114
Bone, 118, 145
Booker, Pte Lew, 180
Booth, L. Cpl Geoff, 149
Bordon, 39, 81
Borgetto, 188
Bou Arada, 139, 172, 173
Bou Dissa, 127
Boulogne, 69
Boultby, Pte Ernie, *11,* 149-50, 155, 158
Boulton, Cpl Louis, 101
'Boxer', Exercise, 95

Bradley, Pte Ronald, 72
Brailsford, 102
Braunschweig (Brunswick), 189
Bresle River, 110
Brighton, 100
British, Dominion and Imperial forces:
   18th Army Group, 140, 164
   British Expeditionary Force (BEF), 26, 43-44, 50, 51, 53, 55, 57, 58, 59, 60, 68, 69, 73, 74, 77, 80, 82, 109, 202n
   Home Guard, 86, 91, 92
   National Defence Companies, 38-39, 91
   Northern Command, 18, 40, 41
   Number 3 North Midland Region, 36
   Territorial Army, 22-23, 26-29, 30, 31, 32-33, 35, 36, 38, 42, 46, 49, 91
   Territorial Force, 19, 22
Armies:
   Eighth Army, 116, 137, 172, 175, 192
   First Army, 117, 121, 136, 172, 175, 204n
Corps:
   I Corps, 73, 76
   II Corps, 17, 73, 93, 94, 95
   III Corps, 73
   V Corps, 117, 137, 160, 172, 173
   IX Corps, 93, 172, 174
   XII Corps, 96, 98, 99, 109
Divisions:
   1st Armoured Division, 109, 114, 172-73, 174-75
   6th Armoured Division, 117, 137, 172-73
   1st Division, 85, 171
   2nd Division, 61, 63
   3rd Canadian Division, 100
   4th Division, 199
   12th Division, 44, 57
   18th Division, 112
   23rd Division, 41, 44, 57, 58
   24th Division, 21
   42nd Division, 85, 94, 109
   45th Division, 94
   46th Division, 20-21, 32, 41, 44, 50, 53, 58, 61, 63, 66-69 *passim*, 73-77 *passim*, 80, 83, 84, 85, 93-102 *passim*, 104, 118, 126, 137, 138, 160, 164, 171-73, 192, 197, 199
   47th Division, 96
   49th Division, 23, 32, 85

Index

50th (Tyne Tees) Division, 85, 96
51st (Highland) Division, 110
55th Division, 41
78th Division, 117, 137, 139
Brigades:
9 Armoured Brigade, 114
1 Army Tank Brigade, 59
26 Brigade, 137
36 Brigade, 122, 123, 127, 157, 165, 171
55 Brigade, 112
128 Brigade, 126, 172
137 Brigade, 50, 97, 126
138 Brigade, 50, 59, 97, 126, 138, 171, 175
139 Brigade, 20, 32-37 *passim*, 41, 50, 51, 53, 55, 57, 58, 60, 61, 62-63, 66, 68, 78, 84-89 *passim*, 93, 94, 95, 103, 109, 118, 121-23, 126-27, 137, 144, 157, 159, 160, 165, 170, 172-73, 176, 193, 197
148 Brigade, 23, 27, 32, 33, 107, 108
151 Brigade, 63, 67, 69
A Infantry Brigade, 110
1 Parachute Brigade, 160, 161, 163, 165, 167, 170, 171
North Midlands Brigade, 18
Units:
17th (Leicestershire) Regiment of Foot, 16
45th (1st Nottinghamshire) Regiment of Foot, 15-16, 18
95th (Derbyshire) Regiment of Foot, 16-18
95th Rifles, 17
8th Argyll and Sutherland Highlanders, 128, 138, 175
Army Air Corps (AAC), 188
Artists Rifles, 59, 70, 84
Borders Regiment, 191
4th Borders Regiment, 110
Buffs (East Kent Regiment), 125, 161, 171
Cavalry Training Regiment, 86
Coldstream Guards, 32
2nd Coldstream Guards, 160
1 Commando, 135, 138, 141, 144, 154
6 Commando, 94
Derbyshire Yeomanry, 29, 30, 175
1/7th Duke of Wellington's (West Riding) Regiment (DWR), 97-98

Durham Light Infantry (DLI), 59, 63, 66
6th DLI, 63
8th DLI, 63, 66, 67, 68-69
9th DLI, 63, 67
16th DLI, 93, 126, 128, 141, 144-45, 148, 155, 157, 158, 159, 160, 165, 167, 169, 172, 173, 176, 193
1st East Lancashire Regiment, 75
1st East Yorkshire Regiment, 199
7th East Yorkshire Regiment, 125
Essex Regiment, 191
1st Green Howards, 99
5th Green Howards, 62
Hampshire Regiment, 126, 176
5th Hampshires, 175
5th (Inniskilling) Dragoon Guards, 78
Inniskilling Fusiliers, 195
Inns of Court Regiment, 46
King's Own Yorkshire Light Infantry (KOYLI), 84
2/4th KOYLI, 126
5th King's Regiment (Liverpool), 125
17/21st Lancers, 137
Leeds Rifles (West Yorkshire Rgt), 48
Leicestershire Regiment:
5th Leicesters, 23
1/5th Leicesters, 107
2/5th Leicesters, 33, 36, 41, 50, 51, 52, 63, 66, 75, 86, 88, 93, 104, 135, 137, 160, 161, 165-69, 172-74, 176, 190, 193
Lincolnshire Regiment, 165, 182
6th Lincolns, 59, 60, 97-98, 103, 126, 138, 141, 144-45, 149, 156-59, 165, 167, 171
1st Loyal Regiment, 75, 78
2/7th Middlesex Regiment, 86
Norfolk Regiment, 161, 171
North Irish Horse (NIH), 158, 161, 167, 171
Parachute Regiment, 170, 194
1st Parachute Battalion, 161, 163, 165, 168
2nd Parachute Battalion, 167, 170
3rd Parachute Battalion, 161, 163, 165, 171
2/7th Queen's Royal Regiment (West Surrey), 96
46th Recce Regiment, 121-22, 141, 173, 193

Rifle Brigade, 17, 49, 137
112th Rgt Royal Armoured Corps, 109
Royal Artillery, 50, 89, 193
  16th Field Rgt, 61, 63, 66, 76
  70th Field Rgt, 86, 133, 151, 156, 161
  172nd Field Rgt, 173
  6th Field Training Rgt, 86
  2 Anti-Tank Bty, 61, 63
  8 Anti-Tank Bty, 61, 63, 73, 76
  229 Anti-Tank Bty, 167
  230 Anti-Tank Bty, 86
  27/72 Bty, 63
  34/86 Bty, 63
  225 Field Bty, 61
  275 Field Bty, 88
  277 Field Bty, 141
  279 Field Bty, 133, 144, 151, 161, 167
  449 Field Bty, 144, 152, 161, 167
  379 Light Anti-Aircraft Bty, 144, 151, 152
  456 Light Bty, 144, 150, 152
  457 Light Bty, 167
  15/17 Medium Bty, 144
Royal Army Medical Corps (RAMC), 37, 43, 101, 102, 195, 197
  183 Field Ambulance, 131
Royal Army Chaplaincy Department, 49, 133
Royal Army Ordnance Corps (RAOC), 43
Royal Army Service Corps (RASC), 43
Royal Electrical Mechanical Engineers (REME), 88
Royal Engineers, 23, 40, 43, 49, 52, 103, 135, 144
  40th (Sherwood Foresters) AA Battalion, 23
  42nd (Robin Hood) AA Battalion, 23
  270 Field Company, 190
Royal Irish Fusiliers, 195
Royal Munster Fusiliers, 47
Royal Scots Infantry Training Centre, 86
Royal Sussex Regiment, 58
48th Royal Tank Regiment, 172
2nd Royal Warwickshire Regiment, 74, 75, 76

Royal Welch Fusiliers, 81
1st Welch Fusiliers, 96
Royal West Kent Regiment, 174
  6th Royal West Kents, 123, 127, 157
Seaforth Highlanders, 49
Sherwood Foresters:
  1st Battalion, 16, 19, 22, 23, 109-10, 116
  1st Volunteer Battalion, 19
  2nd Battalion, 17, 22, 31, 39, 47, 49, 73, 94, 109, 111, 124
  3rd Battalion (2nd Derbyshire Militia), 18, 19
  4th Battalion (Nottinghamshire Militia), 18, 19
  5th Battalion (1st Derbyshire Militia), 18
  5th Battalion (to 1939), 19, 22, 26, 27, 30, 31, 125
  1/5th Battalion, 20, 21, 27, 37, 44, 59, 110-13, 177
  2/5th (later 5th) Battalion:
    A Coy, 27, 32, 47, 49, 50, 55, 68, 75, 125, 134, 144-48, 152-53, 156, 161, 165, 169, 186, 198, 199
    B Coy, 27, 33, 37, 41-42, 47, 55, 56, 58, 66-68, 99, 102, 125, 130, 133, 144, 148, 151, 154, 155, 162-63, 168, 198
    C Coy, 27, 33, 35, 47, 48, 50, 55, 57, 58, 124, 125, 144, 149, 152, 162-64, 168, 169, 172, 183, 198
    D Coy, 27, 30, 47, 49, 55, 70, 101, 144, 149-50, 155, 162, 163, 198
    E Coy, 83
    HQ Coy, 26, 27, 47-49, 55, 95, 123, 125, 154, 159, 194, 198
    Support (S) Coy, 194, 198
    7 Pl., 146-47
    8 Pl., 146
    9 Pl., 130, 146
    10 Pl., 47, 148, 154, 162
    11 Pl., 47, 148, 162, 164, 167
    12 Pl., 47, 151
    13 Pl., 163
    14 Pl., 149, 153
    15 Pl., 149, 155

Index

16 Pl., 90
Admin. Pl., 48, 194
Anti-Aircraft Pl., 48, 51
Anti-Tank Pl., 124, 150, 194
B Echelon, 125, 129, 131, 133, 135, 146, 154, 177, 198
Carrier Pl., 47, 87, 121, 144, 145-46, 156, 194
Intelligence Section, 193
MMG Pl., 123, 194, 204n
Mortar Pl., 47-48, 90, 100, 121, 144, 150, 152, 154, 170, 194
motorcycle pl., 87
Pioneer Pl., 48, 90, 175, 193, 194
Signals Pl., 48, 61, 194
3/5th Battalion, 20
6th Battalion, 19, 22, 23, 27, 45
1/6th Battalion, 21, 94
7th Battalion, 19, 22, 23, 49
2/7th Battalion, 21
8th Battalion, 19, 22, 23, 31, 32, 39, 44, 94, 107-8, 124, 125
2/8th Battalion, 21, 27
9th Battalion, 20, 27, 31, 33, 36, 41, 50-56 *passim*, 62, 66, 72, 73, 75, 84, 86, 93, 109, 113, 126
10th (Home Defence) Battalion, 39, 91
11th Battalion, 21-22, 93
12th Battalion, 21, 113
13th Battalion, 113
14th Battalion, 114
16th Battalion (1942), 110
16th Battalion (Chatsworth Rifles), 20
17th Battalion (Welbeck Rangers), 20
70th Young Soldiers Battalion, 91-92, 102, 110, 124, 125, 145, 171
Sherwood Foresters Infantry Training Centre, 31, 32, 83, 93, 102-3
1/6th South Staffordshire Regiment, 80
Suffolk Regiment, 49
Welch Regiment, 191
West Yorkshire Regiment, 48, 198
York and Lancaster Regiment, 102
6th York and Lancs, 59, 126
Miscellaneous:

268 Squadron RAF, 95
Alien Pioneer Unit, 52
No. 1 Base Ammunition and Base Petrol Dump, 110
Dunbar Officer Corps Training Unit (OCTU), 86
No. 1 Infantry Base Depot, 111
MacForce, 58, 59, 61
17th Motor Coach Company, 94
164 Officer Corps Training Unit (OCTU), 125, 164
Petreforce, 58
Polforce, 58, 61
Scottish Command Central School, 91
38th Signals Training Regiment, 86
Tom Force, 112
Officer Training Corps (OTC), 39, 125
Usherforce, 74
Brittany, 43, 57, 111
Brooke, Field Marshal Alan, 85, 99
Brown Hill, 128
Brown, Sgt Harry, 67
Bruce, Lt Kenneth Ian, 49, 91
Brussels, 53
Brüx, 186
Bruz, 52, 53
Buckshee Road, 129
Bull, L. Cpl Arthur, 132
'Bulldog', Exercise, 94
'Bumper', Exercise, 95-96
Buqueux, 63
Burgermeister, Hauptmann Michael, 140
Burgess, Joan, 179
Burgess, Pte George, 179
Burma, 16, 113
Burton upon Trent, 31, 38, 52
Buttress, Operation, 197
Buxton, 27, 33, 36, 42, 46, 50, 68

'Caesar', Codeword, 41
Cairo, 109, 116
Calais, 69
Camber Sands, 100
Camberley, 80, 106
Cambrai, 54, 57, 58, 178
Cambridgeshire, 96
Canterbury, SS, 110
Cap Serrat, 126, 127, 141, 159
Caporetto (Kobarid), 21

Capua, 183
Cardwell, Edward, 16, 17
Carvin, 60, 63, 66, 67, 69, 70
Casablanca, 192
Case, Capt. Robert Anthony (Bobby), 125, 163, 170
Cassel, 69, 73, 178
Castellette, Pte Arthur, 111, 113
Castle Donnington, 37
Chadwick, Capt., 62, 66
Chamberlain, Neville, 25, 26
Changi, 113
Chapel-en-le-Frith, 33, 36, 37
Chemy, 58
Cherbourg, 51
Chesterfield, 27, 28, 30, 31, 36, 48, 103
Chichester-Constable, Brig. Raleigh Charles Joseph, 60, 63, 76, 85-86, 88, 93, 96, 126, 129, 153, 157, 158
Childers, Hugh, 16, 18
Chinley, 37
Churchill, Winston, 116, 117-18, 126, 191, 192
Civil Defence Scheme 32, 39
Clark, Lt Gen. Mark, 197
'Clive', Codeword, 32
Cockburnspath, 86, 88
Codrington, HMS, 79
Colchester, 125
Colditz, 178
Colver, Lt Cedric, 52, 102
Commando Hill, 161, 162, 163
Connolly, Vice Adm. Richard L., 199
'Conqueror', Exercise, 192-94, *193*, 195
Cooper, Maj. Myles Harry, 49, 71, 73, 83
Cooper, Pte (Sedjenane), 149, 155
Cooper, Pte Sydney, *11*, 50, 53, 55, 76, 79, 81, 100
Corby, L. Cpl Stan, *11*, 164, 168, 169, 172, 195, 197
Cosgrave, Pte Tom, 188-89
Cottesmore, 40
Courrieres, 61, 62, 66, 70
Cousin, Lt Douglas, *11*, 46, 53, 75, 76, 84, 85, 88, 102
Cowderoy, 2nd Lt Bryan, 87
Cowen, Lt Julius, 102, 155, 182, 185, 186
Cowie, Lt Keith, 132, 169, 170
Coxon, Sgt Fred, 148
Cresswell, Pte (Leicesters), 135

Creswick, Sgt John, 75, 84-85
Crete, 140
Crewdson, Brig. Henry Alastair Fergusson, 32, 38, 41, 52, 53, 55, 60
Crews, Capt. Denys, *11*, 120, 125, 148, 154, 164, 194, 198, 199
Crich, 22, 31, 180
Cripps, 2nd Lt George, 59, 70, 90
Cripps, 2nd Lt Percival, 59, 110
Crocker, Lt Gen. John, 194
'Cromwell', Codeword, 89
Curtis, Maj. Gen. Henry Osborne, 50, 52, 53, 58, 60, 61, 69, 75, 82, 85
Cyrenaica, 115, 116
Czechoslovakia, 25, 30

Darwent, Pte Stanley Waine, see Waine, Stanley
Davenport, Capt. George Arthur Keith, *11*, 70, 125, 146, 155, 194
Daventry, 195
Deall, Maj. Eric Noel, 49, 68, 177, 178, 180, 205n.
Death Ridge, 160
Delwari Camp, 113
Derby, 17, 18, 22, 29, 30, 31, 33, 35, 36, 38, 51, 67, 83, 84, 93
Derbyshire, 16, 18, 22, 23, 26, 28-31, 33, 34, 36, 41, 81, 83, 91, 191, 195
Derbyshire, HMT, 118-19, 161, 204n
Derbyshire, trawler, 112
Deule River, 61
Devonshire, Duke of, 18, 20, 31
Dixon, Pte Willis, *11*, 38, 56-57, 61, 74, 75, 148, 162, 163, 174
Djebel Abiod, 123, 127, 138, 139, 141, 157, 160, 161, 162, 165, 167, 170, 199
Djebel Ajred, see 'Baldy Hill'
Djebel Azag, 128
Djebel Aziz, 165, 168
Djebel Bel March, 160, 163, 165, 175
Djebel Bessioud, 173, 174, 176
Djebel Bou Djeblar, 144
Djebel el Azzag, see 'Green Hill'
Djebel Guerba, 141, 144
Donnington Hall, 33
Dooley, Sgt (RA), 76
Douai, 58, 60, 61, 62, 63, 68
Doullens, 58
Dourges, 70
Dove Holes, 33, 35, 37

Dover, 57, 79, 80
'Drake', Exercise, 94
Drem, 86, 90
Drottingholm, SS (Swedish), 180
Dublin, 21, 188
Duke of York, SS, 51
Dunbar, 86, 89, 90
Dunkirk, 62, 69, 71, 73-85, 77, 101, 102, 103, 105, 106, 109-11, 123, 124, 125, 134, 165, 176, 177-78
Dunmow, 59
Durban, 114
Dyle River, 53, 54, 109
Dynamo, Operation, 57, 71

East Anglia, 93, 94, 95, 105, 110, 113, 191
East Dereham, 93
East Lothian, 84, 86
Eban Emael, 140
Edinburgh, 84, 85, 86, 89, 90, 91, 134
Egginton Hall, 38, 94, 99
Egypt, 109, 114, 115, 116, 184
Eisenhower, Gen. Dwight D., 118
El Alamein, 114, 116
El Aouana, 146
El Aroussa, 139
Ellis, Pte F., 196
Enfidaville, 172
Enser, Sgt Maurice, *11*, 134-35, 149, 153, 155, 184-85
Escaut River, 55, 58, 61
Essex, 59, 96, 174
Estevelles, 62, 66, 67
Everard, Lt Col Henry Breedon, 49, 68, 177, 178
Evin Malmaison, 59, 60, 62
Evreux, 111

Fallingbostel, 185
Falmouth, 112
Farnell, Pte Derrick, 50, 68
Fellows, Pte Bob, 134
Fidra, 86
Finningley, 40
Firth of Forth, 89
Flavell, Brigadier Edwin, 160, 163, 165
Fletcher, Cpl Les, *11*, 170
Flude, RQMS Sydney, 154
Folkestone, 80, 81, 96, 100
Forêt de Flines, 58

Fouka, 192
France, 18, 19, 20, 21, 25, 26, 41, 43-56 *passim*, 56, 58, 62, 68, 81, 83, 85, 86, 94, 96, 105, 107, 109, 110-11, 115, 116, 117, 124, 125, 137, 177-79 *passim*, 197, 199, 202n
French forces:
  First Army, 73
  V Corps, 61
  Cavalry Corps, 63
  Corps Franc d'Afrique (CFA), 126, 129, 138, 141, 160, 161, 165, 167
  1st Moroccan Division, 61, 63, 66
  2nd Division Infanterie Nord Africaine, 63
  3rd Division Légère Mécanique, 63
  12th (Motorised) Infantry Division, 63
  40th Artillery Regiment, 63
  99th Infantry Regiment, 62
  106th Motorised Infantry Regiment, 63
  137th Infantry Regiment, 74, 78
  341st Infantry Regiment, 74
  7th Régiment Tirailleurs Maroccains (RTM), 62, 69
  Régiment Tirailleurs Sénégalais, 174
  11th Zouave Regiment, 63, 69
  80th Groupe de Reconnaissance de Division d'Infanterie (GRDI), 62, 66
  Arba Rifles, 144
Freeman-Atwood, Maj. Gen. Harold, 96, 97, 102, 104, 105, 106, 126, 173, 193, 199
Fullwood, Cpl Sam, *11*, 153, 158

Gafour, 172
Gafsa, 175
Galashiels, 93
Gamble, Pte Fred 'Spike', *11*, 204n
Garaet Achkel, 126
Garrett, Lt Richard, *12*, 39, 108, 120, 125, 148, 157
Gazala, 109
Gela, 192
Geneva Convention, 179, 182, 184, 185
Germany, 19, 22, 24-25, 32, 52, 192
German and German Allied forces:
  Luftwaffe, 54, 55, 56, 74, 89, 90, 111, 120, 192, 199
  Armies:
    Fifth Panzer Army, 117, 136, 139
  Corps:

Afrika Korps, 115, 116, 136, 139, 140
Divisions:
  7th Panzer Division, 59, 73
  10th Panzer Division, 136, 145, 173
  15th Panzer Division, 114
  21st Panzer Division, 136
  20th Motorised Division, 76
  18th Infantry Division, 78
  Hermann Goering Division (Luftwaffe), 174
  Division von Manteuffel, 139, 159
Battle groups:
  Kampfgruppe Jefna, 140, 141, 145, 148, 156
  Kampfgruppe Latini, 139, 141, 145
  Kampfgruppe Witzig, 139, 140
Units:
  Barenthin Regiment (Luftwaffe), 140, 141, 145, 148, 156, 158, 176
  I/47th Infantry Regiment, 160
  II/497th Infantry Regiment, 70
  A30 Marsch-bataillone, 139-40, 159, 170
  III/756th Mountain Regiment, 160
  I/69th Panzer Grenadier Regiment (PGR), 163, 168-69, 172
  86th PGR, 172
  11th Parachute Engineer Battalion, 139, 140, 165
  T3 Tunis Field Battalion, 140, 167
  T4 Tunis Field Battalion, 139-40, 167
Miscellaneous:
  Gefahr Lazarett 60, 178
Ghardimou, 122, 123
Ghent, 178
Gibraltar, 15, 119, 192
Gibson, Pte Ernie, *12*, 50, 52, 81
Gilliver, Lt Willoughby, *12*, 134, 146, 148, 153, 157
Glossop, 27, 36
Gloucester Duke of, 88, 93
Goering, Hermann, 140
Goerke, Oberleutnant, 136
Gofton-Salmond, Maj. Geoffrey ('Goofy'), 38, 94, 194
Gommecourt, 20, 21
Gorguechon, 63
Gort Line, 44
Gort, Field Marshal Lord, 44, 53, 57, 58, 69, 76
Gosford, 86

Goubellat, 172
Great Yarmouth, 95
Green Hill, 127, 131, 133-34, 135, 136, 137, 140, 141, 147, 148, 171, 175
Guderian, Generaloberst Heinz, 54, 57-58
Gué de Constantine, 119, 120
Guinness, Revd Paul, 145, 155, 185, 186

Haddington, 84, 89
Haie, Chateau de la, 52
Haldane, Richard Burdon, 19
Halifax (Nova Scotia), 112
Hallett, Pte Eddie, *12*, 145-46, 150
Hamman Lif, 191
Hammond, QM Capt. Richard (Dick), *12*, 48, 125, 154
Hampton, Pte George, *12*, 31, 48, 60, 72, 74, 79, 81, 129
Hanover, 185
Hansell, Pte Horace, 38, 41
'Harold', Exercise, 100, 102, 105
Harris, L. Sgt Ernest, 101
Hartigan, Capt. John Wyndham, 47, 51, 67, 68, 81
Hassell, Lt Col Jacob, 83, 88, 91, 93
Hathersage, 32, 48, 84
Haute Deule, Canal de la, 58, 59, 69, 74
Hawkesworth, Lt Gen. John Ledlie Inglis, 199
Hayes, Pte James, 174
Heanor, 27
Hefford, Lt Col Eric Alfred, 165, 168, 169, 173, 191
Henin-Lietard (Henin-Beaumont), 62, 63, 67
Hennessy, RSM Patrick ('Tara'), 134, 154, 156
Henriques, 2nd Lt David James (Jim) Quixano, 46, 67
Hesse, 179
Hession, Sgt Frank, 48, 49, 74, 81
Higton, Fanny, 30
Higton, Sgt Harry, 30, 111-12, 113, 184, 187
Hill 231 (Sedjenane), 144, 154
Hill, Pte Ernest Briggs, 37
Hindenburg Line, 21, 50
Hine, Capt. Alaric Gordon ('Spotlight'), 87, 121, 125, 159
Hirst, Pte Fred, *12*, 102-3, 118, 119, 120, 125, 129, 131, 148, 154, 159, 162, 164, 165, 167-68, 180, 182, 185

Index

Hitler, Adolf, 24, 25, 31, 90, 116, 196
Hohenzollern Redoubt, 20, 21
Holbrook, Capt. Frank, 124, 135, 167, 170
Holland, 53, 54, 90
Holyhead, 27, 28, 32
Home Defence Scheme 39
Hong Kong, 112
Hope Valley, 27, 32, 33, 36
Horam, 100
Hore-Belisha, Leslie, 26, 29, 31, 32
Horrocks, Lt Gen. Brian, 197, 199
Hotching, Sgt Ted, 172
Houghton, Col Daniel, 15
Howlett, Brigadier Bernard, 157, 165
Hoymille, 75
Hucknall, 30, 35, 37, 40 41
Hudson, Lt Col Charles Edward, 22, 93
Humber estuary, 40
Hunt, Pte Kia, 130
Husky, Operation, 192, 194
Hutt, Cpl Fred, *12*, 130, 131, 169

Iceland, 85
Iden Green, 125
Ilkeston, 30, 46
Inchville, 110
India, 16, 17, 84, 96, 113, 115, 191
Irish Republican Army, 33
Italy, 22, 25, 93, 96, 104, 139, 170, 196, 198, 199

Jackson, Elsie, 164
Jackson, Lt Wilfred Stuart, 125, 164
Jeffery, L. Cpl Fred, *12*, 56, 147
Jefna, 127, 138, 145
Jewkes, L. Sgt Bernard ('Lucky'), 145
Johnson, Pte (Sedjenane), 150
Johore, 112
Jones, Pte Frederick, 68
Jones, Pte Laban, 68
Joumine River, 127
Jukes, Sgt, 32
'Julius', Codeword, 40

Kasserine Pass, 136, 137, 139
Kedleston Hall, 51
Keith-Lucas, Capt. Bryan, 123, 125, 134, 145, 153, 157
Kellett, Sgt Fred, 67
Kent, 80, 96, 98, 102, 108, 113, 125, 134
Kerly, Capt. John, 46, 73, 125, 146-48, 155, 156

Kidger, Cpl Jack, 153
Kiev, 95
Kimberley Hall, 93
King George VI, 106
King Leopold (Belgium), 74
King, Pte Joe, 104
Kingdon, Pte Tommy, 164
Kingsnorth, 97
Kirk, 2nd Lt Mike, 108
Kitchener, Lord Herbert, 19, 20
Knight, Sgt Stan, *12*, 163
Knightsbridge Box, 110
Kolrep, Hauptmann Horst, 70
Kotah, 17
Kristallnacht, 25

La Bassée, 60, 61, 63, 73
La Vacquerie, 63
Lady of Mann, SS, 51
Lakenheath, 93, 94, 95
Lambert, Pte Harold, 149
Lamsdorf (Łambinowice), 178
Lancaster, Capt. Claude Granville, 31, 35
Lancastria, RMS, 111-13
Laufen, 178
Laurence, Capt. Geoffrey, 84, 121, 125
Le Cateau, 17, 57
Le Havre, 110
Le Mans, 111
Le Thelu, 63
Leaver, Lt Horace, 144
Lees, Pte Frank, *12*, 153
Leicestershire, 36, 41
Leith, 89
Leningrad, 95
Leuze, 55
Lewes, 101
Leytonstone, 174
Libercourt, 60
Libya, 115, 184
Liddell Hart, Capt. Basil, 30
Lille, 55, 61, 63, 69, 71, 73, 75
Lillehammer, 107
Lincoln, 92, 102, 104
Lincolnshire, 36
Little Hallam, 46
Little Ouse River, 95
Litton, 2nd Lt Peter, 108
Liverpool, 106, 118
Livorno, 182
Loach, Cpl Steve, 72, 135
Lomme, 73

London, 23, 46, 80, 89, 125, 157
Longnidry, 86
Longstop Hill, 127, 175
Loos, 20, 21, 61, 62
Lord, 2nd Lt Charles Anthony (Tony), 108
Lorraine, 24
Louisbourg, 15
Lulworth Cove, 81
Lympne, 97
Lyon, Pte Robert, 132

Macerata, 183
Macmerry, 86
Macpherson, Pte (Sedjenane), 149
Madden, Lt Keith, 151
Magdala, 16
Maginot Line, 44, 53, 54
Mainz, 178
Maison Carrée (El Harrach), 120, 121, 122, 134
Major, Pte Len, 161
Malaya, 112
Malo-les-Bains, 78, 79, 80
Malta, 187
Manchester, 33, 80, 82, 83
Mansfield, 36
Manteuffel, Col Hasso von, 139, 159
Marchiennes, 58
Mardell, L. Cpl Frank, *13*, 92, 171
Margate, 80
Market Harborough, 41
Markham, CQMS Reg, *13,* 28, 29, 32, , 57, 85, 113, 129, 169, 191
Marshall, Howard, 157
Martin, 2nd Lt John Stanley ('Ginger'), 124, 125, 134
Mason-MacFarlane, Maj. Gen. F. N., 58
Mateur, 122, 123, 126, 127, 139, 156, 172
Mathers, Sgt Jeff, 159
Matlock, 159
Maurice, Sir Frederick, 31
McCall, Maj. Thomas Hardy, 32, 48, 52, 68, 81
McCallun, Sgt R., 155
McCreery, Lt Gen. Richard, 199
McKay, Sgt Pat, *12*, 146
McKechnie, Maj. Alexander, 98, 125
McKerrigan, Capt. John, 164, 172, 195, 196
McQuirt, Pte Bernard, 17

Medjerda River, 127, 172
Medjez-El-Bab, 123, 127, 139, 190
Mellors, Pte Harold, *13*, 108
Mellors, Pte Lewis, 108
Merdelle, 52
Mersey River, 118
Messina, Strait of, 189
Meuse River, 54
Modena, 182
Molde, 107, 108
Mons-en-Pévèle, 61, 63, 71
Montbrehain, 21, 47
Montgomery, Field Marshal Bernard, 116, 165, 197
Montwy, 180
Morocco, 117, 192
Morral, L. Cpl Eric, *13*, 120, 123, 130, 149, 173, 176, 194
Morris, Capt. Charles, 148, 169
Mühlberg, 189
Munich, 25, 26, 30, 31
Murray, Lt (RAMC), 102
Mussolini, Benito, 115

Naples, 182, 186, 197, 199
Neild, Pte A. J. , 149, 155
'Nelson', Exercise, 94, 104
Nelson, HMS, 119
Netherfield, 92
New Mills, 36
Newcastle, 102
Newell, Capt. Joseph Richard (Dick), *13*, 48, 122, 125
Newhaven, 80
Newton, Capt. William Roger (Roger), 49, 125, 144, 155, 158, 163, 164, 179, 194, 198
Nicholson, Brig. Cameron, 137
Nile Delta, 114
Norfolk, 93, 96, 104
Normandy, 109, 197
Normanton Barracks, 17, 22, 30, 31, 38
Northamptonshire, 36
Northern Ireland, 22, 108, 195
Norway, 44, 89, 107-108, 124, 125
Norwegian Division, 2nd, 107
Norwich, 93
Nottingham, 15, 16, 20, 22, 32, 33, 36, 38, 39, 46, 68, 81, 91, 92, 111, 124, 132, 179
Nottinghamshire, 16, 18, 22, 23, 27, 31, 32, 33, 36, 41, 191

Nova Scotia, 15, 112
Nozay, 44, 110

O'Sullivan, Pte Patrick, *13*, 103, 186, 187
Ochsenkopf (Oxhead), Operation, 139, 160
Offiler, Pte Frank, 38, 41, 81, 101, 134, 185, 186
Oignies, 59, 60, 61-62, 63, *64-65*, 66, 68-70, 73, 81, 83, 102, 125, 137, 177-78
Orchies, 58
Orme, Sgt Alan, *13*, 38, 41, 75, 78, 79-80, 84-85, 102, 124, 131, 134, 146-47, 148, 153, 156, 180, 183, 186, 188
Oslo, 107
Oued Sedjenane, 126, 129, 141
Oued Zarga, 123, 190, 191

Paget, Gen. Sir Bernard, 99
Palermo, 182, 187, 189
Palestine, 50, 109, 165, 199
Palmer, Capt. Phillip Claud, *13*, 125, 144, 169
Paris, 54
Park, Capt. Thomas Munro, 185, 197-98
Passchendaele, 21
Patton, Gen. George, 192, 197
Paxton, Pte Leonard, 149
Peacock, Lt John Walter, 194
Peak District, 35, 48
Pearson, Lt Col Alistair, 161
Pearson, Pte Cyril, 180, 183, 186
Peebles, 88
Pegg, Pte Albert, 79, 81
Perry, 2nd Lt Christopher, 87
Pescara, 189
Petre, Maj. Gen. P. L., 58
Pévèle ridge, 62, 63
Phillipeville, 118
Piave River, 22, 93
Pidgeon, Cpl Bill, 155
Pinnock, Cpl Bert, *13*, 133, 134
Plowright, Sgt Phil, *13*, 191
Poland, 26, 31, 69, 178, 179, 180
Pomerania, 24, 69
Pont à Sault, 66
Pont de Beauvin, 66
Pont de la Batterie, 61, 62, 63, 66, 70
Pont de la Briqueterie, 66, 67
Pont du Fah, 173

Pont du Vendin, 61, 62
Pont Maudit, 66
Pornichet, 111
Porton Down, 91
Potter, Maj. John Watts, *13*, 21, 47, 49, 95, 106
PoW Camps (German), 177-179, 180, 183, 184, 185-87
  Dulag XII, 178
  Front-Stalag 101, 178
  Heimatlager, 180
  Oflag 79, 189
  Oflag IV-C, 178
  Oflag IX-A, 180
  Oflag V-A, 185
  Oflag VII-C, 178
  Stalag 357, 185
  Stalag IV-B, 187, 189
  Stalag IV-C, 186
  Stalag IX-B, 183
  Stalag VIII-B, 178
  Stalag XX-A, 178
  Stalag XXI-B, 179
PoW Camps (Italian), 180-188 *passim*, *181*
  H206, 186
  PG47, 182, 185
  PG53, 183, 184
  PG59, 186
  PG66, 183, 184, 185, 186, 189
  PG78, 189
  PG98, 183, 184, 187-89
Poyle, Pte Jim, 33
Poznan, 179
Prague, 25
Prestonpans, 86
Price, L. Cpl George, *13*, 61, 72, 73, 149
Provin, 63

Quebec, 15
Quin, Sgt George, 33

Râches, 58, 60, 61, 62
Ram, Operation, 135
Ramsay, Admiral Sir Bertram, 57
Ramsgate, 79, 80
Ransome, Maj. Gen. Algernon Lee, 32
Rasch, Brigadier G. E. C., 52
Red Cross, 179, 183, 184, 185, 186, 187, 188
Redhill, 80
Reid, Capt. Pat, 178
Rennes, 44, 52, 53, 54, 74, 110

Rider, Sgt Harry, *14*, 159
Ripley, 26, 31, 130
Ripon, 39
Rochdale, 83, 84
Rodney, HMS, 119
Rommel, Field Marshal Erwin, 54, 57, 109, 110, 115-16, 136, 137, 139
Romney, 97
Roome, Cpl Reg, 150
Roosevelt, Franklin D., 116, 192
Rotterdam, 53
Rouen, 111
Rowa, 17
Rugen, 180
Russia, 94, 102, 116, 117
Rutlandshire, 36, 41
Rye, 100

St Amand, 58
Saint-Germain, Treaty of, 25
St Nazaire, 44, 111
St Nicholas de Redon, 53
St Pol, 58
St Quentin, 54, 57
St Quentin Canal, 21
St Thurial, 52
Salerno, 197, 199
Salome, 63
Sapper's Corner, 144, 151
Saxby, Pte Bert, *14*, 154
Sbeitla, 136
Scarborough, 22
Scarpe River, 58, 60, 61, 62
Scheldt River, 57, 61
Schofield, CQMS Jack, *14*, 32, 39, 50, 51, 52, 61, 79, 83, 91, 176, 191
Scorch, Operation, 135-36
Scotland, 84, 85-90 *passim*, 87, 93, 97, 98, 104, 105, 107, 108, 180
Scott, Pte Percy, 67
Scunthorpe, 103
Seclin, 55, 57, 58, 69, 73
Sedan, 54, 57
Sedjenane, 123, 127, 131-34 *passim*, 136,138, 139, 141, *142-43*, 144-59 *passim*, 160, 165, 167, 168, 170-71, 174, 175, 180, 190
Servigliano, 186
Seton Sands, 86
Sforzacosta, 183
Sharpe, Dora, 179
Sharpe, Pte George, 179

Shaw, Pte Ernest, 103-4
Sheppard, Cpl Bill, 30, 45, 87
Sherwood Foresters Association, 38
Sicily, 119, 120, 182, 183, 186, 187, 188, 189, 192, 194, 197
Sidi Abdallah Ben Saiden, 144, 145
Sidi Bou Zid, 136
Sidi Embarek, 122
Sidi Ferruch (Sidi Fredj), 192
Sidi Nsir, 139, 175
Singapore, 107, 112-13, 116
Sissons, Pte John, 120
Smith, Lt Michael Paling, 46, 67
Smith-Dorrien, Gen. Horace, 17
Somme, battle, 20, 21, 32, 199
Somme River, 59, 110
Souk Ahras, 122
Souk el Arba, 123
Soulter, Pte Arthur, 132
South Africa, 16, 17, 18-19
Southampton, 51
Southwell, Bishop of, 22
Soviet Union, see Russia
Spangenburg, 180
Stalingrad, 116, 130
Stansfield, Lt Sydney, 163
Steenvoorde, 73-74
Stirling, 84
Stokes, Sgt George, *14*, 100, 152, 154, 159, 162, 163, 168-69, 190
Storey, Pte Stanley, *14*, 67, 72, 145
Stott, Lt Col Robert Edwin Hugh, *14*, 94, 103, 106, 121, 124, 127, 130, 138, 152-53, 154, 159, 161, 163, 165, 199
Stowmarket, 95
Stuttgart, 185
Sudetenland, 25
Suez, 113, 114, 115, 192
Suffolk, 96
Sugar Loaf Hill, 129
Sulmona, 189
Summers, Pte Gerald, *14*, 99-100, 101, 106, 121, 123, 148-49, 155, 187-89
Supercharge, Operation, 114
Sussex, 100, 106
Sutcliffe, Capt. Geoffrey, 103
Swadlincote, 26
Swanton Morley, 93, 94
Swanwick, 33, 35
Sweden, 108
Switzerland, 179

Tabarka, 123, 159, 164
Talavera, 16
Tamera, 123, 126, 127, 154, 159, 160-72 passim, 166, 174, 175, 180
Tanganyika (Tanzania), 184
Tattersall, Pte, 104
Taylor, Sgt 'Tinker', 130
Téteghem, 75, 76, 77, 78, 79, 84, 85
Thala, 137
Thieulain, 55
Thompson, Pte George, 178
Thorn (Toruń), 178
Tideswell, 37
Tobruk, 107, 109-10, 116.
Tomlinson, L. Cpl Fred, 72, 74, 79
Torch, Operation, 117, 140
Totley, 33, 35, 45
Tottenham, 102
Tournai, 55, 57, 58
Tregantle Fort, 91
Trent, Lord, 36
Trinidad, 112
Tripoli, 116
Tulloch, 2nd Lt Hector ('Heckie'), 108
Tunis, 115, 117, 121, 124, 127, 132, 136, 156, 172, 174, 175, 176, 191
Tunisia, 117, 119, 121-27 passim, 128, 132, 136, 137, 139-41, 157, 158, 170-75 passim, 182, 187, 188, 190-94, 197-98
Tupling, Cpl Victor, *14*, 73, 88
Tynewald, SS, 79

United States Army forces:
  Fifth Army, 197
  Seventh Army, 192
  Ninth Army, 189
  II Corps, 171
  VI Corps, 197
  1st Armored Division, 117
  1st Infantry Division, 192, 194
  9th Infantry Division, 171
  US Rangers, 192
  102nd Mechanised Cavalry Regiment, 192

56th Evacuation Hospital, 197
Upchurch, Pte Dennis, 163
Usher, Col Charles Milne, 74

Vann, Lt Col Bernard, 21
Verity, Lt Bert ('Tich'), *14*, 198-99
Versailles, Treaty of, 24, 25, 69
Viking, SS, 51
Villa Les Floralies, 62, 70
Vyfweg, 74

Waine, Pte Stan, 36-37, 197, 199, 205n
Wainwright, Sgt Bill, 180, 188
Walker, 2nd Lt John Harvey, 49, 68
Walker, Lt John Norman (Johnny), *14*, 125, 150, 151, 152
Walker, Pte John, 101-2
Wall, Capt. Cecil, 48, 73, 125, 159
Wallhead, Sgt Stephen, 156
Ward, Capt. Victor, 28, 47, 49
Waveney River, 94
Weinburg, 185
West Indies, 16
Whalley Bridge, 36
White, Pte Romeo ('Dogger'), 150
Wigram, Capt. Lionel, 98-99
Willett, Pte Dennis Vincent, 132
Williamson, Maj. Charles Arthur Wellesley, *14*, 67-68, 74, 91, 95, 125, 153, 157, 198
Winchelsea, HMS, 80
Winchester, 17
Winnezeele, 73
Witzig, Maj. Rudolf, 140
Wivern, HMS, 51
Wollaton, 124
Wortelager, 179
Worthing, HMHS, 78
Wrexham, 81
Wright, Lt Johnny, *14*, 195
Württemberg, 185

York, 125, 133
Yorkshire, 39, 102
Ypres, 17, 69
Ypres–Comines canal, 73

THE IRON FLUTE

THE IRON FLUTE
War Poetry from Ancient & Medieval China

Selected, translated and introduced by
Kevin Maynard

2019

Published by Arc Publications,
Nanholme Mill, Shaw Wood Road
Todmorden OL14 6DA, UK
www.arcpublications.co.uk

Translation copyright © 2019, Kevin Maynard
Introduction copyright © 2019, Kevin Maynard
Copyright in the present edition © Arc Publications, 2019

978 1911469 10 0 (pbk)
978 1911469 11 7 (hbk)

Design by Tony Ward
Printed in Great Britain by T.J. International Ltd,
Padstow, Cornwall

Cover picture:
Design based on Han dynasty stone rubbing
of a warrior riding to war

This book is in copyright. Subject to statutory exception and to provision of relevant collective licensing agreements, no reproduction of any part of this book may take place without the written permission of Arc Publications.

**Arc Publications 'Anthologies in Translation'
Series Editor: Jean Boase-Beier**

for
Professor J. P. Seaton
and David Su Liqun
苏立群 / 蘇立群

CONTENTS

Introduction / 11
Pronunciation of Chinese Names / 17
Translation Methods / 18
Some Chinese Dynasties / 21

FROM THE SHIJING (Zhao Dynasty)
Fewer and Fewer / 25
Pluck Rusty Ferns / 26
WANG CAN (177-217)
Two Poems from 'The Seven Sorrows' / 28
RUAN JI (210-263)
Two Poems from 'Songs of Tribulation' / 31
BAO ZHAO (?414-466)
Hard Road / 33
Imitation of the Ballad 'Out from the North Gate of Ji' / 35
CHEN SHUBAO (553-604)
Watering My Horse / 37
LU ZHAOLIN (c. 635-689)
Falling Snow / 37
The Black-Maned Bay / 38
Fighting South of the Wall / 38
Moon on the Mountain-Passes / 39
LIU XIYI (c. 651-c. 680)
With the Army / 40
WANG CHANGLING (c. 690-c. 756)
Two Border Poems / 41
Crossing the Border / 42
Boudoir Pangs / 42
LI QI (690-751)
The Squaddie's Ancient Song / 43
WANG WEI (?691-761)
Border Envoy / 44
GAO SHI (704-765)
Yingzhou Song / 45
WANG HAN (fl. 720)
Liangzhou Song / 45

CUI HAO (704-754)
Homage to Wang Weigu / 46
DU FU (712-770)
Insomniac Night / 47
View in Spring / 48
Scanning the Wilderness / 48
LU LUN (748-799?)
Five Frontier Songs / 49
BAO JUNHUI (*fl.* 798)
Moon on the Mountain-Passes / 51
ZU YONG (*fl.* 8th century)
On Sighting Jimen Pass / 52
LI HE (790-816)
Arrowhead / 53
Beyond the Frontier / 55
WEN TINGYUN (801?-866)
Uighur Song: Northern Border / 56
Seeing a Friend Off East / 56
A Song of Distant Rivers / 57
WEI ZHUANG (836-910)
Pity the Ploughman / 59
MA DAI (*fl.* 9th century)
Alone on a Frontier Wall / 59
ZHANG QIAO (Tang Dynasty)
A Report: What Goes On in the Borderlands / 60
LIN KUAN (Tang Dynasty)
On the Border: Replying to a Friend / 61
Setting Out Early Beneath a Mountain Pass / 62
LIU KAI (947-1000)
On the Border / 63
ZHAO BINGWEN (1159-1232)
Under Luzhou's Walls / 64
LIU KEZHUANG (1187-1269)
Bitter Cold / 65
Building Walls / 66
Dying for Your Country / 67
1208: Current Affairs / 68
YELÜ CHUCAI (1190-1244)
A Relative in Mourning / 68

Yuan Haowen (1190-1257)
After the Emperor Left to Tour East: January 1233 / 69
The View from Stone-Ridge Pass / 70
Leaving the City / 72
June 12th, 1233: Crossing North / 73
The Fall of Qiyang: Two Poems / 74
What Those Girls were singing / 76
Duan Keji (1196-1254)
Solace in an Evil Time / 79
Wang Zhong (*fl.* 13th century)
War / 80
Gong Kai (1222-1307)
Starveling Steed / 81
Hao Jing (1233-1275)
Old Horse / 82
Song Wu (1260-c.1340)
Fighting South of the Wall / 83
Zhang Yanghao (1269-1329)
A Song Accompanied by Strings / 84
Zhou Tingzhen (1292-1379)
An Incurable Disease / 85
A Troubled Mind / 86
Liu Ji (1311-1375)
Ballad of the North Wind / 87
Ma Ge (Yuan Dynasty)
Evening March: Zhanggong Village / 88
Gao Qi (1336-1374)
A Soldier's Woman Vents Her Grief / 89
Ma Zhongyang (1450-1516)
Paying Homage at the Temple of the Khan / 90
Li Mengyang (1473-1529)
Crossing the Border / 91
Farewell Commander Li: Off to Yunzhong / 92
On the Border: A Miscellaneous Poem / 93
Mornings Watering My Horse / 94
Gu Lin (1476-1545)
Fighting South of the Wall / 96
Xue Hui (1489-1541)
Following the Army / 97

Xie Zhen (1495-1575)
On the Border: Two Poems / 101
Xu Wei (1521-1593)
Leaving the Border / 102
Xue Lundao (?1531-?1600)
Desolation on the Battlefield / 103
The Old General's Complaint / 104
Ao Ying (Ming Dynasty)
On the Border / 105
Wang Shizhen (1526-1590)
Fighting South of the Wall / 106
Gu Yanwu (1613-1682)
On the Border / 108
Autumn Mountains / 109
Wang Duanshu (1621-1706)
Qiantang Beach-Head Lamentation / 110
Nalan Xingde (1655-1685)
Tune: 'A Love that Never Ends' / 112
Tune: 'Boddhisattva Barbarian' / 113
Xu Lan (17th-18th centuries)
Crossing the Border' / 114

Notes / 115
About the Poets / 117
About the Translator / 124
Alphabetical List of Poets / 125

INTRODUCTION[1]

Many who have little or no knowledge of Chinese culture will still have heard of Sunzi's *Art of War*[1]. But what of the art inspired by war?[2]

The visual arts in China have nearly always avoided depicting scenes of conflict. Its literature on the other hand often finds warfare an irresistibly alluring topic – and in this respect it is of course no different from most other world literatures, whether oral or written.

While Chinese prose has done ample justice to this theme (one has only to think of novels such as *Outlaws of the Marsh* or *The Three Kingdoms*) it is poetry that can boast the most ancient lineage, since it antedates the first Chinese novels by almost two millennia.

Two sub-genres in particular stand out, only one of which has up to now been well served by translators. The first is called 'border poetry' (its Chinese name is 邊塞詩 biānsài shī); this is sometimes also described as the 'frontier style' (邊塞體 biānsài tǐ). The second is known as 喪亂詩 sāngluàn shī – which we have to translate, rather clumsily, as 'poetry of loss and chaos'. Both are species of what we might prefer to call by the more general term of 'war poetry', since both deal with military subjects.

However, they can be differentiated further as follows. The second type of poem lays a much heavier emphasis on the sufferings endured by war's innocent victims (butchered, mutilated or enslaved). The first concerns itself more with both the heroism on the one hand and the privations on the other of the common soldier: frequently driven many hundreds of miles away from home, while defending China's northern borders against nomadic invaders and would-be invaders.

Border poetry can trace its origins right back to the *Shijing* or *Classic of Poetry* (Zhao dynasty: more specifically, 11th–7th centuries BCE); though it was not until the fifth century CE poet Bao Zhao that it really came into its own as a distinct genre[3]. 'Poetry of loss and chaos' is more recent, in that it is particularly associated with the genocidal Mongol invasions of the thirteenth century; though one can add with some certainty that it in its turn derives from earlier poems, such as those written by Du Fu, and other Tang poets.

These were poems that bore witness to the seismic disaster of the An Lushan rebellion (755-763), a catastrophe that well-nigh tore the Tang dynasty apart in the mid-eighth century.

Another way to distinguish these two genres is to state (a little more hesitantly) that *sangluan* poems nearly always tend to be written by eyewitnesses and participants, whereas this is only sometimes true of border poems.

As to the extent whereby either genre can be thought of as something approaching what we in the West consider to be 'protest poetry', that is problematic. Some border poems (as in the case of the Ming loyalist Gu Yanwu) were certainly made use of to complain about wars being waged at the time of composition. However, as was customary with Chinese literature that dared to criticize a contemporary emperor or dynasty, the action of the poem was always pushed back to some much earlier era (Gu Yanwu's poem describes a battle which took place a whole century BCE, though his readers would have suspected, with good reason, that he was actually referring to the defeat of his own Ming dynasty by the Northern Manchu invaders who founded the Qing). Some *sangluan* poems either implicitly or explicitly heap opprobrium on military incompetence, cruelty or cowardice.

But much Chinese war poetry is very far from critical. What is interesting about the two relatively early war poems from that great poet Ruan Ji, as has been pointed out by Stephen Owen (*The Poetry of Ruan Ji and Xi Kang*, Boston / Berlin, 2017, pp. 15-16), is that the second of them already seems closer to that famous quotation of Wilfred Owen's: "My subject is war, and the pity of war", while the first is a conventional gung-ho paean to military prowess. This anthology, I have to admit, is somewhat biased against the second category, though a few such have necessarily been included.

The border peoples with whom Han Chinese living in the north or north-west regions (whether merchants, soldiers, or diplomats) had dealings, were many, and ethnically varied. The 'southern tribes of the Huai' and the northern 'Xianyun' were the twin enemies recognized by the Classic of Poetry. 'Xianyun' seems to have meant irrespectively everyone north of the various Han Chinese states in existence at that time. By the time of the Han the generic term in use was 'Xiongnu'. In subsequent dynasties, as different tribal peoples were distinguished, the names began to multiply: Khitan, Jurchen, Qiang, Uighur, Tangut, Mongols (to use a more recent Western nomenclature). The first two of these invaded large areas of North China and established two Chinese dynasties of their own, the Liao and the Jin respectively. The Mongols, of course, conquered the whole of China in the thirteenth century, and founded the Yuan. A generic term for all such foreign nations was 胡 hú, translated as 'barbarian' or 'nomad'. Something approaching horror was felt by the Han Chinese at these alien peoples' lack of any fixed abode, moving across the steppes as they did, in company with the herds they tended – and living indeed in such close proximity with these animals that they themselves could seem to outsiders almost bestial at times. But along with that initial repulsion, there was also a real and deepening fascination with their 'otherness': their strange but colourful customs, clothing, hairstyles, cuisine, music and dancing. This can be seen in the pictorial art of the Han and the Tang, and it sometimes comes through in their poetry as well. But 'otherness' interpreted as 'savagery' or 'barbarism' has always been how 'civilized' peoples choose to define their own 'superior' identity: Chinese and Romans then, British, French, Germans and Americans more recently.

To write with something approaching relish about the 'savage' and exotic customs of the northern and north-western barbarians, of the bleak terrain they inhabited, the harsh weather that frontier troops had to endure, and of the glory of riding into battle against hopeless odds, might seem to us a very 'Romantic' thing to do. But of course romantic poetry and painting is much older and more widespread than the label 'Western Romanticism' would lead us to believe. Many border poets had never actually visited the remote and colourful places they imagined, though they may have known others who had. My little anthology includes the full range, from what one can only call 'creative variations on a theme' by elegant and effete literati safely ensconced at court in the southern capital (e.g. the piece entitled 'Watering My Horse…' written by Chen Shubao, the last emperor of the sixth century Chen dynasty), to much grittier and more realistic accounts, some of them actually written on campaign and others upon a veteran's return. One thinks of the Tang poets Gao Shi, Cen Shen, and Li Yi who are often praised for the fact that in their border poems they wrote not merely according to literary convention but also from direct personal experience, or of Yelü Chucai, who famously travelled far beyond the north-west frontier while accompanying Genghis Khan as one of his aides[4].

Certain place-names, well-worn poetic formulae and characteristic images return again and again. The bleak and barren terrain, the inclement weather – icy blasts of wind, snow-blizzards one moment and sandstorms the next – the music of the steppes, reed-pipes sounding strange melodies across the frozen wasteland, troops setting out from some barracks on the Wall, never to return, the whitened piles of bones they leave behind after their deaths in battle, the widows and orphans pining for them thousands of miles away... all powerful stuff, though a little of this can go a long way, and there are so many hundreds and hundreds of such poems to choose from that it becomes increasingly hard for the translator to choose. I've avoided many of the most famous contenders (including several of those mentioned in the previous paragraph) since other translators have already done them ample justice. I preferred in the main to concentrate either on those who have never been previously translated, or on those who were writing at the time of the Mongol invasions, a period in which I'm particularly interested at present. Their poems move away from conventional border poetry into eyewitness sāngluàn poetry, as the reader will discover.

During that same Yuan dynasty, a certain scholar and poet, Yang Weizhen, 楊維禎 (1296-1370), is said to have fashioned a flute from an old iron sword. It played the softest music and accompanied him on his wanderings, perhaps providing some small consolation for his lack of employment. (The Mongols mistrusted the whole mandarin class, and preferred to entrust government posts to people from their own ethnic background.) Yang loved this instrument so much that he gave himself the soubriquet 'The Iron Flute Daoist' (tiědí Dàorén 鐵笛道人).There is a famous painting in the Shanghai Museum called 'The Iron Flute' that illustrates this anecdote. It has been attributed to the Ming painter Wu Wei, though American scholars believe it to be a late Qing forgery.

Out of the discord of war we humans can still conjure up sweet music: hence the title of this anthology.

Three war poems by the writer who is arguably China's greatest poet, Du Fu, have been included, though none of them strictly belongs to the genres mentioned above. (Those that do – and there are several famous examples – have already been brilliantly translated by others.) The approach taken in the poems I've chosen is, by contrast, subtler and more oblique. 'Insomniac Night' I consider one of the greatest war poems ever written, though my own translation can't hope to compete with that by Burton Watson. Starting off as what seems like just another 'nature' poem, it leads up slowly but inexorably, by means of a chain of cunningly related images, to a shattering climax. We are made to realize that the whole landscape is threatened by man's destructiveness. It is followed by two other fine poems that are probably already familiar to readers of Chinese poetry in translation via other versions, but which I have come to love so much that I felt I just had to try my hand at them as well.

In conclusion, my hope is that this little selection will at least allow the reader either to discover afresh or to re-experience in a new guise a range of compelling and dynamic voices from medieval China that speak to us not of scenes from a distant age and from faraway places, but of tragic events that we see played out on our television screens on a daily basis. For wherever there are human beings, there will unavoidably be war; and wherever there is war, there will be writers to record it.

NOTES

[1] Other translations of Sun Wu's famous treatise 兵法 bīngfǎ might be 'How to Wage War', 'Military Methodology', or just plain 'Warcraft' (as in the computer game).

[2] The very idea of an 'art' of war is paradoxical. Surely war always degenerates into madness and chaos? But in fact war is willed and organized, sometimes with great ingenuity, by statesmen and military strategists. It is, to them, nearly always considered as a regrettable but necessary extension of diplomacy 'by other means', as von Clausewitz puts it. The battlefield is often seen by such individuals as a sort of chessboard on a larger scale. Moreover, that war can be considered 'beautiful' is a shocking idea to many. Yet just think of the astonishing skill deployed by generations of craftsmen as they forged armour and weapons of great beauty

throughout the ages. Or consider the frequent comparisons made in Chinese and Japanese culture between the way in which a warrior flourishes his sword and the way a calligrapher wields his brush. Think of all those nineteenth century ladies and gentlemen armed with parasols, camp-stools and telescopes who tramped up hills in order to view a distant battlefield, whether Napoleonic or Unionist versus Confederate: colourful well-drilled uniforms moving in strict formation through fire and smoke, troops of infantry and cavalry charging, counter-charging or standing their ground in a disciplined way. Think of British civilians craning their eyes skyward to watch the murderous dogfights taking place high above them, and, yes, finding the spectacle strangely exhilarating. And, just as children enjoy fireworks and a huge bonfire on Guy Fawkes' Night, so Air Raid Wardens during the Blitz sometimes admitted to their diaries how beautiful the sight of a great city engulfed in flames could be, and so, more recently, journalists from hotel rooftops in Baghdad have described the sensual pyrotechnic beauty of American 'Shock and Awe' bombardment, when seen from a relatively safe distance.

The morality of war is similarly paradoxical. Clearly war itself is evil; unless one is a pacifist, it is seen as a necessary evil. But from time immemorial, the bravery of its combatants has rightly been celebrated. Such qualities as loyalty, courage and self-sacrifice have long been recognized as moral virtues and all of them are tempered in the furnace of the battlefield. One wonders from a cynical twenty-first century perspective whether patriotism should be added to the list. In any case, no one doubts that military heroes really do exist, though not all of them get medals. Chinese border poetry often pays tribute to the admirable behaviour exhibited by both the highest-ranking commander and the humblest most anonymous footsoldier; and contrariwise it also allows itself the occasional snort of derision at the laziness and incompetence of bad military leaders. The pity and the horror and the glory and the pointlessness of war: they are all present.

³ At least to begin with, border poetry is nearly always a sub-genre of the ballad form (樂府 yuèfǔ). It begins with one of a range of traditional titles, which never vary in their wording. Here are the main ones: 從軍行 cóng jūn xíng 'With the Army', 關山月 guānshān yuè 'Moon on the Mountain-Passes', 塞上曲 sàishàng qǔ 'Song: On the Border', 出塞 chū sài 'Leaving the Border', 戰城南 zhàn chéng nán 'Fighting South of the Wall', 飲馬長城窟行 yìn mǎ Chángchéng kū xíng 'Watering My Horse in a Niche by the Wall'. One can see at a glance how suggestive such titles are, and can understand why so many poets felt impelled to rise to the challenge they posed. Once the title has been chosen, however, the poet then gets to play a sort of riff on this thoroughly conventional theme. Many such 'variations' when one encounters them in bulk in the anthologies are sufficiently similar to each other to become quite irritating after a while; but good poets always managed to give their versions a fresh twist of some kind.

⁴ Nevertheless, it's worth adding the caveat that all these poets came to the actual frontier armed with expectations that had been coloured and informed by their reading: expectations that couldn't fail to influence what they wrote when they got there. (All I mean by this is that their imaginations had already been heavily impregnated by the thoroughly conventional and 'traditional' ballads they'd learned by heart beforehand. We see what we've been schooled to see. Just as the reader of Wordsworth can't help seeing the Lake District through Wordsworth's eyes, so the

poetizing Tang dynasty border soldier saw the north-western borderlands in and along the Gansu Corridor through the eyes of Southern Dynasties fantasists such as Chen Shubao and Zhang Zhengjian.)

PRONUNCIATION OF CHINESE NAMES

A poem stands or falls by its internal music; and it's important to pronounce more or less correctly the Chinese names included in these translations. Because the Chinese writing system is not primarily phonetic (in that it's very far from being alphabetic), we in the West have had to make use of a number of different transliteration systems over time. The two most popular with translators from the Anglo-Saxon camp have been the Wade-Giles system, which reigned supreme for well over half a century, and the Chinese Romanization system called pinyin, which has now effectively replaced Wade-Giles (though this Victorian relic still has its passionate defenders). Pinyin is what I use throughout this work.

Most of the names the reader will encounter here can be pronounced very much as they are spelled. Three letters in the pinyin alphabet, however, can completely flummox one at a first acquaintance: *c, q* and *x*. The Wade-Giles equivalents were much easier on the eye to a Western reader: *ts', ch'* and *hs* respectively.

So a personal name such as *Cen Shen* should be pronounced *Ts'en Shen*; the *Qin* dynasty is pronounced the *Ch'in* dynasty; a place-name like *Xianyang* should be pronounced *Hsien-yang*, and the *Xianyun* tribes are the *Hsien-yün* (these glosses employ the Wade-Giles method, and they all work very well).

(We Mandarin speakers are always amused at the heavy weather Western journalists and news broadcasters make of the Chinese premier's surname *Xi*. Sometimes it sounds like the name given to the letter 'g', sometimes like the first two phonemes of the word 'cheese'. In fact it should be pronounced 'Hsi': the English word 'sea' spoken with a very faint lisp (thank you again, Professors Wade and Giles).

TRANSLATION METHODS

My practice as a translator varies: the first objective has to be to make a poem that works in English. (I know this is a form of words that greatly irritates many other translators, but I remain unapologetic, since I judge its meaning to be pretty transparent at a first glance, at least in terms of 'ordinary common sense' – itself a phrase that likewise begs a lot of questions.) The second is to use, wherever possible or wherever appropriate, as few English syllables as I can, so as to reproduce, however faintly, the peculiar concision of Chinese classical grammar. However, notice those two qualifying phrases. Occasionally I have had to expand the original a little, in order to incorporate into any lines that required this treatment what would otherwise be ponderous academic footnotes (see below). And in one or two other cases I've amplified a line or several lines purely in order to make the poem 'work' in English, either in terms of its meaning, or of its style:[1] a perilous procedure, and one that calls to mind George Steiner's caveat: "As with a sea-shell, the translator can listen strenuously but mistake the rumour of his own pulse for the beat of the alien sea." A rendering of this kind moves towards what is sometimes called an 'imitation': something earlier generations of poets frequently indulged in, with great success (think of the Augustans). However, the translations that have pleased me most (for what it's worth) are always those that combine the closest fidelity to every character and binome in the original with the fewest words in English, while still 'working' as stand-alone poems in English.

Often I've employed the traditional 'grid', with the hanzi (Chinese characters) in the first row, one per cell, the pinyin below, and the English

---

[1] With older poems I've occasionally opted for something very close to the alliterative accentual-syllabic forms that we associate with our own medieval period (one that started much later than the Chinese 'Middle Ages') – in one case I've even inserted a few end-rhymes, a practice I normally deplore. This inevitably results in a little of the 'padding' that so weighs down and at the same time enervates the Victorian translations of that great Chinese scholar Herbert Giles; though he was making use of late Romantic verse-forms and the poetic diction that went with them: which encouraged a rather different kind of distortion.

in the third row. And underneath this grid (which only provides a literal skeleton) come all the explanatory footnotes, both Chinese and English, from whatever sources are available, if any – and if not, then from my own investigations. A single line or even a single phrase can take a week or more to decipher. At other times, if the source-text is more immediate and 'transparent' I've been a little less rigorous. In either case what usually happens next is that I need a mulling-over period of days or weeks, during which possible solutions to various lines will pop up at different times during the day (and sometimes late at night, or even in the small hours, when you wake up and find that some new arrangement of words has just occurred inside your head while you were sleeping). Finally the whole translation's first draft can come in a rush. But even then, a lot of subsequent tweaking is often required until it meets with my approval.

One occasional technique mentioned above for which no apology is needed: sometimes the translator incorporates what might have otherwise been a 'learned contextual footnote' into the body of the poem. (If the incomparable David Hinton gets away with this sort of thing, then so can I.) Cui Hao's somewhat starstruck paean to his youthful hunting-companion mentions in its very first line that Wang Weigu is already Commander of the Yulin Guard. But 'Yulin' (which translates, not very helpfully as 'Feathered Forest') means nothing to a Western reader. So I've just glossed it as 'Imperial Guard'. The first line of Gu Yanwu's 'On the Border' is an example of this sort of 'footnote expansion'. The Chinese text simply provides us with a three character phrase, 趙信城 'Zhaoxin city'; 'Xiongnu stronghold sacked' is how I've endeavoured to 'unpack' it. A whole episode from the Han war against the Xiongnu is conjured up by this richly associative place-name. The Xiongnu tribe of 'barbarians' was decisively beaten in the Battle of Mobei in 119 BC. Zhaoxin had been their stronghold in the Orkhon Valley beneath the Khangai Mountains. I've tried to compress this story into five syllables. 'Majesty, magnanimous and merciful' is a direct quote from Sima Qian's *Records of the Grand Historian*: a chapter in which a Han general tries to persuade a local king who has joined the Xiongnu to return to the Han emperor against whom he has rebelled. I suspect the phrase is as ironical in Gu Yanwu's poem as it is there. An added layer of complexity is provided, of course, by the poet's own contemporary historical context (see the relevant passage in the main body of my Introduction above).

My sources have sometimes been poetic texts and dictionaries in my own library – particularly, to begin with, the Mathews dictionary (much-maligned in recent decades, though many of us who used it before anything better became available still regard it with affection) – and subsequently the Grand Ricci, Paul Kroll's indispensable *A Student's Dictionary of Classical and Medieval Chinese* and the Taiwanese 中文大辭典 zhongwen da cidian, as well as a wide range of Chinese anthologies and editions of particular poets; but also many online sources, such as the excellent online zdic.net, the Quan Tangshi, Quan Songci and Quan Yuanqu websites provided by xysa.com and the astonishing sou-yun.com anthology of the full range of classical Chinese poets. I've also been fortunate enough to have had access over the years to the richly-stocked library of the School of Oriental and African Studies in Bloomsbury.

SOME CHINESE DYNASTIES

221-206 BCE	QIN (Ch'in) Dynasty	The 'First Emperor' (he unified the country) Capital: Chang'an, present-day Xi'an Qin Shihuangdi dies, 210 BCE.
206 BCE-220 CE	HAN Dynasty	Capitals: 1) Chang'an 2) Luoyang
220-589 CE	Six Dynasties Period (includes famous "Three Kingdoms")	Period of disunity and instability following the fall of the Han; Buddhism introduced to China
618-906 CE	TANG (T'ang) Dynasty	Capitals: Chang'an and Luoyang WANG WEI LI BO DU FU BAI JUYI
960-1279	SONG (Sung) Dynasty	Capitals: 1) Bianjing (present-day Kaifeng) 2) Lin'an (present-day Hangzhou) SU DONGPO [SU SHI]
907-1125 and 1115-1234	Liao and Jin dynasties	Northern 'barbarian' conquest dynasties by the Khitan and Jurchen tribes respectively*
1279-1368	YUAN Dynasty	The reign of the Mongol empire; Capital: Dadu (present-day Beijing)
1368-1644	MING Dynasty	Re-establishment of rule by a Han Chinese emperor; Capitals: Nanjing and Beijing
1644-1912	QING (Ch'ing) Dynasty	Reign of the Manchus (another 'barbarian' conquest dynasty); Capital: Beijing
1912-1949	Republic Period	Capitals: Beijing, Wuhan, and Nanjing
1949-present	People's Republic of China	Capital: Beijing

* Chinese dynasty charts traditionally ignore both dynasties, since in the eyes of many Chinese historians they lacked 'the Mandate of Heaven', and were ruled by non-Han Chinese emperors. To a Western observer, this seems wholly illogical: why include the Yuan and Qing dynasties, then?

THE IRON FLUTE
War Poems from
Ancient and Medieval China

FEWER AND FEWER
    (Songs of the States: 36)

fewer and fewer …
                if we could just go home!
the Leader knows:
                he's why we're all dew-dabbled
fewer and fewer …
                if we could just go home!
it's our Leader needs us:
                he's why we're mired in mud.

式微

式微式微胡不歸
微君之故胡為乎中露
式微式微胡不歸
微君之躬胡為乎泥中

PLUCK RUSTY FERN
(Minor Odes: 167)

pluck rusty fern, pluck rusty fern,
　　pluck it as it's sprouting:
homeward bound, oh homeward bound,
　　when the year's on the turn –
no home and hearth to go to now,
　　thanks to the Xianyun:
nowhere now to settle down,
　　thanks to the Xianyun

pluck rusty fern, pluck rusty fern,
　　pluck it when it's soft:
homeward bound, oh homeward bound,
　　heartsore and weary –
poor hearts pinched and parched,
　　we thirst and we hunger;
border-duties still not done
　　still no news sent home

pluck rusty fern, pluck rusty fern,
　　pluck it now it's hardened:
homeward bound, oh homeward bound
　　when October comes –
the king's affairs unfinished:
　　no chance for us of respite –
such bitter pangs we suffer:
　　set out but don't return

what fancy flower is that?
　　the blossom of the cherry
what equipage is that?
　　that's a great lord's chariot –
his war-chariot made ready:
　　harnessed, his four chargers …
how could we settle down?
　　in one month three engagements

harnessed, his four chargers,
        his stallions so sturdy –
our leader borne behind them,
        underlings to flank him …
those stallions so sturdy,
        bow-nocks of horn, fish-scale quiver,
ever on the watch now:
        the Xianyun probe and harry

back then we sallied forth
        and the willow trees were stirring;
now on our return
        thick snow-flurries afflict us:
our progress home is slow,
        we thirst and we hunger,
heartsore and weary –
        no one to know our sufferings …

From the Shijing (Zhao Dynasty)

駕彼四牡四牡騤騤君子所依小人所腓四牡翼翼象弭魚服豈不日戒玁狁孔棘
昔我往矣楊柳依依今我來思雨雪霏霏行道遲遲載渴載飢我心傷悲莫知我哀

THE 'SEVEN SORROWS': 1

our Western Capital
        collapsed into chaos
wolves and tigers
        have torn it apart
once more escaping
        my Central Plain homeland
Jingzhou my refuge –
        savage asylum:

confronted by grief-stricken
        kinfolk's keening
fetched back by friends
        who clutch at my clothes

I push through the gate –
        desolation surrounds me
white bones, strewn cadavers
        cover the ground …
beside the roadway
        starving widows
let go of their children
        abandoned in bushes

hearing their wailing
        they turn and look back
shed tear after tear
        but cannot return
"I'm off to die somewhere –
        we can't both survive …"

unable to bear this
> I drive my steeds on
I climb Baling Mound
> (a good emperor's tomb)
turn my head round
> gaze back at Chang'an

I know what he meant
> that poet of old
who wrote *'Falling Springs'*
> (Yellow Springs of the Dead)

and venting deep sighs
> my poor heart is torn

    WANG CAN (177-217)

七哀詩三首　王粲

西京亂無象　豺虎方遘患
復棄中國去　遠身適荊蠻
親戚對我悲　朋友相追攀
出門無所見　白骨蔽平原
路有飢婦人　抱子棄草間
顧聞號泣聲　揮涕獨不還
未知身死處　何能兩相完
驅馬棄之去　不忍聽此言
南登霸陵岸　回首望長安
悟彼下泉人　喟然傷心肝

THE 'SEVEN SORROWS': 3

border towns breeding
      hearts that are bitter
– worse for those
      who've been here before:
ice and snow
      to scour your skin
savage winds
      whipped up without pause

not a soul to be seen
      for hundreds of miles
bushes and grasses
      that no one helps grow
climbing the ramparts
      watch-towers in view
light-fluttering dancers:
      flags hoisted aloft

one who wanders
      can't cast a look back –
once through that gate
      stop thinking of home …
sons and brothers
      hauled off as slaves
of weeping and wailing
      there can be no end

no 'happy land' left
      anywhere on earth
why do we linger
      down here so long?
do they suffer at all
      those bugs on the knotweed?
asking no questions
      they scurry to and fro

   WANG CAN (177-217)

七哀詩三首　王粲

邊城使心悲昔吾親更之冰雪截肌膚風飄無止期
百里不見人草木誰當遲登城望亭燧翩翩飛戍旗
行者不顧反出門與家辭子弟多俘虜哭泣無已時
天下盡樂土何為久留茲蓼蟲不知辛去來勿與諮

TWO POEMS from SONGS OF TRIBULATION

1

"no warrior fiercer: his one wish?
        win over the wilds
his chariot driven onward
        on farflung campaigns –
obeying all orders
        forgetful of self
slung over his shoulder
        a good bow called 'Crowcaw'
flash of his breastplate
        like sparkling starlight
reckless in danger
        death lifts sky-souls aloft
why strive to stay alive
        when rushing to the front?
his fealty will linger
        through a hundred generations
his virtues a warranty
        his good name will flourish
posterity to bless him
        a constant memory his courage!"

詠懷詩十三首 其五十三 阮籍

壯士何慷慨志欲威八荒驅車遠行役受命忘自忘良弓挾烏號明甲有精光臨難不顧生身死魂飛揚豈為全軀士效命爭戰場忠為百世榮義使名彰垂聲謝后世氣節故有常

2

when young I studied swordplay
    surpassing ancient masters with my skill

with finesse I sundered rainbows
    made myself a mighty name
        ahead of all my peers …

deserts stretched before me:
    I brandished high my blade

I took my horse to drink
    through China's nine regions

gallantly the banners flew
    drums and gongs the only din I heard

but as for military matters:
    they now just sadden me –

        bitter grief and pity now arise

I think back over my past years:
    prick of conscience springing up within …

            RUAN JI (210-263)

詠懷詩十三首 其四十七 阮籍

少年學擊刺 妙伎過曲城 英風截雲霓 超世發奇聲 揮劍臨沙漠 飲馬九野坰 旗幟何翩翩 但聞金鼓鳴 軍旅令人悲 烈烈有哀情 念我平常時 悔恨從此生

HARD ROAD

who hasn't seen lads
    lusty and mettlesome:
        first you enlisted,
then left for the wars –
    now white-haired vagabonds
        rootless and roofless

heading home never:
    where you first lived
        fades further away
night after night
    day after day
        all news of kinfolk

cut off forever
    countered by rivers
        by peak after peak
north winds howl bleakly
    white clouds skirl by
        screaking of reedpipes

scrannel and keen
    to pierce through this frosty
        frontier sky
you've only to hear it
    and your grief will grow
        but there's nothing for it

what unpicks the past?
    you clamber up high
        to gaze out beyond
soon you'll die trampled
    by hooves of the nomads
        no way of finding

your family at last
>   male offspring fated
>   to ride a rough road
> who would want sons?
>   sorrows unending
>   sigh after sigh

BAO ZHAO (414?-466)

擬行路難十八首 其一十四 鮑照

君不見少壯從軍去白首流離不得還
故鄉窅窅日夜隔音塵斷絕阻河關
風蕭條白雲飛胡笳哀急邊氣寒聽此
愁人兮奈何登山遠望得留顏將死胡
馬跡寧見妻子難男兒生世轗軻欲何
道綿憂摧抑起長嘆

34

IN IMITATION OF THE BALLAD 'OUT FROM THE NORTH GATE OF JI'

from forts on the frontier
   winged missives are issued
      beacon fires flitting
         across to Xianyang
cavalry garrisoned
   in Guanwu –
      to reinforce Shuofang,
         footsoldiers billeted

keen autumn stiffening
   bowstring and bamboo stave
      barbarian warriors
         stubborn as ever
the emperor grasps his
   sword-pommel in fury –
      farflung envoys
         exchange meaning glances

one by one soldiers
   climb boulder-strewn paths
      in single file traversing
         bridges hung high
drums, pipes pulsate
   with Han people's passions
      frontierfrosts mantling
         pennants and plate-mail

sudden blasts hurling
   themselves against border-forts
      flung up from nowhere
         sandstorms come whirling
horsehairs that stiffen
   like spines on a hedgehog
      horntipped bows
         too rigid to bend

in times of great peril:
    the upright and pure
        disorder, upheaval:
            the valiant, the true
to lay down your life
    for a glorious leader –
        to die for your country:

    a noble oblation

BAO ZHAO (414?-466)

代出自薊北門行　鮑照

羽檄起邊亭烽火入咸陽徵騎屯廣武分兵救朔方
嚴秋筋竿勁虜陣精且強天子按劍怒使者遙相望
雁行緣石徑魚貫度飛梁簫鼓流漢思旌甲被胡霜
疾風沖塞起沙礫自飄揚馬毛縮如蝟角弓不可張
時危見臣節世亂識忠良投軀報明主身死為國殤

WATERING MY HORSE IN A NICHE OF THE WALL
   (Ballad)

my charger in an alien land
     – these mountain flowers that glow by night!
no herd nearby, it whinnies at its reflection
     – catching at fresh scents carried by the wind
colours of moonlight lick at the Great Wall's dark
     – along the frontier autumn voices mingle
you'll send what tribute to the Son of Heaven?
     – your own hide wrapping a corpse from the front!

    Chen Shubao (553-604)

FALLING SNOW

autumn now over, the nomads burst through:
a thousand miles of low cloud louring

snows go dark as barbarian sands;
ice as bright as moon on the Han

silver the watchtowers in the steep passes
jade-green the gigantic sweep of the Wall

our fluttering banners and flags have all fallen
our names are a blank to the High Son of Heaven

    Lu Zhaolin (*c.* 635-689)

THE BLACK-MANED BAY
   (Ballad)

glitter of this bay's gold saddle –
          after countless battles, see it enter Gaolan
wind more cutting through these frontier gates –
          waters colder by this never-ending Wall
darkness and snow: your bridle's clink-clink-clink –
          mountain after mountain, your muzzle spouting foam
never hanging back from crossing desert wastes –
          who will ever staunch this endless flow of blood?

    Lu Zhaolin (*c.* 635-689)

FIGHTING SOUTH OF THE WALLS

our general's set off from the Wall
   the tribal chieftain's at Wutan
nomad reedpipes screeching
   northward of Goose Gate

    both wings spread protectively
      south of Dragon City
      carved bows twist and turn by night
        at dawn we loose our cavalry

holding back by day
   then fighting to the death

    Lu Zhaolin (*c.* 635-689)

MOON ON THE MOUNTAIN-PASSES

borderlands' immensity:
    reaching (eastwards, unimpeded)
                     Dolmen Peak
yet still the nomads balk us
    westwards battering Qilian

love-longing travels for a thousand miles
    solitary, luminous
        the moon hangs overhead

among the Altai Mountains
    moonbeams shimmer over Golden Cave
        while all brightness ends
            before Jade Gate

send tidings to my lady in her boudoir:

    tie them to the feet
        of a swan-goose flying home

    LU ZHAOLIN (*c.* 635-689)

關山月　盧照鄰

塞坦通磧石虜障抵祁連
相思在萬里明月正孤懸
影移金岫北光斷玉門前
寄言閨中婦時看鴻雁天

WITH THE ARMY

autumn winds rush by
                        nomad steeds flash past
city walls all sealed
                        troops lost in sudden sallies
into his temple goes the Son of Heaven
                        out from the Gates of Doom his generals plunge
pell-mell they press towards the Yi and Luo
                        horses and chariots by the tens of thousands
striking camp beside the Yellow River
                        morale unbroken charging in broad daylight
their whole lives dreaming of the two-edged sword
                        selflessly the scholar's brush laid by
southward a lone moon climbs above the Han
                        northward thick clouds cluster in Dai County
know well the tactics of those ancient heroes
                        never forget the ancient arts of war
sweep evil from the world a thousand miles –
                        better than sweeping clean your one small room

                                        Liu Xiyi (*c.* 651-*c.* 680)

從軍行　劉希夷

秋天風颯颯群胡馬行疾
嚴城晝不開伏兵暗相失
天子廟堂拜將軍凶門出
紛紛伊洛道戎馬幾萬匹
軍門壓黃河兵氣沖白日
平生懷仗劍慷慨即投筆
南登漢月孤北走代雲密
近取韓彭計早知孫吳術
丈夫清萬里誰能掃一室

TWO 'BORDER POEMS'

   1: Going Up to the Border

locusts churr in the naked mulberry groves:
            September on the Xiao Pass road
frontier-treks: forever to and fro
            everywhere the same bleached reeds and grass
old-time itinerants from You and Bing …
            long since crumbled into dust and sand
roving freebooters – why follow their example?
            swashbucklers bragging of their black-maned bays!

   2: Coming Back from the Border

horses watered at the ford: fall floods
            icy water; kniving wind
sun just sinking under sand-flats –
            as dusk deepens, Lintao's still distinct
those ancient campaigns on the Wall –
            all confident their nerve would hold
days ground to yellow dust …
            white bones strewn among the tangled whin …

                    Wang Changling (*c.* 690-*c.* 756)

塞下曲二首　王昌齡

蟬鳴空桑林八月蕭關道
出塞入塞寒處處黃蘆草
從來幽並客皆共塵沙老
莫學遊俠兒矜誇紫騮好

飲馬渡秋水水寒風似刀
平沙日未沒黯黯見臨洮
昔日長城戰咸言意氣高
黃塵足今古白骨亂蓬蒿

CROSSING THE BORDER

Qin moonlight bright on Han-built fort
They've marched a thousand miles: no going home
If Dragon City's Li Guang came back here
Those nomads wouldn't push through mountain passes

    WANG CHANGLING (*c.* 690-*c.* 756)

出塞　王昌齡

秦時明月漢時關
萬里長征人未還
但使龍城飛將在
不教胡馬渡陰山

BOUDOIR PANGS

young wife at her window
    untouched by sorrow
        spruced up for spring
            in her bright green boudoir
suddenly sees
    at the side of the road
the farewell willow's
        freshest hues …

        kniving pangs:

        why did I pack him off to war
            in search of a title?

    WANG CHANGLING (*c.* 690-*c.* 756)

閨怨　王昌齡

閨中少婦不知愁
春日凝妝上翠樓
忽見陌頭楊柳色
悔教夫婿覓封侯

THE SQUADDIE'S ANCIENT SONG

by day you climb the slope to scan the warning-beacons
come twilight near Jiaohe you water horses

    some squaddie sounds the night-watch,
        bangs his mess-kit gong –

in a sandstorm blackout
    a captive princess vents her many secret sorrows
        by playing on the *pipa*

ten thousand leagues from any city wall your camp
    vast deserts uniform with constant sleet and snow

        Tartar geese fly by each night
            uttering sad cries
        a Tartar youth sheds tears
            with both cheeks streaming

we hear that Jade Gate Pass is to be closed;
yet we're the ones who sacrifice our lives
    behind the general's light chariots

unnumbered years of warfare:
    our bones lie buried under barren skies

what a futile task:
    and all to heap Han tables high

        with foreign grapes

    Li Qi (690-751)

相和歌辭 從軍行 李頎

白日登山望烽火黃昏飲馬傍交河行人刁斗風砂暗公主琵琶幽怨多
野雲萬里無城郭雨雪紛紛連大漠胡雁哀鳴夜夜飛胡兒眼淚雙雙落
聞道玉門猶被遮應將性命逐輕車年年戰骨埋荒外空見蒲萄入漢家

BORDER ENVOY

driving my chariot out to the frontier –
    crossing the Juyan dependency

(puffball tossed past homeland walls;
    wild goose blown through alien skies)

        vast savanna: line of smoke lifts up
        mighty river: orb of fire slides down –

at Xiao Pass troopers tell me:
    "The General's made it to Yanran!"

WANG WEI (691?-761)

使至塞上　王維

單車欲問邊屬國過居延
征蓬出漢塞歸雁入胡天
大漠孤煙直長河落日圓
蕭關逢候吏都護在燕然

YINGZHOU SONG

Yingzhou's young bucks throng the steppes
    beneath the battlements soft fox-fur coats go hunting
nomad liquor never makes them drunk –
    ten years old, their sons can ride a horse

  Gao Shi (704-765)

營州歌　高適

營州少年滿原野
狐裘蒙茸獵城下
虜酒千鐘不醉人
胡兒十歲能騎馬

LIANGZHOU SONG

this fine wine, these goblets   of glittery pearl …
the *pipa* player astraddle his horse   demands that we drink!
Don't laugh if I'm tipsy,   sprawled on the sandy ground
how many soldiers of old   who set out to battle
                  ever returned?

  Wang Han (*fl.* 720)

涼州詞　王翰

葡萄美酒夜光杯
欲飲琵琶馬上催
醉臥沙場君莫笑
古來征戰幾人回

HOMAGE TO WANG WEIGU

he's thirty years old: the Imperial Guard's Commander
    – daily border battles (his life's on the line) …
spring winds flatten these thin grasses
    as he rides out hunting, lithe and spry …
look to the arrows at each shoulder's quiver –
    twang of our newly tightened bows –
the shot elk enters a deep ravine
    so our horses can drink,
        splash into desolate springs:
mounted both, we share a cup of wine,
    eke out our lives with slices of fresh meat;
while watching one another's back,
    when can we properly water our steeds?
        all kinds of savages
                plundering distant Yan
far beacons blazing without stint,
    barbarian hooves raise dust up to the sky
safeguarding the north-east,
    we constantly push onwards
        to end the fighting and preserve the city-walls

we serve our country, strive to keep it safe
    since ancient times we all make common cause

    CUI HAO (704-754)

INSOMNIAC NIGHT

the chill of bamboo
        seeps into my bed
a wilderness moon
        spills over the quad
dense dew trickles
        perfect tiny droplets
sparse stars glimmer, then
        gutter into gloom
self-sparking glow-worms
        flitter through the dark
waterfowl keen
        to each other half asleep …
war and its weapons
        impend over all:
grief blanks out
        as the cool night passes

Du Fu (712-770)

倦夜 杜甫

竹涼侵臥內
野月滿庭隅
重露成涓滴
稀星乍有無
暗飛螢自照
水宿鳥相呼
萬事干戈裏
空悲清夜徂

VIEW IN SPRING

the country crumbles: mountains and rivers remain
city in springtime: grass and trees grow wild

a time of troubles: even the flowers shed tears
pain of apartness: flown bird startles the heart

beacons burning   three whole months
a letter from home   – worth a mint of money

scratched my white hair   *till it's worn quite thin*
not enough left   *to hold one pin*

    Du Fu (712-770)

SCANNING THE WILDERNESS

cloudless autumn –
        yet furthest sight is baffled
the more remote
        the more thick shadows gather …
distant rivers
        blur into the sky –
thick mist shrouds
        a lonely fort
a gust of wind
        sets sparse leaves a-quiver
sunlight sinks
        behind the far-flung hills
a single crane flops home –
        why so late?
crows cluster on black boughs
        as twilight falls

    Du Fu (712-770)

FIVE FRONTIER SONGS

    I

gilded arrows
    fletched with falcon feathers –
        the general's gonfalon,
            embroidered, swallowtailed …
standing alone,
    he bellows his command:
        a thousand soldiers answer
            with a single cry

    II

dark woods –
    breeze that makes the grasses bristle –
        at nightfall, says the legend,
            General Li Guang draws his bow …
dawn comes,
    he hunts for his white fletching:
        fails to find it
            in the stone it sank right through …

    III

a moonless sky:
    wild geese flying high
        all through the night
            the Khan is on the run
longed-for light cavalry
    hasten in pursuit –
        our swords and arrows
            swallowed up in snow …

IV

our troops' tents
    sprawl out across the steppes
        widespread revelry and feasting
            tribute paid for routing nomad tribes
wild dancing and drunkenness:
    armour's gold-glitter
        and drumming's deep thunder
            makes hills and rivers shake

V

muster bowmen; laud the hawk
    make your prowess known
        fly after foxes,
            flush pheasants from their coverts
sweep clean, sweep clean
    those ancient hills –
        until your enemies
            are all wiped out

Lu Lun (748-799?)

塞下曲四首　盧綸

鷲翎金仆姑　燕尾繡蝥弧
獨立揚新令　千營共一呼
林暗草驚風　將軍夜引弓
平明尋白羽　沒在石棱中
月黑雁飛高　單于夜遁逃
欲將輕騎逐　大雪滿弓刀
野幕敞瓊筵　羌戎賀勞旋
醉和金甲舞　雷鼓動山川
調箭又呼鷹　俱聞出世能
奔狐將迸雉　掃盡古丘陵

MOON ON THE MOUNTAIN-PASSES

autumn moon so bright, so high
    shining north of Liaoyang walls

this far-flung border-pass:
    first-watch, brilliance now at the full –
gathering winds –
    moon-halo growing and growing …

sentries gazing down – sweet dreams of home
    stallions startled at the thudding of a drum

north winds bring grief to frontier grasslands
    sandstorms shrouding the nomad camp

frost makes the sword stick to its scabbard
    winds fray to shreds our upland banners …

soon, please, soon to go back to the palace –
    no more to hear the clangour
        of night-watch mess-tins!

    BAO JUNHUI (*fl.* 798)

ON SIGHTING JIMEN PASS

your heart shrinks
    when you leave Yantai
        thudding drums – screak of reed-flutes
           near the general's camp

thousands and thousands of miles:
    freezing light strengthens on bright snow
        as dawn floods borderlands
           and banners flutter high

barbaric moonlight dimmed
    by flaming beacons over battlefields

coastal clouds shroud mountains
    round Jimen Pass's city

I may not be the scholar
    who once flung his pen down
        to enlist

        but I too seek
           the ribbon of renown

  Zu Yong (Tang, 8th century)

ARROWHEAD[1]

char of ashes
    pashed bonedust
        in wet red clay

old blood spilled
    blossoms
        on the bronze

white plumes rotted,
    iron shaft rusted
        in the rains

just this wolf's
    cracked canine left:
        its three blunt points …

two steeds I've raced
    over this flatland
        searching

here by the eastern courier station
    in this tangled ditch
        on the stony field of battle

winds dilate
    as daylight narrows,
        bleak stars blinking on

cloud-skeins unfurl
    banners of black rain:
        night engulfs me

長平箭頭歌　李賀

漆灰骨末丹水沙淒淒古血生銅花白翎金竿雨中盡直余三脊殘狼牙
我尋平原乘兩馬驛東石田蒿塢下風長日短星蕭蕭黑旗雲濕懸空夜
左魂右魄啼肌瘦酪瓶倒盡將羊炙蟲棲雁病蘆筍紅回風送客吹陰火
訪古汍瀾收斷鏃折鋒赤罍曾劇肉南陌東城馬上兒勸我將金換篆竹

and the starved shades keening
   lift and dip
      to right and left[2]

swooping down
   they gulp curds from my pitcher
      guzzle my roast mutton

gnat-swarms settle; set geese screeching
   as reeds and bamboo-shoots
      are flushed with final red

the gale whirls phantom
   firedrakes round me
      to guide me on my way

I've tracked down this ancient lamentation
   to bring it to an end:
      one broken arrowhead

this stark snapped barb
   I take away
      once stuck in living meat

I gain South Street:
   beside the eastern wall
      a boy on horseback

bids me barter
   my metal relic
      for a bamboo tray[3]

   LI HE (791-817)

BEYOND THE FRONTIER

nomad horns reel in
    cold northern winds
        Thistle Gate a-shimmer
            white as rushing water
these skies lap up
    the road to Kokonor –
        along the battlements
            a thousand miles of moonlight
banners drenched
    by dewfall
        night-watches sounded out
            by ice-cold brass
barbarian armour:
    snake's interlocking scales
        horses whinny:
            the exile's green grave whitens
autumn stillness:
    the Pleiad flickers, signifying war
        on far-flung sands
            bleak wasteland of dried grasses
north of nomad tents
    is where horizons end
        rivers flowing on
            beyond all frontiers

    Li He (791 817)

塞下曲　李賀

胡角引北風
薊門白於水
天含青海道
城頭月千里
露下旗濛濛
寒金鳴夜刻
蕃甲鎖蛇鱗
馬嘶青塚白
秋靜見旌頭
沙遠席羈愁
帳北天應盡
河聲出塞流

UIGHUR SONG: NORTHERN BORDER

Uighur gold caps throng our battlements
    Yinshan's barren mountain slopes
snowflakes float outside my tent
    moon-blanched sands beyond the fort

a tribesman's son tootles his jade pipe
    barbarian girls pace flower-strewn brocade
yet laughter's shared:
    me and my southern guest –

don't go home
    until plum-blossom falls

    WEN TINGYUN (801?-866)

SEEING A FRIEND OFF EAST

dead leaves twirl and skitter
  empty barracks square

    leaving this old mountain pass,
      your heart, it swells …

Hanyang ferry:
    howling winds
Yingmen mountain:
    rising sun …

who'll still haunt the riverside
  when, from the back of beyond,
    your sole boat returns?

whenever that may be
  we'll drown our sorrows now
    by drinking deep together

    WEN TINGYUN (801?-866)

A SONG OF DISTANT RIVERS

this year's ninth moon
    the emperor's troops
        plash through distant fords

their horses plough through sand
    wildgeese fly up alarmed

murderous chill blasts
    through empty open country:
        home-thoughts …
            so many miles away …

ramparts mantled by unending frost
    smoke from beacon fires

dry leaves
    shrill winds lamenting
        a whole world withering

not belts made from rhino hide
    nor doublets of sable-fur
        keep them warm

moonglare
    dazzling cold
        saddles worked in gold
their foes' thick dust
    flung up like mist at twilight
        veils our camp from view

remember how the Flying General
    hero of those ancient border wars
        came to Longshou countless times
yet they never hung his image
    in Unicorn Pavilion's
        Hall of Fame

    in high boudoirs
        grieving women
                all still vainly gazing north

WEN TINGYUN (801?-866)

遐水謠　溫庭筠

天兵九月渡遐水馬踏沙鳴驚雁起殺氣空高萬裡情塞寒如箭傷眸子
狼煙堡上霜漫漫枯葉號風天地干犀帶鼠裘無暖色清光炯冷黃金鞍
虜塵如霧罩亭障隴首年年漢飛將麟閣無名期未歸樓中思婦徒相望

PITY THE PLOUGHMAN

name me a dynasty,
    name me a reign
        without war:
never peace
    and plenty ... chaos
        never-ending

more bones than topsoil
    turned up
        by your plough;
and still they come recruiting –
    soldiers

        seeking soldiers

    WEI ZHUANG (836-910)

ALONE ON A FRONTIER-WALL, LOOKING AT THE VIEW

lean on the battlements: look down there –
    rush of regret – a remembered town ...

frost falls on whitened reeds;
    mountains at dusk: mist makes fresh dew ...

Northern geese roost on shores of the river;
    drums set the palisades bristling with spears ...

that one crippled tree, now coloured by autumn –
    a wild song to weep at, to dampen hat-tassels ...

    MA DAI (*fl.* 9th century)

A REPORT: WHAT GOES ON IN THE BORDERLANDS

a bugle's muster-call
                shatters autumn's sparkle
as conscripts lounge at ease
                against watchtowers …
spring breezes now
                caress green burial-mounds –
a spring day sheds its brilliance
                throughout Liangzhou …

no soldiers bar the way
                across these empty wilds
each rover free to roam
                the furthest frontier

those nomads' wanderlust
                runs loose as any river
their only wish, as ever,
                to flow towards the south

Zhang Qiao (Tang dynasty)

書邊事　張喬

調角斷清秋征人倚戍樓
春風對青塚白日落梁州
大漢無兵阻窮邊有客遊
蕃情似此水長願向南流

ON THE BORDER, REPLYING TO A FRIEND

the frontier crossed,
>   boundlessly you roamed –

>   when you got back,
>   your hair had turned quite white

>   encircled now, those nomad tribes
>   (sleep in the saddle while sandstorms flail)

>   grasslands all scorched, bleached –
>   frozen ears can't hear cicadas cry

from here on, you'll put up with penury –
>   *no more prattle, please,*

>   *till more men reach the border*

>   LIN KUAN (Tang dynasty)

塞上還答友人　　林寬

無端遊絕塞歸鬢已蒼然
戎羯圍中過風沙馬上眠
草衰頻過燒耳冷不聞蟬
從此甘貧坐休言更到邊

SETTING OUT EARLY BENEATH A MOUNTAIN-PASS

axle-creak, wheel-clatter …
        shoving, heaving over rugged mountain-paths,
an early solitary start –
        all you hear is water-plash and -chuckle
winds rise
        night-mist scatters
moonglow brightening
        on Hua mountain-slopes
those who travel east and west:
        their hair's gone white
the Yellow River
        continuously cold and clear!
everyone you meet:
        busy, busy, busy:

you're the only one
        who's idle

                                    Lin Kuan (Tang dynasty)

關下早行　林寬

軋軋推危轍
聽雞獨早行
風吹靄散
月照華山明
白首東西客
黃河晝夜清
相逢皆有事
唯我是閒情

ON THE BORDER

the whoosh of whistling arrows
      shot straight up a thousand feet –
  sounding even sharper
                in this tranquil windless sky …

and these blue-eyed nomad youths
      on their three hundred steeds –
all clutching their gold bridles,
      gazing up towards the clouds …

Liu Kai (947-1000)

塞上　柳开

鳴骹直上一千尺天靜無風聲更乾
碧眼胡兒三百騎盡提金勒向雲看

UNDER LUZHOU'S WALLS

dawn: haloed moonglow
       – city under siege
night: high winds
       – camp under attack

hornblasts clanging:
       icy waters shudder
bowstrings' twanging force:
       lone goose startled into flight

sharp arrowbarbs
       impale Wu breastplates
long-poled halberds
       slash and snap Chu chin-straps

       turn round – gaze back upon the battlefield

            dark and comfortless
              at dusk   mists rise

              Zhao Bingwen (1159-1232)

廬州城下　趙秉文

月暈曉圍城風高夜斫營
角聲寒水動弓勢斷鴻驚
利鏃穿吳甲長戈斷楚纓
回看經戰處慘淡暮煙生

BITTER COLD

October:
      filthy frontier weather
our soldiers'
      flimsy winter furs
and is the envoy
      bringing us new clothes or not?
icy scales of armour:
      long insomniac nights

> those ministers in Chang'an:
>   warm and snug
> sun's high: but their red-lacquered gates
>   stay firmly shut
> swathed by screens and curtains
>   fold on fold –
> too drunk to even be aware
>   of all those shivering outside

  L IU K EZHUANG (1187-1269)

苦寒行　劉克莊

十月邊頭風色惡官軍身上衣裘薄
押衣敕使來不來夜長甲冷睡難著
長安城中多熱官朱門日高未啟關
重重幃箔施屏山中酒不知屏外寒

BUILDING WALLS

incessant commotion and clamour
    of thousands of labourers' mallets
        mallets that startle poor mother earth
            with all their thwacking and thumping

everywhere clearing the villagers' land
    constructing clay-kilns belching out smoke
        spying out woodland for timber to fell
            to build up more watch-towers

days so brief
    air so keen
        gangmasters laying about them
            with white rods
hoarse voices upbraiding the workers
        like pelting wind and rain

    "the House of Han's high minister's
        obsessed about the borderlands
    building walls builds us up too
        and wins us high promotion"

long ago the wilderness
    was wide and free of walls

now warning-beacons
    file for miles
        walls must be lined with troops

but you, sir, far away, don't see
    how snaggle-toothed walls look
    how soon they stick up like fish-scales

    walk all along them: empty now

        not a single soldier left

LIU KEZHUANG (1187-1269)

DYING FOR YOUR COUNTRY

our army fought at midnight
    (much blood was shed)

at dawn troops gather up the fallen
    they strip each corpse of armour
before they dig its grave:
    a mass of thickly scattered burial mounds
random cairns piled up on top

– futile hanging up their names
    when tallying your dead
poor families have no salaries sent home
    orphans get no pension

sad that all these generals
    are basking in the high sun's rays –

how can they detect
    the wail of cold and cutting winds
        that summon up
            so many thousand ghosts?

    LIU KEZHUANG (1187-269)

國殤行　劉克庄

官軍半夜血戰來平明軍中收遺骸
埋時先剝身上甲標成叢塚高崔嵬

1208: CURRENT AFFAIRS

poets in this peaceful time
    all sporting silken
        green official jackets:

but this year's treaty with the Jin
    will cost how many bolts of silk?

no more shady willows
    round West Lake
clustered mulberry trees
    on all sides now

        for rearing munching silkworms
  Liu Kezhuang (1187-1269)

A RELATIVE IN MOURNING

desert sands
    for miles and miles and miles –
        a widow's greying hair ...

your broken heart –
    this frontier town
        beneath that moon:
          it drifts by,
            shines down on the wanderer

  Yelü Chucai (1190-1244

AFTER THE EMPEROR LEFT TO TOUR EAST: JANUARY 1233

See them gallop by
    whipping their steeds
        kingfisher feathers stitched
            into their quilted robes
– bury your head in the sand
        to look at the sky!

all I know is
    north of the Yellow River
        the brigands are on their way back
and from the walls of Taicheng
    paper kites flutter and fall
        signalling, 'Help!'

… our ministers worse
than those in Xizong's reign …
when will telling the truth
    guide us back home?
autumn winds travel thousands and thousands of miles:
    all they see is one small fishing boat

YUAN HAOWEN (1190-1257)

壬辰十二月車駕東狩後即事五首其一　元好問

翠被忽忽執鞭戴盆鬱鬱夢瞻天
隻知河朔歸銅馬又說臺城墮紙鳶
血肉正應皇極數衣冠不及廣明年
何時真得攜家去萬裡秋風一釣船

THE VIEW FROM STONE-RIDGE PASS

rattle and creak –
        careening over rock ruts –
                felt-covered wagons

this ancient pass
        still garrisoned and guarded
                by blade and bow

from strung-out encampments below
        sudden dashes of cavalry
                darken the world's red dust

those refugees
        who've donned disguise
                must take the narrow paths
                      much higher up

and as for those
        now turned to wormsmeat
                or to grains of sand

                        don't waste time mourning them –

when preyed upon
        by tigers and by jackals:

                which way to turn?

And yet high up,
   cloud-clad,
      clear as jade,
         in bluest solitude,
            at thirty thousand feet …

Dongshan, the hermit's peak,

   still stands …

YUAN HAOWEN (1190-1257)

石嶺關書所見　元好問

軋軋旃車轉石槽
故關猶復戍弓刀
連營突騎紅塵暗
微服行人細路高
已化蟲沙休自歎
厭逢豺虎欲安逃
青雲玉立三千丈
元隻東山意氣豪

LEAVING THE CITY

In the halls of the Han
            they made sure they heard
the songs of the bard …
                days long gone – today what heroes step forward?

now in the city
        all you can see, high on the roofs,
                flocks of gold siskins

how would they know
        of the tangle of brambles that smother
                    the camels of bronze?

the gods return no more
        to those who drift with the fall winds
wealth and rank are empty and bitter
            an old woman's dream of spring

you pass by Lugou again
        and again you turn
               to look back

over Feng City day
        after day the same
                weird five-coloured clouds

    YUAN HAOWEN (1190-1257)

出都二首　元好問

漢宮曾動伯鸞歌事去英雄不奈何
但見觚棱上金爵豈知荊棘臥銅駝
神仙不到秋風客富貴空悲春夢婆
行過盧溝重回首鳳城平日五雲多

JUNE 12TH, 1233 – CROSSING NORTH: THREE VERSES

corpses sprawled, curled up beside the road
    hordes of half-dead prisoners
        Mongol felt-topped wagons
            plunging past,
                a flood in spate …
weeping women trail
    these Uighur steeds
        for each step taken,
             who won't cast a backward glance?

behind the troops
    bundles of cheap wooden Buddhas – kindling …
        skirl of pipes, bells clanging:
            soldiers pack
                the marketplace aswirl
men of rank imprisoned,
    pillaged homes
        no one knows how many
            all year huge boats
                sailing to Kaifeng

bones stacked high like sticks of hemp
    the homeland's hacked-down mulberries, catalpas
        ferried to Longsha: how long?

    this much I know: north of the Yellow River

our spirit's broken,

    houses smashed –

        thin smoketrails … all that's left of home

YUAN HAOWEN (1190-1257)

THE FALL OF QIYANG: TWO POEMS

hundreds of rivers and mountains – grasses untrampled
for ten years their cavalry darkened the walls of our capital
scan those lands to the west: no letters from Qiyang
Gansu's rivers flow to the east freighted with our tears
sad scrubland tangled with our soldiers' bones
the sun sets over an empty city: why shine at all?
who cries out to the blue inhuman sky,
to ask why Chi You forged the first weapons of war?

from the high passes
    nine tigers's piercing vision:
        nine generals from the past
            watch over these poltroons –
                their paltry strategems

the soil of Yugong's fields … this mighty land
    home of the Han, its frontiers sealed
        as far as Heaven's Peak

blast of north wind's keening reed-flute
    plash of Wei River's icy waters
        plunging over soldiers' bones

thirty-six sharp blade-like ridges,
    reaching up to the sky
        God's Palm to protect us
            … our empty frontiers

YUAN HAOWEN (1190-1257)

歧陽三首　元好問

百二關河草不橫十年戎馬暗秦京
歧陽西望無來信隴水東流聞哭聲
野蔓有情縈戰骨殘陽何意照空城
從誰細向蒼蒼問爭遣蚩尤作五兵

眈眈九虎護秦關儔楚齊屛上看
禹貢土田推陸海漢家封徼盡天山
北風獵獵悲笳發渭水瀟瀟戰骨寒
三十六峰長劍在倚天仙掌惜空閑

WHAT THOSE GIRLS WERE SINGING ...

Wu's young ones singing
             as they trek down the road –
                         mile after mile
                                  the sound of their singing

girls singing as they must,
        softened by the same shared song,
                leaving loved fields, gathered in grief
                          at the loss of their country

day after day riders down from the north,
             piled-up clouds in battle-array:
                    steep banks of a river,
                         a long high wall ...

on countless villages
        a myriad Mongols fall:
                government troops
                        hang back defending the city –

not enough mountain-caves,
        not enough river-boats,
                a single horseman spurs on several thousands ...

those who survive this year,
        who knows if they'll get through the next?

blue hills of the highlands ...
                gazing south,
                      the river never ends
                              that winds round the walls of the city

willing yourself
        to follow that river –
                when it reaches the sea-bed,
                        you know it'll never return

the same sand blown by the wind today
        that blew by yesterday:
                faltering feet of the female slave …
                        the road stretching further and further away

… wild geese wing it together over the river
                their keening cries blend with our songs, with our tears
each autumn they come back, the wild geese,
                en route to the south –
                        once over the ferry from north to south
                                how many of us will return?

how still Zhuxi is: no dust stirs …
        while down there in Jiangnan: spring with its mist and rain –
so sad – today this road is flat as the river
        bristles and briars as far as the eye can see:
                        no sign of life, not anywhere

before they left their fields behind
    marriage-hymns, peace and plenty:
            how they suffer now, those boys and girls!
three centuries they kept things as they'd always been:
                their sheep and kine now all desert sands

carrion birds keep guard where men once were:
>torn shreds of blue cloth ... old headscarves left behind
In June a wind from the south,
>travelling thousands of miles
>>to blow to dust what once was flesh and bone ...

YUAN HAOWEN (1190-1257)

續小娘歌十首　元好問

吳兒沿路唱歌行十十五和歌聲唱得小娘相見曲不解離鄉去國情
北來遊騎日紛紛斷岸長堤是陣雲萬落千村藉不得城池留著護官軍
山無洞穴水無船單騎驅人動數千直使今年留得在更教何處過明年
青山高處望南州漫漫江水繞城流願得一身隨水去直到海底不回頭
風沙昨日又今朝踏碎鴉頭路更遙不似南橋騎馬日生紅七尺係郎腰
雁雁相送過河來人歌人哭雁聲哀雁到秋來卻南去南人北渡幾時回
竹溪梅塢靜無塵楚楚兒郎小小娘三百年來涵養出卻將沙漠換牛羊
太平婚嫁不離鄉楚楚兒郎小小娘三百年來涵養出卻將沙漠換牛羊
饑鳥坐守草間人青布猶存舊領巾六月南風一萬里若為白骨便成塵
黃河千里扼兵衝虞虢分明在眼中為向淮西諸將道不須誇說蔡州功

SOLACE IN AN EVIL TIME

swords and shields surround us:
                     battle-slaughter's blood-stench –
while head still sits on shoulders,
                   a man must follow fame

when sick, you seek a remedy:
               rest is what's required
when jaded, it's your library:
               but sleep's the best solution

the idler: head's turned by,
                eyes catch at
                      all that passes
give him just one cup,
            he's brimful of emotion

this body's only goal now:
         grow old among old mountains
me and mountain flowers:
         we understand each other

     DUAN KEJI (1196-1254)

排悶　段克己

四海干戈戰血腥頭皮留在更須名
病尋藥物為開計悶引文書作睡程
萬事轉頭慵挂眼一杯到手最關情
此身定向山間老我與山英有舊盟

WAR

outcome of those battles undecided:
    so where can I now run?
        completely futile everything I've done –
            my white hair's thin as silk …
Wang Can's, Du Fu's anecdotes about war's chaos:
    I track them both – my poor heart far behind
        who hears the wagtail from a thousand miles away?
           this magpie shivers on one moonlit branch
oh, where's the wine that Daoist sage once brewed
    that kept you sozzled for at least three years?
I'd drink and and drink drink it
    until peaceful times returned

    WANG ZHONG (*fl.* 13th century)

STARVELING STEED

Ever since clouds and mist
     rolled down
          into the stronghold of Sky Pass
see how the Song's twelve stables
     have decayed –

who takes pity today
     on this poor bag of bones?
yet in the sun's last rays
     how vast his shadow on the sandy shore:
         like a mountain!

  GONG KAI (1222-1307)

瘦馬圖　龔開

一從雲霧降天關空盡先朝十二閑
今日有誰憐瘦骨夕陽沙岸影如山

OLD HORSE

strength all spent
        fetched back from
                fourscore battlefields
this worn out warhorse
        overtaken by old age

– hangs its head:
        – old bones once worth their weight in gold ...

    its heart still hungers
           for hundreds
                    and hundreds of miles

veiled its glory-days of yore
            those dusty winds

have drifted off
        – far distant now those frontier walls

short-winded its brief song:
        a hollow pot of silver

yet always it recalls
        the cries of the fallen

    HAO JING (1233-1275)

老馬　郝經

百戰歸來力不任消磨神駿老駸駸垂頭自惜千金骨伏櫪仍存萬里心
歲月淹延官路杳風塵荏苒塞垣深短歌聲斷銀壺缺常記當年烈士吟

FIGHTING SOUTH OF THE WALL

savage fighting by our soldiers
        south of the wall's banked earthwork
horses stumbling to a standstill
        in the snow …

                and now our wall's quite lost to view

frostbitten fingers pluck at bowstrings –
        those fingers then snap off
touch icy metal
        and your skin will crack and blister

no hot meals for seven days:
        with our bare hands
                we slaughter prisoners
                      to swallow their warm blood

we're promised gold
        for all the severed heads we bring
                our horses muffled,
                      by night we infiltrate their lines

gloomy skies above us, darkness here below
        from our saddles hanging:
                lopped mazards streaked with tears

this second-in-command's flayed back
        bears eighty wounds
cadavers swathed in tattered banners
        heaped beside the road

we survivors all resigned to die
        shed tears beneath abandoned walls

… our general is the only one
        who's mentioned in despatches

SONG WU (1260-c. 1340)

A SONG ACCOMPANIED BY STRINGS

    – pity the refugees!
human? barely even human …
    ghosts? they're barely even ghosts …
        – pity the refugees!
the men lack even homespun hempen garb;
    the women's skirts are tattered rags
        – pity the refugees!
their food is peeling bark from trees
    or grubbing grass-roots from the earth
        – pity the refugees!
by day they stumble on without cooked food,
    at night they lodge beneath the stars
        – pity the refugees!
no father's a true father to his son,
    no son's a true son to his parents
        – pity the refugees!
you just can't bear to listen to their speech,
    you just can't bear to hear their shrieks and howls
        – pity the refugees!
each morning guarantees no dusk,
    each nightfall guarantees no dawn
        – pity the refugees!
their dead already clog our roads,
    those left alive themselves close kin to ghosts
        – pity the refugees!
a woman barters for a cup of grain,
    or sells her son there for a few poor coins
        – pity the refugees!
maybe no one wants this,
    but he's now cast aside like roadside dust
        – pity the refugees!

when skies cascade down grain –
    that's when these women might survive … and only then
        – oh, pity the refugees!

ZHANG YANGHAO (1269-1329)

AN INCURABLE DISEASE

soulmates swallowed up
            in slaughter and confusion,
disaster, devastation
            as the old disease digs deeper
vain the conflict
            with all-consuming chaos,
vanished the virtuous
            sages of old
gloaming's fiery glimmer
            alarms poor refugees,
frost at first light
            reminds them of home
bowing and scraping
            for a few pecks of rice –
but this old battered besom's
            still worth a crock of gold

    ZHOU TINGZHEN (1292-1379)

老病　周霆震

喪亂交遊盡艱難老病深寥寥平世策落落古人心
夕照驚岐路晨霜憶故林折腰寧五斗敝帚或千金

A TROUBLED MIND

withered scrub
    where thick mist
        clings
forest campfires'
    fitful
        flicker

fog-banks shrouding
    countless footsteps
        on the move
Jiangsu's war-fever:
    lasting
        how much longer?

ruined villages
    enfeoffed

while barren backlands
    starve

medicine-chests
    all ransacked

    while skilled tacticians
        sit round
            killing time

ZHOU TINGZHEN (1292-1379)

BALLAD OF THE NORTH WIND

beyond the wall
                north winds' mounting howl
across the wall
                blasts buffet soldiers' ears

– *swaddled in snug sable,*
                our general shifts
                              a curtain hung with jade
– *clutches his wine-cup,*
                watches snowflakes
                              flutter down

                                      Liu Ji (1311-1375)

北風行梗　劉基

城外蕭蕭北風起城上健兒吹落耳
將軍玉帳貂鼠衣手持酒杯看雪飛

EVENING MARCH: ZHANGGONG VILLAGE

rotting crops
              travellers few and far between
sequestered hamlet
       hemmed in by high hills
doorways gaping …
          empty streets …

one bird floating by
            beneath banked cloud
– icy howling of the gale …
            one crow's distant glide
                   as daylight swiftly fades

our tract of time a hundred years –
            the *wutong* tree grows old
autumn winds
       across a myriad miles –
            so rice can sprout in spring

Mongol soldiers' trampling
            raises dust
    blurring the road home
        north of the Yellow River:
endless gloomy shoals of sand
              gilded by sun's last rays …

   Ma Ge (Yuan dynasty)

A SOLDIER'S WOMAN VENTS HER GRIEF

did he ever crave promotion or a title, my poor husband?
    the tiger tally of enlistment took him far away
and many nightmares came to haunt my bedroom

now the general's HQ sends a letter:
    our armies all are overthrown …
he's dead, my man – but here's his battledress, at least

a neighbour, his old comrade, brought it back
    I've been a courtesan my whole life long
how can I track his bones down – even find the Wuwei road?

I cut these paper banners
   to summon back his soul

here at the place where once we said farewell

   Gao Qi (1336-1374)

PAYING HOMAGE AT THE TEMPLE OF THE KHAN

Khublai's ancestral hall:
   girdled round
      by nightfall's
         afterglow

Time's green mosses
   suffocate the graven steles

Thistle Gate in Beijing's city-wall
   today we reverence
      the image left behind

why seek those ancient
   burial-grounds?

Mongol characters
   half scored
      upon a temple-pillar

paintings in the porch's gloom:
   General Boyan's armies

sad to see a withered tree
   all its blossoms gone
still spread its branches

by day
   owl's eldritch hooting

         reaches deepest night

   MA ZHONGYANG (1450-1516)

CROSSING THE BORDER

barbarians spread out to the Yellow River's banks
        men of Qin are slain – the Great Wall stays intact

shifting desert sands … a setting sun …
        then icy mists
                as we bed down in watch-towers
                      scattered here and there

scouts to recce the three borderlands:
        a thousand *li* we slash and burn at dusk

our generals lusting for the golden seal of office
        never giving all our dead a moment's thought

                              Li Mengyang (1473-1529)

出塞　李夢陽

胡蔓黃河限秦亡紫塞存
磧沙浮落日寒霧宿疏墩
哨馬三邊動燒荒千裡昏
將軍拜金印白骨不曾論

FAREWELL COMMANDER LI: OFF TO YUNZHONG

yellow winds from the north:
    fog-bale thickens
bold Yunzhou warriors
    blow their horns

the general smooths his sword-blade –
    waits for dawn ...
Hegan mountain shudders
    a waning moon slips down

horses whinny at mangers
    soldiers scoff their provender
once they wore rags
    now furs and embroidery

with loosened reins
    they scud over sands
aim shots at birds of prey

    autumn floods the plain with grasses –

barbarian chieftains run away
    LI MENGYANG (1473-1529)

ON THE BORDER: A MISCELLANEOUS POEM

daily, nightly, beaconfires
        along the borderlands
urgent orders reach us:
        muster your troops!
sheep and oxen now return
        to our lofty stronghold
dogs and poultry
        all sense our alarm
soldiers smooth swordblades,
        hefting them high
our cavalry swoop
        flashing like firedrakes
spearpoints press onward –
        thousands collapsing
we laugh at the fallen:
        they yield up their forts …
all we now live for:
        to capture five chieftains
hauling them home:
        parade them at Court!

  LI MENGYANG (1473-1529)

塞上雜詩　李夢陽

邊烽日夜至飛符來會兵
羊牛入高砦雞犬皆震驚
壯士按劍起鞍馬若流星
鎗急萬人靡笑上受降城
生擊五單于歸來獻天庭

MORNINGS WATERING MY HORSE:
FAREWELL MASTER CHEN, OFF TO THE FRONTIER

mornings take my horse to water
evenings take my horse to water

salty water: will he drink it? no
dried-up grasses: will he eat them? no

all those passing underneath the Wall
               shedding bitter tears …

beside its battlements: strewn corpses: can you tell me whose?

someone says: 'this year's forced labourers –
their only road led far from homes and kinfolk:
not knowing how each man's nine lives
would all be spent
(not one goes back alive)

        and would they mind their bodies crumbling to dust beneath the city-walls?
        this, however – this they do regret:
        all their labour spent for other people's profit and reward

last year bandits plundered Kaifeng county:
      blood gushed beneath Black Mountain
           where savage chieftains' arrows found their mark

across so many miles of yellow dust
      our cries shook heaven

every day they close the city gates: no one dares fight

and so this year they issue orders: "fortify our borders!"
   and navvies toil half-dead before the Wall

blanched grasses north and south of it
   louring clouds at sunset

      clanking, clashing of barbarian flails'

                              LI MENGYANG (1473-1529)

朝飲馬送陳子出塞　李夢陽

朝飲馬夕飲馬
水鹹草枯馬不食行人痛哭長城下城邊白骨借問誰云是今年築城者
但道辭家別六親寧知九死無還身不惜身為城下土所恨功成賞別人
去年賊掠開成縣黑山血逬單于箭萬裡黃塵哭震天城門晝閉無人戰
今年下令修築邊丁夫半死長城前城南城北秋草白愁雲日暮鳴胡鞭

FIGHTING SOUTH OF THE WALL

harsh keen air now:
  autumn arrives
nomads on horseback
  harass our border towns
the emperor's orders
  flash with meteoric speed –
fresh conscripts levied
  at dead of night
and so we push forward:
  strict fish-scale formation
    according to plan
the emperor's guards
  seize their chance – *charge!*
white spear-blades cross:
  as they cross, clashing
each bow curving back:
  moons at the full
their swift- flying barbs
  sing loud before falling
blood gushes out
  reddens the grasses …
deep pits crammed
  brimful of corpses –
soldiers wash themselves
  in Longshui's waters
war-spoils all yielded
  at Chengming Gate
horror, shock and awe:
  our emperor's wisdom
numbing the nomads
  scattered asunder
deep understanding
  informs the whole plan
for this he appointed
  a single great scholar
his strategy smashed them
  those skirmishing bandits

 Gu Lin (1476-1545)

FOLLOWING THE ARMY

when young you lust for glory
        your only topics: warriors and swordplay
with high hopes you enlist
        wrongly dreaming of a marquisate

one fine morning your small squad falls in
        not knowing how much toil and trouble lies in store

        in the southwest scour those distant tribes!
        in the northeast take barbarians captive!
the Martial Emperor has a mighty plan
    he wants to blaze new trails
        and open up new territories …

you follow orders,
    gallop gallant steeds as fierce as you
the generals who command you
    like those of ancient times
(but these same generals take the credit for your feats)

    troops are told to spread beyond the border
    push far east beyond the mountain passes
through barren lands your war machine will clank
that bleak back-country: you'll lay it all to waste

    war's what court-plotters covet most
        carve right through all frontiers whether north or south
equipment's needed urgently – with meteoric speed –
    (but troops pour out for years and years and years)

warships set off into turbid waters
    horses plunge across Tibetan snows
and yet you've still not covered half those rivers, mountains

    you're now so worn out that your hair's quite thin

consumed by frostbite, soldiers' fingers drop off
    their flesh shrivels roasted by hot winds
when sick for home their tears are all dried up
    their hearts are broken when they gaze afar
anger and sorrow: poured-out tears and sweat
    hesitant on cliff-edges, icy and vertiginous
far far away through alien lands
    hazardous pathways leaning to one side

who would enter the cave of a tiger?
    who can subdue the tribes of Guiming?

secret envoys sent
    to set the Kunming savage tribes at odds
armies cut off, bogged down in Kashgar …

    but say the army has some luck –
        the faces of those pen-pushers lose colour

now Fate has murder in her heart:
    she foments heroes' fury
        the tips of arrows loosed in flight
            sound like rushing winds
                blood saturates the garments
                    of all those they impale

five kingdoms always roused to war
    circling round and round to certain ruin

'advance' banners lead you on
    for many thousand miles
till you return with all three armies
    playing victory tunes

that day throughout the borderlands
    war has ceased at last …
"when all the birds are killed,
    the bow is cast aside" …

walk a straight path,
    the penpushers detest you
merit high advancement,
    and your colleagues just feel envy
tick all the boxes for reward,
    you're sure to be excluded:
        letters will defame you, stitch you up
the white-haired soldier who returns:
    a convict standing in the dock condemned!
        strain every sinew for your lord,
            can he even tell the difference
                between the true and the duplicitous?
the stout heart bright as any sun
    the flashing sword of valour,
        heroes mounting to the clouds

        and all of it in vain, in vain

who can determine
    the ways of this world?
who hopes to fathom
    the dictates of destiny?

in that Hall of Fame, the 'Unicorn Pavilion',
    there's one portrait
        you'll surely never see:

        our greatest border general, Li Guang!

            Xue Hui (1489-1541)

從軍行　薛蕙

少小慕功名擊劍復談兵誤信封侯事甘作從軍行一朝備行伍幾處罹辛苦西南通遠夷東北攘驕虜
武帝雄材略土宇新開拓銜命馳嚴霍諸將竟邀功歲歲出臨戎勒兵盈塞外發卒遍關東
騷屑干戈動蕭條田野空廟謀貪戰伐邊隙開胡粤軍興急星火兵連淹歲月戈船下厲水策馬逾蔥雪
山川行未半容鬢驚凋換寒冰手指墮炎風肌肉爛思鄉已淚盡腸斷佛魚泣津凌兢猿眩岸
悠悠歷絕國險道何傾側虎穴詎可入鬼方寧易克間使閉昆明單兵陷疏勒全軍有天幸從吏無人色
天時變殺機壯士奮兵威飛矢風鳴鏑推兵血濺衣長驅五王國大破九重圍萬裡懸旌出三軍奏凱歸
邊垂日無事烏盡良弓棄行直貴臣憎功高同列忌賞格多排沮謗書仍負累白頭還士伍赭衣從吏議
輸力奉明君忠邪不見分丹心徒貫日劍氣枉凌雲人事竟莫測天命諒難聞可憐麟閣上不畫李將軍

ON THE BORDER: TWO POEMS

warfare without end: dry bones …
      clear autumn skies – the steppe goes on and on
soaring eagles circle: barren lands …
      horses whinny – make the deep woods shudder
The Son of Heaven pacified the tribes
      ennobled doughty warriors for their courage
our common world has its own natural limits
      all this crossing borders to invade – what for?

frontier fortress in the fall:
      a hard frost fills the air
daily patrols, reporting back,
      ride through the yamen's gate
bad news from the battle-front
      has blanched the general's hair
no one knows how many soldiers lost …
      battered armour, tattered rags …

   Xie Zhen (1495-1575)

塞上曲　謝榛

百戰多枯骨秋高白草深飛雕盤大漠嘶馬振長林
柔遠君王德封侯壯士心華夷自有限邊徼莫相侵

LEAVING THE BORDER

the general leaves in splendour

    but the borderlands he's quelled
        remain unlovely …

        a barren darkness
          smothered by deep snows
or else beset
        by yellow dust-tornadoes

at dawn beside the river –
    barbarian tents
as night descends,
    those tribal chiefs carouse

        their sons go dancing,
          flapping narrow sleeves
        their matchless sable coats
          smelling of sweet musk …

    Xu Wei (1521-1593)

出塞　徐渭

漢將去堂堂
虜帳朝依水
邊塵靖不揚雪沈荒漠暗沙攬塞風黃
胡酋夜進觴舞兒回袖窄無奈紫貂香

DESOLATION ON THE BATTLEFIELD

swarming round
    the general's feathered banner
scaly armour ripples, glitters

drive on through barbarian lands
    dusk thickening around you

a single tragedy, this battlefield –
    but numberless the tears shed by
these bold souls
    none of whom return
        nameless in the shadowlands below

bleached bones scattered and heaped up
    familiar to the moon
        revisiting
            these frontier passes

rock-piles mark each grave
    raked by blasts of northern wind

darkling clouds
    sandstorms, snowstorms flying overhead
hurtling gales –

    follow that bugle-call

        come to certain grief

  XUE LUNDAO (?1531-?1600)

THE OLD GENERAL'S COMPLAINT

still not put down, those northern tribes?
                brave men inly rage

a waste of time,
        me worrying
                dawn to dusk:

        those savage courts will never swim in blood …

– but to let the dust fly round
                their rank disorder!

                what an insult to the nation!

O once-mighty China:
        where are your heroes now?

our miserable white-polled elders
                      wring their hands

    while glib tongues flatter:

        those pen-pushers'
                billowing black gowns!

    Xue Lundao (?1531-?1600)

【仙呂・桂枝香】宿將自悲　薛論道

匈奴未滅壯懷激烈空勞宵旰憂賢哪見虜庭喋血任胡塵亂飛侮
辱郊社堂堂中國誰是豪傑蕭蕭白髮扼腕滾滾青衫弄巧舌

ON THE BORDER

beside the waters of the Wuding River
        keening winter sounds
                whip above white sands
last month's cities yielded to the foe:
        twilight veils
                the moaning of a flute

atop the general's tent: a star portending war
        – over the Altai mountains
                a V-shaped skein of geese
… and once the campaign's over,
        how many heroes
                ever make it home?

   Ao Ying (Ming dynasty)

塞上曲　敖英

無定河邊水寒聲走白沙受降城上月暮色隱悲笳
玉帳旄頭落金微雁陣斜幾時征戰息壯士盡還家

FIGHTING SOUTH OF THE WALL

South of the Wall we fight,
By the battlements south of the Wall.
North of the wall black clouds lour;
Infantry lurking over to the east,
      waiting for the chance of an ambush
Cavalry scatter over to the west
      harry our flanks without mercy.
Brown dust rising around us –
The sun growing darker and darker –
      the whole sky a haze.
Clamour of gongs and drums:
Shrieks and yells of the dying.
Barbarian horsemen retreating,
Flying back swift as a storm.
The stark trees sickly as weeds,
The grass bleached white and dry.

Who's that crying in the ruck?
A father bears his son's limp corpse.
Wives come seeking their husbands –
Pikes and breastplates in piles,
Skulls smeared red with blood.
Each family summons a soul,
Each company mourns its men.

Go tell our General
If he doesn't know this already.
When living we fought on the frontier
Why should we care
      if they bury us here on the steppes?
The rations in the pot
Grew cold at noon …
Too bad! We sprang to arms,
      and then we parted for ever.
Our meals were left unfinished …

The wind howls over the dunes
> and our souls are running with the wind.

They should go look at the General
Sitting up there in the fort
> under the banner of gold
grasping his ivory baton.
While he lives they'll grant him high titles.
When he dies and goes to his ancestors,
> No shortage of food at *his* grave.

WANG SHIZHEN (1526-1590)

戰城南　王世貞

戰城南城南壁黑雲壓我城北伏兵搗我東游騎抄我西
使我不得休息
黃塵合匝日為青天模糊鉦鼓亂發謹呼胡騎斂飆迅驅
樹若薺草為枯啼者何父收子妻問夫戈甲委積血淹頭
顧家家招魂入隊隊自哀呼
告主將主將若不知生為邊陲士野葬復何悲釜中食午
未炊惜其倉皇遂長訣焉得一飽為野風騷屑魂依之曷
不睹主將高牙大纛坐城中生當封徹侯死當廟食無窮

ON THE BORDER

Xiongnu stronghold sacked:
    snow there's turned to slush
        under Tassel Mountain
            sparrows chirrup spring
March chock-full now
    of orioles and fresh flowers –
        all our slain head south
            to haunt their widows' dreams

say someone follows rank:
    meets with defeat, misfortune –
        his border-spirit rises in the reeds
            nightly with the wildgeese …
Majesty, magnanimous and merciful,
    if you'd not sent so many
            off to slaughter
    maybe fewer living men
        would enter Jade Gate Pass
            never to return

    GU YANWU (1613-1682)

AUTUMN MOUNTAINS

autumn mountains upon autumn mountains …
    autumn rains: thunder rumbles through a mountain range
fighting at the river-mouth, just one day past
    today more fighting on the mountainside
first the right flank's gone, I hear
    now those resisting on the left have been destroyed
earth covers all our banners …
    scaling ladders, battle rams:
        how they dance before the south gate of our city!
            think back to ancient Changping:
                in just one morning genocidal slaughter
            corpses of the vanquished everywhere
                heaped up ever higher, mound on mound
bound northward these three hundred barges –
    each barge laden with our rouge-cheeked girls
        many camels cluster on our quays:
            skreaking foreign fifes pierce Swallow Pass …
                once men of Yan and men of Ying
                      refused to serve the Qin:
south of the capital such warriors still exist …

                        GU YANWU (1613-1682)

秋山　顧炎武

秋山復秋山　秋山秋雨殷
昨日戰江口　今日戰山邊
已聞右甄潰　復見左拒殘
旌旗埋地中　梯衝舞城端
一朝長平敗　伏尸遍岡巒
北去三百舸　舸舸好紅顏
吳口擁橐駝　鳴笳入燕關
昔時鄢郢人　猶在城南間

QIANTANG BEACH-HEAD LAMENTATION

sleek and lush those riverside grasses
        lashing, drumming of torrential rain

cold the spears of all those slain in battle
        yet their hatred burns afresh

sandbank firefly glitter
        scribbles on the moon's reflection

an autumn night in darkened chambers
        wraiths that moan and gibber

on a far peak, struck for the final time
        the gong falls silent and all's still

geese honk winging over
        the stark abandoned village

deep hush now: the baffled spirits
        slide after boats of the vanquished

intense grief-harrowed "droop-headed millet"
        mourning the bows unstrung

bankside wildflower roots
        with just rank blood to drink

dawn wayfarers will groan
        as jet-black demons arise

high hopes have had to follow
        cold mists that move by moonlight

what hope for a fragrant name after death
        when paper banners summon hungry ghosts?

> while from her boudoir window
> > the widow's lonely lamp …
>
> *don't listen to the sound of water*
> > *don't wait up for the evening tide …*
>
> WANG DUANSHU (1621-1706?)

吊錢塘戰場　王端淑

萋萋岸草雨瀟瀟戰死寒戈恨未銷沙際螢光沉月影陰房鬼淚泣秋宵
敲殘遠岫鐘初寂喚徹荒村雁已嘹默默驚魂隨敗楫離離故黍悼空詔
野花根畔惟氊血過客朝吟帶墨妖雄志今隨烟月冷芳名何處紙旛招
深閨亦有孤燈婦莫聽江聲待晚潮

TUNE: 'A LOVE THAT NEVER ENDS'

one uphill journey
one upriver journey

– push your body on towards Yu Pass

      midnight: lampglow
            through a thousand tents

windblast: watchman's drum
snowblast: watchman's drum

to tear the heart
    that dreams of home

          to tear its dreams

home: where such sounds
      are never heard at all

    NALAN XINGDE (1655-1685)

長相思　納蘭成德

山一程水一程身向榆關那畔行夜深千帳鐙
風一更雪一更聒碎鄉心夢不成故園無此聲

TUNE: 'BODDHISATTVA BARBARIAN'

midwinter:
        wild winds pummel the ground

unbuckling your saddle –

crows that bicker …
            darkening skies

  – river flows by icebound

            your sore heart swells and widens

emptiness, barrenness,
    far as the eye can see –

drums and trumpets
          from high city walls

  you reach Chang'an tomorrow

          but your troubles travel on
          NALAN XINGDE (1655-1685)

菩薩蠻　納蘭成德

驚飆掠地冬將半解鞍正值昏鴉亂冰
合大河流茫茫一片愁燒痕空極望鼓
角高城上明日近長安客心愁未闌

CROSSING THE BORDER

lean into this sheer slope
      look down towards the sea
            that ancient frontier sector …

beneath these flapping banners' shade
      see those barrack buildings yonder

behind my horse peach-blossom
      before it, driving snow

dropping down from the pass –
      hard not to cast
           one last backward glance

                        Xu Lan (17th-18th centuries)

出關　徐蘭

憑山俯海古邊州旆影翻飛見戍樓
馬後桃花馬前雪出關爭得不回頭

NOTES ON POEMS

p. 45 Yingzhou Song
Other versions of the first line provide different fifth characters: variously, instead of 滿 'fill', these read in English as 厭 'loathe', 歇 rest' and 愛 'love'. If I'd chosen the last of these, which also works well, my first line would read: 'Yingzhou's young bucks love the open prairies.'

p. 49 – Five Frontier Songs
敲: one source reads "蔽".

p 53 Arrowhead
1. The full title tells us that the arrowhead was found by the poet on the ancient battlefield of Changping (where, a thousand years earlier, some 400,000 Zhao warriors had allegedly been buried alive after surrendering to the forces of Qin – the same forces who, not many decades afterwards, would unify China for the first time at the cost of a huge amount of bloodshed).
2. These two kinds of spirit, the earth-bound hún (to the right) and the heavenly pò (to the left), cannot separate because proper funeral rites had been lacking: they're trapped on the battlefield. Li He will try and appease them.
3. The bamboo tray seems disappointingly anti-climactic until we realize that it would be used to offer up a sacrifice for the dead warriors' souls.
N.B. Careful readers will have noticed how skilfully each image seems to lead to the next: for instance, the 'red clay' (dān shuǐ shā) preceding the 'old blood' (gǔ xuè), and the later red of sunset; the 'steeds' (mǎ) anticipating the 'courier station' (yì); the sinister 'starved shades keening' (pò tí jī shòu) followed immediately by the 'gnat-swarms' (chóng qī) and 'geese' (yàn bìng – literally geese who are either 'distressed' or 'sick'). Li He is known in China as guǐcái or 'demon-gifted', and the creepy, morbid, 'Gothic' atmosphere of this poem is entirely typical of much of his work. Analogies with our own fin-de-siècle poètes maudits and Décadents are often made by modern commentators, and with good reason.

p. 62 Setting out early beneath a Mountain Pass
愛 [?] I've taken the liberty of assuming that line 2 is corrupt: a bold thing for a translator to do. I strongly suspect that 雞 jī is a mistake: chickens on a mountain? But 溱 jí (the trickling sound of a stream as it tumbles over rocks) makes much better sense in this context. There's another onomatopoeic term in the first half of this line, and a second one would balance it. The manuscripts of Tang poems had been copied and re-copied, sometimes over many centuries, before first appearing in print. Textual errors must have proliferated, as in all such manuscript transmis-

sions. Shakespeare scholars have made much more daring suggestions about the texts of many Shakespeare plays – and the First Folio was printed a mere seven years after his death.

p. 73 June 12th, 1233 – Crossing North: Three Verses

A small confession relating to 過去旗車似水流 My first version of this line (the one previously printed in a little magazine) read as follows: 'banners, chariots pouring past, a flood ...' Only later did I become aware that the phrase 旗車 zhān chē in line 2, which does literally translate as "banners and chariots", and would have meant this in any earlier dynasty, had, nevertheless, during the Yuan dynasty, a much narrower and more specialised meaning: it meant the "felt-covered wagons" used then (and still used) by the Mongols. For a long time, I was so pleased with my original version, and particularly with this line as it then stood, that I left the mistake in. To correct it would (or so I rather desperately told myself) have ruined the rhythm. In fact I just thought that the image of 'banners and chariots' was more Romantic (however anachronistic). Willis Barnstone, a fine American translator, recently wrote that "A translator's reward for a mistake must be capital punishment" and fiercely added that there is no "freedom to make errors". In which case I was for a while on Death Row. But I then changed my mind – and I think that now the problem has been solved, albeit at the cost of a little extra (felt) padding.

ABOUT THE POETS

The Shijing ('Classic of Poetry'), from which the first two anonymous poems are taken, is traditionally believed to have been compiled by Confucius. The poems it contains are certainly very ancient, many of them probably more or less contemporaneous with Homer (*c.* 800 BCE). All subsequent Chinese classical poetry stems from this one book.

WANG CAN (177-217) is considered to have been the most outstanding of what were known as the Seven Masters of the Jian'an Era (which covered the end of the Han dynasty and the start of the Six Dynasties). The so-called three 'Seven Sorrows', two of which are included, are among his most famous extant compositions. He threw in his lot with the great general Cao Cao (of 'Three Kingdoms' fame), and was greatly respected by that formidable warlord.

RUAN JI (210-263) is the most celebrated member of that somewhat dissolute group of scholars and poets known as 'The Seven Sages of the Bamboo Grove', and was by far the greatest poet of his era.

BAO ZHAO (*c.* 414-466) was a fifth-century poet who wrote particularly fine 'border poems' in the traditional 樂府 yuèfǔ ('ballad') genre, two of which are included here. Because of his marginal involvement in a rebellion, he was executed in 466.

CHEN SHUBAO (553-604) was the last emperor of the short-lived minor dynasty (557-589) known as the Chen (after his family name). He presided over a court devoted to the arts, and was himself an accomplished minor poet.

LU ZHAOLIN (*c.* 635-689), is another member of one of those quaintly named literary groups of which the Chinese are so fond, in this case 'The Four Paragons of the Early Tang'. Although later dismissed by the great Du Fu as 'not a serious' poet, he was in fact a writer of singular strength and originality. He suffered terribly in his last years from what may have been a crippling form of rheumatoid arthritis. In the end, the pain grew too great for him to bear, and he drowned himself.

Little is known about LIU XIYI 劉希夷 (*c.* 651-*c.* 680) today, though he was highly rated in his own time. Not much of his work survives. He is not to be confused with the homophonous somewhat later and much greater Liu Xiyi 劉禹錫 (772-842). One account of the earlier poet's death states that it occurred as the result of a single, allegedly slanderous, couplet he had written. If true, this would arguably have been taking the literary critic's rôle in life a little too seriously.

WANG CHANGLING (c. 690-c. 756) was an important poet and literary critic, who specialised in 'border poetry'. He was killed during the terrible An Lushan rebellion (755-763). Many of the significant works by him that we know about were lost during the later part of the Tang dynasty.

LI QI (690-751) was a close acquaintance of both Wang Wei and Wang Changling. He was a bit of an eccentric, with eremitic tendencies and a love of alchemy. His work is said to have been strongly influenced by Li Bai (see below).

WANG WEI (?691-761), along with Li Bai and Du Fu, was one of the three titans of High Tang poetry. The stillness, clarity and deep sense of Buddhist negation that one finds, especially in his quatrains but also in much of his other poetry, have endeared him to Chinese and Western readers alike.

GAO SHI (704-765) was yet another member of that circle of High Tang poets mentioned above. Unlike any of the others, he had a distinguished military and political career. He and his contemporary, Cen Shen (not represented in this anthology), have always been coupled together in terms of their fondness for 'border-style' poetry.

WANG HAN (*fl.* 720) was a somewhat debauched figure, only fourteen of whose poems now survive, despite the high reputation he enjoyed in his own day. The seven-word lines of the quatrain translated here comprise his most famous poem.

CUI HAO (704-754). Here we encounter yet another aristocratic poet who believed in living life to the full while challenging social conventions; though his poetry was much less adventurous. He is remembered for one superb poem ('Yellow Crane Tower') which not long afterwards inspired the much greater Li Bai to try and emulate it, though (as Li himself admitted) without success. The poem included here is not so well known, though it is another fine example of 'border' poetry.

DU FU (712-770) and LI BAI (701-762) are often thought of as the two front-runners for the title of 'China's Greatest Poet'. Du's technical mastery and the range and depth of his work set him apart from all of his contemporaries. The An Lushan rebellion made him a refugee and separated him from his family. He wrote powerfully about the experience of fleeing through a country torn apart by conflict.

Lu Lun (748-799?) was a widely travelled poet, whose employment on the staff of the Military Commissioner of Hezhong took him directly into the regions he describes in his lively frontier verses.

Bao Junhui (*fl.* 798), one of the Tang dynasty's relatively small band of female poets, was considered to be a scholar of distinction as well as a talented versifier, and in both capacities she attracted the emperor Dezong's attention.

Zu Yong (*fl.* 8th century). In his childhood he had been a friend of Wang Wei; while still quite a young man, he retired from court, and the majority of his poems adopt pastoral themes. The poem by which he is represented here is in many respects atypical.

Li He (790-816) was one of a group of highly talented late Tang poets whose abstruse and ornately stylized verses often deliberately courted obscurity. He himself was drawn towards the uncanny and the macabre, which helps to explain the considerable attraction his poetry holds for many Western readers, and the glamour that dazzled many later Chinese poets.

Wen Tingyun (801?-866) is a poet whose skimpy biography contains much that is merely anecdotal and about whom, in reality, little is known for certain (he may or may not have earned his later reputation as a rake). What is definite is that he excelled in two genres: the 樂府 yuèfǔ or 'ballad', and, more influentially, the 詞 cí or 'lyric', which he helped to pioneer.

Wei Zhuang (836-910) is best known for the splendid long narrative poem entitled 'Lament by a Lady from Qin', lost for over a millennium, and discovered in the Dunhuang caves at the start of the twentieth century. The much shorter sardonic poem translated here is a tersely worded comment on the folly of all war.

Ma Dai (*fl.* 9th century) was moved around from one minor administrative post to another, suffering the usual vicissitudes of imperial favour, before ending his career as Court Academician in the prestigious 'Taixue' or National University. Little else is known about him.

ZHANG QIAO (Tang Dynasty) lived through the increasingly turbulent final decades of the Tang dynasty. The Huang Chao rebellion ended his hopes of a career in the imperial administration, and from then on he lived in retirement.

LIN KUAN (Tang Dynasty) is shrouded in obscurity and only a few of his poems survive. Both of those included in this anthology suggest personal experience of life in the borderlands.

LIU KAI (947-1000) was, on the one hand, an accomplished scholar and poet and, on the other, a savagely cruel military commander. Such a combination of qualities is by no means unique in Chinese history.

ZHAO BINGWEN (1159-1232) was a distinguished neo-Confucian philosopher as well as one of the leading poets serving under the Jin (Jurchen) dynasty. He was praised by Yuan Haowen (see below), who wrote his biography.

LIU KEZHUANG (1187-1269) was "the most prolific writer of the thirteenth century", according to the *Indiana Companion to Traditional Chinese Literature*. But there was quality in abundance to complement the sheer quantity of his output. He was an important literary critic as well as one of the leading scholars and poets of the Southern Song.

YELÜ CHUCAI (1190-1244) is a most attractive figure in Chinese history. His tall stature, long beard and sonorous voice made him a memorable figure both among his contemporaries and subsequent generations. He persuaded both Genghis and Ögedei Khan that taxing the Han Chinese was much more profitable than slaughtering them in droves; in this way he saved countless lives. He was descended from a long line of Khitan aristocrats. He accompanied Genghis Khan during a long expedition to the remote West in 1218, and wrote an account of it that can still be read with profit and enjoyment today.

YUAN HAOWEN (1190-1257) is a major figure in Chinese literature, not just as a poet, but also as a historian. It is worth noting that the great Japanese scholar Yoshikawa Kōjirō has boldly maintained that he "may well be the foremost Chinese poet from Du Fu to the present". He lived through the calamitous fall of the Jin, the dynasty which he had always served faithfully, and his *sangluan* poetry of witness is unparalleled in its eloquence and compassion. He has hitherto been poorly served by English translators.

Duan Keji (1196-1254) and his brother Duan Chengji, known to their contemporaries as the 'Two Marvels', were the most famous of a group of followers of Yuan Haowen. Like him they lived through a time of genocidal carnage and, wisely one feels, lived lives of retirement from public affairs (keeping one's head down was probably the best way not to lose it to the flash of a Mongol sword).

Wang Zhong (*fl.* 13th century). That he lived towards the very end of the Southern Song, and that his courtesy name was 'Jiweng' is all the information that can currently be gleaned about him.

Gong Kai (1222-1307) was an official under the Southern Song. Intensely loyal to this regime long after it had fallen to the Mongols, he refused to serve under the Yuan, and whereas others in the same predicament turned to writing plays, he took up painting as a means of keeping body and soul together. This poem accompanied his most famous picture, in which the horse is a symbol both of the defeated dynasty and of its now impoverished intelligentsia.

Hao Jing (1233-1275) was a Neo-Confucian scholar and an advisor to Khubilai Khan. On that ruler's behalf, he attempted to effect some kind of reconciliation between the Southern Song and the ascendant Mongols. and was, in other words, a peacemaker. Needless to say, his appeals fell on deaf ears, and he was imprisoned by the Song for a decade and a half.

Song Wu (1260-*c.* 1340), then just a humble clerk in the army, was one of the few survivors of the disastrous armada sent by Khubilai Khan against Japan. His style was heavily influenced by late Tang verse, in particular that of Li He.

Zhang Yanghao (1269-1329) wrote one of the most famous extant 怀古 huáigǔ poems, called 'Lamenting the Past at Tong Pass', of which several English translations exist. The verses he wrote towards the end of his life, when he was a government official in Guanzhong at a time of drought and famine, focus memorably on the sufferings of the common people.

Zhou Tingzhen (1292-1379) is particularly well-known for his 喪亂 sāngluàn poems about the turbulent era through which he lived.

LIU JI (1311-1375) was not just a poet, but also a philosopher and a statesman, who wrote about military strategy while assisting the founder of the Ming dynasty to oust the Mongols from China.

MA GE (Yuan Dynasty), another friend of YUAN HAOWEN, was Assistant Minister in the Ministry of War under the Jin. Like his much more famous friend, he suffered under the Mongol invasions, and wrote well about the privations he endured.

GAO QI (1336-1374) is widely believed to be one of the very greatest Ming dynasty poets. The notoriously cruel Hongwu emperor had him sliced into eight parts for his alleged involvement in a rebellion.

MA ZHONGYANG (1450-1516) was both an imperial Censor and an Assistant Minister in the Ministry of War. But to be an official under the Ming could be dangerous, especially if you fell foul of the eunuchs, who wielded great influence at court. Ma Zhongyang died in prison.

WANG PAN (c. 1470-1530) was a highly cultivated painter and musician, whose one book of poems enjoyed a high reputation among his contemporaries.

LI MENGYANG (1473-1529) was a polymath: cosmologist, historian, philosopher and leader of the 'Archaist' or 'Revivalist' movement in the arts, which favoured injecting more genuine emotion and simplicity into poetry by seeking inspiration from High Tang poets such as DU FU. He was the foremost member of the influential group known as the 'Seven Earlier Masters'.

GU LIN (1476-1545), who hailed from the 'Chinese Venice', Suzhou, was one of the 'Three Masters from Jinling'. He held various high offices, before enjoying a retirement graced by all the arts.

XUE HUI (1489-1541) passed the all-important jìnshì (進士) exam in 1514, and worked in the Ministry of Justice. Like many Chinese scholars, he was of a tolerant, syncretist disposition and leaned equally towards both Buddhism and Daoism.

XIE ZHEN (1495-1575) was one of the 'Seven Later Masters [of the Ming]'. Although what is called a 'commoner poet' (that is, not from a privileged aristocratic background), he achieved considerable fame and popularity for his verses while still in his teens. Later on, he wrote works of literary criticism and espoused influential views on the theory of poetry.

Xu Wei (1521-1593) was a leading dramatist as well as a distinguished essayist, calligrapher and painter. When young, he had been an influential aide to Hi Zongxian, who commanded the armies responsible for defending the south of China. He is also remembered for having murdered his wife, a crime for which he spent a mere seven years in prison, thanks to the intervention of a powerful friend. Strangely, in view of this dubious record on the marital front, the female heroines of his dramas are all feisty and memorable characters, very much the superiors to their male counterparts.

Xue Lundao (?1531-1600) was a soldier for three decades, and rose to the rank of general. He was famous for his mastery of the 散曲 sǎnqǔ genre (a form of lyric poem). One charmingly entitled prose work of his is the 林石逸興 línshí yìxìng 'Taking Pleasure at One's Ease Among Rocks and Groves'. Over a thousand of his poems survive.

Ao Ying (Ming Dynasty) passed his jìnshì (進士) examination in 1522. He was a government official first in Nanjing, and then in Suzhou. He is principally remembered for the prose work entitled Dōnggǔ zhuìyán 東谷贅言 ('Superfluous Words from the Eastern Valley').

Wang Shizhen (1526-1590) was "the dominant figure in Chinese literature during much of the late sixteenth century", according to Daniel Bryant (*The Indiana Companion of Traditional Chinese Literature*). His output alone was on a staggering scale, but equally impressive was the depth and range of his best work.

Gu Yanwu (1613-1682) wrote on a wide range of subjects, among them philosophy, philology, epigraphy, phonetics, history, geography and economics (one wonders how he ever found time for his poetry). He was a Ming Loyalist who refused to serve under the Qing, although, unlike many of his friends (most of whom died for their principles), he did not actively oppose the new regime, but merely retired from public life to pursue a life of study and reflection.

Wang Duanshu (1621-1706) was a well-known Ming Loyalist woman writer, respected for her scholarship and literary accomplishments. She compiled one of the most important seventeenth-century collections of women's poetry.

NALAN XINGDE (1655-1685) was the son of a Manchu Grand Secretary, who mastered the art of the Chinese lyric poem (the 詞 cí) to such an extent by the time of his early death that, in the opinion of the great twentieth-century poet and scholar Wang Guowei, he had become the finest lyric poet since the Northern Song – praise indeed, and richly merited.

XU LAN (17th-18th centuries) was another admirer of the Late Tang poet Li He. He wrote a number of descriptive frontier poems while on an expedition to Outer Mongolia, and the strangeness both of what he saw there and of the language he used in these fine poems excited the admiration of his contemporaries.

ABOUT THE TRANSLATOR

KEVIN MAYNARD was awarded a First Class Honours BA degree at Exeter University and went on to do research into the History of Ideas at the Warburg Institute. Subsequently he became an English teacher and worked in both maintained and independent schools in London and Hertfordshire for over three decades. He came to Chinese literature quite serendipitously in his late forties, and studied Mandarin on a part-time basis at the School of Oriental and African Studies for five years. He has had poems and translations published in a range of magazines, and in 2017 one of the poems included in this anthology ('Building Walls') was 'Commended' in the Stephen Spender Prize Competition.

After spending over three decades in St Albans, Hertfordshire, he now lives on the South Coast in West Sussex.

LIST OF POETS IN ALPHABETICAL ORDER

Anon (*from the* Shijing)	25-6	Wang Shizhen	106
Ao Ying	105	Wang Wei	44
Bao Junhui	51	Wang Zhong	80
Bao Zhao	33	Wei Zhuang	59
Chen Shubao	37	Wen Tingyun	56
Cui Hao	46	Xie Zhen	101
Du Fu	47	Xu Lan	114
Duan Keji	79	Xu Wei	102
Gao Qi	89	Xue Hui	97
Gao Shi	45	Xue Lundao	103
Gong Kai	81	Yelü Chucai	68
Gu Lin	96	Yuan Haowen	69
Gu Yanwu	108	Zhang Qiao	60
Hao Jing	82	Zhang Yanghao	84
Li He	53	Zhao Bingwen	64
Li Mengyang	91	Zhou Tingzhen	85
Li Qi	43	Zu Yong	52
Lin Kuan	61		
Liu Ji	87		
Liu Kai	63		
Liu Kezhuang	65		
Liu Xiyi	40		
Lu Lun	49		
Lu Zhaolin	37		
Ma Dai	59		
Ma Ge	88		
Ma Zhongyang	90		
Nalan Xingde	112		
Ruan Ji	31		
Song Wu	83		
Wang Can	28		
Wang Changling	41		
Wang Duanshu	110		
Wang Han	45		